The Arab Gulf States

The Arab Gulf States

Beyond Oil and Islam

Sean Foley

Viva Books

New Delhi | Mumbai | Chennai | Kolkata | Bangalore | Hyderabad | Kochi | Guwahati

First Indian Edition 2011

VIVA BOOKS PRIVATE LIMITED

- 4737/23 Ansari Road, Daryaganj, New Delhi 110 002
  E-mail: vivadelhi@vivagroupindia.net, Tel. 42242200
- 76, Service Industries, Shirvane, Sector 1, Nerul, Navi Mumbai 400 706
  E-mail: vivamumbai@vivagroupindia.net, Tel. 27721273, 27721274
- Jamals Fazal Chambers, 26 Greams Road, Chennai 600 006
  E-mail: vivachennai@vivagroupindia.net, Tel. 28290304, 28294241
- B-103, Jindal Towers, 21/1A/3 Darga Road, Kolkata 700 017
  E-mail: vivakolkata@vivagroupindia.net, Tel. 22836381, 22816713
- 7, Sovereign Park Apartments, 56-58, K. R. Road, Basavanagudi, Bengaluru 560 004
  E-mail: vivabangalore@vivagroupindia.net, Tel. 26607409, 26607410
- 101-102 Mughal Marc Apartments, 3-4-637 to 641, Narayanguda, Hyderabad 500 029
  E-mail: vivahyderabad@vivagroupindia.net, Tel. 27564481, 27564482
- Beevi Towers, First Floor, SRM Road, Kaloor, Kochi 682 018, Kerala
  E-mail: vivakochi@vivagroupindia.net, Tel: 0484-2403055, 2403056
- 232, GNB Road, Beside UCO Bank, Silpukhuri, Guwahati 781 003
  E-mail: vivaguwahati@[illegible], Tel. [illegible]

www.vivagroupindia.com

Published by arrangement with

Lynne Rienner Publishers, Inc.
1800 30th Street, Suite 314
Boulder, Colorado 80301
USA

ISBN : 978-81-309-1528-9

Published by Vinod Vasishtha for Viva Books Private Limited, 4737/23, Ansari Road, Daryaganj, New Delhi - 110 002. Printed and bound by Raj Press, R-3, Inderpuri, New Delhi - 110 012.

S0000 / S0800 / S0810

Contents

Preface

It was November 2004, and my panel at the annual conference of the Middle East Studies Association (MESA), held that year in San Francisco, had just opened the floor to questions. I was hoping that this part of the panel would go quickly, because I had a job interview later in the afternoon. I delivered a paper that stayed just within my allotted time. When I was done speaking, I breathed a sigh of relief.

But this moment of triumph proved to be short lived. I saw that one of the chief experts on Middle East politics, Greg Gause, was in the room. I had read his work extensively in graduate school, and my paper was, in fact, a response to his seminal text, *Oil Monarchies*. I had just argued that although oil *was* critical to the history and the politics of the Arab Gulf states, as Gause contends, there were other significant factors in their development, including satellite broadcasting, television, and other modern technologies—not to mention the lack of educational and job opportunities for Gulf men and the growing power of women and non-Muslims. I had also argued that scholars would increasingly look at the Gulf states in much the same way that they now look at Mexico, where oil revenues are an important aspect of government budgets but do not exclusively determine national politics.

Since my arguments had little in common with Gause's, my apprehension turned to dread when I saw him raise his hand. He asked the whole panel to explain exactly who we were each challenging in our presentations. Fortunately, I was not required to go first, so I had a moment to think through what I would say. I did not want to avoid the question, but I was reluctant to say to Gause's face that I was challenging *his* ideas. When my time came, however, I decided to take a chance. "You!" I said. I realized I was on safe ground when he smiled and appeared pleased by my answer.

The Arab Gulf States: Beyond Oil and Islam is a product of the conversations with Greg Gause that began that day and that have continued ever since, not only with him but with a host of other scholars, colleagues, and friends. I hope I have presented my arguments with sufficient depth and cogency so that one day, if I am impelled to ask who a young scholar is challenging, the answer will once again be "you."

* * *

Foremost among the scholars, colleagues, and friends alluded to above is John Voll, who was an early proponent of this book and remains one of my most valued advisers. Another early proponent of the book was Jon Alterman, who critiqued my initial proposal for Lynne Rienner Publishers. In addition, I thank Charles Kestenbaum, whom I met in Abu Dhabi in 1996, at which time he helped to spark my interest in Gulf politics. I cannot thank him enough for sharing with me his insights and considerable expertise about the Middle East, the Gulf, and the United Arab Emirates in particular.

There are also four other scholars to whom I owe an enormous debt. For teaching me about global oil markets, strategic and military power, and the challenges facing oil-exporting nations, I thank Anthony Cordesman, Mamoun Fandy, David Painter, and Tarik Yousef.

Paul du Quneoy, Bert Kirby, York Norman, Dan Stigall, Stefan Talke, and Rick Unikel are invaluable friends whose guidance, humor, and companionship helped me through the various trials of writing this book. I particularly thank Paul for reading the final draft of the manuscript and for providing me with much useful feedback. I also thank Lior Strahilevitz for friendship and keen insight into First Amendment issues. Special thanks also go to John Calabrese, Patrick McGreevy, and Barry Rubin for their ongoing support of my scholarship.

Since coming to Middle Tennessee State University (MTSU) in 2006, I have benefited from the friendship, guidance, and support of many faculty members and administrators: Amy Sayward, my department chair; Louie Haas, Ken Scherzer, and my other colleagues in the History Department; Muhammad al-Bakry in the English Department; Samantha Cantrell in the grants development office; Allen Hibbard, the director of the Middle East Studies Center; and John McDaniel, the dean of the College of Liberal Arts.

There were also many other knowledgeable individuals who assisted me: Juan Cole, John Cuddeback, Christopher Davidson, John Esposito, Greg Gause, Fred Lawson, Matteo Legrenzi, Mike Mehlman, Caffey Norman, James Onley, and Hugh Wilford.

I also acknowledge the valuable contributions of Ambassador Nonoo and her staff at the Bahraini Embassy in Washington.

Marilyn Grobschmidt deserves special recognition for first contacting me and for then shepherding me through the process of securing a contract with Lynne Rienner Publishers.

Through the magic of Skype, Paul Weisser, my manuscript editor, provided a valuable sounding board for my ideas and writing style from 2,000 miles away.

This book would not have been possible without the generous financial support of the Smith Richardson Foundation, which provided me a junior faculty research grant in 2006. That grant supplied funds for me to acquire scholarly materials, take research trips to libraries outside of Tennessee, and pay for substantial course release time in 2007 and 2008. My chief contact at the foundation, Scott Boston, was always a pleasure to work with. An MTSU Faculty Research Creative Projects Committee grant in 2008 also aided my research.

I greatly benefited from working with archivists and other librarians in a host of institutions. I especially thank Scott S. Taylor and his colleagues in Georgetown University Library's Special Collections, who readily met my needs as a researcher and provided expert guidance through their archival materials. Their help was very much appreciated. I also benefited from two of the finest libraries of Middle East studies in the United States: the Middle East Institute's George Camp Keiser Library and the Middle East and Africa Reading Room at the Library of Congress. I would like to especially acknowledge the assistance of Simon Braune of the Middle East Institute, who provided a great environment for conducting research and went out of his way to make me feel at home. In addition, I thank the library staff of the University of California at Berkeley, the Truman Presidential Library, and MTSU's interlibrary loan office at the James E. Walker Library.

I am grateful for the friendship of Jol Silversmith, Elizabeth Kimmons, and Anny Kimmons. Their extra bed was always available during my frequent research trips to Washington, and I appreciated their humor and good advice whenever I was in the nation's capital. *Dōmo arigatō!*

I am equally grateful for the help of my parents, Jack and Adelle Foley. Their support and guidance have been instrumental to the completion of this book and to my success throughout every stage of my life. I hope that this "grandbook" brings them much joy and happiness.

My final acknowledgments go to two people who are closely connected to this book and deserve extraordinary recognition: Charles Featherstone and my wife, Kerry Foley.

Charles and I began discussing many of the book's core issues in the late 1990s, when we first met in graduate school at Georgetown University. Over numerous conversations during the years since then, he has freely shared with me his own views and experiences in the Gulf, reminded me of the benefits of taking a contrarian approach, and helped to convince me that my ideas about the Gulf are viable.

I started this project shortly after marrying Kerry, and I cannot thank her enough for her help with every aspect of the book and her willingness to travel with me to Tennessee. Nor can I imagine anyone doing a better job at keeping me happy and focused on finishing the book. It is to Kerry Foley that this book is dedicated.

—*Sean Foley*

1

Introduction

My father rode a camel. I ride a Cadillac. My son flies a jet. My grandson will have a supersonic plane. But my great-grandson . . . will be a camel driver.

—Arab Gulf saying, 1980

I'm from Najran city [in Saudi Arabia], and there are still some houses [that] my father tells me belonged to the Jews who used to live in Najran. The Jews migrated to Israel during the 1950s. My father tells me that they used to live in peace with the rest of the people in Najran.

—An anonymous Saudi, 2007

In 2002, I was in Damascus, Syria, researching the life of a leading nineteenth-century Sufi saint and scholar, Shaikh Khalid Naqshbandi. One day I was invited to visit the home of Shaikh Nazim al-Qubrusi, the most important contemporary figure in Shaikh Khalid's Sufi order, the Naqshbandiyya. When I arrived at the home, I was introduced to the shaikh, who asked me in Arabic about my work on Shaikh Khalid. After we spoke for a few minutes, Nazim switched to English, explaining that it was the only language that everyone present could understand, since some of his followers were Asian Muslims or Western converts to Islam. As Nazim spoke, I noticed that one of his followers was videotaping my conversation with him—to be posted, as I later learned, on YouTube and on his website.[1]

After my conversation with Nazim, I was besieged by several men who attempted to sit next to me, touch my back or arms, or even put their arms around my shoulders. At first, I assumed that the men were enthusiastic followers of Nazim who were displaying Arab social norms, since in Arab societies, from Morocco to Kuwait, heterosexual men engage in far more direct physical interaction than their US counterparts. But when one of the men asked if Nazim had touched my backpack, I understood what was happening: the men believed that Shaikh Nazim—like Shaikh Khalid before him—was a Muslim saint who could confer *baraka,* or blessings from God, onto anyone who interacted with him. By touching me or anything else that had made contact with Nazim, including my bag, they believed that they could benefit from the *baraka* that God conferred to humanity through Nazim.[2]

Shortly after my encounter with Shaikh Nazim and his followers, I, too, was seemingly touched by Nazim's *baraka.* It happened at a newsstand in London's Heathrow International Airport. I would normally have gone straight for the *Economist* and the *Financial Times,* but another magazine caught my attention, the *National Geographic.* The cover was of a senior Saudi prince performing his kingdom's national dance, the *ardha* sword dance, to conclude a camel festival. Its caption read "Kingdom on Edge: Saudi Arabia." Even though I had lived close to the magazine's offices in Washington, DC, when I was in graduate school, I had not read or even looked at *National Geographic* since I was in fifth grade. Had I not stopped at the newsstand at Heathrow, it is unlikely that I would have ever seen that particular issue.[3]

But the magazine caught my attention and held it. The cover highlighted Frank Viviano's article on Saudi Arabia and discussed his recent trip there; it included interviews and photographs of both Saudis and non-Saudis from all walks of life. Men, women (both veiled and unveiled), young, old, commoners, and members of the royal family appeared in rural, urban, public, and intimate settings. There were pictures of things anyone would expect to see: oil fields, deserts, enormous mosques, and palaces. But there were also pictures of things few would expect to see: a family watching Fox News, the crowded and dilapidated homes of foreign laborers, female university students, and a man sporting a colorful Che Guevara T-shirt and jeans rather than the *dishdasha,* the white full-length garment traditionally worn by Saudi men.

As I returned to the article again and again over the following weeks, I was struck by the contrast between the diverse modern society that appeared in Viviano's photographs and the conservative Arab Muslim society that I had found in my reading on Saudi Arabia and its neighbors in my classes at Berkeley and Georgetown. An especially surprising example of Saudi diversity was the name of the family watching Fox News—Naqshbandi—because Shaikh Nazim and the Naqshbandiyya advocate a vision of Islam that is hostile to Wahhabism, Saudi Arabia's state-sanctioned interpretation of Islam. Indeed, adherents to the Naqshbandiyya have reportedly been persecuted in the kingdom,[4] yet the Naqshbandis were presented as a typical Saudi family. They lived in Jeddah, which resembles cities in other parts of the world, with their countless automobiles and traffic congestion, office buildings, mass-produced consumer goods, and low-rise suburban houses. One nighttime picture of the Saudi capital, Riyadh, could easily have been mistaken for Phoenix or Las Vegas.

Equally striking to me was how much Viviano's portrayal of traditional modes of authority undermined the current chief intellectual tool for understanding Gulf states, the rentier model. The rentier model emerged to explain the oil-funded socioeconomic transformation of Iran and what would become the six Gulf Cooperation Council (GCC) states: Bahrain, Kuwait, Oman, Qatar, Saudi Arabia, and the United Arab Emirates (UAE). It by and large ignores traditional modes of authority, such as sword dances at the end of tribal camel festivals, *majlises* (councils in which politicians field requests from ordinary Saudis), direct payments to Saudis in need, and tribal levies guarding vast expanses of desert.

These six states had progressed from poor and isolated communities into wealthy and technologically advanced nations during the 1960s and 1970s. Scholars saw these states, which had tiny indigenous populations and strong monarchies, as so exceptional that they deserved a new scholarly model—the rentier model. In particular, scholars focused on the state monopolies over the fees, or "rents," that foreigners paid for the right to extract oil from the Gulf nations. Scholars argued that these rents permitted monarchs in the Gulf to acquire the resources necessary to govern as police states without taxing their subjects or negotiating with the rest of society, as their counterparts must do in countries without oil. Within the rentier framework, the autonomy of a government vis-à-vis its population correlates to external rents from oil: the greater the revenues from these external rents, the greater the autonomy, and vice versa. If oil revenues decline, rentier governments must make significant concessions to their populations in order to remain in power.[5] The rentier model and oil have even been used to explain patriarchal structures in the Middle East.[6]

Yet events in recent years, as well as statistics compiled by the United Nations, appear to validate Viviano's article and to undermine the rentier model in two key ways. First, most Gulf governments lack one critical element of a police state: robust police.[7] The number of internal security forces per 100,000 residents in most Gulf states is analogous to that of Portugal, Brazil, and Israel—none of which are seen as autocratic police states.[8] Second, although the price of oil and revenues from oil sales increased with breakneck speed between 1999 and the onset of the global financial crisis in 2008, the opposite of what the rentier model predicts has occurred. That is, governments held elections and permitted groups outside of their elites—including women, Shia, foreigners, and religious and secular opposition groups—to take a far more visible public role than before. In June 2008, for instance, Bahrain appointed a Jewish woman to serve as its ambassador to the United States.[9]

Together, these policies suggest that there is more to the politics of these states than oil, and they raise a host of larger questions. To begin with, could the absence of police and other internal security forces tell us something important about the nature of political power and legitimacy in the Gulf? Might the nature of power in the Gulf resemble that of other states that are not rich in oil? Does the diversity of people and workers in the Gulf suggest that discussions of politics and economics in the region require us to consider a host of peoples and traditions besides conservative Sunni Arabs? What about the role of women, especially educated women? Finally, what does the accessibility of Fox and other foreign media mean for the ability of Gulf governments to shape public opinion and to control their own media—both of which are hallmarks of authoritarian police states?

* * *

In this book, I address these questions in a new way. My analysis is based on four core themes.

First, I treat the six GCC countries as normal states that face many of the same social, religious, and economic problems as other states over the past century.

Second, I argue that many of the critical challenges that Gulf states face in the twenty-first century (religious tensions, the role of gender, and existential questions of identity) predate the discovery of oil in 1930 and reflect centuries-old social and cultural factors in the Gulf. Among the most important of these factors are tribal and local customs, patron-client relationships, commercial networks, the hajj, geographic and environmental constraints, familial traditions of governance, and religious and cultural tolerance. These factors, unlike oil, help us to explain, for example, the homosexual practices that F. P. Mackie identified in his 1940 report on Saudi public health; they also suggest why a mass circulation Saudi newspaper regularly publishes schedules for satellite television programs and employs an openly gay Saudi journalist, even though both satellite television and homosexuality are officially illegal in the kingdom.[10]

The record of tolerance in Gulf societies points to my third core argument: we cannot fully understand either past or contemporary realities in the Gulf unless we come to terms with its diversity and investigate the roles of Arab Sunni Muslim men *along with* those of women, non-Arabs, and non-Muslims. Although these last three groups are excluded from regional histories or treated as collective powerless "others" in contemporary political analysis, they have made and continue to make tangible contributions to Gulf societies. Over the past century, women, Western diplomats, Catholic and Protestant Christians, Jews, South Asians, oil company executives, Asian laborers, Shia, overseas investors, and countless others have shaped regional commerce, comforted the sick, inspired political action, educated thousands, and led soldiers into battle. Regional leaders have worked closely with these communities, granted them autonomy, and, at times, adopted them as groups that deserve the protection of the state. Gulf leaders have often provided land and funds for them to construct churches and because of this have been awarded prestigious papal honors usually given to active Catholic laymen, including knighthood in the Order of Pius and the grand cross of the Order of Saint Sylvester.[11]

Another important component of Gulf life and society is the impact of technological change—and this is my fourth core argument. Radio, television, air conditioning, desalinization, satellite broadcasting, the Internet, and cell phones have had at least as important an effect as oil on daily life and on politics in the Gulf. These technological advances have permitted Gulf Arabs to build communities modeled on postwar US suburbs, increase foreign and native populations, and achieve rapid economic growth. Technology has also forced them and others to face a series of cultural, environmental, and political questions that are as difficult to resolve in the twenty-first century as they were in the 1930s, when both radio and the oil industry first appeared in the Gulf. The seriousness of these problems is encapsulated by the fact that, in the 1970s, Gulf Arabs seriously believed that it was possible (in fact, likely) that their descendants would live as Bedouin Arabs—despite the fact that Gulf societies were the wealthiest and most technologically advanced nations on earth at the time.

To support these arguments, I draw on a broad base of primary and secondary sources in Arabic and English: diplomatic correspondence, regional newspapers, poetry, movies, television programs, personal interviews, memoirs, missionary records, and web blogs and other Internet-related materials. I also draw on the records housed in several archives. Georgetown University's William Mulligan Collection is an especially valuable source, since it includes hundreds of classified reports by the employees of the Arab-American Oil Company on virtually every aspect of life in the Gulf, from the books sold in bookstores to the internal politics of royal families. Of particular interest are Phebe Marr's reports on girls and education during a key period for Saudi women—the 1960s—when education was first offered to girls throughout the kingdom.

Another group of sources I use includes the first feature-length Saudi Arabian movie, *Keif al-Hal?* (How Are You?); YouTube videos; and Ahmed al-Omran and other leading Gulf bloggers. These types of popular and alternative media provide information on Gulf society that is not present in other sources and have become an important and controversial outlet for political debate—so controversial that some Gulf governments have imprisoned bloggers and sought to censor the online content.[12]

* * *

My argument is presented in the six chapters that follow. Chapter 2, which charts the history and politics of the Gulf states from the 1920s until the late

1970s, shows how Gulf rulers drew on their families' tradition of governance dating back to the nineteenth century to maintain their authority and to repel rhetorical attacks from Arab nationalists. Rulers reinforced their legitimacy by cultivating various social networks and by promoting Islamic and tribal values. In mosques, sword dances, *majlises,* markets, hajj pilgrimage speeches, royal visits to provincial cities, and welfare institutions, monarchs interacted with ordinary subjects and were thereby confirmed as leaders.

Many rulers further reinforced their authority through a system analogous to a welfare state in which individual subjects and tribes received generous cash subsidies, food, and clothing. Rulers also leveraged their international position and importance to Great Britain, the United States, and South Asian Muslims to win assistance and funds akin to the rents they would later receive from oil. In fact, Saudi Arabia's dependence in the 1930s on the annual fees paid by hajj pilgrims strongly resembled the kingdom's later dependence on the proceeds from the sale of oil.

Although I discuss the importance of oil in Chapter 2, I also argue that the success of the Gulf rulers should be compared to the records of monarchs and presidents elsewhere in the Middle East, who also had access to vast oil revenues but could not maintain political stability. I emphasize several factors that are generally overlooked by historians of this period: the role of the hajj in US-Saudi relations, the importance of air conditioning, the impact of US missionary hospitals and schools, and Jewish and South Asian dominance of Gulf commerce between 1900 and the 1950s. In addition, I stress the importance of radio and other mass media, which took root in the 1930s and were, by the 1960s, as much an aspect of daily life in the region as the call to prayer and Quran readings. The Gulf states treated the mass media as an aspect of sovereignty and competed fiercely with one another, as well as with Western oil companies, Arab nationalists, and regional US military bases, over stations and channels. The result was that Arabs in the Gulf—much like East Germans during the Cold War—had access to broadcasts in their native language from terrestrial radio and television stations based in neighboring states. Although regional governments heavily censored domestic radio and television content whenever they could, they did not in fact control everything that was broadcast within their national borders. Instead, they were forced to compete for domestic audiences, which overwhelmingly preferred foreign television and radio broadcasts.

Chapter 3 explores the nexus of political events, economic factors, and new forms of media that appeared in the Gulf from the Iranian revolution in 1979 until the year 2000. This nexus fundamentally altered which foreign and domestic groups could demand access to state resources; it also ensured that government decisions respected the interests and views of those groups. The new media—foreign and Gulf-based—pursued their own agendas and were sometimes funded by governments and organizations that differed considerably from those of other Gulf states. They gave a platform to dissident voices and employed Arabic-speaking journalists who could follow their own inclinations. Unlike Western journalists, Arab journalists did not depend on guides and translators. If that meant interviewing Bin Laden or covering anti-US protests in Bahrain, the stories went on the air.

In Chapter 4 I discuss strategies that Gulf states have undertaken since 2000 to address the growing imbalances in their societies and to take advantage of the steep increases in the price of oil from 1999 until mid-2008. From the start, many of these policies produced unintended socioeconomic and political outcomes, some of which undermined the stability of the GCC societies. Although the decision of the Gulf states to maintain close ties with the United States may have deterred Iran or Iraq from attacking them, it also enraged important segments of GCC public opinion, convincing some people to support Al-Qaida and other organizations dedicated to using violence to overthrow Gulf regimes. Initiatives designed to reduce the dependence of Gulf economies on the proceeds from exporting oil joined with an influx of expatriate labor to reopen social divisions, since few GCC nationals were qualified to work in the positions created by the booming private sector. Moreover, the private sector's dependence on foreign direct investment has left the GCC states open to the whims of foreign investors, especially after oil prices declined rapidly and a world financial crisis erupted in 2008. Without the benefit of new oil proceeds and foreign investment, formerly booming economies in the Gulf slowed, companies collapsed, and thousands of workers lost their jobs. Even the Gulf's most dynamic and modern economy, Dubai, had to borrow billions of dollars from its neighbor, Abu Dhabi, just to pay its short-term debt payments to foreign creditors.

Perhaps the principal beneficiaries of the political and economic reforms in Gulf societies since the late 1990s have been women, the subject of Chapter 5. The chapter focuses on four key themes. First, many women in the Gulf in the past, especially before the discovery of oil, served as teachers, entrepreneurs, and political leaders. Second, issues of gender—such as the veil or gender-separated schools—are often miscast as women's issues when in reality they are part of a social system in which both women and men are expected to act modestly. The male *dishdasha* and the accompanying headgear, which are symbols of Gulf Arab identity, cover nearly as much of the body as a veil does. Third, women in Gulf societies acquired ever greater socioeconomic power in the 1990s because they were the only group beside expatriates who were able to fill the positions created by the private sector. Women benefited from the enormous investments made in education in the 1970s, especially in secondary and postsecondary schools. Since younger women on average are more literate and stay in school longer than their male counterparts, this gap will only widen in the future, especially in advanced industries, where women already dominate the workforce. Fourth, the problem of how to reconcile the desire to utilize educated women effectively with the conservative framework of Gulf society remains an important and troubling question for GCC governments and their peoples. Extending the right to vote to women and permitting them to drive—issues that make headlines today—will look minor in comparison to those issues facing the GCC states when women emerge as the only segment of the indigenous population qualified to work in modern economies. Indigenous men show few signs of wishing to compete with them, preferring to work in family businesses, the army, or the government, occupations that do not require extensive education.

In Chapter 6 I investigate the role of non-Arabs, non-Muslims, and Shia in Arab Gulf societies along with the relationship of these groups to indigenous Sunni Arab peoples. US Protestant missionaries, Indian merchants, Jewish pearl dealers, South Asian business consultants, and Western oil executives have thrived in the Gulf and have built important institutions. Many of these people still make contributions to the region. Although Gulf peoples, and Saudis in particular, have a reputation for religious intolerance, the ruling families in Saudi Arabia and other Gulf states have readily integrated non-Muslims into their societies and granted them wide cultural freedoms and, over time, direct state protection and citizenship. Shia have faced official hostility, but they have also benefited from the rise of the oil industry and the opportunities it has provided them for rapid socioeconomic advancement. Just as indigenous Sunni Arabs have been affected by the technological and rapid political changes in the Middle East since 1990, non-Muslims and Shia have, too. These individuals can turn not only to international media and nongovernmental organizations to promote better labor practices in the Gulf but also to the Shia government in Iraq, to India, and to other states that send workers to the Gulf. Many expatriates also maintain extensive communal organizations in the Gulf and have representatives in their home country's parliament. The demographic presence of foreigners (as much as 70 percent of the population in some states) and their sociopolitical activities have not gone unnoticed by the indigenous Sunni Arabs. Although some fear that the expatriates will lead to the eventual extinction of indigenous Gulf society, others have sought to incorporate Indian democratic traditions into civil society and to give foreigners the opportunity to become citizens. How well indigenous Gulf Arabs (and expatriate workers) reconcile these issues will play an important role in the future of the region.

In Chapter 7 I argue that the GCC states are normal—not exotic—societies, which face many of the same challenges that other states have faced for decades. Although there is little doubt that petroleum will play a role in their economies for years to come, I show in this book that there are significant benefits to adopting an approach to the Gulf that does not effectively begin and end with oil. It is worth noting here that the demographic and socioeconomic concerns of Gulf Arabs are analogous to those of Europeans, who fear that their nations are evolving into a giant Euro Disney that will be run by foreign hordes.[13] Similarly troubling is that young men in the Gulf are more interested in reckless driving, drug abuse, and other dangerous forms of behavior than in earning a college education or competing in the modern workforce—much like many of their counterparts in North America. In Georgia and other US states, men have been disproportionately affected by the recent global financial crisis and have fallen far behind their female peers in educational achievement.[14] Globalization has also forced Gulf Arabs, much like other peoples, to address aspects of their past that had long been ignored or hidden, aspects such as the Jews who lived in Najran and in Manama. Such problems will continue to vex scholars for years to come as the Gulf diversifies economically and becomes a region in which oil will play a significant but less vital role over time. The economic and political structures of the GCC states may eventually resemble that of contemporary Mexico, where oil revenues allow the national government to provide social services at a lower rate of taxation but do not determine the political and economic structures of the nation's society.

The present moment is an especially exciting one in Gulf history, since states that were made suddenly wealthy by the presence of petroleum must ponder the many questions that arise as their ancient traditions come into uneasy contact with both modernity and money.

Notes

1. For more on Shaikh Nazim and his use of technology, see Sean Foley, "The Naqshbandiyya-Khalidiyya, Islamic Sainthood, and Religion in Modern Times," *Journal of World History* 19, no. 4 (December 2008): 521–545.

2. Ibid.

3. Frank Viviano, "Kingdom on Edge: Saudi Arabia," *National Geographic* 204, no. 4 (October 2003): 3–41.

4. US Department of State, Under Secretary for Democracy and Global Affairs, Bureau of Democracy, Human Rights, and Labor, "International Religious Freedom Report 2005: Saudi Arabia" (available at http://www.state.gov/).

5. The leading proponents of the rentier model are Hazem Beblawi, Kiren Chaudhry, Jill Crystal, Gregory Gause, and Giacomo Luciani. Even the recent work of Michael Herb, which investigates the institutional development of the states' monarchies and compares Kuwait and the UAE, accepts the guiding assumptions of the rentier model as accurate. The same can be said of the Italian scholar Matteo Legrenzi, who has done the most in-depth recent work on the GCC. One scholar who has sought to move away from the rentier paradigm in regards to Saudi Arabia is Pascal Ménoret. Together, these studies have yielded important insights into the institutional constructions of GCC states, such as the political and economic dangers of state dependence on oil sales and the problems arising from weak societal institutions. For more on these works, see Hazem Beblawi and Giacomo Luciani, eds., *The Rentier State* (New York: Routledge, 1987); Kiren Chaudhry, *The Price of Wealth: Economies and Institutions in the Middle East*

(Ithaca, NY: Cornell University Press, 1997); Jill Crystal, *Oil and Politics in the Gulf: Rulers and Merchants in Qatar* (Cambridge: Cambridge University Press, 1995); Gregory Gause, *Oil Monarchies: Domestic and Security Challenges in the Arab Gulf States* (New York: Council on Foreign Relations, 1994); Michal Herb, *All in the Family: Absolutism, Revolution, and Democracy in the Middle Eastern Monarchies* (Albany: State University of New York Press, 1999); Matteo Legrenzi, *The Gulf Cooperation Council: Diplomacy, Security and Economy in a Changing Region* (London: I. B. Tauris, 2008); Pascal Ménoret, *The Saudi Enigma*, trans. Patrick Camiller (London: Zed Books, 2005).

6. Michael Ross, "Oil, Islam, and Women," *American Political Science Review* 102, no. 1 (February 2008): 107–123.

7. This type of misperception is hardly unique to Gulf states. Imperial Russia, which is often portrayed as an autocratic police state, had significantly fewer police officers per capita in the first decades of the twentieth century than democratic states, such as Great Britain or France. For more on this paradox and the surprising weakness of Russia's police forces in relation to its civil society before World War I, see Paul du Quenoy, *Stage Fright: Politics and the Performing Arts in Late Imperial Russia* (University Park: Pennsylvania State University Press, 2009).

8. All of these statistics are approximate and based on the following: Anthony Cordesman and Khalid al-Rodhan, *Gulf Military Forces in an Era of Asymmetric Wars* (Washington, DC: Center for Strategic and International Studies and Praeger Security International, 2007); United Nations Office of Drugs and Crimes, *Surveys of Criminal Trends and Operations of Criminal Justice Systems* (see http://www.unodc.org/); the work of scholars with Vision of Humanity (see http://www.visionofhumanity.org/).

9. Nora Boustany, "Barrier-Breaking Bahraini Masters Diplomatic Scene: Nonoo Is First Jewish Ambassador from an Arab Nation," *Washington Post*, December 19, 2008.

10. Mackie notes in the report: "In a country where certain proclivities are tolerated one would expect to find (amongst boys and young men who are passive agents) the rectal complications peculiar to this disease, but I only once heard of stricture of the rectum in a youth but was not able to see him." F. P. Mackie, *Report to the Saudi Arabian Mining Syndicate on Saudi Arabia's Public Health*, March 7, 1940; reprinted in United States Department of State, *Records of the Department of State Relating to Internal Affairs of Saudi Arabia, 1930–1944* (Washington, DC: National Archives, National Records and Archives Service, General Services Administration, 1974), Reel 3.

11. Victor Sanmiguel, *Christians in Kuwait* (Beirut: Beirut Press, 1970), 69–70.

12. Faiza Saleh Ambah, "Saudi Activist Blogger Freed After 4 Months in Jail Without Charge," *Washington Post*, April 27, 2008; "Internet Is New Frontline in War for Human Rights: Amnesty," Agence France-Presse—English, May 23, 2007.

13. For more on European fears of a demographic and cultural catastrophe on the continent, see Russell Shorto, "No Babies?" *New York Times*, June 29, 2008.

14. Sarah Baxter, "Women Are Victors in 'Mancession'; Economics and Gender Roles Are Being Rewritten in America as Men Bear the Brunt of Job Losses," *Sunday Times* (London), June 7, 2009; Janell Ross and Heidi Hall, "After Unemployment, Many Men Struggle with New Family Role," *Tennessean*, August 2, 2009 (available at http://www.tennessean.com/).

2

The Emergence of the Modern Gulf, 1930–1981

The new method [i.e., radio] of receiving the news of the world in Arabic, with Egyptian comments thrown in, is not only significant but contains very great possibilities for both good and harm. Let us hope that the Egyptian broadcasting service is under proper control.

—British agent, Kuwait, 1935

Praise Allah, Praise America.

—Hajj pilgrims, Beirut International Airport, 1952

Oil revenues and the popularity of the automobile and bottled soft drinks have not drastically changed the social and moral patterns [in Saudi Arabia], which are closely tied to conservative Islamic thought. Indeed, it is television which may ultimately make the greatest contribution to . . . change.

—Douglas Boyd, *Journal of Broadcasting,* 1970–1971

In late August 1952, Edward Debbas faced a challenge. The Harvard-educated[1] head of Lebanon's international airport and the interim head of the country's airline authority had to figure out how to transport thousands of hajj pilgrims camped at the still unfinished airport to Mecca with only a week left before the start of the hajj.[2] These individuals were among the tens of thousands of additional pilgrims who had decided to go on the hajj in 1952, when Saudi Arabia eliminated pilgrimage dues and Turkey's government allowed its citizens to make the pilgrimage for the first time since the 1920s.[3] As the sea and land routes to Mecca became overwhelmed with pilgrims, thousands went to Beirut, which had air service to Jeddah, the traditional gateway to Mecca.

Less than half of the hajj travelers even knew Arabic.[4] Among the many dignitaries at Beirut's airport was Mullah Kashani, the speaker of the Iranian parliament and a fierce critic of US policy in the Middle East. King Ibn Saud of Saudi Arabia personally promised Kashani that he would travel to Jeddah by a special plane from Beirut, and so the mullah, along with all of the other pilgrims, arrived at the airport with ticket in hand.[5]

Initially, the ten daily DC-3 flights flown by Air Liban, Middle East Airlines, and Saudi Arabian Airlines could handle the travelers wishing to go to Jeddah. But as thousands arrived at the airport, it was clear what had happened: the airlines had oversold tickets, in part because of a dispute between Lebanese and Saudi airlines over how to divide the profits and fly pilgrims to Saudi Arabia.[6] Britain and France could not extend state support, and Western airlines refused Debbas's appeals for aid, insisting "that all their planes were required for existing commitments, that longer notice would have been needed, and besides, ferrying pilgrims did not offer much commercial incentive."[7] As the deadline for the hajj loomed, pilgrims began to fear that they would never make it and asked increasingly angry questions about when they could go to Jeddah.[8]

With days left before the start of the hajj, Debbas suggested to the Lebanese Foreign Affairs Ministry that it ask the US government for assistance. After the Saudi government approved Debbas's idea, the Lebanese foreign minister asked the US minister to Lebanon, Harold Minor, for help.[9] Minor, who had already tried to secure seabound shipping for pilgrims, sent an overnight telegram to Washington, recommending US assistance via military aircraft as a goodwill gesture.[10] The State Department gave an immediate positive response, and hours later, thirteen US C-54 military transport planes arrived at Beirut's airport.[11] US officials also sent technical, mechanical, and cleaning crews to work with Debbas and other Lebanese airport employees.[12] When Debbas told the hajj pilgrims that the Americans would fly them to Jeddah, many yelled out praise for Allah and for the United States.

For the next four days, a C-54 took off every hour from Beirut for the ten-hour round trip. Lebanese and US personnel devised a system of rope sequencing that allowed groups of eighty pilgrims at a time to be loaded efficiently.[13] Following the insistence of the US military, no additional commercial airline tickets were sold, and the $260,000 of proceeds from the tickets already sold were donated to a Muslim charity.[14] US planes carried as many pilgrims in four days as the local airlines had carried in three weeks, and each hajj pilgrim received a lunch courtesy of the American Friends of the Middle East.[15] Each pilgrim in Beirut who already had a ticket for Jeddah arrived safely, with the last plane landing only hours before the hajj was to officially start. The Saudi government did its part, too, granting the United States Air Force full access to its airfields and extending the hajj deadline a day to facilitate the pilgrims stranded in Lebanon.[16]

Both *Time* and *Life* magazines ran stories on the airlift, highlighting the fact that Kashani kissed the cheeks of both the pilot, Alfred Beasley, and his co-pilot, Angelo Elmo, upon arriving in Jeddah.[17] Lebanon's mufti, Muhammad Alaya, told Minor that Muslims must include the US people—"infidels though they are—in their prayers."[18] A Turkish pilgrim cabled his nation's prime minister and president: "The Beirut-Jedda air-bridge constitutes real international cooperation. At no time in history has so much help been offered from so far away and for such a large number of people in such a noble cause. Muslims, the whole world over, and this year's pilgrims in particular, will not forget this gesture."[19] British officials coldly reported that the airlift "added much to American prestige" in Saudi Arabia at London's expense.[20] The US Defense Department concurred with this assessment of the operation and noted that the airlift was the most cost-effective action undertaken in years to win support for US policies in the Middle East and the broader Muslim world.[21] In the eyes of US diplomats and scholars in Lebanon, the airlift displayed the "power and organizational ability of the United States in the best possible way."[22]

Perhaps no people were more impressed than the Saudis, especially the man charged with administering the hajj, Prince Faysal. He had much at stake in the hajj, since the one a year earlier had been a disaster and great embarrassment for the kingdom, which defined itself at home and abroad as the protector of Mecca, Medina, and the pilgrimage. In fact, British diplomats regularly referred to the 1951 hajj as the "holocaust," because 5,000 to 7,000 pilgrims had died from heatstroke.[23] Even Faysal's father, King Ibn Saud, had only escaped death from heatstroke because his guards promptly covered him with ice.[24]

The hajj went off smoothly in 1952, however. Pilots in the United States Air Force, as well as some working for the Arab-American Oil Company (ARAMCO), the US oil company in Saudi Arabia, flew pilgrims to Jeddah and directly to Mecca in US planes. In addition, US-supplied trucks moved pilgrims from Jeddah to Mecca on roads constructed by Bechtel, the US engineering firm.[25] The US government had acted in Saudi Arabia's time of need, sparing Faysal and his government considerable humiliation at the most important event of the year for Saudis. This would be a lesson that the Saudi royal family would not soon forget, even after US secretary of state John Foster Dulles decided in 1953 that the United States Air Force would never fly hajj pilgrims to Jeddah again.[26]

It is significant that the 1952 airlift was not the first time that Washington had lent assistance to Saudi Arabia's hajj, nor was it the first time that the US government had contemplated using airplanes to ferry pilgrims to Jeddah. In 1943, Archibald Roosevelt, who was an intelligence officer in North Africa, proposed—with the blessing of the US legation in Tangier—that a US plane fly prominent North African Muslims to Jeddah for the hajj.[27] Roosevelt, who was the grandson of Theodore Roosevelt and the cousin of Franklin Delano Roosevelt, thought this would be a goodwill gesture that would also counteract a Free French airlift of notable African Muslim pilgrims.[28] Also during the 1943 hajj, Faysal and Ibn Saud lobbied US officials in Saudi Arabia and Washington for US financial assistance and modern transportation for the pilgrims.[29]

Although Great Britain readily provided assistance for that 1943 hajj, receiving prominent mention for it in Ibn Saud's annual hajj speech, Wallace Murray and other senior State Department officials refused to assist Saudi Arabia. They argued that US assistance was impractical politically and that air travel was inconsistent with Muslim ideals of suffering while on the hajj. At that time, Saudi Arabia lay within Britain's sphere of influence, and so it was up to London to address problems there. Furthermore, Murray observed, ARAMCO had won its contract in Saudi Arabia to explore for oil precisely because the United States *lacked* influence in the kingdom, and therefore Americans were not seen as a threat to its independence. If the US government were to become more involved in Saudi Arabia or its neighbors in the future, even larger oil concessions in the region might go to US competitors. Why take the risk?[30]

* * *

The stark difference between the reactions of senior US officials in 1943 and nine years later to assisting Saudi Arabia with the hajj is central to understanding the development of the kingdom and its five Gulf state neighbors (Bahrain, Kuwait, Qatar, Oman, and the United Arab Emirates) in the half century between 1931 and 1981. During those five decades, the six states built wealthy, stable, and technologically advanced societies with modern bureaucracies and cities. Despite frequent predictions of their imminent demise, they weathered rapid socioeconomic change and the challenges posed by the collapse of the pearling industry, the rise of oil, military conflicts, the Cold War, Arab nationalism, decolonization, and Islamism. None of the states collapsed or faced a threat to its authority analogous to the revolutions that toppled the monarchies in Egypt (1952), Iraq (1958), Libya (1969), and Iran (1979). In 1981, the Gulf regimes were, in the words of Jill Crystal, "anachronistically stable monarchical regimes."[31] They were also far more stable and cohesive politically than they had been before Britain's appearance in the region in the nineteenth century.

To explain the remarkable record of continuity of these regimes, scholars universally point to one factor: the revenues that rents from petroleum extraction generated for the region's ruling monarchies. Although Crystal, Gregory Gause, and many other scholars have marshaled impressive evidence to support this claim, we should bear in mind that monarchies in Iran, Libya, and Iraq also had access to vast oil revenues and powerful international allies but could not maintain enough political stability to survive. One could say the same thing about the dictatorial regimes in Mexico, Russia, or Venezuela, which ushered in oil development in the early twentieth century and had grown rich from it but had long been confined to the dust heap of history by 1981.

By contrast, Morocco's monarchy, which had *no* oil revenues, withstood the same political, social, and economic currents that crushed other long-standing monarchies in the Middle East between 1931 and 1981. Samuel Huntington and other Western scholars long looked at Morocco's regime as anachronistic and medieval, since its claim to legitimacy rested on Islam and the king's status as sharif, the direct descendant of the Prophet Muhammad. Morocco's government appeared weak, compared to modern regimes in Egypt, Iraq, and South Yemen, which rejected religion in favor of popular sovereignty. But instead of collapsing in the face of modernity, Morocco's monarchy flourished in the twentieth century, utilizing the police and other clearly modern tools of political control with premodern links and retaining support throughout the diverse society. By 1981, Morocco's monarchy—much like those in the Arab Gulf—was much stronger than it had been before European colonization at the turn of the twentieth century.

The close similarities between Morocco and the Arab Gulf states suggest that there are factors other than oil that contribute to state formation, new governing institutions, co-option of elites, and the maintenance of ruling coalitions. The most important of these factors is the "anachronistic" or "medieval quality" of governance, long seen as the states' biggest weakness. But this weakness also created a vast well of historical or institutional legitimacy, which the monarchies could use to govern or to counteract political crises. Along with the sultanate of Morocco, the ruling families in the Arab Gulf were the only national leaders in the Arab world after 1960 who could legitimately claim a tradition of governance over their national territories that dated back to the nineteenth century. Rulers of seemingly stronger modern states in the Middle East could only achieve a comparable level of legitimacy by framing themselves and their governments within the tradition of ancient, often pre-Islamic heroes, peoples, and states.[32]

Governing in the Gulf in the twentieth century, however, involved much more than drawing on historical legitimacy, no matter how secure and broad such legitimacy was. As this chapter will show, rulers reinforced their legitimacy by cultivating tribal, familial, ethnic, religious, and commercial networks and by promoting Islamic and tribal values. In mosques, sword dances, salons (councils or *majlises*), markets, hajj pilgrimages and speeches, royal visits to provincial cities, and welfare institutions, ordinary subjects interacted directly with monarchs, thereby conferring legitimacy on them. Many rulers further reinforced their authority through a system analogous to a welfare state, in which individual subjects and tribes received generous cash subsidies, food, and clothing. Rulers also leveraged their international positions to win assistance akin to the rents they would later receive from oil. In fact, Saudi Arabia's dependence in the 1930s on the annual fees paid by hajj pilgrims—many of whom were subjects of Britain's vast empire traveling to Jeddah on European ships—mirrored the kingdom's high dependence on the proceeds from ARAMCO's sale of Saudi oil in the 1970s.

The British Raj in the Gulf

"Under British Protection, but not British Protectorates"

For much of the century between the 1820s and the 1920s, the Gulf was a "British lake," which—as James Onley has recently shown in *The Arabian Frontier of the British Raj*—was closely tied administratively to the British Empire's possessions in India, Iran, East Africa, and elsewhere. From Kuwait all the way to Oman, political residents and naval steamers projected Britain's power and worked to maintain a framework by which ruling families were, in the words of one US diplomat, "under British protection, but not British protectorates."[33] As Lord Curzon, the famous viceroy of India, remarked, London "upheld the independence" of several Arab Gulf principalities, but British influence "remained supreme."[34]

To maintain their empire in the Gulf, British officials followed a multilayered strategy that utilized both hard and soft power. Even though Britain generally avoided involving itself in the internal politics of the Trucial States, it capitalized on the fact that shaikhs in Kuwait, Bahrain, and elsewhere in the Gulf were often weak rulers, whose power was regularly challenged in their own families and by nearby leaders. Britain helped rulers to distribute state income from land, possessions, and minor taxes to family members and other leaders of the community. (Some shaikhs literally counted every Indian rupee paid by the British government or oil companies well into the late 1950s.[35]) The wealth of Gulf merchants, however, usually dwarfed that of the shaikhs, and therefore the former could resist "oppressive" policies and flee excessive taxation.[36] Merchants also forced local rulers to acknowledge their authority via elected consultative councils and other traditions of mutual consultation.

British officials managed the foreign affairs of Bahrain, Kuwait, Qatar, Oman, and the Trucial States, often making decisions without consulting local leaders.[37] For example, the Kuwaiti emir was not consulted when Sir Percy Cox agreed in 1922 to cede half of Kuwait's territory to what would become Saudi Arabia. British officials worked tirelessly to exclude other powers from gaining influence in the region and discouraged both Europeans and Americans from visiting. US attempts to establish consuls in Bahrain, Muscat, and Kuwait before and even after World War II met with stiff British resistance despite the long-term presence of US missionaries in each territory. In addition, British officials asserted jurisdiction over foreigners in the Gulf through a system of extraterritorial laws akin to the systems in place in French North Africa and British India.[38]

The Gulf's geography, climate, and socioeconomic structure cemented Britain's ability to dominate the region without directly administering large regions of it. The area had little arable land, few skilled laborers,[39] and no manufacturing, so Gulf populations imported most of their food[40] and labor from abroad and depended on rent-seeking activities to survive: pilgrimage fees, transit trade, herding, pearling, and raiding.[41] Whenever skilled or unskilled labor was needed, it had to be imported, often from British territories.

Poor climate also provided few opportunities for European settlement. The region's population remained small because of the dearth of resources, the harsh climate, and the frequent outbreaks of disease, including cholera, syphilis, gonorrhea, and the plague. The region's far-flung population centers, being dependent on seaborne commerce, were vulnerable to external attack from neighboring states or tribes. Two-thirds of Gulf Arabs lived nomadic or seminomadic lives and were therefore well out of state control. Sunni Muslims were by far the largest population, but there were also Jews, various Christian denominations, Hindus, and other non-Muslims. In addition, Shia Muslims were important, especially in Bahrain and Kuwait.[42]

Gulf merchants further reinforced Britain's soft power in the Gulf, as South Asians and other British subjects provided modern goods, services, and transportation. As James Onley has demonstrated, merchants served as British consuls in the Gulf and were valuable sources of intelligence, which was "needed to sustain [Britain's] informal empire."[43] Merchants in Jeddah and other Gulf communities often sent their sons and daughters to British-run schools in Egypt and other parts of the empire.[44] They also depended on Indian flour, grain, and rice controlled by the empire.[45] Indian rupees and other British imperial currencies were the monetary exchange of choice in Bahrain, Kuwait, Qatar, and Oman. British shipping transported passenger and commercial traffic to Europe, Asia, and beyond via British-controlled sea lanes, territories, canals, and straits. These types of overlapping commercial and transportation networks allowed London to control the Arab Gulf, even though it did not directly administer wide areas of the region or have formal political ties with some of its governments. In fact, Great Britain did not have a permanent representative stationed on the Trucial Coast until 1939 and lacked treaty relations with Fujairah until 1950.[46]

World War I and New Technologies

The settlement arrangements at the end of World War I seemingly strengthened Britain's position in the region. The collapse of the Ottoman, German, and Russian empires during and after the war eliminated Britain's principal Great Power competitors in the Gulf. Not only did London maintain its power in Kuwait, Qatar, Bahrain, Oman, Iran, and the Trucial Coast, but it gained new bases in Iraq and new influence in the interior of the Arabian Peninsula. Britain's extension of power in Iraq and the Gulf benefited from three technical innovations that gained in importance in the years after the war: airplanes, wireless communication (telegraphs and radios), and air conditioning. British officials in the region were especially aggressive in maintaining influence after 1933, when London switched responsibility for setting policy in the Gulf from the Foreign Office to the India Office.[47] Foreign Office diplomats were sensitive to Britain's relationship with the United States and other great powers, but India Office bureaucrats saw no reason to yield British influence to anyone in the region.

The first two innovations, airplanes and wireless communication, greatly expedited imperial communications, allowing Britain to project its military might over large areas more swiftly than before. For example, in Iraq, airplanes and wireless communication allowed the British-backed Sunni monarchy to overcome geographical barriers in the north and south that had long impeded the ability of a centralized government to rule the nation. In time, Iraq would provide a useful model for dealing with rebellious tribesmen in Kuwait, Saudi Arabia, and other states in the Gulf that faced similar geographic challenges. Airplanes were also an issue when Iran forced Britain to move its imperial air route from Iran's Gulf coast to the Trucial States on the Arabian Peninsula in 1933. To accommodate the new route, Britain had to build airfields and establish permanent facilities in Sharjah and other areas of the Trucial Coast for the first time.[48]

The third innovation, air conditioning, permitted Britons and other westerners to work year-round in Sharjah and other areas of the Gulf without suffering the often disabling effects of extreme and prolonged exposure to heat. In a region where humidity can reach as high as 90 percent and daytime temperatures can regularly reach 100 degrees Fahrenheit, this technology was a major advance. For decades, the Arab Gulf was known as a "white man's grave." During the nineteenth century, as Onley observes, every British "political officer assigned to the Gulf suffered seriously from ill health at some point during his assignment."[49] Air conditioning in offices, homes, and work camps reduced the incidents of illness from unimaginable levels to those on a par with those in Europe and North America. A British diplomat visiting the Arab Gulf in 1940 noted that air conditioning aided efficiency and was worth an extra "two hours' useful work a day during the summer."[50]

Britain, the Oil Companies, and the Gulf

Air conditioning proved especially important to the rise of the oil industry, which utilized modern machinery, employed scores of Western workers, and came to dominate the Arab Gulf's economy and very identity. Britain played an integral role in the industry from the start with the formation of the Anglo-Persian Oil Company (APOC) in 1909 and the Turkish Petroleum Company (TPC) in 1912 (later the Iraq Petroleum Company, or IPC). In the years immediately before World War I, Britain secured rights to extract oil from the Arab Gulf states along with promises that no future concessions would be granted to anyone else without consulting London first. Even more significant was the British Admiralty's decision in 1912 that turned oil into the most prized strategic commodity in the world by transforming the British fleet's steam turbine engines from coal to oil. In a single stroke, Britain ensured that the Arab Gulf would play a paramount role in global affairs over the next century.

Yet the importance of the supplies of petroleum in the Gulf was hardly obvious at the time and was dwarfed by larger supplies of oil in the Americas, Russia, Iran, and other states in the Middle East. Major British companies showed little interest in the Arabian side of the Gulf coast until the discovery of petroleum in commercial quantities in 1932 by the Bahrain Petroleum Company (BAPCO), a Canadian-chartered subsidiary of US Standard Oil of California (now Chevron).

Throughout the 1930s and 1940s, oil companies were formed in the Arab Gulf states, such as the Kuwait Oil Company (KOC). Modeled on APOC and IPC, KOC and its fellow oil companies had Western (usually British) management, were headquartered in the British Empire, and employed local (Arab and non-Arab) workers along with expatriates, many of whom were South Asian. The Western compounds of these companies in Dhahran, Saudi Arabia, Awali, Bahrain, and elsewhere in the Gulf featured modern schools, Western-style housing, air conditioning, electric lights, paved streets, buses, trees, and grass.[51] Air conditioning was especially important to the new compounds, as a former Dhahran resident remembered: "There are a few small squares, which in European towns would contain parks or cafes; in Dhahran they have large buzzing air conditioning units."[52] Over time, the compounds and their air conditioning provided a blueprint for a new mode of living in the Gulf that would have more in common with US suburbs than with cities of the Arab world.

After the onset of the Great Depression in the 1930s, oil companies gained enormous power, equal to that of many sovereign and independent states—what a Western diplomat characterized with the Latin legal term *imperium in imperium* (sovereignty within sovereignty).[53] In fact, the oil companies developed a degree of socioeconomic and political power equivalent to that of the Canal Company in Panama and the United Fruit Company in Guatemala. This power soared as three principal sources of income for the region evaporated. The slowdown in the global economy immediately curtailed pilgrimage traffic and transitory commerce. At the same time, Japanese entrepreneur Kokichi Mikimoto's success in developing cultured pearls produced a crash in the price of pearls. Tens of thousands of divers, merchants, and other businesses were destitute as rulers scrambled to find alternative sources of income. Oil companies quickly provided an almost miraculous source of jobs, a demand for goods, and government revenue. The change in Bahrain's fortunes in the 1930s was so dramatic that Stephen Longring argues that "no community and government had been more suddenly and timely rescued from disaster than [Bahrain]."[54]

Oil revenues also produced two key changes in Gulf societies. First, as Jill Crystal and others have noted, oil revenues transformed the power dynamics in the Arab Gulf states by concentrating wealth in the hands of the rulers, who for the first time had a source of secure income that could dwarf those of the merchants. Second, the oil industry stimulated the mass migration of South Asians to the Gulf, helping to create one of the defining features of modern life in the region, the preponderance of South Asian laborers. The mass migration reflected London's attempts to check rising US commercial influence in the Arab Gulf and vast shortages of labor in the Gulf. Recruitment networks arose in which merchants bought certificates that allowed them to import South Asian workers into Gulf territories under British influence: a system that would be replicated in the 1960s and 1970s by independent Arab Gulf states in the form of the *kafala* system. Moreover, British officials used formal and informal agreements to pressure regional leaders and oil companies to open recruiting stations in South Asian cities as well as to use British subjects as clerical staff, craftsmen, and unskilled and semiskilled laborers.[55]

By the end of the 1930s, British policies had achieved their desired results. South Asians represented more than 90 percent of clerical and technical employees at BAPCO and dominated clerical, technical, and artisan positions in both Qatar and Kuwait.[56] In both states, oil companies employed many unskilled South Asians. Indian contracting firms also often met the needs of expanding oil companies. In all cases, the factor that drove South Asian migration to the Gulf—as it would for decades—was money. South Asians working in Bahrain or Kuwait earned double the salary of comparable workers in Indian cities. In January 1948, for example, Indian clerks in Kuwait earned around 210 rupees a month in salary plus food and housing, whereas Indian clerks in South Asia earned on average 60 to 70 rupees a month.[57]

Yet the oil companies' use of South Asian and other expatriate workers produced a national and socioeconomic backlash among local Arabs, who felt that it was only fair that companies should prefer local workers over expatriates. As early as 1938, Sunni and Shia Bahrainis called on BAPCO to replace foreign workers with Bahrainis, recognize a union, and standardize pay and benefits. BAPCO balked at these demands, arguing, as private employers in the Gulf today still do, that South Asians and other expatriates were far better employees than the Bahrainis were.[58] Eventually, the British resident, Charles Belgrave, mediated and solved the dispute, winning a pledge by BAPCO to hire more Bahrainis at higher wages. But the basic issues of the dispute—the clash between the expectations of ordinary Gulf Arabs and the interests of private employers—continue to haunt the region. Plans to replace expatriates with local workers in Bahrain and other Arab Gulf states are part of a process that is decades old.[59]

Britain and the Rise of the Saudi Welfare State

Oil and expatriate laborers were equally important to Bahrain's neighbor, Saudi Arabia. Although the kingdom was an independent state and would develop a partnership with a US oil consortium (ARAMCO), Britain's influence in Saudi Arabia was as strong as it was in the Arab Gulf states, with which it had treaty relations and resident political agents. That relationship began in the first decades of the twentieth century, when King Ibn Saud, after seizing Riyadh in 1902 and reconstituting a state in the Najd, sought an alliance with Great Britain. This lasted for half a century, during which British power fundamentally shaped Saudi society, politics, and economic life.

Ibn Saud viewed Great Britain as critical for recreating the Saudi-Wahhabi emirate, which his family had governed in the eighteenth century. That emirate had conquered much of the Arabian Peninsula, including the Hijaz, but had created powerful enemies because of its frequent raids on surrounding territories and its seemingly fanatical religious views. Egyptian armies, using European weapons and advisers, crushed the emirate in 1811 with the full support of the Ottoman Turkish government and other Muslims. Ibn Saud was determined that his state would not fall to a similar coalition or be surrounded by the Turks again, lack powerful European allies, or go into battle without the latest European weapons and military technology.[60] He hoped that Great Britain would back his state, but also he sought assistance from the Turks, Poles, Germans, White Russians, Soviets, Dutch, and Americans.[61]

The logic of a Saudi-British alliance was sufficiently strong for both sides to realize the benefits of partnership, so, in 1915, the two sides reached the first of a number of bilateral agreements. In exchange for Ibn Saud's support of Britain's goals against the Ottoman Empire in World War I and his assurance that he would not invade Britain's Arab Gulf dependencies, the Saudi monarch received an annual subsidy, ammunition, and modern weapons.[62] British support allowed Ibn Saud's army to seize strategic territories, such as the city of Hail, and to pacify his tribes, which for years had been raiding urban communities, neighboring territories, rival tribes, and hajj pilgrims.[63] To keep the tribes from returning to their old ways and provoking a devastating British attack, Ibn Saud implemented a three-part strategy. First, using motor travel and wireless (i.e., radio) technology, he deployed force against unruly tribesmen. Second, he built an efficient intelligence service[64] and, third, a welfare state[65] in which his power and legitimacy, according to a Muslim Dutch visitor to Riyadh in 1931, rested "on his ability to pay, pay, pay."[66] In 1941, the king warned a British diplomat "that if he were to remain strong in his own country," as the British government desired, "he must be generous in his distribution of food and money to his tribes."[67]

It should come as no surprise that from the 1920s until the 1950s, Ibn Saud provided generous grants of cash, foodstuffs, tea, sugar, and textiles to tribes, along with subsidized or free food to the populations of Jeddah, Riyadh, Mecca, Taif, and other Saudi towns.[68] In November 1931, Ibn Saud gave 4,000 tribesmen a large meal every day and an annual "allowance" of cash.[69] By 1941, he was providing subsidies to more than half a million people and feeding 30,000 people daily in Riyadh alone, which was virtually the entire population of the Saudi capital.[70] Subsidies to Saudi tribes accounted for a staggering 80 percent of the kingdom's annual budget in 1943.[71] A decade later, subsidies to tribes were still a heavy charge on government revenues.[72] Under this system, domestic taxation was unthinkable, and so accounted for less than 5 percent of royal income.[73] Indeed, the modern Saudi welfare state was in place long before oil was the dominant factor in the kingdom's economy.

Britain, the Hajj, and the Rise of Modern Saudi Identity

The Saudi welfare state faced a near fatal crisis in the mid-1920s, when the British government ended the subsidy it had paid to Ibn Saud since World War I. Subsequent requests for assistance or loans were refused by London. In response, Ibn Saud, who no longer feared British financial reprisals, seized a neighboring territory that had been part of the original Saudi state, the Hijaz, and expelled its longtime rulers, the Hashemites. This coastal state had forms of income far more lucrative than Ibn Saud's one-time British subsidy: hajj pilgrimage taxes, customs duties, and funds from pious endowments around the Muslim world designated for the upkeep of the Hijaz's two holy cities, Mecca and Medina. By 1926, Ibn Saud had full control of the Hijaz, and in 1932 he merged his original Riyadh-based state, the Najd, with the Hijaz and other Arabian regions into a new kingdom that bore his family's name, Saudi Arabia.[74] Although the new state had a reputation for adhering closely to a very conservative vision of Islamic law and society, the decree establishing Saudi Arabia announced that the date of the kingdom's founding was specifically timed to correspond to an important date in a non-Islamic calendar: the first day of the constellation Libra.[75]

The new state's populations were just as diverse as those of its neighbors in the region and the broader Middle East. Non-Arabs, Jews, Christians, Shias, and Ismailis were all Saudi subjects, with non-Muslims required to pay the traditional *jiziya* tax instead of the *zhakat*—much as they had done for centuries under Ottoman rule. Greeks were among the merchants in Jeddah's main market in 1943.[76] Non-Sunni Muslim communities were strong in al-Hasa and Najran, whose Jewish population had maintained warm relations with local tribal chiefs for generations and had been the only gunsmiths.[77] Homosexuality was so tolerated and pervasive that F. P. Mackie, a US doctor, expressed surprise in a report he wrote on diseases in the kingdom that he did not find "rectal complications" and other conditions commonly linked to homosexuals.[78] (Natana DeLong-Bas notes in *Wahhabi Islam* that the founder of Wahhabis, the eighteenth-century scholar Muhammad ibn Abd al-Wahhab, advised toleration of gay men so long as they kept their behavior private.[79]) US Christian missionaries visited various parts of the kingdom and were invited to the royal court. Diversity extended to the royal family itself, for some of Ibn Saud's favorite wives and slaves were Armenian Christians.[80] Ibn Saud would later tell his British confidant, St. John Philby, that he would readily marry a Jewish woman, who would "have full liberty of belief and conscience."[81]

The relative tolerance of the Saudi state, which I will discuss in greater detail in Chapter 6, reflected in part the financial and political significance of the kingdom's most diverse region, the Hijaz. Following the conquest of the region, Ibn Saud understood that the hajj pilgrimage would be of no value unless he could restore order and safety to the annual event, which had been plagued for a decade by thieves and robbers. Thanks to Saudi military power, Ibn Saud achieved this goal, allowing Muslim participation in the hajj to rise dramatically. Although the number of pilgrims had declined precipitously during the final years of Hashemite rule in the mid-1920s (there were virtually no overseas pilgrims in 1925), an average of 101,563 Muslims participated in the first four hajj pilgrimages under Saudi Arabian administration from 1927 to 1930.[82] Each hajj pilgrim spent an average of nearly US$2,000 (all references to dollar figures are in US dollars) in the kingdom during his or her stay, with Saudi merchants marketing trinkets and "holy" dates and figs to pilgrims.[83]

As the number of hajj pilgrims skyrocketed, their receipts dominated Saudi annual revenues in much the same way that oil would in the post–World War II period. By the mid-1930s, hajj pilgrimage fees constituted 50 percent of all Saudi revenues.[84] Customs duties, most of which were tied to hajj-related trade and imports, often accounted for another third of Saudi revenues. Hajj-related income was 80 percent of annual Saudi revenues, much higher than any other source, and allowed the state to demand a remarkably low level of internal taxation from the population.[85] (This would remain a significant portion of the kingdom's budget decades after the start of the oil era in the 1930s.[86]) For all intents and purposes, Saudi Arabia had become a rentier state economically, with hajj dues serving as the exogenous rent that permitted the government to forgo internal taxes. This model of government finance, built on external income and low domestic taxation, would eventually be adopted by every Arab Gulf state in the twentieth century.

Even though the seizure of the Hijaz provided a much needed source of revenue for Ibn Saud to use to replace Britain's subsidy, it presented a series of complex economic, foreign, and domestic challenges, the most vexing of which was the hajj itself. Because of the enormous time and expense involved in making the pilgrimage, Muslims would not take the trip if economic circumstances became unsettled or if travel to Saudi Arabia were unsafe. As a British economic report noted, Saudi Arabia's dependence on the hajj and its minimal reliance on internal taxation left the kingdom's government "particularly exposed to the consequences of any world-wide trade recession."[87] The potential consequences of this arrangement were borne out after the start of the Great Depression and World War II, when the number of pilgrims declined from 220,000 in 1927[88] to 50,000 in 1933[89] and 9,024 in 1940.[90] Pilgrimage fees and other customs duties dried up, collapsing royal finances.[91]

Another vexing problem that the Hijaz presented to Saudi Arabia was the fact that it was economically and socially an appendage of Europe's overseas empires—especially Britain's empire—because of the number of hajj pilgrims who traveled from European-held territories in Asia and Africa.[92] Since the nineteenth century, Europeans had been using the fear of epidemics of plague and other diseases associated with hajj pilgrims to win control of the official quarantine station on the Red Sea island of Kamarān, which regulated who could enter the Hijaz by sea. Although the Saudis partially circumvented Kamarān by building their own quarantine station at Jeddah, they could not avoid the facts that 50 to 75 percent of hajj pilgrims originated in British or Dutch territories and that an equally high percentage of hajj fees were paid in sterling, the rupee, or European-related currencies.[93] Many of the charitable foundations that provided funds for the poor and other vulnerable citizens of Mecca, along with maintaining mosques and schools in the city, were located or administered in the British Empire.[94]

An equally important issue was that Saudi Arabia could not escape the facts that British ships carried 49 to 77 percent of hajj pilgrims traveling to the Hijaz[95] or that the British Navy made an official visit to the kingdom every Ramadan.[96] To address the problem of British power, Riyadh encouraged wealthier pilgrims to travel on European ships and discouraged destitute Muslims from doing so. Riyadh actively lobbied the Office International d'Hygiene Publique (the predecessor to the World Health Organization) to increase the size of cabins on hajj transport ships in order to raise the cost of traveling to Jeddah.[97] The Saudis allowed a film to be made of the hajj to publicize the event abroad[98] and replicated the Ottoman strategy of providing means of transport over land to serve as an alternative to European shipping. Yet it was still a British operation through and through. Britain's role was clear in 1942, when Ibn Saud personally thanked the British government for providing food and transportation to hajj pilgrims during his annual address to Muslim dignitaries on the hajj in Mecca.[99]

Overcoming dependence on hajj receipts and Britain for the pilgrimage, however, paled in comparison to the challenge of establishing Ibn Saud's legitimacy in the hajj. Here, too, the British were significant players because of their influence on Saudi Arabia's neighbors to the south and east—Bahrain, Oman, the Trucial States, Yemen, and Qatar—and two northern neighbors, Iraq and Jordan. The final two were governed by members of the Hashemite family, who had long administered the Hijaz before being expelled by Ibn Saud in 1926.[100] For Ibn Saud, the proximity of two Hashemite states seriously complicated his efforts to govern, because they provided a viable alternative source of authority in the Hijaz, especially since they were among the most prominent families in the Arab world and sought to retake the territory.[101] In fact, the Hashemites directly and indirectly supported opposition movements to Saudi rule in the Hijaz and other parts of the kingdom.[102] Ibn Saud survived several assassination attempts allegedly tied to the Hashemites.[103]

To counteract the Hashemite appeal, Ibn Saud pursued a four-part strategy that came to define Saudi national identity. First, he maintained close relations with the British government, hoping that it would keep Hashemite rulers in check. In particular, he treated the British ambassador in Jeddah as his virtual personal attorney on all matters and rejected favorable trade deals with Japan and Germany in the 1930s in order to maintain London's friendship.[104]

Second, he participated in Bedouin war dances in Mecca and elsewhere to prove his strength and vigor and did not impede many tribal legal traditions.[105]

Third, he and his sons emphasized his family's tradition of governing in association with Wahhabi religious authorities and their resistance to Turkish and European imperialism. In conversations with US and British officials, Ibn Saud and his son, Emir Faysal, stressed their family's centuries-old rivalry with the Turks and Ottoman Empire and their vigorous support for the Arab revolt.[106] Integral to Saudi notions of governance (and those of its Arab Gulf neighbors) were the ideal of equality and the principle that government leaders should be directly accountable to their subjects. Like other Arab rulers, the Saud family maintained open courts and frequently traveled to various regions of the kingdom. These rituals reinforced tribal loyalties and group solidarity (*asabiyya*) and gave subjects opportunities to seek personal redress for their grievances and even to challenge a monarch's policies or actions to his face.[107]

Finally, Ibn Saud emphasized his personal piety and religious idealism. Although he refused to accept a position as eminent as caliph (the religious and political head of the global Muslim community),[108] he referred to himself as the "Herald of Islam" and the "Imam of the Hijaz." He also adopted a role that the Ottoman rulers had utilized to legitimize their presence in the Hijaz: custodian of the two holy places and all the Muslims therein.[109] Each year, in an address delivered in Mecca at the start of the pilgrimage, Ibn Saud and his successors have reaffirmed their commitment to protect the holy places and the hajj. From the 1930s forward, the Saud family and their state defined themselves and their place in the world through their ability to manage the hajj pilgrimage for Muslim visitors, whom Saudis termed "God's guests." For the Hijazis, the promise to help Muslims fulfill an obligation from God helped them as well, because of their dependence on the hajj trade.[110]

Irrespective of the value of the title of "Herald of Islam" at home and abroad, it left a larger question: how to reconcile the central role of the hajj in Saudi life with the fact that Saudis could not care for God's guests without British assistance. This question became a central element in Saudi foreign policy throughout World War II and the postwar period—an element that would take precedence over virtually everything else and shape the relationship of Saudi Arabia and its Arab neighbors with Britain and other states, including the United States.

Britain's Silent Partners

When Saudi Arabia adopted its new identity in the early 1930s, few would have predicted that the United States would take a leading role in Saudi Arabia and the other Arab Gulf states. Although Saudis and other Gulf Arabs readily bought US automobiles, kerosene, petroleum, textiles, radios, and other consumer goods, few Gulf products besides hides, skins, and pearls arrived in the United States.[111] British investments in the region's oil industry dwarfed those of US firms, which felt that they profited from the continuation of Britain's imperial presence in Iraq, Kuwait, and elsewhere in the Gulf. With the notable exception of the wealthy philanthropist Charles Crane, very few Americans traveled to the region or called on Washington to exercise financial or political influence in the Gulf the way it had done in Latin America and Asia. It was not until World War II that there was a permanent US diplomatic representation in the region outside of Iraq.

But the lack of official US presence in the Gulf masked a significant US presence on which Great Britain came to depend. Starting in 1891, the Dutch Reformed Church of America sent dozens of doctors and nurses to its mission stations in Kuwait, Bahrain, and Oman. Few Gulf Arabs converted to Christianity, but thousands took advantage of the modern medical care provided by the church's doctors. In the 1920s, Louis Dame, Harold Storm, Gerald Nykerk, Paul Harrison, and Esther Barny, among others, provided medical care to Ibn Saud and other Gulf monarchs. Sara Hosman spent many decades on her own, deep in the interior of Sharjah, serving Bedouin women and men as a doctor, despite the fact that she had a wooden leg.[112] Similarly, Burwell M. (Pat) Kennedy and his wife ran a mission and hospital in Buraimi, a desert oasis located in a disputed border area between Abu Dhabi, Oman, and Saudi Arabia.[113] These missionaries kept in close contact with friends and family in the United States, promoted US trade, and occasionally provided intelligence to US diplomats stationed in Baghdad and Cairo.

US Protestant missionaries, along with Catholics, also founded and administered some of the first modern schools and hospitals in the Gulf. Enrollment in the schools included a broad cross section of Gulf peoples: Sunnis, Shia, various Christian sects, Jews, and Hindus. Bahrain's Mason Memorial Hospital was the first to offer both basic dental care and x-rays in the Gulf. Missionary doctors regularly served 80,000 to 90,000 patients every year and conducted 1,500 surgeries in the Gulf annually, a remarkable number, given that the population of the region stood at only 3.6 million at the time. Christian schools, hospitals, and mobile medical missions helped lay the foundation for the contemporary educational and health-care systems in Kuwait, Bahrain, and Oman. Even after the Kuwaiti government built its first modern hospital in the late 1930s, US missionaries annually served 67,000 patients, which was then "approximately equal to treating every man, woman, and child in Kuwait once a year."[114]

The mission facilities not only provided education and health care to Britain's officials and their families in the Arab Gulf but also allowed Britain to reinforce its authority in regions that its officials feared to visit without considerable military support.[115] It is worth noting that Britain's attempt to enforce an arms prohibition in Dubai in 1908 met with fierce resistance, and British officials refused to station a permanent representative anywhere on the Trucial Coast until 1939 out of fear that any such individual would be killed.[116] By contrast, US missionaries worked for decades on the Trucial Coast, building enduring institutions that freed London from the obligation of investing in medical and educational facilities there. Because British resources were overstretched in other parts of the world, the work of US missionaries was a welcome way for London to maintain its position in the Gulf cheaply.

Missionary doctors, however, were hardly the only Americans in the Gulf who facilitated British dominance in the region. After World War I, US oil companies realized that they could not depend entirely on US suppliers to remain competitive in Asia and Europe. Middle East oil fit the needs of US companies, so after furious lobbying of British officials by Anglo and US petroleum companies and US officials under the rubric of the Open Door Policy, a series of deals was struck. US companies got access to oil fields in Iraq and Bahrain in exchange for investments in Britain's empire, especially in the City of London, which was rapidly losing its position to New York as the center of world business.

An implicit aspect of these deals was London's belief that it could not easily maintain its empire in the Middle East economically, politically, or strategically unless it gave Washington a tangible stake in the maintenance of British imperial assets in the region. For their part, US officials welcomed the new arrangements because they believed that Washington lacked the resources and will to defend US overseas assets and that the British were the only ones who could do that. In addition, Washington permitted British diplomats in the Gulf to administer the oath of allegiance to acquire new US passports, register marriages between US citizens, and certify various types of forms for US customs agencies. Just like US missionaries, government officials of the United States and the country's oilmen were effectively silent partners in Britain's Raj in the Gulf.[117]

"Gently" Pushing for ARAMCO

It is within the context of the US-UK partnership that we can better come to terms with the rise of what came to be known in Saudi Arabia as ARAMCO. Although Britain wielded enormous influence in Saudi Arabia through the hajj and by controlling the territories that surrounded the kingdom, Anglo-Saudi relations were far from smooth in the 1930s and 1940s. During that period, Ibn Saud persistently sought British financial and military assistance,[118] warning of the dangers to London if his regime weakened or collapsed. Following the establishment of a Soviet embassy in Jeddah in the 1920s, he even sought to use the specter of communist infiltration into the Middle East and the hajj to win more assistance from Great Britain.[119]

Time after time, British officials politely rebuffed Ibn Saud's requests or provided aid that fell far short of Saudi expectations.[120] London felt that its limited financial resources were better deployed elsewhere and that Saudi Arabia could ill afford to lose Britain's protection, regardless of how much British support was given. The strategic value of Saudi oil reserves was not at all clear in the interwar period, and British-controlled reserves in Iraq and Iran appeared larger than anything else in the Middle East. IPC was the only major British company interested in Saudi oil reserves, but its board of directors moved slowly on Saudi Arabia's proposals to develop the kingdom's oil fields. Furthermore, IPC's representative in the kingdom, Stephen Longring, reportedly hunted wild animals in the desert, went on fishing trips, and made few official contacts when Saudi officials made their decision in 1933 as to which company would receive the kingdom's concession to export oil.[121]

The attitude of Longring and British diplomats in the Gulf reflected their irritation with Ibn Saud and the seemingly medieval quality of life in his kingdom. When Ibn Saud asked their opinion about his desire to award the Saudi concession to a US oil company, Standard Oil of California, they gave it their full blessing. At the time, British officials privately expressed their relief that the Saudi king would be someone else's responsibility. Over the next decade, these officials "gently" pushed Ibn Saud toward "greater understanding and cooperation" with ARAMCO and the United States, even when he preferred to work with Britain or keep Washington at a distance because of its support of a Jewish state in the Palestinian mandate territory.[122] Indeed, British officials were so committed to a Saudi-American partnership that they provided both planes and ships for Emir Faysal to travel from Saudi Arabia to the United States on a state visit in 1943.[123]

For its part, Standard Oil of California took advantage of the opportunity that the British government had offered it. Years before the first barrel of oil was pumped out of the ground, company officials established firm ties with the Saudi government and did what London had hoped they would do: namely, they lent Ibn Saud millions of dollars annually to prop up his welfare state. Standard Oil's investment took a lead role in various aspects of Saudi society, from economic development, to agriculture, to transportation for the royal family and the hajj pilgrims. Company officials usually blurred the lines between Saudi interests and those of the company, which was, for all practical purposes, a sovereign, independent entity operating within Saudi Arabia. By 1940, the company's chief representative had amassed more power and influence than any foreign diplomat except Britain's.[124] And it was not unheard of for ARAMCO to host senior foreigners in the kingdom and introduce them to Ibn Saud. British policy in Saudi Arabia in the 1930s was an unqualified success: the kingdom's government, a British ally, remained stable with little direct cost to the British treasury.

World War II, the Mass Media, and a New Arrangement in the Gulf

In many ways, the Anglo-American partnership forged in Saudi Arabia and the rest of the Gulf during the interwar years strengthened during World War II, but it also evolved in important ways that would transform the region in the postwar period. Washington deployed military and diplomatic assets in Bahrain, the Trucial Coast, Iran, and other nearby areas to help Britain protect its communication and supply routes and oil fields, which briefly came under Italian attack in 1943. For the first time, Washington no longer had to depend on the British Navy to protect US overseas commercial assets in the Middle East. It could depend on the power of the United States Navy and later the United States Air Force. During the war, Washington established a naval base in Bahrain and an airfield in Saudi Arabia. The military power of the United States in the region was beginning to match its economic clout there.

Washington and London also cooperated in containing the economic dis ruption that resulted from Japanese and German attacks on Allied shipping. Additional problems were inflation, especially in the Gulf, and the severe shortage of oil tankers and hajj transport ships. In some parts of the Gulf, inflation grew fourfold in sterling and 50 percent in gold between 1939 and the mid-1940s.[125] A US report noted in 1944 that inflation and rising food prices during the 1940s had overwhelmed the Saudi welfare state and resulted in malnutrition among adults in the kingdom and acute food shortages in Riyadh.[126] To address these problems, Britain and the United States gave financial, agricultural, technical, and administrative aid to the Gulf regimes.[127] Saudi Arabia was especially hard hit, since it suffered a severe drought and, because of the war, was unable to take full advantage of oil royalties and as many hajj fees as normal.[128] London provided most of the early assistance—approximately £10 million between 1941 and 1943, which was made possible by a US loan to Great Britain.[129] ARAMCO provided an additional $3 million loan in 1941 and 1942, based on leveraged future oil exports.[130]

Saudi and other Gulf leaders also looked to London and Washington for assistance with a problem that originated far away from the Gulf: foreign radio broadcasts. US officials estimated that at least 500 shortwave radios existed in Saudi Arabia in 1941, along with hundreds more throughout the Gulf.[131] Radios frequently appeared in the advertisements of the official Saudi newspaper, *Um al-Qura*.[132] Some radios could pick up broadcasts from as far away as Iowa,[133] and Arabs in the Gulf frequently listened to foreign broadcasts with their families and also at work and in social organizations, such as Bahrain's "youth" clubs.[134] The appearance of radios in the Gulf in the 1930s led monarchs and their officials to grasp the power of radio to shape public opinion and to undermine governments.[135] For example, radio broadcasts discussing League of Nations deliberations on Ethiopia had led to riots and hoarding of food in Jeddah and Mecca in 1935.[136] During that same year, Britain's political agent in Kuwait observed that the new Egyptian radio broadcasts could cause great harm should they fall into the wrong hands.[137]

Ibn Saud took this threat as seriously as the British political agent in Kuwait did. The Saudi king received three to four reports daily on foreign radio transmissions and closely monitored who listened to German and Italian broadcasts among his kingdom's elite.[138] In 1935, he authorized the two Saudi official newspapers, *Um al-Qura* and *Saut al-Hijaz*, to publish weekly news bulletins,[139] and in 1937, he authorized the construction of a powerful radio station in Mecca to compete with foreign broadcasters.[140] He also ordered that his population be closely monitored for any signs of Axis sympathies.[141] Although few prominent Saudis espoused subversive views drawn from Axis radio broadcasts, the question of how to deal with external media continued to plague Ibn Saud (and his successors) for decades to come, especially after Egypt and other Arab nations built their own radio stations.

These types of political sensitivities explain why Ibn Saud and his family reacted quickly when Axis radio broadcasts alleged that Britain and other Allied states, with whom Saudi Arabia was firmly allied, had purposely hindered the hajj. During Saudi prince Faysal's state visit to the United States in 1943, he requested US assistance for the hajj,[142] and Ibn Saud focused on the hajj during his meeting in the same year with President Franklin Roosevelt's representative, Lieutenant Colonel Harold Hoskins.[143] From these consultations, Hoskins and his superiors quickly understood the seriousness of the hajj to the Saudis.[144] Although the Americans did not fly hajj pilgrims to the Hijaz, Washington did meet Saudi requests for currency, medicine, and ground transport for hajj pilgrims.[145] US trucks and US-printed Saudi riyals made it to the Hijaz in time for the hajj of 1943.[146] The United States played an even more prominent role in the 1944 hajj,[147] seeking, in cooperation with Britain, to establish a Saudi currency board or monetary authority, in order to address a problem that had plagued Saudi Arabia every hajj season—namely, ensuring that there were enough Saudi riyals in circulation to accommodate the financial needs of thousands of overseas pilgrims.[148] In 1952, under close US guidance, these discussions led to the creation of the Saudi Central Bank and the Saudi Arabian Monetary Agency (SAMA).[149]

The US decision to assist Saudi Arabia was part of an important shift in policy in the region, and in Saudi Arabia in particular. Washington had earlier turned down Saudi and ARAMCO requests for aid, including a 1942 request for a $10 million loan for Saudi Arabia and membership in the Lend-Lease Program.[150] The Roosevelt administration argued that Washington had higher priorities, that Saudi Arabia was not engaged in the war, and that London was responsible for the kingdom's welfare, since Britain was the dominant power in the Gulf.[151] In a letter to ARAMCO, Roosevelt noted that Saudi Arabia was "a little far afield for us!"[152]

Official US views changed rapidly as Americans began to seriously worry that British representatives in Saudi Arabia were taking credit for US assistance and doing everything they could to incorporate the kingdom (and its oil supplies) into the British Empire.[153] By 1944, US assistance outpaced British assistance with substantial increases in Lend-Lease payments, commodity credits, military assistance, and outright loans.[154] A year later, US officials stated that US aid was meant to prevent Britain from gaining "an inside track in the world's richest oil area."[155] In an apparent zero-sum game over oil in the Gulf region, Washington had no intention of losing to London. By 1946, Washington had amassed sufficient power in Saudi Arabia that a British official observed that the Americans had a financial "noose" around Ibn Saud's head.[156]

For its part, London could not stop the rising influence of the United States in Saudi Arabia, but it was able to retain tight control over the rest of the Gulf, because it was clear by the mid-1940s that Arab oil reserves were large enough to accommodate the needs of Great Britain *and* the United States. In both formal and informal agreements, Britain accepted US preeminence in Saudi Arabia, and the United States withdrew proposals to establish consulates in Bahrain and the other Gulf states. Nor did US diplomats protest when British officials barred them from visiting Qatar and the Trucial Coast in 1946.[157]

Britain's position in the Gulf received a further boost by the onset of the Cold War at the end of World War II. In light of the growing conflict between the United States and the Soviet Union, Great Britain's control of the oil fields and the Gulf no longer appeared to be a challenge to US interests. Quite the opposite was now true: the British presence served Washington's interests by checking Soviet influence in a strategically important region of the world that was critical to US plans for reconstructing Europe.[158] US officials could not ignore Soviet pressure in Greece and Turkey or the strength of the Communist parties in two states that bordered the Gulf, Iran and Iraq.

Within this new political environment, Britain exercised its authority and power in its Gulf territories more openly than ever before. After rarely intervening in the internal politics of the region's 350,000 residents for decades, British officials regularly overthrew weak leaders, determined labor contracts and royal budgets, served as mediators between local elites and oil companies, and reached strict bilateral treaties with each emirate.[159] London funded medical and educational facilities in the Gulf, especially in areas where US missionaries lacked a permanent presence.[160] These investments (and the positive publicity they generated) were now too important to be delegated to others. Despite two world wars, the Depression, and the onset of the Cold War, Great Britain's presence in the Gulf had held firm and, with the exception of Saudi Arabia, looked even stronger in 1945 than it had in 1930.[161]

The Long Road to Sovereignty

Decolonization and the Arab-Israeli Conflict

Two and a half years after the end of World War II, two events fundamentally altered Britain's position in the Gulf: decolonization and the Arab-Israeli conflict. In 1947, Great Britain withdrew from South Asia, where two new nation-states, India and Pakistan, took the place of Britain's Raj. These nation-states inherited the Raj's vast trade networks and bureaucracy, including the administration of South Asian pilgrims' trips to Mecca. British- and European-controlled shipping lines passed into Indian, Pakistani, Malaysian, Turkish, African, and Greek hands. Although £13 million of the £15 million collected in hajj fees in 1952 came from sterling regions of the world,[162] Britain (and Europe generally) had lost a century-old dominance over Islam's annual pilgrimage. The hajj ceased to be emblematic of European power and instead became a symbol of Muslim independence, pride, and even national rivalries.

As other states from West Africa to Southeast Asia similarly became independent of European empires, the states of the Gulf region sought to take advantage of these events to exercise sovereignty over British-owned industries and take control of Britain's territories in the Gulf, especially those linked to oil. Starting in the late 1940s, Tehran claimed Bahrain and nationalized British-owned oil facilities in Iran. During this same period, Iraq claimed Kuwait as its nineteenth province, Pakistan sought Oman's territory in Gawadar, and Saudi Arabia sent military forces into the Buraimi oasis and threatened to seize parts of the Trucial Coast. In each instance, Britain responded forcefully both militarily and diplomatically, and with the exception of the Buraimi oasis, avoided conflict. London's solutions to these conflicts, however, rarely won broad international acceptance and often postponed conflicts instead of solving them. In the long run, Britain's decisions set the stage for border disputes involving every Arab Gulf state and for the first Gulf War, the defining moment in the region over the past quarter-century.

No place where decolonization occurred was more contentious for the Middle East and the Gulf than the British mandate of Palestine, where two populations, Jews and Palestinian Arabs, sought to create mutually exclusive nation-states, Israel and Palestine. As the dispute in Palestine reached a boiling point after World War II, Gulf Arabs reacted with considerable alarm. They were familiar with the conflict and for years had followed the fate of the Palestinian Arabs and the rise of Zionism in Palestine.[163] Ibn Saud, who viewed Zionism as a surrogate or Trojan horse for Soviet communists, expressed his bewilderment that Washington supported Israel's independence while simultaneously opposing communism elsewhere.[164] The Saudi king also feared Zionists and repeatedly warned US officials of the consequences domestically and regionally if a Jewish state were to come into existence.[165] His fears were well founded, for Zionists sought to assassinate him in 1947,[166] and the plight of the Palestinians became the chief ideological cause of Western-trained intelligentsia and military officers throughout the Arab world who wanted to overthrow Arab monarchies after World War II.

When Israel gained its independence in 1948, Gulf leaders refused to recognize the new state, threatened to boycott Western companies that did business with the Jewish state, and accepted thousands of Palestinian refugees. Saudi officials publicly voiced exceptionally harsh anti-Jewish views and falsely asserted that Jews had always been forbidden from entering the kingdom, repeating a prophetic tradition that no religion other than Islam was permitted to exist in the Arabian Peninsula.[167] They also refused to issue visas to US Jews, including members of Congress, despite considerable US pressure to do so. In 1946, in a bitter exchange with ARAMCO executives and E. A. Locke, a private adviser to President Harry Truman, Saudi officials ridiculed Truman for ignoring their advice and threatened to revoke the company's concession immediately. Although Saudi officials never carried out their threat, they refused to join formal regional military and political alliances with London or Washington. Instead, they conducted informal public ties with Western nations—often through oil companies.[168]

The "50-50" Split

Senior US policymakers, understanding the potential danger of these threats, promoted a political and economic arrangement that would provide a progressively higher percentage of the benefits of oil profits to governments in the Gulf states and allow Western oil companies gradually to abandon their role in the region. In the eyes of these policymakers, retreat was inevitable: Saudi Arabia and other Gulf states were certain to follow the path of oil-producing nations in Latin America, such as Mexico, which nationalized its oil production in 1938, and Venezuela, which agreed to split proceeds from oil sales equally with foreign companies in 1943. It was far better to manage this decline than to lose control altogether, even though it meant significantly increasing the amount of royalties paid to local governments and reducing the amount of taxable profits that ARAMCO and other companies paid annually to the United States Treasury. Furthermore, US officials argued that this arrangement was in the long-term interests of the United States because it reduced the amount of foreign assistance that Washington would be required to provide to maintain pro-Western governments in the Gulf. This was an argument similar to the one used a generation earlier by the British government to support US involvement in Saudi Arabia.[169]

By the end of the 1940s, having taken note of the changes in Latin America, Gulf oil producers sought increases in the oil royalties paid to governments, the salaries of workers, and greater input into company management. Although London, ARAMCO, and other Western oil companies opposed these requests, Washington's pressure eventually won over the obstinate parties. In 1950, ARAMCO accepted the Saudi request that it share royalties with the kingdom evenly (the so-called 50-50 split), an arrangement that was quickly requested by Kuwait, Bahrain, and the other oil-producing states under British administration.[170] Soon this arrangement was replicated in other Middle Eastern oil-producing states.

Significantly, the 50-50 split coincided with a dramatic upswing in global demand for petroleum and energy after World War II. The upswing represented a nexus of economic and cultural factors that intensified energy consumption while limiting the use of coal, especially in the cities of North America and Europe. Shortages of coal after the war, an enormous global increase in the number of automobiles, and solid economic growth drove demand for oil to unforeseen levels. Public outcries about pollution from coal forced governments to convert to oil for many fuel purposes, especially after 4,000 people perished in one week from a coal-induced smog cloud in London in December 1952.[171]

The following statistics suggest how dramatic a shift this international transformation was. In 1950, coal provided 75 percent of the energy for the Western world, whereas oil provided only 23 percent. By the 1970s, oil provided 60 percent of the West's energy needs, whereas coal provided only 22 percent. Furthermore, oil from the Gulf provided 90 percent of Japan's oil needs and 55 percent of Western Europe's. Between 1960 and 1970 alone, oil use in noncommunist nations increased by 21 million barrels a day. During the same period, Western European oil consumption grew fifteenfold, and even faster in Japan.[172]

The results of the shift to petroleum and the 50-50 split were dramatic, both in terms of production and income, for the Gulf states. Kuwaiti revenues from oil doubled in 1952 and expanded by 34 percent between 1955 and 1960. Revenues from oil sales in Saudi Arabia went from $31.5 million in 1948 to $170 million in 1952.[173] Three years later, Saudi revenues from oil sales grew to $288 million.[174] They grew again to $334 million in 1960 and $663 million in 1965.[175] In Bahrain, oil revenues grew from $9 million in 1955 to $13 million in 1960 and $20 million in 1965.[176] In Qatar, oil revenues soared from $34 million in 1955 to $54 million in 1960 and $77 million in 1965.[177] Finally, Abu Dhabi and Oman, which had no oil revenues in 1955, respectively earned $84 million and $50 million from oil in 1967.[178]

The Challenge of Arab Nationalism

The rise of the Gulf oil industry not only brought enormous wealth into the region; it also raised the profiles of Kuwait, Saudi Arabia, and other oil-producing Arab Gulf states in the eyes of Arab nationalists. Born in the first decades of the twentieth century, Arab nationalism was a synthesis of secular European nationalism, socialism, and positivism, on the one hand, with Arab historical and cultural experience, on the other. The ideology deliberately downplayed an Islamic identity in favor of one based on language and culture, in which Arabs of all faiths could unify economically, socially, and politically. Although the ideology was neither fully socialist nor communist, Arab nationalists cooperated with the Soviet Union. They were horrified by the Arab loss in the 1948 Arab-Israeli war, which they believed embodied the corrosive corruption of the Arab world, the injustices of Zionism and Israel, and the need to rid the region of anachronistic monarchies.

Once Arab nationalists came to power throughout the Arab world in the 1950s, Egypt's Gamal Abdel Nasser and other Arab leaders worked hard to transform their states into entities that were consistent with modern, Western, social democratic models. Unable to win financial and military support from the West, they turned to the Soviet Union and its allies for weapons and economic development. (Nasser's first arms purchases were from Czechoslovakia.) New government bureaucracies, schools, and parties arose throughout the region to mobilize the masses to make this vision a reality. Given their personal youth and that of their regimes, Arab nationalists legitimized their actions by arguing that they upheld the glories of ancient figures and traditions, including some pre-Islamic traditions: Salah al-Din, Ibn Khaldun, Queen Zenobia, and the glories of ancient Babylon and Egypt.

Cognizant of the political potential of radio, Arab nationalist leaders utilized the medium aggressively, broadcasting messages that called for Arab unity and the overthrow of governments opposed to their programs. On such shows as *From the Wealth of Arab Lands, Radio Cairo, Voice of the Arab Na-*

tion, and *Voice of South Arabia and the Gulf,* Arab nationalists singled out Saudi Arabia and Britain's Arab Gulf dependencies for special criticism because of their links to so-called imperialist Western nations and because their authority rested on religion and autocracy rather than "modern" concepts such as popular sovereignty. Within this framework, Gulf governments were not legitimate; they were "artificial" or medieval entities that served foreigners and the foreign desire to control Arab resources. In other words, these governments were Western surrogates who wasted valuable petrodollars that should have gone to Arab development. They were definitely not progressing as fast as Egypt and other secular Arab republics.

Arab nationalists reinforced the power of their arguments by specifically gearing comic books and radio shows to Gulf audiences.[179] For example, in Baghdad, dissident Saudis published their own journal, *Sawt al-Tahi'a,* and broadcast radio messages calling for Arab unity and the overthrow of the Saudi monarchy.[180] Although announcers in Cairo and Damascus did not always get Gulf geographical names right (e.g., they falsely referred to Abu Dhabi and Dubai as "Abu Dubai"),[181] they usually employed local accents correctly. Rarely would one hear a speaker use Egyptian or Syrian Arab accents in programs beamed to the Gulf.[182] Arab nationalist radio programs appealed to the sensibilities of ordinary Gulf Arabs with stories of official and religious corruption and hypocrisy. In one program, *Voice of the Arab Nation* satirized the legitimacy of one of the most powerful institutions in Saudi Arabia—the Mutawwa'a (the religious police)—through a story that blended satire and colloquial Saudi Arabic. An ARAMCO report about this program noted:

> A laborer in Saudi Arabia was driving his motorcycle past the house of a Mutawwa' [*sic*]. . . . Disturbed by the motorcycle's noise, the Mutawwa' stopped the poor laborer, beat him, and damaged his motorcycle, calling it the devil's horse. When the Mutawwa' said motorcycles are forbidden, the laborer retorted that it was a machine only, just like any other, or like the automobile. The Mutawwa' disagreed, saying that automobiles are allowed. The laborer asked on what grounds? "Because," said the Mutawwa', "they are mentioned in the Quran." The laborer was astonished and asked to cite the verse. The Mutawwa' said there is a verse in which God said, "And Cadillacs are the reward for the righteous" (this phrase appears in the Quran a number of times, as in Cattle, 84). But removing the dot from the Arabic letter di in the word kadilika ("thus, likewise") the word becomes kadallik, the plural form of Cadillac in Saudi colloquial. The Mutawwa' explained to the laborer that the term was originally Kadallik but that some compiler of the Quran mistakenly put a dot over the letter dal making it a dhal.[183]

Other insults were far more personal and unsettling to those in power. For example, announcers stated that the harem of the Saudi king or that of King Hussein of Jordan was composed of Jewesses from Israel, Yemen, and Europe.

They similarly argued that Gulf leaders fleeced the oil wealth and that the US dollar was the shrine to which they "perform the pilgrimage."[184]

Arab nationalists benefited from two broad social trends in the Gulf. First, radio fit a natural inclination in the Gulf populations toward indoor café- or home-based entertainment, especially because of the soaring heat.[185] Second, radio listenership grew exponentially after World War II in the Gulf because radios were easily transportable and provided information to people who were both semiliterate and, with rare exceptions, without access to daily newspapers and weekly magazines until the 1970s.[186]

Furthermore, Arab nationalist arguments resonated in the Gulf among the growing population of guest workers from Egypt, Syria, and other areas of the Arab world as well as among the local Arab populations themselves.[187] During crises in 1952 and 1956 in Egypt, riots erupted in Bahrain and other parts of the Gulf. These riots, which included men and both veiled and unveiled women, paralyzed Bahraini society.[188] In Kuwait, US missionaries reported that large pictures of Nasser were hung everywhere during the Suez Canal crisis of 1956. Even in the Trucial State of Abu Dhabi, one of the most isolated areas in the Trucial Coast, leaflets circulated widely that called on Arabs to kill British oil executives.[189] Such threats also occurred to oil executives in other Gulf states, which, despite their severe repression of workers' rights, faced serious ongoing tensions among oil industry workers in the 1950s. After a coup toppled a seemingly strong regime in Iraq in 1958, it seemed to be only a matter of time before the far weaker Arab Gulf states would also fall—no matter how generously oil companies split their profits with the regional governments.

The Power of History

In fact, the coups never occurred because governments in Saudi Arabia and the Arab Gulf were *old.* A generation after the rise of the Arab nationalist regimes, every Arab Gulf royal family remained firmly in power. Much like the monarchy in Morocco, whose identity rested on centuries-old religious and tribal traditions, Gulf monarchs could draw on incremental but still highly symbolic assertions of sovereignty and an ancient web of governance that brought together a commitment to Islam, rituals of mutual consultation, tribal loyalties, and religious movements. These various elements, which were at the core of Saudi Arabia's welfare state under Ibn Saud, allowed monarchs to pursue seemingly contradictory policies while maintaining public support without the assistance of bureaucracies, political parties, and other instruments of modern state power. It is striking that monarchs in the Gulf never faced what Samuel Huntington called the "King's Dilemma" in which Saudi Arabia and other monarchies in the 1960s had to choose between centralizing and modernizing their societies or maintaining traditional modes of authority and power.[190]

In reality, from the start, the most vexing challenge for the Arab Gulf elites was to balance the desire of their populations for the chief promises of Arab nationalism—freedom from Western imperialism and restoration of the Palestinians' rights—with the need to maintain the links to the West that were necessary for security and economic growth. To address these concerns, leaders publicly differentiated themselves from the West, promoting the dignity and national rights of their subjects against Euro-American power while delivering results that Arab nationalists promised to deliver only *after* seizing power.

Ordinary Saudis and others in Arab Gulf societies accepted these contradictory policies because their governments regularly consulted them and asserted national sovereignty. For example, the Kuwaiti royal family relentlessly lobbied KOC to hire more Kuwaitis, reinvigorated the emirate's participatory political institutions, and provided $500 million in financial aid to developing nations throughout Asia and Africa, including Kuwait's large neighbor, Iraq, and the most powerful Arab state, Egypt.[191] Qatar's rulers systematically ignored British advisers, and Abu Dhabi's rulers camped far outside of the capital for months, effectively denying the British resident an opportunity to lend "advice" and thereby exercise traditional British power.[192] Some rulers also mirrored Ibn Saud's practice of providing meals to entire communities on religious holidays.[193] By pursuing these policies, rulers exercised a fundamental aspect of sovereignty—the ability to say no to another state, no matter how powerful—and made clear that they could offer something tangible to their populations.[194]

Baubles, Baseball, and Bin Laden

No society in the Arab Gulf felt more intensely the transformation produced by oil wealth, the rise of Arab nationalism, and the need to assert national sovereignty than the one legitimately independent state in the Gulf: Saudi Arabia. Not only did portions of the population question the legitimacy of the Saudi monarchy, but Americans had also built a political apparatus parallel to that of France's Morocco protectorate. In this system, Americans wielded power and influence indirectly as advisers to seemingly independent government departments, and the US ambassador advised Saudis on all international, legal, and economic issues.[195] In the words of British diplomats, who knew what an empire looked like, US officials were building their own "empire in the Kingdom"—and they were not intent on sharing with anyone, especially the British.[196]

Starting with Prince Faysal's visit to the United States in 1943, Americans sought to convince Saudis of US military power and the benefits of what British diplomats termed "the baubles of American civilization—Coca-Cola, Cadillacs, and the rest."[197] With the assistance of ARAMCO and other US advisers, using the wealth generated by oil production, Riyadh began an unprecedented program to bureaucratize its governing institutions and to realize the vision of "US modernity" that was shown to Faysal in 1943.[198] Riyadh and other Saudi cities emerged as sprawling communities similar to Los Angeles, cooled by air conditioning and built around automobiles, supermarkets, suburban housing developments, and fast-food restaurants. US influence impacted every aspect of daily life, including the most popular Arabic books sold in Riyadh, many of which were secular and translations of English-language US texts.[199]

The foundation of the US presence in Saudi Arabia, as Robert Vitalis notes in his recent brilliant book *America's Kingdom,* was ARAMCO. The company's officials interacted with the Saudi government as if ARAMCO were "an autonomous state" and dealt with the US ambassador only when it suited them.[200] ARAMCO's Arabic nickname suggested tremendous power and influence—*Um ARAMCO* (mother ARAMCO).[201] The company's Dhahran compound was a physical manifestation of its influence and the ideal picture of bourgeois US culture, with air-conditioned homes, manicured lawns, Little League baseball teams, Western movies, bowling alleys, and swimming pools. Building on a tradition of Saudi-Wahhabi tolerance of religious minorities, the company won the right for its employees to practice Christianity in the kingdom and to hire Christian clergy. One Little Leaguer in Dhahran, Joe Williamson, pitched a no-hitter in 1956 and was then prominently featured in an exhibit on Little League baseball in the Baseball Hall of Fame in Cooperstown, New York.[202]

Although these outward manifestations of influence and power were analogous to those of other Western oil companies in the Gulf, ARAMCO's regional knowledge and local impact were unrivaled. The company's Arab Bureau employed a staff of Orientalists, translators, public relations specialists, and local informants to produce detailed reports on every possible subject relevant to the company's operations.[203] ARAMCO could determine which individuals and regions would succeed in the long run. Among the Saudis who were linked to the company was Suleyman Olayan, one of ARAMCO's earliest employees and the most successful businessman in Saudi history. Muhammad bin Laden, who founded a large Saudi construction company and fathered the most infamous Saudi today, Osama bin Laden, also benefited from ties to the company. During the 1930s and 1940s, Bin Laden became a prominent builder, partly thanks to his work for ARAMCO.[204] Because of the company's size and influence, it could generate fierce resistance among conservatives: Shaikh Abu Bahz, a religious leader, repeatedly charged in public—and to Ibn Saud's face at his court in 1944—that ARAMCO enslaved Saudis and contradicted basic Islamic practices.[205]

Answering Abu Bahz

Although Ibn Saud readily silenced Abu Bahz with the assistance of the kingdom's ulama (Muslim clerics), the Saudi state knew that it needed a far better long-term response to conservative charges.[206] The answer was to prove that the monarchy could control an institution central to the kingdom's identity: the hajj. To achieve this goal, Saudi Arabia needed to create a national airline, Saudi Arabian Airlines. Taking shape at the end of World War II, it was a partnership between the Saudi government and a US airline, Trans World Airlines (TWA).[207] By using US pilots and TWA's DC-3 aircraft,[208] Saudi Arabian Airlines flew foreigners and Saudis, including Ibn Saud, to Mecca and other locations, starting in 1946.[209] When Saudi Arabian Airlines could not fly thousands of pilgrims from Beirut to Jeddah in time for the 1952 hajj, the United States Air Force filled in the gap. The US airlift was not only one of the most spectacular of its time, but it also proved decisively that Saudi Arabia could carry out a hajj successfully without British or European help.

A generation later, Saudi Arabian Airlines maintained one of the largest and most modern fleets of aircraft in the Middle East. By 1983, it was carrying more than 10 million passengers per year—the largest ridership in the region[210]—and facilitated the growth of the hajj pilgrimage from 50,000 in 1933 to 400,000 in 1970 and more than a million in 1983.[211] Thanks to jet aircraft and US assistance, Riyadh could attest that it had achieved in twenty years what the Ottoman Empire and its Hijaz railroad had been unable to accomplish in more than a century: total Muslim control over all transportation routes to the hajj pilgrimage. For the first time since the establishment of Saudi Arabia in 1930, Saudis could rest assured that they were truly custodians of Mecca, Medina, and the hajj and did not need European assistance for the annual pilgrimage. Never again would a Saudi king have to thank Great Britain for help with an annual event that was at the heart of the kingdom's identity.[212]

The success of Saudi Arabian Airlines dovetailed with the rise of an institution that was central to the political life of the kingdom and that of its neighbors—the national armed forces. The new military institutions also helped the other Gulf states to define themselves vis-à-vis their neighbors and British colonialism. From Kuwait to Oman, rulers called on Gulf Arab youths to join their military forces and receive Western military training, a process that was often woven into a governing metanarrative that stretched back decades and even centuries. Whenever possible, rulers channeled ambitious nobles and promising officers to the air force, an institution that clearly projected modern military power to their public but that was not likely to provide the nucleus for the types of coups that had overthrown other regional monarchies. Gulf armies, which existed alongside paramilitary units, remained just large enough to maintain domestic order. This reduced the probability of coups but meant that in times of crisis the states were permanently dependent on outside military assistance, at first British and later US.

In Saudi Arabia, Ibn Saud kept his army modest in size and balanced it with a national guard composed of loyal tribal levies. He also linked military recruitment drives to public celebrations of "the newfound strength of Saudi Arabia and the Arabs" and maintained his family's close alliance with Wahhabism, an alliance that dated back to the eighteenth century. History textbooks in Saudi primary schools reinforced these messages, describing the Wahhabi-Saud alliance as the "greatest . . . and most successful movement for independence in the Arab countries."[213] It was the "torch" that lit the "path of liberation" of the Arab world from Turkish rule and European imperialism.[214] The message of Ibn Saud and his family was clear: Arab nationalists might assert a desire to liberate and unify the Arab world, but no one could match the royal family's record of support for the Arab cause over time. In other words, Ibn Saud, his family, and the family's allies were more authentic Arab nationalists than Nasser and his cohort of Western-educated military officers.

Throughout the 1950s and 1960s, Ibn Saud, his family, and his fellow Gulf monarchs utilized their military forces to reinforce their own political legitimacy. In 1952, Ibn Saud appealed to his people to contribute to a special fund to support Saudi Arabia's nascent air force. In a short time, this fund accumulated the equivalent of £54,000 sterling—a staggering sum in the 1950s—from a cross section of Saudi society: elite princes, bureaucrats, merchants, religious figures, and ordinary people, some of whom donated just a few riyals.[215] Just nine years later, in 1961, the Saudi state further built on that enthusiasm when it announced on Radio Mecca that the Royal Saudi Air Force was "fully capable of defending" the kingdom by itself.[216] Riyadh then requested the withdrawal of US forces from the Dhahran Air Base—long a prime symbol used by Arab nationalists to tie Riyadh to Washington and to criticize the lack of true Saudi sovereignty.[217] Saudi Arabia could finally say no to a foreign presence and carry on its proud "tradition" as the torch of anti-imperialism in the Arab world.

Mass Media

For Saudi Arabia and its neighbors, sovereignty did not end with military power: it also included mass media, especially television. By the 1960s, television had established itself thoroughly in the region. A Western researcher noted that it was as much an aspect of daily life in Saudi Arabia as "the call to prayer and Koran readings."[218] Gulf Arabs had a host of program choices decades before the rise of satellite television: ARAMCO shows in Arabic and English,[219] US military television, and about ten state-run television networks.[220] Enough Egyptians watched ARAMCO's Arabic shows in the 1950s that a leading Egyptian newspaper publicly complained to the *New York Times* about the pro-Western content of the shows.[221]

It should therefore come as no surprise that governments in the Gulf saw radio and television broadcasting as an aspect of politics, national sovereignty, and self-defense. Kuwait and Saudi Arabia invested heavily in radio and television in the 1950s and 1960s to compete with foreign broadcasters, resist propaganda, and provide an alternative to movie theaters, which were then banned in the kingdom.[222] Under the leadership of King Faysal, who became king in 1964, no expense was spared in radio and television broadcasting. A deputy treasury secretary oversaw the construction of the broadcast stations, which had direct access to "unlimited funds" and utilized the most modern US technologies.[223] When Riyadh opened its television transmitter in Damman (then the largest in the world) in 1969, it was meant "not so much to give Eastern Province Saudis a better TV picture as to reach Kuwait."[224] The official Saudi view of radio and television was expressed by Fuad al-Farsi, Saudi information minister, who, when asked about privatizing television and radio, said that it was impossible in Saudi Arabia because they "were a manifestation of sovereignty."[225]

As other Gulf states gained wealth from oil sales in the 1960s, they, along with individual emirates in the UAE, followed Kuwait and Saudi Arabia's lead. Qatar, Bahrain, Abu Dhabi, Sharjah, and others built radio and television transmitters near international borders to make certain that their television programs could compete in the region.[226] Dubai television began to transmit in color in 1974 and, in 1978, became the first Arab-owned station in the Arab world to broadcast in English.[227] Within a week of Sultan Qaboos's ascension to the throne in Oman in 1970, he started radio broadcasts in Arabic and other languages from Oman.[228]

Gulf Arab nations also turned to print media to express their sovereignty, founding magazines and daily newspapers aimed not only at local audiences but also at the wider Arab world. Saudi Arabia was the most successful at these "pan-Arab" projects, but it was hardly alone. The Qatari government sports magazine *al-Sakir* (The Falcon) became the most successful sports magazine ever published in the Arab world, with a circulation of 100,000 readers. A generation before al-Jazeera became a household name around the globe, *al-Sakir* showed Qatar's potential to serve as a base for pan-Arab media.[229]

Although Gulf governments heavily censored domestic television and radio content, one could not say that they controlled what was on television within their national borders, as Egypt and other Arab states did. In reality, the situation in the Gulf was akin to that of East Germany, whose television programs competed with West German television for viewers. There is also a parallel to the situation between China and Taiwan, whose citizens can see each other's broadcasts. For this reason, the best an Arab Gulf state could hope for was to get its voice onto the airwaves, where its subjects could hear it. Whether those subjects or anyone else in the region tuned in or cared was an entirely different matter.

The Second Oil Era

"No Leverage Other Than Force"

Just as the Gulf states competed for influence (and often failed) in the airwaves of the region, British officials wondered if anyone cared or respected *their* power in the late 1950s and throughout the 1960s—even as their nation's financial interests and ties expanded in the Gulf. Kuwait, Qatar, and other Arab Gulf oil exporters that had treaty relations with Britain provided a welcome market for British goods while simultaneously investing in the London stock market, especially in British corporations. Although British officials recognized that maintaining a position in the Gulf "opened them up to charges of imperialism," they did not see withdrawal as a viable option, since the Gulf, according to Prime Minister Anthony Eden, was "vital to the very existence of the United Kingdom."[230] To friend and foe alike, Great Britain portrayed itself as a benevolent actor that would guarantee a better future for the Arabs of the Gulf region, protect them from communism and predatory neighbors, and bring all the benefits of modernity, including democracy.

Yet by 1960, it was already clear that British officials were rapidly losing their ability to get things done the way they had for decades—that is, by "advising." Many Gulf Arab rulers did not need British money and no longer feared their neighbors as they once had. It was now the other way around: Gulf rulers were now investors in British securities and worked closely with former rivals—to the exclusion of Britain. By the mid-1960s, Kuwait alone had more than $1 billion in investments in the United Kingdom, and British companies conducted $500 million in business annually in the Gulf states.[231] Kuwait and other Arab Gulf states—even those that were not formally independent—were also increasingly important players in the world economy because of their oil exports and the emergence of the Organization of Petroleum Exporting Countries (OPEC), which was founded in 1960 to manage global oil markets. Kuwait and Saudi Arabia were among the first members of OPEC, which by the early 1970s would grow to include every Arab Gulf state.

As billions of dollars poured into the region, the new wealth allowed the Arab Gulf states to adopt an unheard-of degree of autonomy from Britain, much to the chagrin of British officials in the region. The inability of the British resident in Qatar in 1960 to reform a highly unpopular monarch, who was clearly spending state money irresponsibly, or even to get a royal audience to officially submit his own resignation was especially disheartening.[232] Equally discouraging was Britain's failure to suppress the rebellion in the interior of Oman without having to resort to promising significant financial rewards to the Trucial Coast Arabs, who had already received substantial developmental and military assistance from London.[233] As early as 1961, British officials opined in private conversations that they were already thinking about how to withdraw from the Gulf, since they increasingly had "no leverage other than force" over Britain's Gulf dependencies.[234]

The pressures pushing for British withdrawal from the Gulf intensified in the 1960s. The success of Kuwait's transition to independence in 1961—despite Iraq's threats—and the fact that Kuwait continued to invest in British securities suggested that London could maintain very profitable commercial ties with the Gulf even after it no longer maintained an empire there. British withdrawals from Malaysia and elsewhere and ongoing domestic financial problems raised questions at home and abroad about the worth of the empire in the Gulf. Furthermore, Britain's diplomats found that their empire in the Gulf damaged their nation's reputation in both the Arab world and the United Nations. Within Britain, there was also an increasing "ideological aversion to the practice of empire," especially in the ruling Labour Party—epitomized by British prime minister Harold Wilson's observation in 1967 that Great Britain's international "commitment is not to police the world."[235]

If these pressures were not enough to compel Britain's withdrawal from the Gulf, London's ability to project force there was deteriorating rapidly. The government of Iraq in 1958 and the government of South Yemen in 1967 denied Britain access to military bases that it had long used to project force into the Gulf. At the same time, Iran, Saudi Arabia, Iraq, and other states were purchasing advanced Soviet and US weapons systems that were sometimes more advanced than those used by the British. Just to maintain their nation's one advantage in the Gulf—force—British officials faced the unpleasant prospect of having to compete in an arms race against wealthy oil states. Even worse was the prospect of having to fight against adversaries who had superior military technology.[236]

Britain's Withdrawal from the Gulf

All of the factors discussed above help to explain why it was relatively easy for the British government to implement a quick withdrawal from the Gulf in 1967, when serious financial problems were threatening the British economy, necessitating severe budget cutbacks and the devaluation of the British pound (which was lowered from $2.80 to $2.50 in a single day).[237] A British government report stated in February 1968 that Britain's security lay in Europe, and so the nation should withdraw from the Gulf by 1971. Stunned Arab Gulf states, including Abu Dhabi (which had experienced a British-engineered coup in 1966), pressed London to reconsider its decision, offering to defray the costs of British forces remaining in the Gulf. US officials, then preoccupied with the war in Vietnam and unwilling to take on new problems, also pushed for Britain to remain in the region. But Whitehall refused to bow to pressure.

Between 1968 and 1971, Britain's top negotiator in the Gulf, Sir William Luce, worked tirelessly with diplomats from the United States, the Soviet

Union, Iran, Saudi Arabia, and the other regional powers to secure a viable future for each of the new Arab Gulf states. Luce successfully won recognition for Oman and Qatar, convinced the shah of Iran to abandon his claim to Bahrain, and created a loose federation of Trucial States, the United Arab Emirates, foremost of which was Abu Dhabi. In 1971, four new states—Oman, Qatar, Bahrain, and the United Arab Emirates—were recognized and found easy entry into the United Nations and other international bodies. With small populations and enormous oil wealth, these new states would naturally become key international players, just like the already independent Arab Gulf states of Kuwait and Saudi Arabia. Equally important was the fact that most of the new states did not have much of a relationship with either Washington or Moscow and therefore could stay neutral in the Cold War.

It was far more difficult to find a workable solution for the set of islands in the Gulf known as Abu Musa and the Greater and Lesser Tunbs. These islands, which produced some oil, had been claimed by Sharjah, Ras al-Khaimah, and Iran for years. After months of diplomacy, Luce yielded to Tehran's desires because Britain was not strong enough to risk a confrontation with Iran. He advised Sharjah and Ras al-Khaimah to negotiate, warning that Britain would not protect them from Iran. Sharjah took his advice, reaching an understanding with Iran; Ras al-Khaimah did not, pledging resistance. The Iranian military occupied the three islands shortly before Britain's formal withdrawal from the Gulf in December 1971. The images of officials in Ras al-Khaimah resisting Iranians resonated throughout the Gulf, leaving a bitter memory for many in the UAE, especially after London's large arms deal with Tehran became public in late 1971. The large Arab states, including Egypt and Iraq, denounced Iran and Britain, and Arab youth in the UAE stoned Iranian businesses. It was an inglorious end to Great Britain's empire in the Gulf—which had been a defining institution in the region for many decades—and an inauspicious start to the modern Gulf.[238]

"Relatively Unresponsive to U.S. Power"

The decisive factor in Britain's decisions regarding its withdrawal from the Gulf nations was the opinion of Britain's closest ally, the United States. Initially, the British hoped that the United States would use its enormous military and political power to convince Iran and other states to support the new Arab states and their claims to the Gulf islands. Sir Alec Douglas-Home, Great Britain's foreign secretary in 1971 and a former prime minister, repeatedly asked the Nixon administration to do just that. But President Richard Nixon, who had been a close friend of the shah of Iran since the 1950s, refused to become involved in the dispute. Nixon and his national security adviser, Henry Kissinger, saw Iran as the "preponderant power" in the Gulf and the West's best hope in future years for retaining influence and stability. following

Britain's withdrawal.[239] They would have preferred cooperation between Washington's closest allies in the region, Saudi Arabia and Iran, but they recognized that it was unlikely that Saudi Arabia would project military power effectively or would see much long-term benefit from working with the shah, who ruled a Shia nation that was aligned closely with Israel.

Nixon and Kissinger's views reflected the nuanced position of US policymakers as they sought to craft a realistic response to Britain's decision to withdraw. On the one hand, they understood that the region's oil was extremely important to key allies in Europe and Asia, as well as for US business and the war in Vietnam (89 percent of the oil used by US forces in Southeast Asia came from the Gulf). In 1970, US oil companies controlled 55 percent of the region's oil industry and had $1.5 billion in assets in the Gulf. US officials also feared Soviet support of dissident groups in the Gulf and the possibility that the monarchs of Bahrain and Saudi Arabia might fall.[240]

On the other hand, there was very little that US officials thought they could do about the various problems. The US government had few military assets in the region at the time and only a scant diplomatic presence in the lower Gulf. As Kissinger noted in a 1970 national security memo to Nixon, "While the Persian Gulf is important to U.S. allies and friends, its potential instability seems relatively unresponsive to U.S. power."[241] Britain had long-term diplomatic and political relationships in the region, which it planned to use to provide military assistance in the future. States flush with oil proceeds had little interest in Washington's chief tool for increasing influence overseas: foreign assistance. At best, Kissinger argued, Washington could increase its diplomatic presence in the region and look for ways to provide technical and educational assistance.[242] Nobody contemplated the massive military commitments of the 1990s and 2000s. Invitations from Bahrain, Kuwait, and other states to increase Washington's military presence in the region were generally rebuffed by US policymakers, who were far more worried about preparing for a day when Iran would be the sole US ally in the Gulf.

New Wealth and Global Power

Two factors radically altered US policy in the Gulf, the value of the Gulf states to Washington, and the wealth of those states. The first factor was that domestic US oil production peaked at approximately 9.63 million barrels a day in 1970 and thereafter continued on a steady decline, forcing Washington (and the West generally) to import more petroleum, especially from the Gulf.[243] Western petroleum imports jumped from 11 percent of petroleum used in 1970 to 21 percent by 1973.[244] And the numbers continued to grow: between 1972 and 1980 alone, 43 percent of Saudi oil exports went to Europe, 33 percent went to Asia, and 18 percent went to the United States.[245] Oil in the Gulf was becoming critical to the economic well-being of the United

States and its key allies and would become critical to the maintenance of US power.

The second factor was that global petroleum markets in 1973 and 1974 underwent their most important shift since the 50-50 split of the 1950s. "For the three decades prior to 1974," an ARAMCO study noted, "petroleum prices had been between $2 and $4 a barrel; fluctuations of $1 or more were a major shock to the petroleum markets around the globe."[246] In 1970, the average price was $1.80.[247] But this dynamic changed during the 1973 Arab-Israeli war, when Saudi Arabia and the other Arab Gulf states refused to sell oil to the United States along with several Asian and European states. Despite his decades-long alliance with Washington, King Faysal felt that it was imperative to show solidarity with the Arab states that were fighting (and losing to) Israel, as well as to emphasize his and his people's anger at Washington for its support of Israel in the war. The price of a barrel of oil rose from $2.90 to $5.12 in October 1973 and to $12 by January 1974.[248] A Saudi oil official made the terms of the embargo clear to the Japanese government with the following explanation: "If you are hostile to us, you get no oil. If you are neutral, you get oil but not as much as before. If you are friendly, you get the same as before."[249]

The threats were not idle ones. Although the embargo was lifted in 1974, after just five months, the costs to the United States and other developed economies were staggering. Within the United States alone, gas prices shot up from thirty cents a gallon to well over a dollar.[250] As a consequence, US inflation jumped from 3.3 percent in 1972 to 11 percent in 1974.[251] The US economy lost 500,000 jobs and $10 billion to $20 billion in gross domestic product (GDP).[252] Washington had little choice but to address Arab concerns and to find ways by which events and governments in the Gulf would respond to US power. Secretary of State Kissinger conducted shuttle diplomacy between the warring parties and initiated a dialogue with Egypt that led to the Camp David Accords in 1979. Saudi Arabia and the Arab states had gotten a superpower to change course by adopting a policy that was more consistent with their own views of the world. King Faysal—like his father, Ibn Saud—had demonstrated that a "traditional" Gulf monarchy could defend Arab honor and dignity far better than Egypt and other modern Arab states could.

The boycott not only demonstrated the awesome potential economic and political power of the Arab Gulf states but also gave those states full control of their most vital resource: oil. Gulf states began aggressively to acquire stakes in the national oil companies, with Kuwait and Saudi Arabia leading the way. In 1974, both countries purchased 60 percent of the national oil companies operating in their borders, KOC and ARAMCO, respectively. During the next two years, Kuwait bought the remaining 40 percent of KOC, and Saudi Arabia ended ARAMCO's concession in the kingdom. In 1980, Riyadh bought all of ARAMCO's Saudi holdings. A symbol of US power and influence in the Middle East—a virtual state within a state—was now firmly in Saudi hands.[253]

With greater prices at the pump and nearly full ownership of oil production, the Arab Gulf states reaped benefits from oil that dwarfed the 50-50 split of the 1950s. Between 1972 and 1980, Saudi Arabia's annual oil revenues rose from $3.1 billion to $102 billion.[254] Bahrain's earnings leaped from $68 million in 1972 to $528 million in 1977.[255] Other oil-producing Arab Gulf states witnessed similar windfalls from oil sales in the 1970s. For example, in 1978, Kuwait's per capita income ($17,100) was the largest in the world, very much ahead of that of the United States at the time ($10,630).[256] The windfall from oil in the 1970s constituted, in the words of Kiren Aziz Chaudhry, the "largest and most rapid transfer of wealth in the twentieth century."[257]

Modern Gulf Society Comes into View

The wealth domestically accelerated several dynamics that had begun in the 1930s. To begin with, monarchs could overwhelm the entire economy of their own nations, using their oil wealth to outpace all other financial actors, including the commercial families, who had once been more powerful than the monarchs. These families were either bought off or else they missed out on enormous and highly lucrative government contracts to build modern cities and vast modern infrastructures, including roads, bridges, ports, airports, hospitals, schools, and mosques. In addition, the governments provided cradle-to-grave social services in a host of fields, including health care, education, housing, food, unemployment insurance, utilities, and other municipal services. Sections of government dedicated to collecting taxes stopped functioning, since the state no longer needed these for revenue. Although this new system spread wealth from oil, it was not accompanied by new consultative political institutions. This was a rentier state system par excellence—little different from that employed by Ibn Saud when he used hajj pilgrimage fees in the 1930s.

Nevertheless, the system of wealth distribution reinforced conservative social values, seeking to prevent socialist, Marxist, religious, and Arab nationalist groups from influencing Gulf populations. This trend was most intense in Bahrain and Kuwait, which had elected legislatures. Bahrain's legislature included groups that promoted Marxism, women's rights, labor unions, and Shia populations. When those groups challenged the government's authority in 1975, the emir dissolved the legislature with the support of the Sunni Arab religious groups. When Kuwaiti legislators tied to leftists challenged the monarchy's hold on power in 1976, Kuwait's emir dissolved the parliament and then allied himself firmly with the one sector that did not oppose his decision—apolitical Sunni religious groups. He did this principally by appointing the head of the Islam and Social Reform Society, Yosuf al-Hajji, the minister of pious endowments. Monarchs in other Gulf nations struck analogous agreements with domestic Islamist leaders and granted asylum to foreign Islamists, including members of the Egyptian Muslim Brotherhood.

Making the system work, however, forced Gulf leaders to face an old problem: the dearth of skilled and unskilled labor. With the exception of Kuwait, no state in the region could boast a literacy rate higher than 45 percent of the population, with the UAE and Oman closer to 20 percent. Large portions of the population lacked modern education, lived in rural areas, or worked in family businesses. As early as 1950, British officials noted that women dominated the upper levels of Western schools in the Gulf, since most male students dropped out of school to work in family businesses after they gained minimal levels of literacy.[258] Except in the fields of medicine and education, using the few educated Gulf women to work in the modern economy was out of the question.

Importing workers from other Arab states offered a solution that was consistent with the Gulf states' public commitment to Arab nationalism and to assisting the Palestinians. But importing expatriate Arab laborers, some of whom had already worked in the region for some time, carried steep risks in the 1970s, because many Arabs believed in the secular and nationalist ideas that the Gulf states had hoped to keep out of their societies. Thousands of expatriate workers offered Egypt and other large Arab states opportunities to influence the politics of the Gulf—opportunities that might prove dangerous to the Gulf states, thanks to the difference in wealth between them and other Arab states. Arab nationalists had spent decades broadcasting radio messages into the Gulf, calling for the overthrow of monarchies.

A natural alternative to importing foreign Arab workers was to resurrect the employment networks created by Britain for the region's oil industry in the 1930s, using South Asians. Thousands of turbaned Sikh carpenters, Malay nurses and typists, Pakistani businessmen, Goan secretaries, and many other South Asians arrived in the Gulf.[259] In the 1950s, there had been approximately 8,000 Indians and Pakistanis in Kuwait; by 1975, there were 50,000.[260] Overall, the number of South Asian workers in the Gulf rose from 50,000 in the mid-1970s to 395,682 in 1980, constituting as much as two-thirds of any particular state's workforce.[261] Another group that benefited from the influx of foreign workers was Filipinos, of whom there had been 7,813 in the Gulf states in 1976; by 1980 there were 132,044.[262] In 1970, there were 685,000 foreigners of all types in the six Gulf states; a decade later, there were 2.7 million.[263] In the period between 1975 and 1980, foreign workers' total share of employment in the region jumped from 50.5 percent to 70 percent.[264]

Expatriates found work through Gulf sponsors that participated in the *kafala,* a network of regional employers and workers that was similar to that used by British officials and merchants forty years before to bring South Asians to the Gulf to work in the oil industry. In this system, every worker who came from outside the Gulf was required to demonstrate that he or she had a legal guarantor (or *kafel*)—usually a private citizen or a private or state institution—before receiving a residency permit, the *iqama*. A *kafel* would attest to a foreigner's employment status, agree to pay for his or her return trip home, and notify authorities if the worker moved or changed jobs. Workers were thus significantly tied to their employers and could not freely switch positions unless their *kafel* agreed to it. By the early 1980s, the *kafala* system had become, in the words of sociologist Anh Nga Longva, a defining "institution" for Gulf life and its image to the outside world.[265]

Because the Gulf states only permitted their own citizens to serve as *kafels,* the *kafala* system seemingly invested enormous socioeconomic power in the hands of Gulf nationals, although they represented less than 50 percent of the population in Kuwait, Qatar, and the UAE and as little as 15 percent of the workforce in Kuwait. Gulf employers or sponsors could control virtually every aspect of their workers' lives, with little fear that the workers would quit, since Gulf wages were usually higher than those in most other parts of the world. Expatriate workers were expected to surrender their passports to their sponsors, who saw the documents as a guarantor of good behavior and an assurance that the foreigners would not leave before the expiration of their work contracts. Nor was it uncommon for foreigners, from factory workers to highly educated strategic analysts, to have to accept six-day workweeks and being locked in their place of employment throughout the workday. Domestic servants were especially vulnerable to physical and sexual abuse, because they worked in private settings far from public view.[266]

For business and political leaders in the Gulf, South Asians and Filipinos presented a number of key advantages. They spoke English (unlike comparable workers from, say, Thailand and Korea), they accepted far lower wages than Europeans or Americans, they had a strong work ethic, they were highly familiar with the region, they had no claim to permanent settlement, and they could be expelled more easily than Arabs or westerners. Furthermore, South Asian states and the Philippines depended on the Gulf for oil and on remittances from their workers there to meet their international financial obligations. After 1976, the remittances represented Pakistan's largest single source of export earnings.[267] Indians in the Gulf annually sent $1.6 billion home in remittances, of which $500 million flowed into one Indian state, Kerala.[268] Any limitations on migration to the Gulf met with fierce resistance among ordinary citizens, who looked at the region as an untapped frontier. Consequently, there was little that India, Pakistan, or other South Asian states could do for their citizens—even when their rights were openly and wantonly violated.

The logic of using South Asian workers in the Gulf states was confirmed by ARAMCO in 1970, when it designed a linear programming model to determine which workers would be the most cost efficient for the company's future workforce. The answer was that South Asians were by far the lowest-cost solution for ARAMCO, so the company should fire and replace most of its current employees, who were either Americans or Saudis.[269]

A Temporary Situation

The fact that ARAMCO chose to ignore the results of its model and sought to increase Saudi participation in the company's workforce illustrates the types of social pressures that faced the Gulf states in the 1970s. From the start of the influx of South Asian workers, Gulf governments, many of which had recently gained independence from Britain, reassured their populations that the new workers were just a temporary solution. Importing them, in other words, was just a rational response to the lack of education of the indigenous populations and their small size. Expatriates would build the modern economies and educate a new generation of Gulf Arabs, who would then have the skills to assume full control of their societies in short order. ARAMCO, the signature corporation of the largest state in the Gulf, understood that it had to hire more Saudis, especially in management positions, as it came under full Saudi control.

To meet the challenges of running ARAMCO and other modern concerns within their rapidly modernizing societies, the Gulf states followed a clear two-part strategy. First, they encouraged their populations to increase rapidly and gave women generous financial incentives to remain at home to raise large families. Between 1970 and 1990, Saudi Arabia's population rose from 5.74 million to 16.5 million inhabitants.[270] During the same time, Kuwait's population grew from 760,000 to 2.11 million, the UAE's population increased from 505,000 to 1.75 million, Qatar's population jumped from 171,000 to nearly 420,000, Oman's population rose from 750,000 to 1.39 million, and Bahrain's population grew from 282,000 to 510,000.[271] These statistics are even more noteworthy when one bears in mind that the population of the UAE grew by just 6,000 people between 1900 and 1960.[272]

As educated Gulf nationals came of age, they were in a strong position to take advantage of the second part of the strategy: laws that gave them preferential treatment in public- and private-sector hiring, particularly for management positions. The programs had different names—to Emiratize, Omanize, or Saudize—but were the same in scope and approach throughout the Gulf. In much the same way that Malays had replaced ethnic Chinese and others in Malaysia after the introduction of the New Economic Policy in 1969, Gulf Arabs were to replace South Asian and other expatriate workers in every sector of the economy, from the highest paid officials to ordinary laborers. It would all be done quickly, within less than a decade. This was such a widely accepted assumption that the state governments in India failed to develop a tax structure to take advantage of the millions of dollars in remittances from the Gulf, since policymakers expected these revenues to soon disappear.[273]

But there were already indications in the early 1970s that replacing South Asian and other expatriate workers with local Arabs would not be possible in the near or medium term. Increasing a population was one thing; educating and getting that population to accept positions in the private sector over secure government positions was a completely different matter. The same ARAMCO analysts who had determined that the most cost-effective future workforce for the company would be South Asians also concluded that the company could not expect Saudis to assume a sizable portion, let alone a majority, of its managerial and professional positions before 1990. And this estimate was widely considered to be far too optimistic by many within the company, whose senior managers feared that Saudi college graduates would advance "five to ten years earlier than their American counterparts did in the past."[274] An ARAMCO report in 1973 observed that hiring Saudi college graduates would prove to be a challenge:

> The Saudi Arabian government continues to maintain and exercise first lien on the emerging Saudi Arab college graduates, ninety-five percent of whom are readily employed in its many offices and agencies. The remaining . . . come from prosperous families generally well established in on-going businesses and more often than not, the fresh graduates prefer to work for their own businesses. As you know, we have been cautioned not to proselytize the former and cannot very effectively attract the latter smaller group because not only is their first loyalty to their family enterprise, but, logically enough, one's business holds promise of greater financial reward than going to work for a salary.[275]

With large government contracts for family businesses and a growing public sector, there was no reason for young, educated Saudis and other Gulf Arabs to seek employment with ARAMCO or far less prestigious companies. Qatar was typical in the 1970s, in that half the local labor force worked in government.[276] Most Gulf nationals had little desire to become ordinary day laborers. That work, they felt, was for someone else to do.

For individuals who could not immediately find employment or whose education did not prepare them for work in the modern economy in the Gulf, there was little reason to worry. Generous government benefits covered them until they found suitable work. This system suited private-sector employers as well, since they had no desire to hire local workers, who had to be paid higher salaries than expatriates and could not be fired as easily. So long as oil revenues continued to increase, Gulf governments had adequate resources to make this system work smoothly.

The Iranian Revolution and a New Course in the Gulf

The politics of the Gulf region remained remarkably stable in the early and middle 1970s after Britain's departure in 1971. For many Gulf states, the Pax

Iranica was not much different from the century-long Pax Britannica, since the shah's armed forces guaranteed Western interests in the Gulf and the free flow of oil through the Straits of Hormuz. But this order collapsed in 1979, when Ayatollah Ruhollah Khomeini and his fellow clerics toppled the shah's regime and established the Islamic Republic of Iran.[277]

Initially, the Gulf countries cautiously welcomed Iran's new government and were particularly pleased with the new defense minister, Seyed Ahmad Madani, who formally rejected Iranian nationalism, announcing that his nation "no longer wished to be the gendarme of the Persian Gulf."[278] He also canceled all military orders, paid or unpaid, and transferred Iran's large Indian Ocean navy base, Chah-Bahar, to the Southern Fishery Company. Other officials assured the Gulf states that Iran did not have any designs on their independence, integrity, or even their wealth. New Iranian president Muhammad Ali Rajai was even quoted as saying that Iran's Islamic Republic would reconsider the question of sovereignty over the islands of Tunbs and Abu Musa. Many in the Gulf states hoped Abu Musa or the Tunbs would be restored to Arab sovereignty.[279]

These hopes were soon dashed by the increasingly radical tone of the regime. Iranian officials now actively promoted the revolution's ideas and urged Gulf Shias, who had decades of disagreements with Sunni governments, to follow Iran's example. Religion provided a useful cover for long-held Iranian national desire to control the Gulf. Ayatollah Sadegh Rouhani perfectly articulated this concept when he threatened to annex Bahrain unless the island's rulers adopted a more Islamic form of government. And many Iranians—even those who adamantly opposed the Islamic revolution—did not doubt the legitimacy of Iran's claims to the islands in the Gulf.

The radicalization of the Iranian revolution also surprised the United States. The Carter administration had weathered the crisis that led to the downfall of the shah remarkably well and had even retained influence in the new government of Prime Minister Mehdi Bazargan. But President Jimmy Carter and his advisers had a much more difficult time addressing the international implications of the revolution after fifty-two Americans were taken hostage in the US Embassy in Tehran in early November 1979. This event signaled to US officials that Iran was quickly becoming a hostile power that could threaten vital US interests in the Gulf and in the Straits of Hormuz. Equally alarming was the Soviet Union's invasion of Afghanistan in January 1980.

To meet these two concerns, the administration announced that any attempt to win control over the Gulf would be regarded as an assault on the vital interests of the United States and "would be repelled by any means necessary, including military force."[280] This new policy, which became known as the Carter Doctrine, soon represented a significant departure from previous US policy in the Gulf. Henceforth, the US government viewed the security and stability of Saudi Arabia and the other Gulf states as vitally linked to its own.

Never again would it permit another power to take the territory of any of these states by force, as Iran had done in 1971 with Abu Musa and the Tunbs. This new policy, in turn, put the Arabs in a much stronger position, since it compelled the United States, much like Britain before it, to support them in any border dispute with Iran.

Sensing Iran's weakened position, the Gulf states gradually took a tougher line toward that nation. When Iraq invaded Iran in the fall of 1980, the Gulf states sided with Saddam Hussein's government, which had prudently cited the liberation of Abu Musa and the Tunbs as one of its principal war aims. With the outbreak of war, the Gulf states also profited handsomely, since the price of petroleum more than doubled, climbing from nearly $13 to $30 a barrel in less than a year. The oil income of the Saudi government increased by 77 percent between 1979 and 1980.[281]

In May 1981, Saudi Arabia, Kuwait, the United Arab Emirates, Oman, Qatar, and Bahrain formed the Gulf Cooperation Council, a regional alliance whose members portrayed it as a first step toward a broader Arab economic and political organization. The member states also sought to synthesize their military forces while providing millions of dollars in aid to the Iraqi war effort and continuing to invest in modern weapons. In the 1970s, Saudi Arabia spent between $9 billion and $16 billion annually on weapons, an amount equal to as much as 19.1 percent of its GDP.[282] Between 1971 and 1980, Kuwait spent $7.63 billion on weapons, Oman spent $5.48 billion, the UAE spent nearly $4.27 billion, Qatar spent $2.07 billion, and Bahrain spent $253 million.[283] Although individual GCC armies were small compared to the armies of Iran or Iraq, they were gargantuan in relation to their domestic populations. In fact, Oman, Kuwait, and the UAE had among the highest number of soldiers per 1,000 residents in the world.[284]

Saudi Arabia, Oman, and Bahrain supplemented their arms purchases by reaching informal defense arrangements with the United States and Great Britain. Washington pledged to defend these states' security should Iran or the Soviet Union seek to control the Gulf region. Under this arrangement, Bahrain, Oman, and Saudi Arabia stored material for the US military (and later the British) to use in a crisis, while simultaneously keeping their diplomatic distance publicly from Washington's strong support for Israel. US soldiers remained stationed far outside the region but regularly conducted exercises in the Gulf and could deploy there if a crisis erupted. The arrangement came to be called the "over the horizon" defense, whereby Gulf populations did not see US and other Western forces permanently stationed in their region, but Gulf governments could rest assured that Western military aid would be forthcoming if needed.

A State of Unease

For the Shia Muslims of Iran and elsewhere in the Gulf, the message was clear: only Sunni Arab Muslims would be permitted to participate in the economic and political life of the Gulf region. It is not surprising that Tehran did not take a positive view of the GCC and its new security arrangements with Washington. Iranian officials chastised Arab Gulf regimes for permitting a foreign power to establish a presence in the region and for not defending "true Islam." Diplomatic relations between Iran and the Arab Gulf states deteriorated rapidly, especially after Iran repeatedly called on Gulf nationals to press their governments to end their support of Iraq and to support Iran.

These developments were a disaster for the Shia Arabs of the Gulf, since they had always been suspect in the eyes of Sunni governments and now were regarded as "potential fifth columnists" who merited open discrimination and harsh official treatment. The response of these Shia Arabs was to erupt in mass demonstrations throughout the Gulf. For example, in Saudi Arabia, there was an *intifada* (uprising) in the Eastern Province in 1979. In Bahrain, there were large protests in both 1979 and 1982, and the Sunni-dominated government foiled a coup in 1981 by Shia who were dedicated to establishing an Islamic fundamentalist state and expelling the US naval presence there. Arab Sunni retributions in Bahrain were fierce and swift: senior members of Shia religious elites were executed, and dozens of Shia activists were forced to flee the archipelago, mostly to Lebanon and England.

Kuwait's Shia increasingly labored under similar prejudices. Having built a positive role for themselves in postindependence Kuwait, they now found themselves caught between foreign Shia activism and the fears of mainstream Sunni society. That situation reflected a combination of factors: Kuwait's steadfast support of Iraq in the Iran-Iraq war, the flood of exiled Iraqi Shia activists into Kuwait, and the frustration of educated Shia over their inability to advance in Kuwaiti society. From 1983 to 1989, largely foreign-led militant Shia groups in Kuwait established cells, recruited Kuwaiti Shia, and staged terrorist attacks that targeted oil facilities, Western interests, Saudi Arabia, and the Kuwaiti emir. Although most Shia condemned the protests, the government responded with mass arrests, convictions, and deportations. Shia Kuwaitis in the oil industry lost their jobs, and government surveillance of the Shia community increased markedly.[285]

Nevertheless, the Shia were hardly the only groups in Arab Gulf life to be affected by the revolution in Iran. That event became a catalyst for growing tensions between the rapid modernization of daily life, on the one hand, and Islamic and tribal values, on the other. The unease was especially apparent in the seizure of the Grand Mosque in Mecca in 1979 by conservative Sunni activists. Launched on the same day as the intifada in the Eastern Province, the seizure shook the foundations of Saudi Arabia and the Gulf. The seizure of the mosque challenged the religious legitimacy of the Saudi state and its modernization programs as well as alleging high-level official corruption and excessive foreign influence. It is significant that these criticisms were shared by many secular and Western-oriented Saudis, including the kingdom's leading novelist, Abdelrahman Munif. For example, the final scene of his novel, *Cities of Salt,* depicts a group of oil workers, aided by a mythical airborne creature, attacking a US oil facility and the leadership of a corrupt monarchy that is clearly modeled on Saudi Arabia.[286]

The real-life attack on Mecca's Grand Mosque, which appeared live on television around the world, challenged Saudi Arabia's claim to protect Islam's holiest cities, Mecca and Medina. Therefore, Riyadh had no choice but to react with force, using Saudi soldiers to storm the mosque and either kill or capture the participants. (The Saudi defense minister, Prince Sultan, successfully rallied his troops by appealing to their patriotism, saying, "You can go home. You needn't fight, but what am I to do? Send for the Pakistanis?"[287]) Supporters of the seizure, such as Shaikh Abdullah bin Zaid al-Mahmud, were exiled to neighboring Qatar. At the same time, with the support of religious elites, Riyadh launched a series of Islamic cultural, educational, social, and political reform programs, including substantial support for the Afghanis who were fighting against the Soviet invasion. Although that support came mostly in the form of weapons and financial aid, there were examples of Gulf Arabs who were combatants in Afghanistan, including the scion of a wealthy Saudi family, Osama bin Laden.

The scale and ambitions of the Islamist programs dwarfed any comparable project that had been attempted previously in the region, transformed the landscape of whole cities (women virtually disappeared from public places), and led to restrictions on personal freedoms for men and women, down to the very clothes they could wear in public. Saudi contributions to infrastructure projects that had been meant to link the GCC states (such as the causeway connecting Bahrain to Saudi Arabia) and assistance to poorer Arab Gulf communities reinforced Saudi and other conservative voices in the Gulf. A new generation of Gulf Arabs came of age in societies that were more conservative religiously and socially and more segregated by gender than ever before. The groundwork for mass support of Al-Qaida and other similar groups in the Gulf that espoused conservative Islamic principles and anti-American views was now in place. Male and female voices that might have provided an effective counterweight to such groups were effectively silenced throughout the region.

Conclusion

As dangerous as the Islamist groups would prove to be, they and the values they upheld served two goals for the Arab Gulf states after the 1979 Iranian revolution. The physical and vigorous rhetorical manifestations of the Arab Gulf states' conservative Islamic ideals signaled their continued determination to uphold national sovereignty and to offer their national publics something that others could not: stability. This was a powerful rhetorical tool for populations that were uneasy about the breathtaking changes that were taking place in the socioeconomic structures of their states and about how long their newfound wealth would really last. This unease emerged in a common prediction among Gulf Arabs in the 1970s that their grandchildren would not live in modern luxurious cities instead but live in the desert and ride camels—just as generations of Gulf Arabs had done before the twentieth century.[288]

The same prediction also points to a remarkable fact: Gulf Arabs believed that it was possible (in fact, likely) that their societies would revert back to their way of life before the twentieth century despite fifty years of changes. In half a century, from 1930 to 1981, the Arab Gulf states had transformed from impoverished and thinly populated states that were firmly within Britain's Indian empire into wealthy independent states that could revolutionize global politics. Using the proceeds from oil sales and new technologies such as air conditioning, Gulf states had undergone rapid socioeconomic change, imported millions of non-Arab immigrants, attained the highest per capita incomes in the world, and compelled one of the two strongest global powers, the United States, to alter its positions in the Arab-Israeli conflict and to commit to defending them from attack.

None of these changes were enough, however, to convince Arab Gulf nationals that the socioeconomic conditions and the political structures of their states had changed beyond all recognition. At least, the changes were not so irreversible that these societies could not easily re-embrace the Bedouin lifestyle of their fathers and grandfathers. Although the outside world may have seen these states chiefly through the lens of petroleum, Arabs in the Gulf no more defined their communities by oil than did Americans, Western Europeans, or others who lived in societies in which the consumption of oil had become central to every facet of daily life since World War II. Instead, Gulf Arabs defined themselves and their leaders through traditional customs, values, and rituals, including religion, tribe, national sovereignty, government assistance for the community, and the defense of Muslim and Arab rights. Although Gulf societies adopted increasingly conservative Islamic traditions in the 1970s, they retained the flexibility that had allowed them in the past to welcome a host of non-Sunni minority groups—notably, Hindus, Shia Muslims, Christians, and Jews.

Thus, the success of Gulf Arab monarchies during the period from 1930 to 1981 can be explained by their ability to adhere to traditional values while using new technologies and streams of revenue to reinforce existing centers of power. From the start, these monarchies benefited from their age and the legitimacy afforded by their long-standing tradition of governance. By doing so, Gulf states succeeded in much the same way that Great Britain, Japan, Morocco, and Thailand had—by modernizing their societies in the twentieth century while retaining governing traditions and monarchies. Though Arab nationalists, utilizing radio, offered the hope of a brighter and better future throughout the 1950s and 1960s, the Gulf monarchies countered these arguments by pointing to their recent accomplishments, especially the modernization of national armies, the nationalization of oil companies, the creation of indigenous radio programs, resistance to British administrators, and winning control of the hajj. This final accomplishment was most important to Saudi Arabia, since it defined itself as the defender of the hajj and the two holiest cities in Islam, Mecca and Medina.

As peripheral as oil may have appeared to some segments of Arab Gulf societies, it still mattered. When oil's price and demand declined in the early 1980s, that had a dramatic impact on political and economic life in the region. What had been favorable balances of payments turned negative, and budget deficits soared, forcing unpleasant choices for states that had promised vast social welfare protections to their people. The Iran-Iraq war ensured that Sunni-Shia tensions remained intense and kept regional relations equally strained. Despite their official Islamic rhetoric, Gulf governments faced ongoing challenges to their Islamic credentials from vocal minorities, who utilized new communication technologies, including the Internet and satellite television, to question their legitimacy. All these factors haunted Gulf societies throughout the 1980s and 1990s, particularly after one of the defining events of the modern era: Iraq's invasion of Kuwait.

Notes

1. Debbas, a Christian Lebanese, earned a B.A. and an M.S. from the American University in Beirut and came to the United States in 1947 on a Department of State scholarship. He first studied at Lehigh University and then earned an M.S. at Harvard University in 1949. Edward Debbas, in discussion with the author, October 17, 2009.

2. "U.S. Is the Pilgrim's Friend in Need," *Life Magazine*, September 8, 1952, 29–31; Nick Nolte to Walter S. Rogers, "Operation Hajj," September 5, 1952, Institute of Current World Affairs Collection of Letters, RHN–45, 2 (available at http://www.icwa.org/).

3. "Tidings for the Muslims: Royal Decree of the Canceling of Pilgrimage Dues," *Um al-Qura*, May 23, 1952, 5; Nolte, "Operation Hajj," 2–3; Carp, U.S. Consulate Istanbul to Washington, "Pilgrimage to Mecca," no. 174, September 16, 1952, reprinted in Alan de Lacy Rush, ed., *Records of the Hajj: A Documentary History of the Pilgrimage to Mecca*, vol. 8, *The Saudi Period (Since 1952)* (Cambridge: Cambridge University Press Archive Editions, 1993), 100–103.

4. Edward Debbas, in discussion with the author, October 17, 2009.

5. Nolte, "Operation Hajj," 5.

6. As early as July 1952, US diplomats had noted that Saudi Arabia's insistence that 50 percent of all pilgrims transported by air would go by Saudi Arabian airlines had the potential to cause serious disruptions. Crawford, "Annual Pilgrimage," US Embassy Jidda to Washington, no. 345, July 24, 1952, reprinted in Rush, *Records of the Hajj*, vol. 8, *The Saudi Period*, 21–22.

7. Nolte, "Operation Hajj," 3. In a 2009 interview, Debbas did not remember

asking specifically for assistance from French or US airlines. Edward Debbas, in discussion with the author, October 17, 2009.

8. A Lebanese newspaper estimated that at least 34,000 pilgrims from Turkey, Iraq, Iran, and Afghanistan arrived in Lebanon in the days before the airlift. "Biggest Flying Bridge for Transport of Pilgrims to Mecca," *al-Bilad,* September 1, 1952, reprinted in Rush, *Records of the Hajj,* vol. 8, *The Saudi Period,* 59.

9. Debbas also asked Minor directly for US assistance. The two men were friendly, and Debbas remembers regularly visiting Minor's home in 1952. Edward Debbas, in discussion with the author, October 17, 2009.

10. "Airlift for Allah," *Time,* September 8, 1952, 34; United States Congress, House Committee on Foreign Affairs, *Mutual Security Act of 1958: Hearing Before the Committee on Foreign Affairs: House of Representatives, 85th Congress, Second Session* (Washington, DC: United States Government Printing Office, 1958), 690–691, 824–826.

11. Minor, Embassy Beirut to Washington, "USIS Story on Meccan Airlift," no. 364, August 25, 1952, reprinted in Rush, *Records of the Hajj,* vol. 8, *The Saudi Period,* 53; Walter J. Boyne, "The Pilgrim Airlift," *Air Force Magazine Online* 90, no. 3 (March 2007): 82. The US operation included 80 officers and 129 enlisted men.

12. Edward Debbas, in discussion with the author, October 17, 2009.

13. Ibid.

14. Minor, Embassy Beirut to Washington, "Meccan Airlift," no. 422, August 30, 1952, reprinted in *Records of the Hajj,* vol. 8, *The Saudi Period,* 58; Hare, Embassy Beirut to Washington, "Progress Report on Use of Mecca Airlift Fund," no. 164, September 9, 1954, reprinted in Rush, *Records of the Hajj,* vol. 8, *The Saudi Period,* 76–77.

15. For more on this organization and its close ties to the Central Intelligence Agency (CIA), see Hugh Wilford, *The Mighty Wurlitzer: How the CIA Played America* (Cambridge, MA: Harvard University Press, 2008), 126–127, 137, 236–247.

16. Nolte, "Operation Hajj," 4; Boyne, "The Pilgrim Airlift," 83.

17. "Airlift for Allah."

18. Ibid., 34.

19. Nolte, "Operation Hajj," 5.

20. Pelham to Eden, "Annual Report on the Pilgrimage to the Holy Places in the Hejaz for 1952," no. 21, ES 1781/4, Jeddah, February 2, 1953, reprinted in *British Documents on Foreign Affairs: Reports and Papers from the Foreign Office Confidential Print,* ed. Paul Preston and Michael Partridge, pt. 5: *From 1951 Through 1956,* Series B: *Near and Middle East, 1953,* ed. Bülent Gökay, vol. 6: *Arabia, Lebanon, Israel, Syria, and Jordan, 1953* (Bethesda, MD: University Publications of America, 1992), 65.

21. William Foster, Deputy US Secretary of Defense, to Secretary of the Army, Secretary of the Navy, Secretary of the Air Force, and Joints Chiefs of Staff, "Psychological Significance of the Mecca Airlift," October 1, 1952. I thank the Truman Presidential Library for providing me with a copy of this document.

22. Nolte, "Operation Hajj," 5.

23. Pelham to Eden, "Annual Report on the Pilgrimage to the Holy Places in the Hejaz for 1952," 62–63.

24. Ibid.

25. Trott to Bevin, "Pilgrimage to the Hejaz, 1950," no. 140, ES 1782/33, Jeddah, October 24, 1950, reprinted in *British Documents on Foreign Affairs: Reports and Papers from the Foreign Office Confidential Print*, ed. Paul Preston and Michael Partridge, pt. 4: *From 1946 Through 1950*, Series B: *Near and Middle East, 1950*, ed. Malcolm Yapp, vol. 10: *Israel, Syria, Arabia, General, Jordan and Arab Palestine and the Lebanon, 1950, January 1950–December 1950* (Bethesda, MD: University Publications of America, 1999), 231.

26. While Dulles does not explain why he chose not to renew the mission, he might have believed that it violated the First Amendment of the US Constitution. The airlift was not a normal humanitarian operation but a special case in which the US government—by flying pilgrims to Mecca as opposed to their homes—could be seen as using official funds to promote a specific religion (in this case, Islam). The operation could thus be seen as a violation of the First Amendment of the US Constitution, and the American Civil Liberties Union would certainly initiate legal action were a similar airlift undertaken today. Whether such a case would override the humanitarian and foreign policy concerns related to the airlift in US courts is a different matter. I thank Lior Strahilevitz and Bert Kirby for helping me understand the potential constitutional issues connected to the 1952 Hajj airlift. Dulles to Certain American Diplomatic and Consular Posts, "Circular Airgram," no. 851, June 5, 1953, reprinted in Rush, *Records of the Hajj,* vol. 8, *The Saudi Period,* 71; Minor, US Embassy Beirut to Washington, no. 128, July 31, 1953, reprinted in Rush, *Records of the Hajj,* vol. 8, *The Saudi Period,* 73; United States Congress, House Committee on Foreign Affairs, *Mutual Security Act of 1958,* 824–826.

27. Kirk, US Legation Cairo to Washington, no. 1540, August 27, 1943, reprinted in United States Department of State, *Records of the Department of State Relating to Internal Affairs of Saudi Arabia, 1930–1944* (Washington, DC: National Archives, National Records and Archives Service, General Services Administration, 1974), Reel 5; Hull, Washington to US Consul Algiers, no. 890, September 8, 1943, reprinted in United States Department of State, *Records of the Department of State Relating to Internal Affairs of Saudi Arabia, 1930–1944*, Reel 5; Wallace Murray to Berle and Dunn, US Department of State, October 2, 1943, reprinted in United States Department of State, *Records of the Department of State Relating to Internal Affairs of Saudi Arabia, 1930–1944*, Reel 5; Wallace Murray, US Department of State, "Memorandum of Conversation—Arthur Sweetser and Wallace Murray: Proposed Pilgrimage to Mecca by Army Transport Planes Carrying the Sultan of Morocco, the Bey of Tunis and High Moslem Ecclesiastics of French North Africa Under the Auspices of the Office of War Information," 890F.404/33, October 2, 1943, reprinted in United States Department of State, *Records of the Department of State Relating to Internal Affairs of Saudi Arabia, 1930–1944*, Reel 5.

28. The French delegation was paid for by a committee headed by Henri Giraud and Charles de Gaulle. Wiley, Algiers to Secretary of State, November 2, 1943, reprinted in United States Department of State, *Records of the Department of State Relating to Internal Affairs of Saudi Arabia, 1930–1944,* Reel 5; Murphy, Algiers to Secretary of State, A-93, November 18, 1943, reprinted in United States Department of State, *Records of the Department of State Relating to Internal Affairs of Saudi Arabia, 1930–1944*, Reel 5; and Wilson, Algiers to Secretary of State, A-29, no. 120, December 28, 1943, reprinted in United States Department

of State, *Records of the Department of State Relating to Internal Affairs of Saudi Arabia, 1930–1944*, Reel 5.

29. US Legation Cairo to Washington, no. 890, October 4, 1943, reprinted in United States Department of State, *Records of the Department of State Relating to Internal Affairs of Saudi Arabia, 1930–1944*, Reel 5.

30. Elmer Davis to Sweetser, "Proposed Pilgrimage to Mecca," September 28, 1943, reprinted in United States Department of State, *Records of the Department of State Relating to Internal Affairs of Saudi Arabia, 1930–1944*, Reel 5; Murray, "Memorandum of Conversation—Arthur Sweetser and Wallace Murray."

31. Jill Crystal, *Oil and Politics in the Gulf: Rulers and Merchants in Qatar* (Cambridge: Cambridge University Press, 1995), 187.

32. A good example of this process is in Iraq, where President Saddam Hussein consciously defined himself as the new Nebuchadnezzar. For more on this process, see Amatzia Baram, *Culture, History, and Ideology in the Formation of Iraq* (New York: St. Martin's Press, 1991).

33. Alexander Sloan, US Legation in Baghdad to Washington, "British Officials' Conferences with King Ibn Saud Persian Gulf," no. 151, March 12, 1932, reprinted in United States Department of State, *Records of the Department of State Relating to Internal Affairs of Saudi Arabia, 1930–1944*, Reel 1.

34. Newton to Halifax, no. 139, E1637/1637/91, Baghdad, March 31, 1940, reprinted in *British Documents on Foreign Affairs: Reports and Papers from the Foreign Office Confidential Print*, ed. Paul Preston and Michael Partridge, pt. 3: *From 1940 Through 1945*, Series B: *Near and Middle East*, ed. Malcolm Yapp, vol. 4: *Eastern Affairs, January 1940–December 1941* (Bethesda, MD: University Publications of America, 1997), 95–97.

35. Susan Hillyard, *Before the Oil: A Personal Memoir of Abu Dhabi, 1954–1958* (Bakewell, Derbyshire, UK: Ashridge Press, 2002), 144.

36. For example, see the events in Qatar outlined in A. A. Russell, "Summary of News from the Arab States for the Month of September, 1928," no. 7, 1928, reprinted in *Political Diaries of the Arab World: The Persian Gulf*, vol. 8, *1928–1929* (Farnham Common, England: Archive Editions, 1990), 160.

37. For an excellent example of how this system worked, see T. C. Fowler, Political Resident at Bahrain to India Office, E3248/269/91, Camp Bahrain, May 12, 1935, reprinted in *British Documents on Foreign Affairs: Reports and Papers from the Foreign Office Confidential Print*, ed. Kenneth Bourne and D. Cameron Watt, pt. 2: *From the First to the Second World War*, Series B: *Turkey, Iran, and the Middle East, 1918–1939*, ed. Robin Bidwell, vol. 10: *Eastern Affairs, December 1933–June 1935* (Bethesda, MD: University Publications of America, 1985), 374–376.

38. A good example is Newton to Halifax, "no. 139, E1637/1637/91," 96.

39. For example, in 1940 there were no individuals trained in modern trades in the Hejaz and just 610 masons, 310 carpenters, 23 blacksmiths, 36 tinsmiths, and 27 wood turners out of a population of more than a million people. Raymond Hare, US Legation Cairo to the Secretary of State, "Labor Conditions in Saudi Arabia: Builders and Contractors at Jeddah," no. 2025, March 18, 1940, reprinted in United States Department of State, *Records of the Department of State Relating to Internal Affairs of Saudi Arabia, 1930–1944*, Reel 5.

40. British diplomatic documents indicate that much of the Gulf's overseas trade in the 1930s was food imports from the British Empire. Calvert to Eden, no.

O.T. 20, E5488/1041/25, Jeddah, June 26, 1936, reprinted in *British Documents on Foreign Affairs: Reports and Papers from the Foreign Office Confidential Print*, ed. Kenneth Bourne and D. Cameron Watt, pt. 2: *From the First to the Second World War,* Series B: *Turkey, Iran, and the Middle East, 1918–1939,* ed. Robin Bidwell, vol. 11: *Eastern Affairs, June 1935–December* 1936 (Bethesda, MD: University Publications of America, 1985), 355–361.

41. Indeed, Hijazis paid for the goods they imported almost entirely using the money from hajj pilgrims. David Hogarth, *Hejaz Before World War I: A Handbook* (Oxford: Falcon-Oleander, 1978; first published in 1917 by Arab Bureau, Cairo), 79–80. Citation is to the 1978 edition.

42. Parker Hart, US Consulate Dhahran, "General Observations Regarding Dhahran, Bahrain," no. 51, December 20, 1944, William Mulligan Papers, Georgetown University Library Special Collections, Box 7, Folder 6.

43. James Onley, *The Arabian Frontier of the British Raj: Merchants, British, and Rulers in the Nineteenth-Century Gulf* (Oxford: Oxford University Press, 2007), 219.

44. Phebe Marr, "Girls' Schools—The Hijaz," April 8, 1961, William Mulligan Papers, Georgetown University Library Special Collections, Box 3, Folder 6.

45. Hogarth, *Hejaz Before World War I: A Handbook,* 79–80.

46. Bevin to Hay, "Future Judicial Arrangements in the Persian Gulf States," November 20, 1950, EA 1643/76, reprinted in *British Documents on Foreign Affairs: Reports and Papers from the Foreign Office Confidential Print*, ed. Paul Preston and Michael Partridge, pt. 5: *From 1951 Through 1956,* Series B: *Near and Middle East, 1952,* ed. Bülent Gökay, vol. 4: *Arabia, Lebanon, Israel, Syria, Jordan, and General, 1952* (Bethesda, MD: Lexis-Nexis, 2005), 10–12; Hay to Bevin, "His Majesty's Government's Future Policy in the Trucial States and Central Oman," November 25, 1950, EA 1057/12, no. 83, reprinted in Gökay, vol. 4: *Arabia, Lebanon, Israel, Syria, Jordan, and General, 1952* (Bethesda, MD: Lexis-Nexis, 2005), 12–15.

47. Secretary of State for the Colonies to the Acting Resident of the Persian Gulf, Bushire, no. 16, E4217/305/91, Colonial Office (London), July 29, 1933, reprinted in *British Documents on Foreign Affairs: Reports and Papers from the Foreign Office Confidential Print*, ed. Kenneth Bourne and D. Cameron Watt, pt. 2: *From the First to the Second World War,* Series B: *Turkey, Iran, and the Middle East, 1918–1939,* ed. Robin Bidwell, vol. 9: *Eastern Affairs, June 1933–May 1934* (Bethesda, MD: University Publications of America, 1985), 65–66.

48. This process forced British officials to work more closely with ruling families in the Trucial Coast than they had done in the past. For more on these problems, see Political Resident in the Persian Gulf to the Foreign Secretary to the Government of India, "Policy on the Trucial Coast," E7156/2240/91, Bahrain, November 16, 1934, reprinted in *British Documents on Foreign Affairs: Reports and Papers from the Foreign Office Confidential Print*, ed. Kenneth Bourne and D. Cameron Watt, pt. 2: *From the First to the Second World War,* Series B: *Turkey, Iran, and the Middle East, 1918–1939,* ed. Robin Bidwell, vol. 10: *Eastern Affairs, December 1933–June 1935* (Bethesda, MD: University Publications of America, 1985), 58–60; Hay to Bevin, "His Majesty's Government's Future Policy in the Trucial States and Central Oman," 8.

49. Onley, *The Arabian Frontier of the British Raj,* 68.

50. Newton to Halifax, "no. 139, E1637/1637/91," 96.

51. Clarence J. McIntosh to McIntosh Family, August 16, 1944, Clarence J. McIntosh Papers, Georgetown University Library Special Collections, Box 2, Folder 24, Letter 27.

52. Nora Johnson, *You Can Go Home Again* (New York: Doubleday Books, 1982), 40.

53. Makins to Eden, "Report on a Visit to the States of the Persian Gulf Under British Protection with Some Observations on Iraq and Saudi Arabia and with Conclusions and Recommendations," no. 12, March 20, 1952, reprinted in *British Documents on Foreign Affairs: Reports and Papers from the Foreign Office Confidential Print*, ed. Paul Preston and Michael Partridge, pt. 5: *From 1951 Through 1956*, Series B: *Near and Middle East*, ed. Bülent Gökay, vol. 4: *Arabia, Lebanon, Israel, Syria, and Jordan, 1952* (Bethesda, MD: Lexis-Nexis, 2005), 35.

54. Quotation cited in Mahdi al-Tajir, *Bahrain: 1920–1945: Britain, the Shaykh, and the Administration* (New York: Routledge, 1987), 177.

55. Ian J. Seccombe and R. I. Lawless, "Foreign Worker Dependence in the Gulf, and the International Oil Companies: 1910–50," *International Migration Review* 20, no. 3. (Autumn 1986): 550–553, 560.

56. Ibid., 563–565.

57. Ibid., 568.

58. One saw similar controls in Saudi Arabia. For more on this issue, see Bullard to Halifax, no. 100, E3334/1698/25, Jeddah, May 17, 1938, reprinted in *British Documents on Foreign Affairs: Reports and Papers from the Foreign Office Confidential Print*, ed. Kenneth Bourne and D. Cameron Watt, pt. 2: *From the First to the Second World War*, Series B: *Turkey, Iran, and the Middle East, 1918–1939*, ed. Robin Bidwell, vol. 12: *Eastern Affairs, June 1936–June 1938* (Bethesda, MD: University Publications of America, 1986), 438–439.

59. Al-Tajir, *Bahrain: 1920–1945*, 173–180; Seccombe and Lawless, "Foreign Worker Dependence," 560.

60. In a meeting with US Undersecretary of State Edward Reilly Stettinius in May 1943, Ibn Saud's son, Faysal, voiced concern that Saudi Arabia would be surrounded in much the same way the Turks had surrounded the previous Saudi states. US Department of State, Department of Near Eastern Affairs, "American Policy in the Near East: Meeting Prince Faisal, Mr. Stettinius, Mr. Berel, Mr. Murray, Mr. Alling," November 1, 1943, reprinted in United States Department of State, *Records of the Department of State Relating to Internal Affairs of Saudi Arabia, 1930–1944*, Reel 3.

61. Ibn Saud allowed the Soviet Union to set up a steamship line from Odessa to Jeddah and to import goods into Saudi Arabia, including substantial quantities of petroleum. Gill to Simon, Jeddah to London, no. 485, E82/82/25, December 20, 1932, reprinted in *British Documents on Foreign Affairs: Reports and Papers from the Foreign Office Confidential Print*, ed. Kenneth Bourne and D. Cameron Watt, pt. 2: *From the First to the Second World War*, Series B: *Turkey, Iran, and the Middle East, 1918–1939*, ed. Robin Bidwell, vol. 8: *Eastern Affairs, December 1931–June 1933* (Bethesda, MD: University Publications of America, 1986), 268–269; Ryan to Simon, no. 66, E1488/1225/25, February 28, 1933, reprinted in *British Documents on Foreign Affairs: Reports and Papers from the Foreign Office Confidential Print*, ed. Kenneth Bourne and D. Cameron Watt, pt. 2: *From the First to the Second World War*, Series B: *Turkey, Iran, and the Middle East, 1918–1939*, ed. Robin Bidwell, vol. 8: *Eastern Affairs, December 1931–June 1933*

(Bethesda, MD: University Publications of America, 1985), 287–288; Bullard to Eden, no. 38e, E1869/115/25, Jedda, March 11, 1937, reprinted in *British Documents on Foreign Affairs: Reports and Papers from the Foreign Office Confidential Print*, ed. Kenneth Bourne and D. Cameron Watt, pt. 2: *From the First to the Second World War*, Series B: *Turkey, Iran, and the Middle East, 1918–1939*, ed. Robin Bidwell, vol. 12: *Eastern Affairs, June 1936–June 1938* (Bethesda, MD: University Publications of America, 1985), 152–155.

62. Shafi Aldamer, *Saudi Arabia and Britain: Changing Relations, 1939–1953* (Reading, England: Ithaca Press, 2003), 6.

63. James Moose, US Department of State, Financial Division, "General Considerations in Connection with Economic or Financial Assistance to Saudi Arabia," no. 890, April 3, 1943, reprinted in United States Department of State, *Records of the Department of State Relating to Internal Affairs of Saudi Arabia, 1930–1944*, Reel 5.

64. Alexander Kirk, US Legation, Cairo to Secretary of State, "Situation in Saudi Arabia," no. 110, September 11, 1941, reprinted in United States Department of State, *Records of the Department of State Relating to Internal Affairs of Saudi Arabia, 1930–1944*, Reel 3.

65. Louis Dame, who visited Saudi Arabia in the 1920s, noted that 70 percent of Saudis lived at the expense of Ibn Saud. He also discussed an "idle" population, who acted in ways familiar to twenty-first-century observers of Gulf Arabs: "All they do is . . . stand in the most prominent places in the mosque to say their prayers. . . . Work is beneath their dignity, but if [Ibn Saud] should cut them off his list of retainers, they would be paupers." Louis Dame, "Intolerance in Inland Arabia," *Neglected Arabia* 117 (April–May–June 1921): 11–12.

66. Ryan to Henderson, Jeddah to London, May 28, 1931, no. 200, E3267/1600/25, reprinted in *British Documents on Foreign Affairs: Reports and Papers from the Foreign Office Confidential Print*, ed. Kenneth Bourne and D. Cameron Watt, pt. 2: *From the First to the Second World War*, Series B: *Turkey, Iran, and the Middle East, 1918–1939*, ed. Robin Bidwell, vol. 7: *Eastern Affairs, June 1930–June 1932* (Bethesda, MD: University Publications of America, [illegible]), 207–209.

67. Stonehewer-Bird to Halifax, no. 8, E945/252/25, Jeddah, February 6, 1940, reprinted in *British Documents on Foreign Affairs: Reports and Papers from the Foreign Office Confidential Print*, ed. Paul Preston and Michael Partridge, pt. 3: *From 1940 through 1945*, Series B: *Near and Middle East*, ed. Malcolm Yapp, vol. 4: *Eastern Affairs, January 1940–December 1941* (Bethesda, MD: University Publications of America, 1997), 63–66.

68. A longtime resident of Saudi Arabia told US officials in the 1940s that Ibn Saud provided subsidies to at least 500,000 people and fed 30,000 people in Riyadh alone. James Moose, US Legation of the United States of America Jeddah to Washington, "Comment on Request of King Ibn Saud for American Military Mission," no. 52, October 25, 1943, reprinted in United States Department of State, *Records of the Department of State Relating to Internal Affairs of Saudi Arabia, 1930–1944*, Reel 4; J. S. Carter, US Department of State, "Memorandum on Saudi Arabia Based on Conversation with Longtime Resident in Saudi Arabia," October 28, 1941, reprinted in United States Department of State, *Records of the Department of State Relating to Internal Affairs of Saudi Arabia, 1930–1944*, Reel 3.

69. Calvert to Sir John Simon, "Jedda Report for November 1934," no. 354, E7515/715/25, December 3, 1934, reprinted in *British Documents on Foreign Affairs: Reports and Papers from the Foreign Office Confidential Print*, ed. Kenneth Bourne and D. Cameron Watt, pt. 2: *From the First to the Second World War*, Series B: *Turkey, Iran, and the Middle East, 1918–1939*, ed. Robin Bidwell, vol. 10: *Eastern Affairs, December 1933–June 1935* (Bethesda, MD: University Publications of America, 1985), 245–247.

70. Carter, "Memorandum on Saudi Arabia Based on Conversation with Longtime Resident in Saudi Arabia."

71. James Moose, US Legation, Jeddah to Washington, "Budget of Saudi Arabia in 1943 and Proposed Budget for 1944," no. 91, January 12, 1944, reprinted in United States Department of State, *Records of the Department of State Relating to Internal Affairs of Saudi Arabia, 1930–1944*, Reel 5; James Moose, US Legation, Jeddah to Washington, "1944 Budget to Saudi Arabia," no. 154, April 13, 1944, reprinted in United States Department of State, *Records of the Department of State Relating to Internal Affairs of Saudi Arabia, 1930–1944*, Reel 5.

72. Wells Hangen, "Arabia Preparing Extensive Reform," *New York Times*, December 11, 1953, 12 (from a database called "Historical New York Times" administered by ProQuest; hereafter *Historical New York Times*).

73. As of 1937, there were only four sets of taxes in Saudi Arabia: the tithe on crops, dates, and cattle; tax on fishing (20 percent of value); monthly tax of 15 percent on boats; and a tax of 10 percent on mariners. Other taxes were collected by municipal authorities. Lee J. Callahan, US Consul, Aden to Washington, "Taxes in Saudi Arabia," no. 24, April 7, 1934, reprinted in United States Department of State, *Records of the Department of State Relating to Internal Affairs of Saudi Arabia, 1930–1944*, Reel 2; and Pelham to Eden, no. 57E., "Saudi Arabian Budget, April 1952–March 1953," April 29, 1952, reprinted in *British Documents on Foreign Affairs: Reports and Papers from the Foreign Office Confidential Print*, ed. Paul Preston and Michael Partridge, pt. 5: *From 1950 Through 1956*, Series B: *Near and Middle East*, ed. Bülent Gökay, vol. 4: *Arabia, Lebanon, Israel, Syria, and Jordan, 1952* (Bethesda, MD: Lexis-Nexis, 2005), 5–7.

74. For more on the British subsidy and the other factors that prompted Ibn Saud to invade the Hijaz, see Joseph Teitelbaum, "Pilgrimage Politics: The Hajj and the Saudi-Hashemite Rivalry, 1916–1925," in *The Hashemites in the Modern Arab World: Essays in Honor of the Late Professor Uriel Dann*, ed. Asher Susser and Aryeh Shmuelevitz, 75–84 (London: Frank Cass, 1995); Clive Leatherdale, *Britain and Saudi Arabia: The Imperial Oasis* (London: Frank Cass, 1983), 16–29.

75. Astrology is still important to Saudi society, despite the fact that senior Saudi religious scholars have linked it to sorcery and other sinful acts. The Saudi Arabian daily newspaper, *The Saudi Gazette*, regularly published horoscopes in the 2000s, and the characters in Rajaa al-Sanea's novel, *The Girls of Riyadh*, discuss their horoscopes and those of potential husbands. For more on astrology and Saudi Arabia, see Amos Peaslee, *The Constitutions of Nations*, 2nd ed., vol 3: *Nicaragua to Yugoslavia* (The Hague: M. Nijhoff, 1956), 276; Rajaa al-Sanea, *Girls of Riyadh*, trans. Rajaa al-Sanea and Marilyn Booth (New York: Penguin Press, 2007), 53–55; and Natana DeLong-Bas, *Wahhabi Islam: From Revival and Reform to Global Islam* (Oxford: Oxford University Press, 2004), 73–75.

76. Clarence J. McIntosh to McIntosh Family, February 14, 1943, Clarence J. McIntosh Papers, Georgetown University Library Special Collections, Box 1,

Folder 7, Letter No. 7. McIntosh noted in the letter that a Greek store in Jeddah's *souq* (market) carried imported food from the United States.

77. H.St.J.B. Philby, *Arabian Highlands* (Ithaca, NY: Cornell University Press for the Middle East Institute, 1952), 277; Joseph Tobi, *The Jews of Yemen: Studies in Their History and Culture* (Leiden: Brill, 1999), 22; Christoph Wilcke, *The Ismalis of Najran* (New York: Human Rights Watch, 2008), 10.

78. F. P. Mackie, *Report to the Saudi Arabian Mining Syndicate on Saudi Arabia's Public Health*, March 7, 1940, reprinted in United States Department of State, *Records of the Department of State Relating to Internal Affairs of Saudi Arabia, 1930–1944* (Washington, DC: National Archives, National Records and Archives Service, General Services Administration, 1974), Reel 3, 11.

79. Ibn Wahhab, however, saw homosexuality as sinful behavior and did not condone it. His comments on the subject emerge in a response to a question from a follower about whether it is appropriate to invite a man who has effeminate behavior or who is known to be bisexual to a wedding party. For more on Wahhab and homosexuality, see DeLong-Bas, *Wahhabi Islam*, 165–166; Nadya Labi, "The Kingdom in the Closet," *Atlantic Monthly*, May 2007 (available at http://www.theatlantic.com/).

80. Aden to Washington, "Summary: Ibn Saud's Family," August 15, 1932, reprinted in United States Department of State, *Records of the Department of State Relating to Internal Affairs of Saudi Arabia, 1930–1944*, Reel 1; Dame, "Intolerance in Inland Arabia," 14; Louis Dame, "A Trip to Central Arabia," *Neglected Arabia* 167 (January–February–March 1934): 19; "Reader Bullard to Family, June 14, 1938," in Reader Bullard, *Two Kings in Arabia: Letters from Jeddah: 1923–5 and 1936–9*, ed. E. C. Hodgkin, 232–233 (Reading, UK: Ithaca Press, 1993).

81. Yitzhak Nakash, *Reaching for Power: The Shi'a in the Modern Arab World* (Princeton, NJ: Princeton University Press, 2006), 44.

82. Ralph Chesbrough, US Legation Beirut, "The Economic Resources and Commercial Activities of the Kingdom of the Hedjaz, Nejd, and Dependencies," no. 16, June 30, 1930, reprinted in *Records of the Department of State Relating to Internal Affairs of Saudi Arabia, 1930–1944*, Reel 1; Stonehewer-Bird to London, "Report on the Pilgrimage of 1927," E4387/249/91, September 24, 1927, reprinted in Robin Bidwell, ed., *British Documents on Foreign Affairs: Reports and Papers from the Foreign Office Confidential Print*, pt. 2: *From the First to Second World War*, Series B: *Turkey, Iran, and the Middle East, 1918–1939*, vol. 14: *The Pilgrimage in the Reign of Ibn Saud, 1927–1939* (London: University Press of America, 1989), 1; Stonehewer-Bird to London, "Report on the Pilgrimage, 1928," E4867/58/91, September 12, 1928, reprinted in Bidwell, *British Documents*, pt. 2, Series B, vol. 14, 27; Ryan, "Report on the Pilgrimage 1929," E2421/54/91, April 3, 1930, reprinted in Bidwell, *British Documents*, pt. 2, Series B, vol. 14, 51; Ryan "Report on the Pilgrimage of 1930," E3460/100/25, reprinted in Bidwell, *British Documents*, pt. 2, Series B, vol. 14, 83–116; and Ryan, "Report on the Pilgrimage 1931," E3460/100/25, November 26, 1931, reprinted in Bidwell, *British Documents*, pt. 2, Series B, vol. 14, 117.

83. Chesbrough, "The Economic Resources and Commercial Activities of the Kingdom of the Hedjaz, Nejd, and Dependencies."

84. Calvert to Eden, "no. O.T. 20, E5488/1041/25," 342.

85. Ryan to Simon, "Hejaz-Nejd: Annual Report, 1931," E 2429/680/25, Foreign Office, May 18, 1932, reprinted in Penelope Tuson and Anita Burdett, ed.,

Records of Saudi Arabia: Primary Documents, 1902–1960, vol. 4: *1926–1932* (Oxford: Archive Editions, 1992), 606.

86. As late as 1972, hajj payments were nearly nine-tenths of the total revenue provided by oil. A decade later, Saudi Arabia earned more than $76 million from Southeast Asian pilgrims alone. Gerald Blake and Russell King, "The Hijaz Railway and the Pilgrimage to Mecca," *Asian Affairs* 3, no 3 (1972): 325, reprinted in Rush, "Records of the Hajj," vol. 8, *The Saudi Period*, 577; Fred R. von der Mehden, *Two Worlds of Islam: Interactions Between Southeast Asia and the Middle East* (Gainesville: University of Florida Press, 1993), 22–23.

87. Grafftey-Smith to Bevin, "Annual Economic (A) Report on Saudi Arabia, 1946," no. 89, E5274/2574/25, June 14, 1947, reprinted in *British Documents on Foreign Affairs: Reports and Papers from the Foreign Office Confidential Print*, ed. Paul Preston and Michael Partridge, pt. 4: *From 1946 Through 1950*, Series B: *Near and Middle East*, ed. Malcolm Yapp, vol. 4: *Eastern Affairs, January 1947–December 1947* (Bethesda, MD: University Publications of America, 2001), 82.

88. Ryan, "Pilgrimage Report A.H. 1350 (1932)," September 2, 1932, E4942/103/25, reprinted in Bidwell, *British Documents*, pt. 2, Series B, vol. 14, 164–212; Ryan to Simon, "Pilgrimage of A.H. 1351 (1933)," Jeddah, July 29, 1933, E4704/30/25, reprinted in Bidwell, *British Documents*, pt. 2, Series B, vol. 14, 213–256.

89. Ryan to Simon, "Pilgrimage of A.H. 1351 (1933)," 214.

90. Blake and King, "The Hijaz Railway and the Pilgrimage to Mecca," 576.

91. Gill to Reading, no. 346, E4677/2064/25, Jeddah August 29, 1931, reprinted in *British Documents on Foreign Affairs: Reports and Papers from the Foreign Office Confidential Print*, ed. Kenneth Bourne and D. Cameron Watt, pt. 2: *From the First to the Second World War*, Series B: *Turkey, Iran, and the Middle East, 1918–1939*, ed. Robin Bidwell, vol. 7: *Eastern Affairs, June 1930–June 1932* (Bethesda, MD: University Publications of America, 1985), 280. Between 1929 and 1931, Saudi customs revenues in the Hijaz dropped from £1.17 million to £880,320.

92. Ibn Saud had considerable support in South Asia, and British policy toward him impacted Muslim opinion of Britain there. For more on this issue, see Government of India to Secretary of State for India, no. 707s, E1215/387/25, Delhi, March 9, 1931 reprinted in *British Documents on Foreign Affairs: Reports and Papers from the Foreign Office Confidential Print*, ed. Kenneth Bourne and D. Cameron Watt, pt. 2: *From the First to the Second World War*, Series B: *Turkey, Iran, and the Middle East, 1918–1939*, ed. Robin Bidwell, vol. 7: *Eastern Affairs, June 1930–June 1932* (Bethesda, MD: University Publications of America, 1985), 139.

93. Stonehewer-Bird, "Report on the Pilgrimage of 1927," 1–26; Stonehewer-Bird, "Report on the Pilgrimage, 1928," 31; Ryan, "Report on the Pilgrimage 1929," 51, 54–55; Ryan, "Report on the Pilgrimage of 1930," 88–90; Ryan, "Report on the Pilgrimage of 1932," 166–194; Calvert to Simon, "Report on the Pilgrimage of 1933," 213–220; Calvert, "Report on the Pilgrimage of 1934," August 11, 1934, E5550/148/25, reprinted in Bidwell, *British Documents*, pt. 2, Series B, vol. 14, 257–263; Calvert, "Report on the Pilgrimage of 1935," E5154/74/25, August 4, 1935, reprinted in Bidwell, *British Documents*, pt. 2, Series B, vol. 14, 289–297; Calvert, "Report on the Pilgrimage of 1936," E5367/27/25, August 3,

1936, reprinted in Bidwell, *British Documents*, pt. 2, Series B, vol. 14, 290–291; Trott, "Report on Pilgrimage of 1937," E4922/201/25, August 9, 1937, reprinted in Bidwell, *British Documents*, pt. 2, Series B, vol. 14, 356–362; Trott, "Report on Pilgrimage of 1938," August 16, 1938, reprinted in Bidwell, *British Documents*, pt. 2, Series B, vol. 14, 383–389; and Trott, "Report on Pilgrimage of 1939," September 5, 1939 reprinted in Bidwell, *British Documents*, pt. 2, Series B, vol. 14, 410–416. For an in-depth study of Holland's role in the hajj, see Michael Miller, "Pilgrims' Progress: The Business of the Hajj," *Past and Present* 191, no. 1 (2006): 189–228.

94. For instance, British-controlled Muslim pious foundations for Mecca and Medina existed in Egypt, Burma, and India. For more on these ties, see "Record of Third Meeting with the Hejaz-Nejd Delegation Held at the Foreign Office at 11:30 AM on May 13, 1932," E2404/1494/25, May 13, 1932, reprinted in *British Documents on Foreign Affairs: Reports and Papers from the Foreign Office Confidential Print*, ed. Kenneth Bourne and D. Cameron Watt, pt. 2: *From the First to the Second World War,* Series B: *Turkey, Iran, and the Middle East, 1918–1939*, ed. Robin Bidwell, vol. 8: *Eastern Affairs, December 1931–June 1933* (Bethesda, MD: University Publications of America, 1985), 87–88.

95. The numbers are startling in the 1920s and 1930s: 73 percent of all seaborne hajj pilgrims arrived on British ships in 1923, 63 percent in 1924, 60 percent in 1927, 58 percent in 1928, 68 percent in 1929, 66 percent in 1930, 56 percent in 1931, 75 percent in 1932, 77 percent in 1933, 62 percent in 1934, 61 percent in 1935, 59 percent in 1936, 58 percent in 1937, 48 percent in 1938, and 47 percent in 1939. Bullard, "Pilgrimage Report for 1923," no. 100, E/25/91, December 18, 1923, reprinted in *British Documents on Foreign Affairs: Reports and Papers from the Foreign Office Confidential Print,* ed. Kenneth Bourne and D. Cameron Watt, pt. 2: *From the First to the Second World War,* Series B: *Turkey, Iran, and the Middle East, 1918–1939*, ed. Robin Bidwell, vol. 4: *The Expansion of Ibn Saud, 1922–1925* (Bethesda, MD: University Publications of America, 1985), 16–61; Bullard, "Pilgrimage Report for 1924," E1779/25/91, February 27, 1925, reprinted in *British Documents*, pt. 2, series B, vol. 4, 249–260; Stonehewer-Bird, "Report on the Pilgrimage 1927," 7–13; Stonehewer-Bird, "Report on the Pilgrimage, 1928," 29–51; Ryan, "Report on the Pilgrimage 1929," 51–62; Ryan, "Report on the Pilgrimage of 1930," 86–91; Ryan, "Report on the Pilgrimage of 1932," 172–173; Calvert to Simon, "Report on the Pilgrimage of 1933," 219–220; Calvert, "Report on the Pilgrimage of 1934," 257–263; Calvert, "Report on the Pilgrimage of 1935," 295–297; Calvert, "Report on the Pilgrimage of 1936," 328–331; Trott, "Report on Pilgrimage of 1937," 360–363; Trott, "Report on Pilgrimage of 1938," 387–390; and Trott, "Report on Pilgrimage of 1939," 415–416.

96. The 1932 hajj report noted: "The customary naval visits during the pilgrimage were paid by Captain C. S. Sandford." Ryan, "Report on the Pilgrimage of 1932," 166.

97. Stonehewer-Bird to Viscount Halifax, "Political Review of Events in Saudi Arabia for the Year 1939," no. 62, E2720/1194/25, Jeddah, July 18, 1940, reprinted in *Records of Saudi Arabia: Primary Documents: 1902–1960*, ed. Penelope Tuson and Anita Burdett, vol. 7: *1938–1946,* 5–13 (Cambridge: Archive Editions, 1992).

98. William Ochsenwald, "Islam and Loyalty in the Saudi Hijaz, 1926–1939," *Die Welt des Islams* 47, no. 1 (2007): 1–32.

99. "Ibn Saud's Speech at the Royal Banquet for the Visitors to the Kabba," *Um al-Qura,* December 19, 1942 (Du al-Hijja 11, 1361), 6.

100. Henderson to Ryan, British Foreign Office to Jeddah, nos. 44 and 45, E1149/387/25, March 7, 1931, reprinted in *British Documents on Foreign Affairs: Reports and Papers from the Foreign Office Confidential Print,* ed. Kenneth Bourne and D. Cameron Watt, pt. 2: *From the First to the Second World War*, Series B: *Turkey, Iran, and the Middle East, 1918–1939*, ed. Robin Bidwell, vol. 7: *Eastern Affairs, June 1930–June 1932* (Bethesda, MD: University Publications of America, 1985), 7–8.

101. US Department of State, "American Policy in the Near East: Meeting Prince Faisal, Mr. Stettinius, Mr. Berel, Mr. Murray, Mr. Alling."

102. A good example is the Ibn Rifada rebellion. Ryan to Simon, no. 247, E3494/76/25, June 14, 1932, reprinted in *British Documents on Foreign Affairs: Reports and Papers from the Foreign Office Confidential Print,* ed. Kenneth Bourne and D. Cameron Watt, pt. 2: *From the First to the Second World War*, Series B: *Turkey, Iran, and the Middle East, 1918–1939*, ed. Robin Bidwell, vol. 8: *Eastern Affairs, December 1931–June 1933* (Bethesda, MD: University Publications of America, 1985), 121–123; Ray Atherton, US Embassy London to Secretary of State, "Attempted Assassination of King Ibn Saud," no. 1306, March 21, 1935, reprinted in United States Department of State, *Records of the Department of State Relating to Internal Affairs of Saudi Arabia, 1930–1944*, Reel 1; Bullard to Halifax, no. 55, E2059/1573/25, Jeddah, March 22, 1938 reprinted in *British Documents on Foreign Affairs: Reports and Papers from the Foreign Office Confidential Print*, ed. Kenneth Bourne and D. Cameron Watt, pt. 2: *From the First to the Second World War*, Series B: *Turkey, Iran, and the Middle East, 1918–1939*, ed. Robin Bidwell, vol. 12: *Eastern Affairs, June 1936–June 1938* (Bethesda, MD: University Publications of America, 1986), 428–429; Trott to Halifax, E6447/549/25, Jeddah, August 22, 1939, reprinted in *British Documents on Foreign Affairs: Reports and Papers from the Foreign Office Confidential Print*, ed. Kenneth Bourne and D. Cameron Watt, pt. 2: *From the First to the Second World War*, Series B: *Turkey, Iran, and the Middle East, 1918–1939*, ed. Robin Bidwell, vol. 13: *Eastern Affairs, December 1937–September 1939* (Bethesda, MD: University Publications of America, 1986), 400–401.

103. Atherton, "Attempted Assassination of King Ibn Saud."

104. Memorandum J. A. Moffett to President Roosevelt (signed later by Wallace Murray), April 16, 1941, reprinted in United States Department of State, *Records of the Department of State Relating to Internal Affairs of Saudi Arabia, 1930–1944*, Reel 5.

105. Ryan to Henderson, "Present Conditions in the Hejaz," no. 95, E1790/1600/25, Jeddah, March 14, 1931, reprinted in *British Documents on Foreign Affairs: Reports and Papers from the Foreign Office Confidential Print*, ed. Kenneth Bourne and D. Cameron Watt, pt. 2: *From the First to the Second World War*, Series B: *Turkey, Iran, and the Middle East, 1918–1939*, ed. Robin Bidwell, vol. 7: *Eastern Affairs, June 1930–June 1932* (Bethesda, MD: University Publications of America, 1985), 152–155.

106. During a banquet in May 1931, Ibn Saud pointed to a Turkish prince, Ahmad Wahid al-Din Hafid, and described how his ancestors had fought those of the prince rather than call themselves servants of the commander of the faithful. "The Address of the King to the Royal Banquet," *Um al-Qura,* May 10, 1931, 6;

and US Department of State, “American Policy in the Near East: Meeting Prince Faisal, Mr. Stettinius, Mr. Berel, Mr. Murray, Mr. Alling.”

107. For a discussion of this process in Oman, see Dawn Chatty, “Rituals of Royalty and the Elaboration of Ceremony in Oman: View from the Edge,” *International Journal of Middle East Studies* 41, no. 1 (February 2009): 39–60.

108. There were constant rumors to the contrary, especially in Syria, Egypt, and North Africa. See Vaughan-Russell to Macdonald, Damascus to London, no. 9, October 21, 1924, reprinted in *British Documents on Foreign Affairs: Reports and Papers from the Foreign Office Confidential Print*, ed. Kenneth Bourne and D. Cameron Watt, pt. 2: *From the First to the Second World War*, Series B: *Turkey, Iran, and the Middle East, 1918–1939*, ed. Robin Bidwell, vol. 4: *The Expansion of Ibn Saud, 1922–1925* (Bethesda, MD: University Publications of America, 1985), 110; Halifax to M. Lampson, no. 416, E1527/1034/65, Foreign Office, April 4, 1938, reprinted in, *British Documents on Foreign Affairs: Reports and Papers from the Foreign Office Confidential Print*, ed. Kenneth Bourne and D. Cameron Watt, pt. 2: *From the First to the Second World War*, Series B: *Turkey, Iran, and the Middle East, 1918–1939*, ed. Robin Bidwell, vol. 13: *Eastern Affairs, December 1937–September 1939* (Bethesda, MD: University Publications of America, 1986), 63; Lampson to Halifax, No. 459, E2504/1034/65, April 22, 1938, reprinted in Bidwell, *British Documents*, pt. 2, series B, vol. 13, 85; Charles Heisler, Consul, American Legation to Tunis, “Efforts of the Moslems to Reestablish the Caliphate,” Tunis to Washington, no. 189, August 9, 1939, reprinted in United States Department of State, *Records of the Department of State Relating to Internal Affairs of Saudi Arabia, 1930–1944*, Reel 1.

109. In a speech delivered at the royal banquet in Mecca on April 4, 1933, Ibn Saud stated that he was “the herald of Islam . . . an Arab Muslim who served Islam and who worked for the spread of Islam and for Muslim Unity. . . . He did not aim to be a chief on earth. . . . It had been said that he claimed to be Caliph over all of Islam. He made no such claim. The Caliph must enforce the commands of the Islamic religion over the whole world of Islam, and this was possible in the time of the Khalifat: but was there a man who could do so at the present time? It was clearly impossible and all that he desired was unity and cooperation among Muslims.” “Address of the King to Royal Banquet,” *Umm al-Qura*, April 6, 1933, 1.

110. Increased trade, however, did not mean that Hijazi grievances disappeared. Well into the 1940s some Hijazis called themselves “Ibn Saud’s stepchildren.” Grafftey-Smith to Bevin, no. 80, E5722/5722/25, Jeddah, June 17, 1946, reprinted in *British Documents on Foreign Affairs: Reports and Papers from the Foreign Office Confidential Print*, ed. Paul Preston and Michael Partridge, pt. 4: *From 1946 Through 1950*, Series B: *Near and Middle East, 1946*, ed. Malcolm Yapp, vol. 2: *Eastern Affairs, April 1946–December 1946* (Bethesda, MD: University Publications of America, 1999), 8–9; Trott to Bevin, “Unity of Saudi Arabia: Danger from the Hejaz Constitutional party,” no. 170, E11803/10169/25, Jeddah, December 3, 1947, reprinted in, *British Documents on Foreign Affairs: Reports and Papers from the Foreign Office Confidential Print*, ed. Paul Preston and Michael Partridge, pt. 4: *From 1946 Through 1950*, Series B: *Near and Middle East*, ed. Malcolm Yapp, vol. 4: *Eastern Affairs, January 1947–December 1947* (Bethesda, MD: University Publications of America, 2001), 97.

111. Cloyce Huston, American Vice Consul, US Legation to Aden, “Suggested Recognition by the United States of the Government of the Hedjaz and of the

Nejd," no. 208, May 6, 1930, reprinted in United States Department of State, *Records of the Department of State Relating to Internal Affairs of Saudi Arabia, 1930–1944*, Reel 1.

112. William E. Mulligan, "Arabian Affairs Division: Sarah Hosman," March 8, 1961, William Mulligan Papers, Georgetown University Library Special Collections, Box 3, Folder 6.

113. John R. Jones, "Local Government Relations," March 30, 1969, William Mulligan Papers, Georgetown University Library Special Collections, Box 7, Folder 21.

114. Dr. Mylrea, "Annual Report of the Arabian Mission for 1938: Kuwait," *Neglected Arabia* 185 (April–May–June 1939): 9.

115. Rosemarie Zahlan, "Anglo-American Rivalry in Bahrain, 1918–1947," in *Bahrain Through the Ages*, ed. Shaikh Abdullah bin Khalid al-Khalifa and Michael Rice (London: Kegan Paul International, 1993), 568.

116. Hay to Bevin, "Boundaries of the Trucial Coast Shaikhdoms," no. 20, E5370/60/91, Bahrain, April 20, 1948, reprinted in *British Documents on Foreign Affairs: Reports and Papers from the Foreign Office Confidential Print*, ed. Paul Preston and Michael Partridge, pt. 4: *From 1946 Through 1950*, Series B: *Near and Middle East*, ed. Malcolm Yapp, vol. 6: *Arabia, Iraq, Palestine and Transjordan, Syria, the Lebanon, and General, 1948* (Bethesda, MD: University Publications of America, 1997), 7–9; Bevin to Hay, "Future Judicial Arrangements in the Persian Gulf States," 9–12; Hay to Bevin, "His Majesty's Government's Future Policy in the Trucial States and Central Oman," 12–15; and Hay to Eden, "Recognition of Fujairah as a British-Protected State," no. 25, EA 1057/5, Bahrain, April 2, 1952, reprinted in *British Documents on Foreign Affairs: Reports and Papers from the Foreign Office Confidential Print*, ed. Paul Preston and Michael Partridge, pt. 5: *From 1951 Through 1956*, Series B: *Near and Middle East*, ed. Bülent Gökay, vol. 2: *Turkey, Jordan, Arabia, Lebanon, Israel, and Syria, 1951* (Bethesda, MD: Lexis-Nexis, 2005), 52.

117. To get an idea of how much power US diplomats ceded to their British counterparts in the Gulf, see the US State Department's response to Rose Mae Ashby's request for information on visiting the Gulf in 1938. J. C. Satterhwaite, American Consul, US Legation to Iraq, "Transmitting Information Concerning Visa and Travel Requirements in al-Hasa and the Independent Sheikhdoms of the Persian Gulf," no. 1156, November 10, 1938, reprinted in United States Department of State, *Records of the Department of State Relating to Internal Affairs of Saudi Arabia, 1930–1944*, Reel 1.

118. Stonehewer-Bird to Viscount Halifax, no. 22, E541/252/25, Jeddah, February 5, 1940, reprinted in *British Documents on Foreign Affairs: Reports and Papers from the Foreign Office Confidential Print*, ed. Paul Preston and Michael Partridge, pt. 3: *From 1940 Through 1945*, Series B: *Near and Middle East*, ed. Malcolm Yapp, vol. 4: *Eastern Affairs, January 1940–December 1941* (Bethesda, MD: University Publications of America, 1997), 56; Stonehewer-Bird to Halifax, no. 8, E945/252/25, 63–66.

119. Such threats were rebuffed by British officials, who noted that Soviet policies were "very different than those" of Ibn Saud. Bullard to Chamberlain, E3518/2442/91, May 18, 1925, reprinted in, *British Documents on Foreign Affairs: Reports and Papers from the Foreign Office Confidential Print*, ed. Kenneth Bourne and D. Cameron Watt, pt. 2: *From the First to the Second World War*,

Series B: *Turkey, Iran, and the Middle East, 1918–1939*, ed. Robin Bidwell, vol. 4: *The Expansion of Ibn Saud, 1922–1925* (Bethesda, MD: University Publications of America, 1985), 287–289; and Stonehewer-Bird to Chamberlain, no. 49, E3363/332/91, April 9, 1928, reprinted in *British Documents on Foreign Affairs: Reports and Papers from the Foreign Office Confidential Print*, ed. Kenneth Bourne and D. Cameron Watt, pt 2: *From the First to the Second World War*, Series B: *Turkey, Iran, and the Middle East, 1918–1939*, ed. Robin Bidwell, vol. 6: *Eastern Affairs, January 1928–June 1930* (Bethesda, MD: University Publications of America, 1985), 35–36.

120. "Record of Third Meeting with the Hejaz-Nejd Delegation Held at the Foreign Office," 87–88.

121. Ray Fox, American Counsul, Aden to Secretary of State, "Oil Concession for the al-Hassa Area of Saudi Arabia," no. 19, June 24, 1933, reprinted in United States Department of State, *Records of the Department of State Relating to Internal Affairs of Saudi Arabia, 1930–1944*, Reel 2; Daniel Yergin, *The Prize: The Epic Quest for Oil, Money, and Power* (New York: Free Press, 1991), 291.

122. Jordan to Eden, no. 21, "Annual Report for Saudi Arabia for 1943," Jeddah, February 15, 1944, reprinted in Tuson and Burdett, *Records of Saudi Arabia,* 7:19–21.

123. N. Walmsley Jr., American Vice Consul, Aden to Washington, "Summary: Ibn Saud's Family," no. 91, August 15, 1932, reprinted in United States Department of State, *Records of the Department of State Relating to Internal Affairs of Saudi Arabia, 1930–1944,* Reel 1.

124. Pelham to Eden, "Position of America in Saudi Arabia," no. 153, ES 1051/188, reprinted in *British Documents on Foreign Affairs: Reports and Papers from the Foreign Office Confidential Print*, ed. Paul Preston and Michael Partridge, pt. 5: *From 1950 Through 1956*, Series B: *Near and Middle East*, ed. Bülent Gökay, vol. 4: *Arabia, Lebanon, Israel, Syria, and Jordan, 1952* (Bethesda, MD: Lexis-Nexis, 2005),144–148.

125. Crafftey Smith to Bevin, "Annual Economic (A) Report on Saudi Arabia 1946," 81.

126. William Eddy, Special Assistant US Legation Jidda to Washington, "Memorandum on Malnutrition and the Cost of Food in the Hejaz," no. 147, April 6, 1944, reprinted in United States Department of State, *Records of the Department of State Relating to Internal Affairs of Saudi Arabia, 1930–1944*, Reel 5.

127. Halifax to Stonehewer-Bird, no. 20, E1039/252/25, Foreign Office (London), March 7, 1940, reprinted in *British Documents on Foreign Affairs: Reports and Papers from the Foreign Office Confidential Print*, ed. Paul Preston and Michael Partridge, pt. 3: *From 1940 Through 1945*, Series B: *Near and Middle East*, ed. Malcolm Yapp, vol. 4: *Eastern Affairs, January 1940–December 1941* (Bethesda, MD: University Publications of America, 1997), 68–69.

128. Kirk to US Secretary of State through US Legation in Cairo, June 26, 1941, reprinted in United States Department of State, *Records of the Department of State Relating to Internal Affairs of Saudi Arabia, 1930–1944*, Reel 5.

129. Paul Alling to Berele and Acheson, "Lend-Lease for Saudi Arabia," no. 141, December 14, 1942, reprinted in United States Department of State, *Records of the Department of State Relating to Internal Affairs of Saudi Arabia, 1930–1944*, Reel 4; Wikely to Eden, "Annual Summary of Events in Saudi Arabia During 1942," no. 8, E1102/1102/25, Jeddah, January 27, 1943, reprinted in

British Documents on Foreign Affairs: Reports and Papers from the Foreign Office Confidential Print, ed. Paul Preston and Michael Partridge, pt. 3: *From 1940 Through 1945*, Series B: *Near and Middle East*, ed. Malcolm Yapp, vol. 6: *Eastern Affairs, July 1942–March 1943* (Bethesda, MD: University Publications of America, 1999), 394–396.

130. Carter, "Memorandum on Saudi Arabia Based on Conversation with Longtime Resident in Saudi Arabia."

131. Ibid.

132. A good example is the advertisement for radios on page 8 of *Um Qura*, December 25, 1942, No. 939, 8.

133. A US diplomat stationed in Jeddah and later Dhahran told his family that he could hear broadcasts from Iowa, Palestine, Cairo, India, Germany, Italy, London, and the Belgian Congo. Clarence J. McIntosh to McIntosh Family, November 21, 1943, Clarence J. McIntosh Collection, Georgetown University Library Special Collections, Box 1, Folder 33, Letter No. 38, and Clarence J. McIntosh to McIntosh Family, January 20, 1944, Clarence J. McIntosh Collection, Georgetown University Library Special Collections, Box 2, Folder 3, Letter No. 3.

134. Max Thornburg, "Notes on Certain Aspects of the Current Situation in the Middle East (Arab Countries) and the Views of Max W. Thornburg, Vice President of Bahrain Petroleum Co., LTD, Dictated at the Request of Major Roscoe B. Gaitehr on October 28, 1940," October 30, 1940, reprinted in United States Department of State, *Records of the Department of State Relating to Internal Affairs of Saudi Arabia, 1930–1944*, Reel 3.

135. Elizabeth Calverley, "My Visit to Arabia," *Neglected Arabia* 189 (July–August–September 1940): 10; Hodgen, "Kuwait Intelligence Report: For the Period 1st January to 15th January 1935," no. 1, January 25, 1935, reprinted in *Political Diaries of the Arab World: The Persian Gulf*, vol. 11: *1934–1935* (Cambridge: Cambridge University Press, Archive Editions, 1989), 384–385.

136. Calvert to Hoare, no. 271, E6153/5599/25, Jeddah, October 1, 1935, reprinted in *British Documents on Foreign Affairs: Reports and Papers from the Foreign Office Confidential Print*, ed. Kenneth Bourne and D. Cameron Watt, pt. 2: *From the First to the Second World War*, Series B: *Turkey, Iran, and the Middle East, 1918–1939*, ed. Robin Bidwell, vol. 11: *Eastern Affairs, June 1935–December 1936* (Bethesda, MD: University Publications of America, 1985), 80.

137. Hodgen, "Kuwait Intelligence Report."

138. Wells Thomas, "From a Doctor's Journal," *Neglected Arabia* 180 (October–December 1937): 10; Bert Fish, Consul, US Legation Cairo to Secretary of State, "Remarks of Mr. St. John Philby at Jeddah," no. 2019, March 9, 1940, reprinted in United States Department of State, *Records of the Department of State Relating to Internal Affairs of Saudi Arabia, 1930–1944*, Reel 3.

139. Calvert to Hoare, no. 290, E6546/5599/25, Jeddah, October 15, 1935, reprinted in, *British Documents on Foreign Affairs: Reports and Papers from the Foreign Office Confidential Print*, ed. Kenneth Bourne and D. Cameron Watt, pt. 2: *From the First to the Second World War*, Series B: *Turkey, Iran, and the Middle East, 1918–1939*, ed. Robin Bidwell, vol. 11: *Eastern Affairs, June 1935–December 1936* (Bethesda, MD: University Publications of America, 1994), 104–105.

140. Saudi Arabia's religious establishment initially thought of radios and cars as satanic until Ibn Saud convinced them otherwise. For more on this episode in

Saudi history, see Guido Steinberg, *Religion und Staat in Saudi Arabien: Die wahhabitischen Gelehrten, 1902–1953* (Würzburg: Ergon, 2002), 548; David B. Levis, US Vice Consul France, to the Department of Commerce, "Radio and Islam," no. 11592, May 27, 1937, reprinted in United States Department of State, *Records of the Department of State Relating to Internal Affairs of Saudi Arabia, 1930–1944*, Reel 2.

141. Thornburg, "Notes on Certain Aspects of the Current Situation in the Middle East."

142. US Legation Cairo to Washington, no. 890, October 4, 1943.

143. Wikeley to Eden, "Record of a Conversation Between His Majesty King Ibn Saud and Lieutenant-Colonel Hoskins," no. 68, E5552/506/65, Jeddah, September 1, 1943, reprinted in *British Documents on Foreign Affairs: Reports and Papers from the Foreign Office Confidential Print*, ed. Paul Preston and Michael Partridge, pt. 3: *From 1940 Through 1945*, Series B: *Near and Middle East*, ed. Malcolm Yapp, vol. 7: *Eastern Affairs, April 1943–December 1943* (Bethesda, MD: University Publications of America, 1997), 171–174. Two of the first three issues Ibn Saud asked Hoskins about dealt with the hajj.

144. Ibid.

145. James Moose, US Consulate Jidda, to Washington, "The 1943 Pilgrimage to Mecca," no. 21, August 17, 1943, reprinted in United States Department of State, *Records of the Department of State Relating to Internal Affairs of Saudi Arabia, 1930–1944*, Reel 5; Harry Shullaw, US Consulate Jidda to Washington, no. 151, October 2, 1943, reprinted in United States Department of State, *Records of the Department of State Relating to Internal Affairs of Saudi Arabia, 1930–1944*, Reel 5.

146. Cordell Hull, Washington to US Embassy London, January 4, 1944, reprinted in United States Department of State, *Records of the Department of State Relating to Internal Affairs of Saudi Arabia, 1930–1944*, Reel 6; James Moose, US Legation Jeddah to Washington, no. 195, November 24, 1943, reprinted in United States Department of State, *Records of the Department of State Relating to Internal Affairs of Saudi Arabia, 1930–1944*, Reel 6.

147. Jordan to Eden, "Annual Report on Saudi Arabia for 1943," E1293/1293/25, February 28, 1944, reprinted in Tuson and Burdett, *Records of Saudi Arabia*, 7:23–28.

148. US Department of State, "Treaty Plan for Establishment of Central Bank in Saudi Arabia: Memorandum of Conversation: Messrs White, Bernstein, Friedman, and Glendenning (Treasury Department); Messrs Landis, Livesey, Parker and McGuire (State Department)," January 19, 1944, reprinted in US Department of State, *Records of the Department of State Relating to Internal Affairs of Saudi Arabia, 1930–1944*, Reel 6; Trott to Bevin, "Pilgrimage to the Hejaz, 1950," 231.

149. Pelham to Eden, "Saudi Arabia Annual Review for 1952," no. 4, ES 1011/1, Jeddah, January 1, 1953, reprinted in *British Documents on Foreign Affairs: Reports and Papers from the Foreign Office Confidential Print*, ed. Paul Preston and Michael Partridge, pt. 5: *From 1950 Through 1956*, Series B: *Near and Middle East*, ed. Bülent Gökay, vol. 6: *Arabia, Lebanon, Israel, Syria, and Jordan, 1953* (Bethesda, MD: Lexis-Nexis, 2005), 53–57.

150. For more on these requests, see Bert Fish, US Legation to Cairo to Washington, Wallace Murray, Chief of Near Eastern Affairs Division, March 8, 1940, reprinted in United States Department of State, *Records of the Department of State*

Relating to Internal Affairs of Saudi Arabia, 1930–1944, Reel 5; Kirk to US Secretary of State through US Legation in Cairo, June 26, 1941, reprinted in United States Department of State, *Records of the Department of State Relating to Internal Affairs of Saudi Arabia, 1930–1944*, Reel 5.

151. Memorandum J. A. Moffett to President Roosevelt; Cordell Hull, Department of State, to United States Legation in Cairo, "Advance to Saudi Arabia," no. 18786, August 21, 1941, reprinted in United States Department of State, *Records of the Department of State Relating to Internal Affairs of Saudi Arabia, 1930–1944,* Reel 5.

152. Douglas Little, *American Orientalism: The United States and the Middle East Since 1945* (London: I. B. Tauris, 2003), 48.

153. James Moose, US Legation to Jeddah, "Policy of British Minister in Saudi Arabia," no. 153, April 13, 1944, reprinted in United States Department of State, *Records of the Department of State Relating to Internal Affairs of Saudi Arabia, 1930–1944,* Reel 4; James Moose, US Legation to Jeddah, "Statements of King Ibn Saud on Needs of Saudi Arabia," no. 169, May 2, 1944, reprinted in United States Department of State, *Records of the Department of State Relating to Internal Affairs of Saudi Arabia, 1930–1944,* Reel 4.

154. Jordan to Eden, "Annual Report on Saudi Arabia for 1944," 23–28; James Moose, US Legation Jeddah to Washington, "Budget of Saudi Arabia in 1943 and Proposed Budget for 1944," no. 91, January 12, 1944, reprinted in United States Department of State, *Records of the Department of State Relating to Internal Affairs of Saudi Arabia, 1930–1944*, Reel 5.

155. Edward Stettinius to President Roosevelt, US Department of State, "Memorandum for the President: Proposals for the Extension of Long-Range Financial Assistance to Saudi Arabia," December 21, 1944, reprinted in United States Department of State, *Records of the Department of State Relating to Internal Affairs of Saudi Arabia, 1930–1944,* Reel 4.

156. Smith to Bevin, "Annual Report on Saudi Arabia, 1946," no. 14, E1095/1095/25, Jeddah, January 26, 1947, reprinted in *British Documents on Foreign Affairs: Reports and Papers from the Foreign Office Confidential Print,* ed. Paul Preston and Michael Partridge, pt. 4: *From 1946 Through 1950*, Series B: *Near and Middle East,* ed. Malcolm Yapp, vol. 4: *Eastern Affairs, January 1947–December 1947* (Bethesda, MD: University Publications of America, 2001), 66.

157. Hay to Bevin, "His Majesty's Government's Future Policy in the Trucial States and Central Oman," 10–12.

158. Hay to Bevin, "Annual Review of Political Events in the Persian Gulf During 1949," no. 10, EA 1011/1, Bahrain, January 31, 1950, reprinted in *British Documents on Foreign Affairs: Reports and Papers from the Foreign Office Confidential Print*, ed. Paul Preston and Michael Partridge, pt. 4: *From 1946 Through 1950,* Series B: Near and Middle East, 1950, ed. Malcolm Yapp, vol. 10: *Israel, Syria, Arabia, the Middle East (General), Jordan and Arab Palestine and the Lebanon, January 1950–December 1950* (Bethesda, MD: University Publications of America, 1999), 197–201.

159. Makins to Eden, "Report on a Visit to the States of the Persian Gulf Under British Protection with Some Observations on Iraq and Saudi Arabia and with Conclusions and Recommendations," 34–40; Burrows to Eden, "Persian Gulf: Annual Review for 1953," no 30, EA 1011/11, March 12, 1954, reprinted in *British*

Documents on Foreign Affairs: Reports and Papers from the Foreign Office Confidential Print, ed. Paul Preston and Michael Partridge, pt. 5: *From 1951 Through 1956*, Series B: *Near and Middle East*, ed. Bülent Gökay, vol. 8: *Arabia, Lebanon, Israel, Syria, and Jordan, 1954* (Bethesda, MD: Lexis-Nexis, 2005), 28–36; Burrows to Eden, "Review of Events in the Persian Gulf During the Past Year and Some Thoughts on the Future," no. 87, EA 10113/1, August 26, 1954, reprinted in *British Documents on Foreign Affairs: Reports and Papers from the Foreign Office Confidential Print*, ed. Paul Preston and Michael Partridge, pt. V: *From 1950 Through 1956*, Series B: *Near and Middle East*, ed. Bülent Gökay, vol. 8: *Arabia, Lebanon, Israel, Syria, and Jordan, 1954* (Bethesda, MD: Lexis-Nexis, 2005), 83–89.

160. The Dubai facility was housed in a building donated by the city's shaikh. Within four days of its opening in 1939 there were almost 150 outpatients, and the stock of drugs provided for a year was expected to run out in five months. Barrett, "Intelligence Summary of the Political Agent Bahrain for June 1939," no. 12, July 4, 1939, reprinted in *Political Diaries of the Arab World: The Persian Gulf*, vol. 13: *1938–1939* (London: Archive Editions, 1990), 368–369.

161. The strength of Britain's postwar position is revealed in diplomatic dispatches from the Gulf and internal British discussions about the Gulf. For example, see Bevin to Hay, "Future Judicial Arrangements in the Persian Gulf States," 10–15.

162. Pelham to Eden, "Saudi Arabia: Annual Review for 1952," no. 3, ES 1011/1, Jeddah, January 1, 1953, reprinted in *British Documents on Foreign Affairs: Reports and Papers from the Foreign Office Confidential Print*, ed. Paul Preston and Michael Partridge, pt. 5: *From 1951 Through 1956*, Series B: *Near and Middle East*, ed. Bülent Gökay, vol. 6: *Arabia, Lebanon, Israel, Syria, and Jordan, 1953* (Bethesda, MD: Lexis-Nexis, 2005), 53–57.

163. Ryan to Eden, no. 128, E2838/608/25, Jeddah, May 1, 1936, reprinted in, *British Documents on Foreign Affairs: Reports and Papers from the Foreign Office Confidential Print*, ed. Kenneth Bourne and D. Cameron Watt, pt. 2: *From the First to the Second World War*, Series B: *Turkey, Iran, and the Middle East, 1918–1939*, ed. Robin Bidwell, vol. 11: *Eastern Affairs, June 1935–December 1936* (Bethesda, MD: University Publications of America, 1994), 215.

164. Smith to Bevin, "Annual Report on Saudi Arabia, 1946," 98–99.

165. Niles Lind, Attaché of US Legation to Jeddah, "Memorandum: King Abdul Aziz-Saud's Remarks About Jews," October 30, 1944, reprinted in United States Department of State, *Records of the Department of State Relating to Internal Affairs of Saudi Arabia, 1930–1944,* Reel 3 enclosed within William Eddy, US Legation to Jeddah, "Remarks About Jews Made by King Abdul Aziz al-Saud," no. 30, October 30, 1944, reprinted in United States Department of State, *Records of the Department of State Relating to Internal Affairs of Saudi Arabia, 1930–1944,* Reel 3.

166. Trott to Bevin, UK Embassy Jeddah to London, "Saudi Arabia, Annual Report for 1947," PRO: 371/68779, reprinted in, Penelope Tuson and Anita Burdett, ed, *Records of Saudi Arabia: Primary Documents, 1902–1960*, vol. 8: 1946–1953 (Oxford: Archive Editions, 1992), 133.

167. Bullard to Halifax, no. 116, E3791/10/31, Jeddah, June 6, 1938, reprinted in *British Documents on Foreign Affairs: Reports and Papers from the Foreign Office Confidential Print*, ed. Kenneth Bourne and D. Cameron Watt, pt. 2: *From the*

First to the Second World War, Series B: *Turkey, Iran, and the Middle East, 1918–1939*, ed. Robin Bidwell, vol. 13: *Eastern Affairs, December 1937–September 1939* (Bethesda, MD: University Publications of America, 1986), 40–44; Bullard to Halifax, no. 164, E6860/1/31, Jeddah, November 16, 1938, reprinted in *British Documents on Foreign Affairs: Reports and Papers from the Foreign Office Confidential Print*, ed. Kenneth Bourne and D. Cameron Watt, pt. 2: *From the First to the Second World War*, Series B: *Turkey, Iran, and the Middle East, 1918–1939*, ed. Robin Bidwell, vol. 13: *Eastern Affairs, December 1937–September 1939* (Bethesda, MD: University Publications of America, 1986), 200; Bullard to Halifax, no. 174, E7036/1/31, November 24, 1938, reprinted in *British Documents on Foreign Affairs: Reports and Papers from the Foreign Office Confidential Print*, ed. Kenneth Bourne and D. Cameron Watt, pt. 2: *From the First to the Second World War*, Series B: *Turkey, Iran, and the Middle East, 1918–1939*, ed. Robin Bidwell, vol. 12: *Eastern Affairs, June 1936–June 1938* (Bethesda, MD: University Publications of America, 1986), 206–207.

168. William Mulligan to F. W. Ohliger, February 8, 1948, William Mulligan Papers, Georgetown University Library Special Collections, Box 1, Folder 50.

169. Yergin, *The Prize*, 445–449.

170. Hay to Eden, "Persian Gulf: Annual Review For 1951," no. 5, EA 1011/11, Bahrain, January 17, 1952, reprinted in *British Documents on Foreign Affairs: Reports and Papers from the Foreign Office Confidential Print*, ed. Paul Preston and Michael Partridge, pt. 5: *From 1950 Through 1956*, Series B: *Near and Middle East*, ed. Bülent Gökay, vol. 4: *Arabia, Lebanon, Israel, Syria, and Jordan, 1952* (Bethesda, MD: Lexis-Nexis, 2005), 25–30.

171. J. R. McNeil, *Something New Under the Sun: An Environmental History of the Twentieth Century* (New York: W. W. Norton, 2001), 64–71.

172. Arthur P. Clark, et al., *A Land Transformed—The Arabian Peninsula, Saudi Arabia, and Aramco* (Dhahran: Saudi Arabian Oil Company; Houston: ARAMCO Services Company, 2006), 253–256.

173. Pelham to Eden, "Saudi Arabian Budget," 5–7.

174. Central Intelligence Agency, *National Intelligence Estimate: The Persian Gulf States*, No. 30-1-67, May 18, 1967, 15 (available at https://login.library.lausys.georgetown.edu/).

175. Ibid.

176. Ibid.

177. Ibid.

178. Ibid., 11, 15.

179. Helen Metz, "Report on *The Series of the Free, No. 1: The Greatest Drama, The Story of a Nation*" (printed in Riyadh 5 Rajab 1382/December 2, 1962), September 23, 1964, William Mulligan Papers, Georgetown University Library Special Collections, Box 3, Folder 22. The comic had pictures suggesting that Egypt was modern and had rockets and skyscrapers while Saudi Arabia was governed by a morally bankrupt and sex-obsessed royal family.

180. Mordechai Abir, *Saudi Arabia in the Oil Era: Regime and Elites: Conflict and Collaboration* (Boulder, CO: Westview Press, 1988), 112.

181. Peter Lienhardt, *Sheikhdoms of Eastern Arabia*, ed. Ahmed al-Shahi (New York: Palgrave, 2001), 10.

182. "Radio of the Arab Nation," December 6–19, 1961, William Mulligan Papers, Georgetown University Library Special Collections, Box 3, Folder 10.

183. J. R. Jones, "Voice of the Arab Nation," November 14, 1961, William Mulligan Papers, Georgetown University Library Special Collections, Box 3, Folder 10.

184. Ibid.

185. Naomi Sakr, *Satellite Realms: Transnational Television, Globalization, and the Middle East* (London: I. B. Tauris, 2001), 5.

186. Ibid,, 5–6. The growing importance of radio in the Gulf is further illustrated by Madawi al-Rasheed. He notes that a former ARAMCO worker told him that all he wanted to buy for himself in the 1950s was a radio, so "he could hear what was going on in Palestine and Egypt." Madawi al-Rasheed, *A History of Saudi Arabia* (Cambridge: Cambridge University Press, 2002), 97.

187. A good example of these types of tendencies is the Dubai National Front, which organized in 1953 to oppose the influence of non-Arabs in the city as well as to reduce the influence of Great Britain and the ruling family. For more on this movement, see Christopher Davidson, *Dubai: The Vulnerability of Success* (New York: Columbia University Press, 2008), 43–50.

188. Salman Sau'd Halib (F. S. Vidal edited), "Events in Bahrain," November 5, 1956, William Mulligan Papers, Georgetown University Library Special Collections, Box 2, Folder 54.

189. Hillyard, *Before the Oil,* 159.

190. Samuel P. Huntington, *Political Order in Changing Societies* (New Haven, CT: Yale University Press, 1968), 177.

191. Bell, "Confidential Annex to Kuwait Diary No. 11 Covering the Period October 28 to November 28, 1956," November 28, 1956, reprinted in *Political Diaries of the Arab World: Persian Gulf,* vol. 20: *1955–1958* (Oxford: Archive Editions, 1990), 253; Halford, "Confidential Annex to Kuwait Diary, No. 6: Covering the Period May 19 to June 19, 1958," June 19, 1958, reprinted in *Political Diaries of the Arab World: Persian Gulf,* vol. 20: *1955–1958* (Oxford: Archive Editions, 1990), 655–657; Halford, "Kuwait Diary No. 9: Covering the Period August 26, 1958 to September 25, 1958," no. 1014/58, September 24, 1958, reprinted in *Political Diaries of the Arab World: Persian Gulf,* vol. 20: *1955–1958* (Oxford: Archive Editions, 1990), 707–708; Middleton, "Annual Review Kuwait: 1958," no. 1 1012/59, Kuwait, January 6, 1959, reprinted in *Political Diaries of the Arab World: Persian Gulf,* vol. 21: *1947–1958,* ed. Robert Jarman (Wilts, UK: Archive Editions, 1998), 297–327; John Jones, "Notes on Kuwait Oil Company Relations," June 23, 1965, William Mulligan Papers, Georgetown University Library Special Collections, Box 3, Folder 24.

192. Hay to Bevin, "Annual Review of Political Events in the Persian Gulf During 1949," 19; William Mulligan, "Confidential Memorandum: Conversation with Dhahran Consul W. K. Schwinn," November 22, 1958, William Mulligan Papers, Georgetown University Library Special Collections, Box 2, Folder 61.

193. Susan Hillyard noted that every year shaikhs took turns providing a day's worth of food for the entire town of Abu Dhabi. Hillyard, *Before the Oil,* 140–142.

194. These policies were sufficiently successful that some Gulf leaders could even deny in public that the British presence in the Gulf was "colonialism." This view persists among many Gulf Arabs. An Emirati intellectual observed in 2009 that his people lack the "colonial" baggage of other Arab states. Neil Patrick, "Nationalism in the Gulf States" (research paper, Kuwait Programme on Development, Governance and Globalisation in the Gulf States, 2009), 28.

195. Pelham to Eden, "Position of America in Saudi Arabia," 144–148.

196. Ibid.

197. Displays of US wealth included flying fresh vegetables and eggs from Eritrea. Ibid.

198. Pelham to Eden, "Saudi Arabia: Annual Review for 1952," 14.

199. A. H. Kemal, "Books and Bookstores in Riyadh," March 14, 1966, William Mulligan Papers, Georgetown University Library Special Collections, Box 3, Folder 28.

200. Pelham to Eden, "Position of America in Saudi Arabia," 144–148.

201. Francis Meade, *Honey and Onions: A Life in Saudi Arabia* (Philadelphia: Xlibris Corporation, 2004), 67.

202. William E. Mulligan, "A Sport . . . a Rite of Passage . . . a Way of Life," *The Arabian Sun,* January 24, 1973, William Mulligan Papers, Georgetown University Library Special Collections, "Arabian Sun Articles," Box 16, Folder 7.

203. Pelham to Eden, "Position of America in Saudi Arabia," 146.

204. Raymond Hare, US Legation Cairo to Secretary of State, "Labor Conditions in Saudi Arabia: Builders and Contractors at Jedda," no. 2025, March 18, 1940, reprinted in United States Department of State, *Records of the Department of State Relating to Internal Affairs of Saudi Arabia, 1930–1944,* Reel 5.

205. David Commins, *The Wahhabi Mission and Saudi Arabia* (New York: I. B. Tauris, 2006), 101–102; William Eddy, US Legation Jidda to Secretary of State, "Complaints by Central Arabian Fanatics That King Abdul Aziz Is Surrendering His Land to Unbelievers," no. 35, January 19, 1945, reprinted in United States Department of State, *Records of the Department of State Relating to Internal Affairs of Saudi Arabia, 1930–1944,* Reel 3.

206. Ibid.

207. Grafftey-Smith to Bevin, "Annual Report on Saudi Arabia 1946," 84; Pelham to Eden, "Position of America in Saudi Arabia," 145.

208. Among the American pilots who flew Ibn Saud was Joe Grant. As of November 2009, he was 101 years old and healthy enough to host a book signing at the Smithsonian Air and Space Museum in Washington, DC. For more on Mr. Grant's life and the aircraft he flew in Saudi Arabia, see Michael Saba, *King Abdulaziz . . . His Plane and His Pilot* (Sioux Falls, SD: GulfAmerica Press, 2009). I thank Jol Silversmith for alerting me to Mr. Grant and to his book.

209. Trott to McNeil, "Saudi Arabia: Annual Review for 1949," no. 45, ES 1011/1, Jeddah, February 22, 1950 reprinted in *British Documents on Foreign Affairs: Reports and Papers from the Foreign Office Confidential Print*, ed. Paul Preston and Michael Partridge, pt. 4: *From 1946 Through 1950*, Series B: *Near and Middle East,* 1950, ed. Malcolm Yapp, vol. 10: *Israel, Syria, Arabia, the Middle East (General), Jordan and Arab Palestine and the Lebanon, January 1950–December 1950* (Bethesda, MD: University Publications of America, 1999), 218–221.

210. R.E.G Davies, *Saudi Arabian Airlines, an Airline and Its Aircraft: The Illustrated History of the Largest Airline in the Middle East* (McLean, VA: Paladwr Press, 1995), 44.

211. Blake and King, *The Hijaz Railway and the Pilgrimage to Mecca*, 576; Ryan to Simon, "Pilgrimage of A.H. 1350 (1933)," 213–256; Eleanor Doumato, "Saudi Arabia: The Society and Its Environment," in *Saudi Arabia: A Country Study*, ed. Helen Metz, 93 (Washington, DC: Library of Congress Federal Research Division, 1992).

212. More hajj pilgrims arrived by air than any other means of transport as early as the 1960s. Blake and King, *The Hijaz Railway and the Pilgrimage to Mecca,* 577.

213. A. H. Kemal, "Modern History as Taught in Saudi Arabian Elementary Schools," January 14, 1966, William Mulligan Papers, Georgetown University Library Special Collections, Box 3, Folder 28.

214. Ibid.

215. Pelham to Eden, "The Development of the Saudi Armed Forces," no. 12, ES 1202/1, Jeddah, January 14, 1953, reprinted in *British Documents on Foreign Affairs: Reports and Papers from the Foreign Office Confidential Print*, ed. Paul Preston and Michael Partridge, pt. 5: *From 1951 Through 1956,* Series B: *Near and Middle East,* ed. Bülent Gökay, vol. 6: *Arabia, Lebanon, Israel, Syria, and Jordan, 1953* (Bethesda, MD: Lexis-Nexis, 2005), 61–62. Some contributions were as little as five Saudi riyals.

216. "Saudi Arabia Cancels Dhahran Airbase Agreement," March 26, 1961, William Mulligan Papers, Georgetown University Library Special Collections, Box 7, Folder 23.

217. Ibid.

218. Douglas Boyd, "Saudi Arabian Television," *Journal of Broadcasting* 15, no. 1 (Winter 1970–1971): 77.

219. The initial ARAMCO Arabic television programs were introduced primarily for the company's 9,000 Saudi Arab employees and their families, but its 12-kilowatt power was sufficient to reach 350,000 potential viewers in eastern Saudi Arabia and neighboring lands. Daniel Da Cruz, "T.V. in the M.E.," *Aramco World* 18, no. 5 (1967): 19–25 (available at http://www.saudiaramcoworld.com/).

220. Ibid.; William E. Mulligan, "The TV Picture in Arabia," *Arabian Sun,* March 6, 1974, William Mulligan Papers, Georgetown University Library Special Collections, "Arabian Sun Articles," Box 16, Folder 7.

221. Dana Schmidt, "Arabian Town Is Like a U.S. Suburb," *New York Times,* November 23, 1959, 3 (*Historical New York Times*).

222. Kuldip R. Rampal, "Saudi Arabia," in *Mass Media in the Middle East*, ed. Yahya R. Kamalipour and Hamid Mowlana, 249–250 (Westwood, CT: Greenwood Press, 1994); William Rugh, *Arab Mass Media* (Westwood, CT: Greenwood Publishing Group, 2004), 192.

223. R. Metz, "Report: April 24, 1963," April 24, 1963, William Mulligan Papers, Georgetown University Library Special Collections, Box 6, Folder 12; Boyd, "Saudi Arabian Television," 74–75.

224. Rugh, *Arab Mass Media,* 192; Mulligan, "The TV Picture in Arabia."

225. Rugh, *Arab Mass Media,* 209.

226. Ibid., 192–193.

227. Ibid., 193.

228. Hana al-Deen, "Oman," in *Mass Media in the Middle East*, ed. Yahya R. Kamalipour and Hamid Mowlana, 190–191 (Westwood, CT: Greenwood Press, 1994).

229. Mohamed Arafa, "Qatar," in *Mass Media in the Middle East*, ed. Yahya R. Kamalipour and Hamid Mowlana, 234–235 (Westwood, CT: Greenwood Press, 1994).

230. "Memorandum of a Conversation, White House, January 30, 1956," February 7, 1956, reprinted in United States Department of State, *Foreign Relations*

of the United States: 1955–1957, vol. 13: *Foreign Relations: Near-East, Jordan*, (Washington, DC: United States Government Printing Office, 1989), 327–328.

231. Central Intelligence Agency, *National Intelligence Estimate: The Persian Gulf States*.

232. William Mulligan, "Memorandum to the File: Talk with Walter K. Schwinn, Counsul General," January 18, 1960, William Mulligan Papers, Georgetown University Library Special Collections, Box 2, Folder 64; William Mulligan, "Talk with Walter K. Schwinn, Consul General," January 31, 1960, William Mulligan Papers, Georgetown University Library Special Collections, Box 2, Folder 64.

233. Elie Salem, "Interview with the Imam of Oman," January 7, 1960, William Mulligan Papers, Georgetown University Library Special Collections, Box 2, Folder 64; Robert Headley Jr., "Visit to the Imam of Oman," January 10, 1960, William Mulligan Papers, Georgetown University Library Special Collections, Box 2, Folder 64.

234. Mulligan, "Talk with Walter K. Schwinn," January 18, 1960.

235. Glen Balfour-Paul, *End of Empire in the Middle East* (Cambridge: Cambridge University Press, 1999), 124.

236. Ibid., 132–133.

237. Abdullah Taryman, *The Establishment of the United Arab Emirates, 1950–1985* (London: Croom Helm, 1987), 66–68.

238. Muhammad Abdullah, *The United Arab Emirates* (New York: Barnes and Noble, 1978), 280–284.

239. National Security Council, "U.S. Policy Options Towards the Persian Gulf," October 19, 1979, PA/HO Declassified, 12938, June 21, 2006, 1–9 (available at https://login.library.lausys.georgetown.edu/).

240. Ibid.

241. Henry Kissinger, "Memorandum to the President: The Persian Gulf," October 22, 1970, PA/HO Declassified, 12938, June 21, 2006, 1 (available at https://login.library.lausys.georgetown.edu/).

242. Ibid., 3–4.

243. Clark, et al., *A Land Transformed*, 254.

244. Ibid.

245. Ibid., 258.

246. Ibid., 254.

247. Yergin, *The Prize*, 625.

248. Ibid.

249. Ibid., 628.

250. Ibid., 617.

251. Mary Beth Norton, et al., *A People and a Nation: A History of the United States*, vol. 2: *Since 1865*, 3rd ed. (Boston: Houghton Mifflin, 1990), 971.

252. Ian J. Bickerton and Carla L. Klausner, *A History of the Arab-Israeli Dispute*, 5th ed. (New York: Pearson Prentice Hall, 2007), 172.

253. Yergin, *The Prize*, 646–648, 651–652.

254. George Phillip, *The Political Economy of International Oil* (Edinburgh: Edinburgh University Press, 1994), 173.

255. J. S. Birks and C. A. Sinclair, "Preparations for Income After Oil: Bahrain's Example," *British Journal of Middle East Studies*, no. 1 (1979): 39–57.

256. Myron Weiner, "International Migration and Development: Indians in the Persian Gulf," *Population and Development Review* 8, no. 1 (March 1982): 9.

257. Kiren Chaudhry, *The Price of Wealth: Economies and Institutions in the Middle East* (Ithaca, NY: Cornell University Press, 1997), 1.

258. Hay to Bevin, "Social and Political Effects of the Development of the Oil Industry in the Persian Gulf," no. 34, EA 10110/2, Bahrain, April 24, 1950, reprinted in *British Documents on Foreign Affairs: Reports and Papers from the Foreign Office Confidential Print*, ed. Paul Preston and Michael Partridge, pt. 4: *From 1945 Through 1950*, Series B: *Near and Middle East, 1950*, ed. Malcolm Yapp, vol. 10: *Israel, Syria, Arabia, the Middle East (General), Jordan and Arab Palestine and the Lebanon, January 1950–December 1950* (Bethesda, MD: University Publications of America, 1999), 203–204; Hay to Bevin, "Future Relations Between His Majesty's Government and the Shaikhdoms," no. 13, EA 1511/11, Bahrain, January 29, 1951, reprinted in *British Documents on Foreign Affairs: Reports and Papers from the Foreign Office Confidential Print*, ed. Paul Preston and Michael Partridge, pt. 5: *From 1951 Through 1956*, Series B: *Near and Middle East*, ed. Bülent Gökay, vol. 4: *Arabia, Lebanon, Israel, Syria, and Jordan, 1952* (Bethesda, MD: Lexis-Nexis, 2005), 18–19.

259. Sharif Mukaddam, "Spotlight on Indians in the Arab World," *Clarity*, November 1, 1975, William Mulligan Papers, Georgetown University Library Special Collections, Box 10, Folder 1.

260. Seccombe and Lawless, "Foreign Worker Dependence," 565; Weiner, "International Migration and Development: Indians in the Persian Gulf," 8.

261. Fred Arnold and Nasra M. Shah, "Asian Labor Migration to the Middle East," *International Migration Review* 18, no. 2 (Summer 1984): 296.

262. Ibid.

263. J. S. Birks, I. J. Seccombe, and A. Sinclair, "Migrant Workers in the Arab Gulf: The Impact of Declining Oil Revenues," *International Migration Review* 20, no. 4 (Winter 1986): 811.

264. Ibid.

265. Anh Longva, *Walls Built on Sand: Migration, Exclusion, and Society in Kuwait* (Boulder, CO: Westview Press, 1997), 78; Anh Longva, "Keeping Migrant Workers in Check: The Kafala System in the Gulf," *Middle East Report* 211 (Summer 1999): 20–22.

266. Daromir Rudnyckyj, "Technologies of Servitude: Governmentality and Indonesian Transnational Labor Migration," *Anthropological Quarterly* 77, no. 3 (2004): 425.

267. Haider Yusufzai, "Pakistani Labour Migration to the Middle East," *Economic Review*, April 1997 (available at http://findarticles.com/); Fred Halliday, "Labor Migration in the Arab World," *MERIP Reports* 123 (May 1984): 9; Arnold and Shah, "Asian Labor Migration to the Middle East."

268. Weiner, "International Migration and Development: Indians in the Persian Gulf," 4.

269. Joseph A. Mahon, oral interview by Robert Norberg, August 16, 1994 (revised July 12, 1995), Joseph A. Mahon Papers, Georgetown University Library Special Collections, Box 1, Folder 47, 45.

270. International Monetary Fund, *International Financial Statistics Online*, "Saudi Arabia, 1945–2003" (available at https://login.library.lausys.georgetown.edu/).

271. International Monetary Fund, *International Financial Statistics Online*, "Bahrain, 1945–2003" (available at https://login.library.lausys.georgetown.edu/);

International Monetary Fund, *International Financial Statistics Online*, "Kuwait, 1945–2003" (available at https://login.library.lausys.georgetown.edu/); International Monetary Fund, *International Financial Statistics Online*, "Oman, 1945–2003" (available at https://login.library.lausys.georgetown.edu/); International Monetary Fund, *International Financial Statistics Online*, "Qatar, 1945–2003" (available at (https://login.library.lausys.georgetown.edu/); International Monetary Fund, *International Financial Statistics Online*, "UAE, 1945–2003" (available at https://login.library.lausys.georgetown.edu/); United Nations Department of Economic and Social Affairs, Population Division, *United Nations' World Population Prospects* (New York: United Nations Publications, 2007), 130.

272. Eric Hooglund and Anthony Toth, "United Arab Emirates," in *Persian Gulf Studies: Country Studies,* ed. Helen Metz, 208 (Washington, DC: Library of Congress Research Division, 1993).

273. Weiner, "International Migration and Development: Indians in the Persian Gulf," 2–3.

274. "ARAMCO Managerial and Professional Work Force—1/1/1972–12/31/1972," Joseph A. Mahon Papers, Georgetown University Library Special Collections, Box 1, Folder 24, 8.

275. Ibid.

276. Weiner, "International Migration and Development: Indians in the Persian Gulf," 10.

277. Maqsud al-Hassan Nuri, "Regional Military Involvement: A Case Study of Iran Under the Shah," *Pakistan Horizon* 37, no. 4 (1984): 32–45.

278. Sean Foley, "History, Oil, and Ethnicity: The Story of Abu Musa and the Tunbs Islands," *Politica* 2, no. 2 (Spring 1996): 75.

279. Ibid.

280. Michael T. Klare, *Rising Powers, Shrinking Planet: The New Geopolitics of Energy* (New York: Metropolitan Books, 2008), 180.

281. Clark, et al., *A Land Transformed*, 261.

282. United States Arms Control and Disarmament Agency, *World Military Expenditures and Arms Transfers, 1971–1980* (Washington, DC: United States Government Printing Office, 1982), 65.

283. Ibid., 39, 55, 62, 64, 70.

284. Ibid., 55, 62.

285. Graham Fuller and Rend Francke, *The Arab Shi'a: The Forgotten Muslims* (New York: Macmillan, 2001), 155–165.

286. Abdelrahman Munif, *Cities of Salt*, trans. Peter Theroux (New York: Vintage Books, 1989), 616.

287. Robert Lacey, *The Kingdom: Arabia and the House of Saud* (New York: Avon, 1983), 485.

288. Weiner, "International Migration and Development: Indians in the Persian Gulf," 11. This prediction is also similar to Ibn Khaldun's famous sociological and historical theory about the rise and fall of ruling families in four generations. For more on this issue, see Ibn Khaldun, *The Muqadimah*, trans. Franz Rosenthal (Princeton, NJ: Princeton University Press, 1967), 105–107.

3

Globalization, Wars, and a Telecommunications Revolution

> *Kuwait's first and second lines of defense are diplomatic. The military comes a poor third.*
>
> —Nawaf al-Ahmad al-Jaber al-Sabah,
> Kuwaiti minister of defense, 1988

> *All we do is tell the truth and nothing but the truth.*
>
> —Muhammad Jassem al-Ali,
> director of al-Jazeera Television, 2001

Between the late 1970s and the start of the twenty-first century, an intersection of political events, domestic and economic factors, and new forms of media transformed the GCC states. This process began to fundamentally alter which foreign and domestic groups could realistically demand access to state resources and also ensured that government decisions respected the interests and views of these groups. The most important events of this period were the Iran-Iraq war from 1980 to 1988 and Iraq's invasion of Kuwait in August 1990. The latter brought unprecedented global public attention to GCC societies and heralded the rise of satellite news channels and other new forms of delivering information, such as the Internet and mobile phones.

Throughout this period, the Gulf's regimes remained remarkably stable. With the exception of Iraq, whose government was overthrown by a US invasion in 2003, the same regimes were in place in 2004 that had been there in 1980 in the GCC states and their neighbors. In some cases, the same leaders who had been in power in 1970 and 1979 were still in power in 2000. The regimes of the GCC states had never been absolute monarchies, in which power and authority were vested in a single leader or group of leaders, although increased oil wealth may have made it appear that this was the case. Instead, individual states had been a coalition of various tribes, groups, constituencies, and sometimes parliaments that lent authority to a specific ruling family.

The diffusion of power explains in large part why the Gulf states liquidated their overseas holdings and cut capital improvement projects after it became clear that their populations were unwilling to countenance any reductions in welfare spending. This was true even as oil prices and government revenues collapsed in the 1980s. Although continual government spending guaranteed stability and generated economic growth, this policy became much harder to sustain after the onset of another major decline in petroleum prices in the late 1990s. By the turn of the twenty-first century, poverty and income inequalities in the Gulf were impossible to ignore and a source of social tension. The opponents of Gulf regimes won significant public support during this period by linking the declining standards of living and other social problems to official corruption and long-standing alliances with Washington. Benefiting from new technology, these opponents posed as powerful a threat to the Gulf governments' legitimacy as Arab nationalism had a generation earlier.

The Gulf in the 1980s

Doors to Knowledge and Enlightenment

In July 1986, Islamist political movements were still several years away, as King Fahd of Saudi Arabia addressed foreign Muslims assembled in Mecca for the hajj pilgrimage. The speech—like those his father and brothers had given to hajj pilgrims—was a major address that reiterated the government's commitment to protecting the hajj and Islam's two holiest cities, fostering global diplomacy, and promoting the welfare of the kingdom's people. But he especially emphasized the result of the kingdom's development programs and vast social welfare network:

> We have opened the doors of knowledge and enlightenment . . . to every citizen and have set up health centers and made available medicines to the sons of our people without effort. The wheels of industry have turned under the hands of our sons in all fields in order to meet the homeland's requirements in products and essential goods, in a serious effort to achieve self-sufficiency and self-reliance. . . . We have made light reach the villages and rural areas . . . through electrification networks. We have linked the nearest and most remote parts of the Kingdom with a modern communication network.[1]

Even though Fahd's speech overstated the success of his government's development programs, his boasts were not empty rhetoric. Rather, they reflected the results of Saudi and Gulf socioeconomic development plans, which were among the most successful ever undertaken in the twentieth century. In less than a decade, the Arab Gulf states' programs had produced gains in both physical infrastructure and human capital that more developed societies had needed many decades to achieve. From the mid-1970s until the mid-1980s, one could see real improvements in social indicators, from literacy to female education, to infant mortality, to life expectancy. The Gulf states also boasted a variety of modern non-oil industries, including mechanized agriculture. For a region whose people had regularly experienced food shortages and hunger as recently as the 1940s, self-sufficiency in crops such as wheat was a critical marker of progress and future stability.

As successful as the development plans and social welfare programs were in modernizing Gulf life, their financial costs were enormous and grew exponentially. Just as during the reign of Ibn Saud, the state had to "pay, pay, pay." Although not every development project was funded, many were, regardless of the cost.[2] And constructing modern cities and growing wheat and other crops in the Gulf's arid climate necessitated gargantuan investments in water, electrical generation, telecommunication, housing stock, and transportation networks. Between 1974 and 1984, the Saudi development programs cost \$500 billion.[3] That figure, however, did not include the large costs of maintaining infrastructure and subsidies that provided medical care and opened the "doors of knowledge and enlightenment."[4] The per capita costs and percentage of national budgets of these subsidies rose by astonishing rates in the 1970s and 1980s.

One subsidy illustrates this process well: fuel. In 1975, the Saudi government spent 0.8 percent of its national budget on fuel, with a per capita subsidy of \$25. In 1979, the fuel subsidy represented 5.8 percent of the Saudi national budget, and the subsidy per capita was \$152. Four years later, in 1983, the subsidy grew to 32.8 percent of the national budget, and the per capita subsidy was \$692—a twenty-seven-fold increase from 1975. There were similar increases in subsidies for other basic utilities, including water and electricity. Collectively, these subsidies represented 1.4 percent of the Saudi national budget and \$41 per capita in 1975. Four years later, in 1979, they accounted for 31.9 percent of the Saudi budget and \$674 per capita.[5]

The Oil Crash

From the vantage point of the late 1970s and early 1980s, the increases in subsidies and the vast investments in infrastructure, although expensive, were affordable in the eyes of most Arab Gulf state leaders. Between 1972 and

1980, the price of a barrel of oil had gone from $3 to $35 and state oil revenues in the Gulf had increased correspondingly: Saudi Arabia's went from $3.1 billion in 1972 to $102 billion in 1980; Kuwait's, from $1.7 billion to $17.9 billion; Qatar's, from $300 million to $5.5 billion; and the UAE's, from $600 million to $26 billion.[6] The rise in petroleum revenues was especially steep between 1978 and 1980: Saudi Arabia's income increased 35 percent; Kuwait's, 45 percent; the UAE's, 41 percent; and Qatar's, 40 percent.[7]

By the early 1980s, the UAE's per capita income was $29,000, one of the world's highest; at $18,000, that of Saudi Arabia roughly equaled that of the United States.[8] Saudi leaders and economists worried about the inflationary pressure of absorbing too many financial assets. US analysts worried whether the UAE and Kuwait would continue to produce oil at the then current levels, since, in the words of a US Central Intelligence Agency report, they could almost "live off their financial assets without much further need for oil revenue."[9] Throughout the 1970s, oil demand increased by 3.5 percent annually, and few observers expected either global demand for oil or its price to decline in the 1980s.[10] The finance and economic minister of Saudi Arabia, Muhammad Abu al-Khalil, wrote in 1979 in *International Affairs* that "the use of oil is the use of a fixed stock of capital" (i.e., oil consumption would remain constant and not decline), and senior oil company executives and national petroleum ministers lamented the fact that oil had been so cheap for so many years.[11] It was widely assumed that the United States and other developed nations would simply have to adjust to the new market conditions, in which energy remained expensive. Analysts with the World Bank and the Central Intelligence Agency concluded that prices would increase in the 1980s, with the World Bank predicting that the price of oil would be more than $47 per barrel by 1985.[12] After the start of the Iran-Iraq war in 1980, such estimates were seen as far too conservative, since it was likely that major oil fields might be damaged in the fighting. Under these conditions, the Arab Gulf states would have more than enough oil revenues to maintain their welfare systems and continue investing in new ambitious development programs.

But the price of oil never reached $47 in the 1980s, and, by the time of Fahd's speech in 1986, it was well under $10.[13] The reasons for the decline in prices were simple: (1) an increase in the production of oil from non-OPEC producers,[14] as well as from Iran and Iraq, both of which needed all the money they could get to fight their war; and (2) a decrease in oil demand worldwide. Central bankers in the United States, Western Europe, and Japan responded to inflationary pressures tied to high oil prices by increasing interest rates, which slowed economic activity, including oil consumption. Between 1980 and 1985, global oil consumption dropped an average of 1.4 percent each year.[15] Even after the developed nations' economies recovered economically in the mid-1980s, their oil consumption remained below previous levels until 1990. Energy conservation and other alternative sources of power had permanently reduced demand for petroleum—just as societal pressure a generation earlier to abandon coal had led to an increase in global oil consumption. Worldwide consumption of oil, especially from OPEC nations, was not fixed and would not necessarily continue the dramatic upward trajectory of the 1945–1980 period.

Although oil prices would stabilize at $18 per barrel by late 1986, the damage had been done. Between 1980 and 1986, global oil prices declined by 61.4 percent, leading to steep declines in the revenues of the Arab Gulf states.[16] From a high in 1981 of $113.2 billion, Saudi oil revenues collapsed to $42.3 billion in 1985 and $20 billion in 1986.[17] Other Arab Gulf states experienced similar declines in oil income between 1980 and 1986: Kuwait's went from $17.9 billion to $6 billion; the UAE's, from $19.5 billion to $7 billion; and Qatar's, from $5.5 billion to $1 billion.[18] All the increases in the price of oil between 1978 and 1980 were erased.

This decline in prices had an appreciable impact on Gulf finances, which by 1986 were more connected than ever to petroleum. Oil and gas revenues that year were 43 percent of Kuwait's total state revenues, 58 percent of Bahrain's, 58 percent of Saudi Arabia's, and 78 percent of Oman's.[19] Naturally, government revenues declined throughout the Gulf in the 1980s: by 4.6 percent in Bahrain, 31.6 percent in Kuwait, almost 60 percent in the UAE, 69 percent in Qatar, and 77 percent in Saudi Arabia.[20] The decline in oil prices was reinforced by a weakening of the US dollar, the currency in which the Gulf states were paid for oil.[21] This left them at an additional disadvantage because they imported most of their goods from European and Asian nations, whose currencies had simultaneously appreciated vis-à-vis the dollar.

The Arab Gulf governments could not escape the fact that they were far less wealthy in real terms than they had been before the early 1980s. This was especially true of the UAE and Kuwait. The former's GDP shrank from $29 billion in 1983 to $21.5 billion in 1986; its trade surplus declined by 58 percent between 1985 and 1986 alone.[22] Kuwait's real estate index, a broad measure of demand for housing and commercial buildings in the country, collapsed in the mid-1980s, standing at 3,438.81 in April 1982, but at only 594.96 in January 1985.[23] For societies that as recently as 1981 had been the wealthiest in the world, worrying about the effects of amassing too much capital, the change in status came as an enormous shock. The subsidies and investments that King Fahd had lauded were clearly no longer within the means of most Arab Gulf governments. Although they were free of the huge debts that Mexico and other Latin American oil exporters had amassed, it was clear that the Arab Gulf states were, for the first time since the 1960s, genuinely short of funds.

At that moment of crisis, the Gulf governments found it very difficult to pursue the most logical approach to dealing with their budgetary shortfalls—

namely, reducing spending and imposing income and other taxes, which had virtually disappeared in the Gulf during the 1970s. Even proposals to tax expatriate workers found little public support. As Kiren Chaudhry shows in *The Price of Wealth,* merchants and other Gulf elites who had supposedly been coopted by the Gulf governments refused to accept reductions in government spending, on which they had depended for more than a decade.[24] The once seemingly all-powerful Gulf states had to back down, maintaining chronically large budget deficits throughout the 1980s.

To finance those deficits, most Gulf states froze infrastructure projects and, whenever possible, liquidated their overseas assets, reduced foreign aid commitments, sold development bonds, and exported *more* oil. All the Gulf governments benefited from the fact that their national budgets did not have to be transparent, so they could control what was known about them. Money derived from the sale of oil and reported in national balance-of-payment statistics often failed to appear in the oil revenues of state budgets. At times, the gap between what was earned and what was reported could be considerable: 29.5 percent of the total in Saudi Arabia; 29 percent, for the UAE; 23.7 percent, for Kuwait; 18.7 percent, for Qatar; 18.4 percent, for Bahrain; and 8.8 percent, for Oman.[25] Still, the post-1986 oil crash policies worked to maintain social stability.

Diplomacy Is the Principal Defense

Social stability was crucial to the success of the Arab Gulf states as they approached a difficult regional political environment in the 1980s. Although the GCC represented a political alliance, divisions remained among its members regarding international borders and interpretations of Islam. Qatar gave refuge to lèading Islamists from around the world, such as the Egyptian scholar Yusuf al-Qaradawi, as well as Shaikh Abdullah bin Zaid al-Mahmud, who was exiled from Saudi Arabia, along with several other Saudi Muslim clerics, after the seizure of Mecca's Grand Mosque in 1979. Shaikh Abdullah eventually became Qatar's most senior Muslim scholar.[26]

The war between Iran and Iraq reinforced GCC divisions because member states could not reach a common policy on the conflict. Kuwait, Saudi Arabia, Bahrain, and Qatar supported Iraq out of fear of Iran's revolutionary government. Kuwait permitted transshipments of goods across its borders for Iraq and, along with Saudi Arabia, lent Baghdad $60 billion for its war with Iran.[27] Saudi Arabia also constructed pipelines to ship Iraqi oil to the Red Sea. By contrast, Oman and the UAE emirates of Dubai, Sharjah, and Ras al-Khaimah maintained ties with both Iran and Iraq, professing neutrality in the war.[28] The UAE emirates feared that they would disrupt their own Iranian and Shia populations and thus their profitable re-export trade with Iran.[29]

These fissures became especially important in 1984 with the start of the four-year "Tanker War" phase of the Iran-Iraq war. This phase started when Iraq attacked Iranian tankers in the Gulf and Iran's oil terminal at Kharg Island in retaliation for Iran's blockade of Iraq's exports of oil through the Shatt-al-Arab waterway. Iran responded by attacking tankers carrying Iraqi oil from Kuwait and tankers of the Gulf states supporting Iraq. Although the attacks did little to either the war efforts or the economies of either side, the Iranian actions became a significant nuisance by destroying a handful of Arab Gulf offshore oil facilities and tankers, including twenty-one Kuwaiti tankers in the six months preceding April 1987. Each of these attacks reverberated throughout the Gulf, raising the specter that Tehran might choose to close the Straits of Hormuz to all Gulf shipping. For Kuwait and other states that lacked alternatives for their oil exports, such an event would have been a catastrophe.[30]

Tense relations between Tehran and the Arab Gulf states supporting Iraq were approaching a boiling point in the late 1980s after terrorist attacks in Kuwait were linked to Iran. Furthermore, in 1987, Iranian aircraft violated Saudi airspace, and a demonstration by Iranian hajj pilgrims deteriorated into a riot and a violent confrontation with Saudi police, in which 400 Iranian pilgrims were killed. According to the Saudis, the riot marked the culmination of nearly a decade of Iranian challenges to Saudi control of the two holy cities. Throughout this period, Iran sent more than 100,000 pilgrims to Mecca for the hajj, who then staged demonstrations and provoked Muslims from other nations. The violence in 1987 came at a sensitive political moment for the Saudi royal family, since King Fahd had formally adopted the title "Custodian of the Two Holy Places" only a year before. Moreover, Tehran explicitly and implicitly threatened the internal stability of the Arab Gulf states with its ability to rally their Shia populations to repeat the violence of the late 1970s and early 1980s in Bahrain and Saudi Arabia.[31]

To combat Iran, however, the Arab Gulf states had few realistic options. They already provided significant financial and logistical support to Iraq's war efforts and had no desire to directly confront Iran, which had an army of 500,000 soldiers. By comparison, Saudi Arabia, which maintained the largest GCC army, had only 45,000 soldiers, two-thirds of whom were non-Saudis. Most other GCC states had no more than 20,000 troops each.[32] There was the joint-GCC military unit, the Peninsular Shield force, but that was mostly composed of Saudis and had only 10,000 soldiers.[33]

The Gulf states were also already devoting considerable sums to weapons: between 1985 and 1990, Saudi Arabia bought $106 billion worth of new weapons; the UAE, $10.6 billion; Oman, $9 billion; Kuwait, $2.04 billion; and Bahrain, $1.07 billion.[34] Although these sums had produced modern land, sea, and air forces, there was no way they would produce military might equal to Iran's. As the Kuwaiti officials often noted, their state's best means of defense was diplomacy.[35]

It is not surprising that the Gulf states chose to confront Iran through interactions with the Great Powers. In 1987, Kuwait asked the Soviet Union, the United States, and Great Britain to protect Gulf shipping. Fearful that Moscow might gain a foothold in the Gulf, Washington provided Kuwait with an immediate affirmative reply. Building on the informal "over the horizon" alliance that had been developed in the 1970s, the US Navy deployed to the Gulf, using facilities in Bahrain, Oman, the UAE, and elsewhere. To facilitate US operations, the GCC states had as many as half of their tankers temporarily fly the US flag. Although US naval escorts were involved in a number of clashes with Iranian forces, Iran generally avoided interfering with these Gulf ships.[36]

Iraq's Invasion of Kuwait

Finances, Borders, and Oil

Tensions in the Gulf eased in 1988 and 1989. Exhausted by years of fighting, Iraq sued for peace. Following Khomeini's death in 1989, Iran accepted a United Nations–negotiated cease-fire with Iraq. The war ended in a stalemate, with neither side able to declare a decisive victory. With the end of the Cold War, the Iran-Iraq war also coincided with a marked improvement both in US-Soviet and in US-Iraqi relations. In the late 1980s, US-Iraqi trade soared, with the United States purchasing Iraqi oil, and Iraq becoming one of the largest markets for US agricultural and manufactured products. Iraq, which had been a traditional client of the Soviet Union, began to seek closer ties with the United States.[37]

At the same time, Iranian relations with the Arab Gulf states and with Washington began to improve in significant ways. In June 1990, both Iranian president Ali Akbar Hashemi Rafsanjani and King Fahd publicly emphasized a deep desire for improved bilateral relations, to "eliminate all cause of current dispute" in Fahd's words.[38] In 1991, in a clear sign of improved bilateral ties, Iran ended its self-imposed ban on Iranians' traveling on the hajj. For the first time since the hajj riots in 1987, Iranians resumed going on the hajj.[39] Saudi officials welcomed the Iranian pilgrims and permitted them to hold a peaceful rally in Mecca, in which they shouted "Death to America" and "Death to Israel."[40] In his inaugural address in 1989, US president George H.W. Bush promised that "good will begets good will," a statement some interpreted as offering Iran and other "pariah" nations an opportunity for improved ties with the United States if they "moderated" their behavior in international affairs.[41]

Although the international relations of the Gulf appeared to be improving, there was one significant problem: Iraq's finances. Following the war with Iran, Baghdad launched an ambitious civilian and military development program, which was well beyond its means. Although Iraq earned $13 billion from oil revenues in 1989, its civilian and military imports and debt repayments were more than $20 billion. Iraq's debt was staggering. It owed more than $50 billion to the Soviet Union and Western creditors and tens of billions more to Kuwait and Saudi Arabia. Iraq's refusal to demobilize its army and reduce its military budget further exacerbated its financial problems. Its military budget ($12.9 billion) was equivalent to $700 per capita, a significant number when one considers that Iraqi per capita income in 1990 was $1,950.[42]

By early 1990, Iraq understood that its financial position was untenable and needed immediate relief, especially as the price of oil began to collapse. In January 1990, the price of oil stood at $21 a barrel; by March, it was below $18; and by summer, it was $11. At that rate, Iraq would go bankrupt without significant financial assistance. Inflation at that time was running at 40 percent in Iraq, and Baghdad only had enough cash reserves to buy the equivalent of three months of necessary imports. Borrowing more funds was becoming increasingly difficult, too. As Iraqi leaders surveyed their dire financial position, they were clear who was responsible for Iraq's problems—namely, the Arab Gulf states, especially Kuwait and the UAE. In February 1990, Saddam Hussein demanded that the Gulf states put a moratorium on their wartime loans to Iraq and provide his country with a $30 billion gift for postwar reconstruction.[43]

As Iraq made these demands, it framed them within three sets of grievances. First, Baghdad alleged, rightly, that Kuwait and the UAE had exceeded their OPEC quotas in 1990, thereby contributing mightily to the decline in world oil prices. Official Iraqi requests that Kuwait adhere to its quotas remained unanswered. Second, Baghdad claimed, again correctly, that Kuwait had stolen oil from Iraq located just inside the Iraqi border. Third, although Kuwaitis did not expect Iraq to repay the wartime loans, they nonetheless refused to officially forgive Iraq the debt. This weakened Baghdad's credit rating, which made borrowing far more expensive, because foreign lenders counted Iraq's debt to Kuwait as part of the nation's liabilities when deciding terms for new loans. (By contrast, the Saudis were willing to officially forgive Iraq's debt to them.)[44] In May 1990, Saddam Hussein voiced his and his countrymen's frustrations when he said: "War is fought with soldiers, . . . but it is also done by economic means. . . . This is in fact a kind of war against Iraq."[45] For its part, Kuwait believed that it had the right to export as much oil as it wished, especially since Iraq had done precisely that in the 1980s during its war with Iran. Furthermore, the exact location of the Kuwaiti border with Iraq remained an issue open to considerable debate. Loan forgiveness in Kuwaiti eyes was one of its few bargaining chips with its large and powerful neighbor. If Kuwaitis were to give that up, they required something tangible in return. After all, Iraqis felt that Kuwait had been stolen from their country in the nineteenth century by Britain, and they had a low regard for the Kuwaiti royal family.

By summer 1990, ever more frustrated, the Iraqi leaders decided to go to war to address their grievances. After Kuwait again refused to limit its output of oil and to provide an acceptable solution to the debt and border issues, Baghdad sent a letter to the Arab League on July 15, 1990, laying out its case against Kuwait. A week later, Iraqi military units deployed to the border, and by the end of the month, there were enough forces to occupy all of Kuwait. Iraqi officials publicized the troop movements and deployed their most battle-tested and politically reliable troops to emphasize the seriousness of their intensions. In response, US and Arab diplomats tried to mediate the dispute. Declassified diplomatic documents from the period indicate that US officials fully understood the seriousness of Iraq's financial difficulties and the genuine anger of Iraqi officials. Yet even the most prescient US officials did not foresee a war under any circumstances. When Kuwait again refused to provide everything that Iraq demanded at a bilateral meeting on July 31, 1990, the Iraqis decided to invade.[46]

Things Fall Apart

On August 2, 1990, Iraqi soldiers invaded Kuwait and shortly thereafter reached Kuwait City. Along the way, they secured Kuwait's oil fields and strategic facilities. They then established an interim administration and began the process of bringing Kuwait's population firmly under Iraqi control. Kuwait's army and security forces put up little resistance because of their poor training, weak command and control, and an overly centralized logistical system. The Kuwaiti army's central complex was inexplicably vulnerable to air attack—a vulnerability the Iraqis ruthlessly exploited.[47] Bedouin tribesmen and foreigners, who made up much of the Kuwaiti army, deserted in droves, having little reason to remain loyal to Kuwait's government, which had mistreated them for years. Most of those who did not desert their posts were killed or retreated with the rest of the Kuwaiti military to Saudi Arabia.

Civil defense and paramilitary forces were of little help to the Kuwaitis who did not escape the occupation. These citizens provided the only resistance to Iraq's invasion while contending with a collapse in government services. Because most leading Kuwaiti males either fled or were taken into custody by the Iraqis, women, especially pious women, took the lead in violent and nonviolent resistance. Throughout the occupation, Kuwait City earned the nickname the "City of Women," and Kuwaiti resistance fighters became known as the *samidun* (or the religiously faithful).[48] Outside the country, both male and female Kuwaitis trained with US Special Forces and lobbied the government in exile to restore suspended democratic freedoms and institutions after the occupation.[49] In a series of unprecedented public meetings in Saudi Arabia between ordinary Kuwaitis and their government, the Kuwaiti royal family agreed to hold elections after the liberation of the country.[50]

The resistance of ordinary Kuwaitis became one of a litany of problems for the Iraqis in Kuwait. When Iraqi soldiers reached Kuwait's National Bank, they found nothing of value, since Kuwaiti leaders had already transferred the bank's holdings to overseas financial institutions, prudently changing the passwords to access the emirate's various accounts. This action effectively barred Iraq from having any access to more than $100 billion in official Kuwaiti assets. With the help of computer networks and overseas banks, the Kuwaiti government reconstituted itself overnight in Saudi Arabia and worked to win international support against the invasion. Ultimately, Kuwait's employment of banking and computer technology would be a preview of the paramount impact of modern technology on the politics of the Gulf in the 1990s.[51]

Within two days of the invasion, Kuwait's diplomacy, "its first and second lines of defense," yielded immediate benefits. The United Nations Security Council unanimously called on the Iraqi government to withdraw unconditionally from Kuwait and for member states to impose economic sanctions against Iraq until it did so. Except for limited quantities of food and medicine, Iraq could not export oil or import any goods to rebuild its economy or to supply its forces in Kuwait. Iraq may have physically held Kuwait, but it could not touch Kuwait's billions in overseas assets or sell Kuwaiti oil. The ban on selling oil was especially important, since oil was paramount to Iraq's economy, and Kuwait and Iraq together held 20 percent of global oil reserves. Washington also worked closely with Moscow to win UN Security Council authorization to use force against Iraq if it did not withdraw from Kuwait.[52]

A Fateful Choice

The Iraqi occupation of Kuwait forced the GCC to face a crisis that it was ill prepared to address. In the past, the GCC states had only had to deal with occasional violations of their airspace or the sinking of oil supertankers. Throughout the eight-year Iran-Iraq war, the GCC states had looked to Iraq to counter Iran. Now Iraq controlled a GCC state (Kuwait) and sought the backing of Palestinians, Yemenis, and other expatriate workers in the Gulf states by threatening to attack Israel.[53] To make matters worse, Baghdad reached an agreement with Tehran that concluded the 1988 UN-negotiated cease-fire, allowing Iraq to focus on defending its gains in Kuwait and potentially moving farther southward toward Saudi Arabia.[54]

Even though the GCC states uniformly condemned Iraq's invasion, they could not agree on a coordinated response to the attack aside from strengthening the Peninsular Shield force. But the force never deployed—despite the fact that it was based in Hafr al-Batin, a Saudi city 95 miles from Kuwait on a modern highway that connected Iraq, Kuwait, and Saudi Arabia. At no time in 1990 or 1991 would the Gulf states cooperate to deal with the Iraqi threat. Even more disturbing to the GCC leaders than the failure of the GCC military to repel Iraq's army was the fact that Kuwait fell before US military forces could intervene. New approaches were clearly needed to meet the GCC's security needs and to free Kuwait.[55]

This dilemma was especially acute for Saudi Arabia. In the days shortly after the Iraqi invasion, senior Saudi leaders feared that they would face a ground war with Iraq—a ground war they felt they would lose. Although it was seen as unlikely that Iraq would annex all of Saudi Arabia the same way it had annexed Kuwait, the Saudis worried that Iraq would attack the oil-rich Eastern Province. And they had good reason to worry, for Iraq had 6,000 tanks and more than a million men under arms. By contrast, Saudi Arabia only had an army of 68,000 men.[56] Even if an Iraqi attack on Saudi Arabia never materialized, the GCC governments lacked the resources to expel Iraq from Kuwait.

The occupation also held considerable symbolic importance to Saudi Arabia and its fellow GCC states. Every day that the members of Kuwait's ruling family remained out of power meant that it would be that much harder to reinstate them. This was not a minor issue for the GCC states, all of which were monarchies. In the previous forty years, they had witnessed other pro-Western monarchies fall in the Middle East, including the Hashemite family in Iraq in 1958, King Idris in Libya in 1969, and the shah of Iran in 1979. After these monarchies were overthrown, none of them ever came back to power.

Under these conditions, Saudi Arabia made the fateful decision to issue a formal invitation for Washington to deploy US soldiers as part of a multinational coalition, including some Arab armies, to defend the kingdom. Riyadh understood that both regional and global Muslim opinion would not welcome the presence of thousands of US soldiers in the same kingdom as the holy cities of Mecca and Medina. But Saudi Arabia had a decades old relationship with Washington, and it was clear that the US military had sufficient assets both to defend the kingdom and to expel Iraq from Kuwait. Saudi Arabia, which borders Iraq and Kuwait, was the logical place from which to launch such a military operation. Riyadh's decision was also consistent with the diplomacy of other Gulf states, which, following Iraq's annexation of Kuwait, had upgraded their diplomatic relations with Washington and were hosting nearly half a million US soldiers, airmen, and sailors.[57]

When we consider this Saudi decision to invite in the US military, we should bear in mind that Saudi Arabia and its GCC allies had few viable options for dealing with Iraq in 1990 other than working with Washington. For example, although Egyptian or Syrian soldiers would not have raised significant religious qualms, it is unclear if Saudi Arabia and the other GCC states were willing to pay the price that Cairo or Damascus would certainly have demanded to bail out Kuwait, in the form of military subsidies, financial assistance, preferential trade agreements, and so on. It is also not clear how those armies could have been deployed without US military assets. A potential GCC alliance with Iran was perhaps even more fraught with peril. Without the check of Iraq, Iran would dominate the region and form alliances with the Shia in the Gulf states. Another option would have been to accept Osama bin Laden's offer to use his organization of Arab veterans of the jihad in Afghanistan, Al-Qaida, to liberate Kuwait. This offer was not taken seriously, since no one could fathom how Bin Laden and his followers could possibly defeat the Iraqi army in Kuwait.[58]

The War and Gulf Society

Mixed Reactions

US military power remained the only viable option for evicting Iraq, and the popular narrative that took shape around the Gulf War, which began in January 1991, was defined by logical calculations. The United States and its allies had the resources to evict Iraq from Kuwait, and Saudi Arabia and the other GCC states did everything to make that possible.

From August 1990 forward, the GCC governments housed more than 600,000 US and other foreign soldiers. In September 1990, the GCC governments opened their naval and air facilities to US and coalition aircraft, including the airfields adjacent to Mecca and Medina. Dubai's Jebel Ali port was especially important to the US Navy because it was the only facility in the Gulf region large enough to berth an aircraft carrier. By 1992, Jebel Ali was the largest port of call for the US Navy. The US military was now in plain sight—no longer "over the horizon" as it had been in the 1970s and 1980s.[59]

Although the Shia populations in Saudi Arabia and Bahrain welcomed the actions against Iraq's government, the Gulf monarchies understood that they faced elite and popular opposition among some Sunni Arabs to the decision to attack Iraq and ally with the United States. To offset this opposition, the Saudi government followed the same strategy it had used with ARAMCO and Abu Bahz in the 1930s—that is, it asked the senior religious figure in Saudi Arabia to support its actions. The grand mufti of Saudi Arabia, Shaikh 'Abd al-'Aziz ibn Bahz, penned a *fatwa* (religious opinion) that authorized a jihad against Iraq, even if that meant cooperating with non-Muslims.[60]

The *fatwa* did not, however, prevent Gulf Arabs from discussing in the media and in Friday sermons, as well as informally, essentially the same question that Prince Sultan had asked his soldiers in 1979. Was it legitimate to ask non-Saudis and other Gulf Arabs (especially non-Muslims) to fight other Muslims? Furthermore, were Muslim governments that resorted to such measures still legitimate?[61] These questions echoed throughout the Gulf. For example, UAE emirate governments publicly expressed reservations over Washington's threats to attack a fellow Sunni Arab state. The UAE foreign ministry also initially shared those concerns until strong lobbying from the al-Maktums, the royal family of Dubai, convinced the UAE federal government to support the US position vigorously. The al-Maktums' argument was simple: in a time of crisis, it was imperative for the UAE elites to support a fellow royal family.[62]

Yet the most strident of the criticisms did not appear in official channels. Building on the conservative milieu and ethos promoted by Gulf governments since the late 1970s, popular preachers gained an audience by criticizing US and Arab Gulf state actions in specifically Islamic terms. They utilized the same technology that Ayatollah Khomeini and his followers had employed a decade earlier during the Iranian revolution—cassette tapes and pamphlets. Safar al-Hawali, the dean of Islamic College at Umm al-Qura University in Mecca, released an audiotape in which he argued that the crisis pointed to the kingdom's dangerous dependence on Western military power. In his eyes, Iraq's actions were not justified, but Saudi Arabia's invitation of US troops meant that the kingdom had turned to an "evil greater than Saddam—that is, the U.S.A."[63] Other, younger preachers and teachers raised similar concerns in their cassettes and pamphlets about dependence on US power and the corrupting influence of Western culture.[64]

These criticisms gained substantial credibility among Gulf Arabs in the months immediately after the invasion and defined the outlook of the region's political activists for a generation. Not only did Saudi Arabia and other Gulf states open their territory to foreign military forces, but they also provided subsidies to Western states for their military expenses. Saudi Arabia alone provided nearly $15 billion, and the UAE provided $10 billion. Bahrain and Dubai indirectly paid billions as well after their tourism and service sectors collapsed in 1990 and 1991. But the costs of the Iraqi occupation, dealing with Kuwaiti refugees, and funding Western military deployments in the region fell most heavily on Kuwait itself. The Kuwaiti government ended up paying $66 billion in increased governmental expenditures, transfer payments, and various subsidies.[65]

Even though the Gulf states were relatively wealthy by global standards, these were very heavy burdens for them to bear, especially after years during which they had reduced their overseas assets and foreign currency reserves because of the oil bust of the 1980s. For the first time, Saudi Arabia had to take out loans from the World Bank and other international creditors.[66] Before the war, Kuwait's reserve Fund for Future Generations had stood at a healthy $100 billion (for a native population of less than 2 million).[67] Following the war, this had been reduced to only $35 billion.[68] Kuwait also took out more than $5.5 billion in loans in 1991 from international creditors.[69] Saudi and Kuwaiti loans reinforced the fears about their governments' dependency on the West and increased suspicions about the rationale for the billions of dollars in arms sales from the United States and other nations in the 1970s and 1980s. It appeared to al-Hawali and other critics as if the region's vast oil resources were destined, both in peacetime and in wartime, to go to the West and not to the societies where the oil originated. Such a system was indicative, in their eyes, of the corruption of the Gulf's political leaders and their desire to please Washington more than their own peoples.[70]

The critics were equally wary of the economic changes that the Gulf states implemented during the war. In a dramatic reversal of decades of economic policy, Saudi Arabia and the other GCC states expelled more than a million Yeminis, Palestinians, and other expatriates whose loyalties were suspect. A new class of expatriates replaced them, many of whom were neither Arab nor Muslim. In September 1990, Saudi Arabia encouraged its government agencies to accept female volunteers for the social and medical professions as a way of freeing up positions for Saudi men in the military services. In November 1990, partially in response to this appeal, as well as to the global media attention given to the kingdom over the Iraqi crisis, forty-five elite and educated Saudi women violated the semiofficial ban on women driving. The Saudi government quickly arrested the women and then publicly humiliated and shunned them. For Islamist activists and critics of the Gulf regimes, the message was clear: women provided tools with which they could challenge the legitimacy of any regime in the region.[71]

CNN: A Media Revolution

Islamic activists could also not escape the emergence of a new element in their societies: satellite news television, especially the US satellite channel Cable News Network (CNN). Gulf Arabs, like other peoples around the world, tuned in to CNN because there was no alternative to its live coverage of events during the Kuwait crisis. The network also benefited from technological advances that reduced the costs of accessing satellite television programming. What had once been mockingly called the Chicken Noodle Network had earned tremendous credibility at home and abroad.[72] The network had become so important that the George H.W. Bush administration requested the Finnish government, the host of a US-Soviet summit in September 1990, to wire President Bush's guesthouse specially so he could see CNN.[73] During the initial days of the war, it was equally important for the Kuwaiti emir to show that he was following events closely in Kuwait by watching CNN in his hotel room in Washington.[74]

Although Ted Turner and the executives at CNN had originally conceived of cable as a platform to deliver their news service to the US public, they quickly understood the commercial and content possibilities of providing news internationally via satellite. Unlike terrestrial television, satellite television is not regulated under international law, nor can countries regulate its content. Neither could countries bring suit in any court, international or domestic, against corporations or other nations for broadcasting inflammatory or politically sensitive programming into national territories. For news broadcasters such as CNN, satellite broadcasting was the perfect vehicle to deliver information across national borders.

In 1990, CNN began to broadcast to the Gulf twenty-four hours a day via a transponder owned by ARABSAT (Arab Satellite Communications Organization), a leading Arab satellite communications company based in Saudi Arabia. Prior to the Gulf War, neither the Gulf governments nor private entrepreneurs had expressed much interest in satellite television, in part because the costs of owning a satellite dish were extremely expensive.[75] Within weeks of its introduction to the Gulf states, however, CNN outshone its competitors in the region's highly competitive media market with far sleeker presentations, higher production values, more professional announcers, and a wider array of experts than anything anyone in the Arab world had seen before.[76] When Iraq invaded Kuwait in August 1990, CNN had correspondents reporting live from Kuwait and Iraq. By contrast, Saudi state television waited for several days before reporting that Iraq had invaded Kuwait. The difference was highly reminiscent of the period before the 1950s, when European, Egyptian, and other foreign broadcasters dominated the airwaves of the Gulf and shaped how the region's peoples looked at the world.[77]

This time something was different. The tens of thousands of professional workers in the Gulf who had studied and worked in the United States or Western Europe regarded the delays of Saudi and other state television networks as totally unacceptable, pressured for better coverage, and got it.[78] Local broadcasters in Bahrain eagerly agreed, when given the chance by CNN, to pass the US network's satellite feed directly to their viewers.[79] Terrestrial stations in Egypt, Qatar, and several other parts of the Arab world also provided CNN programming directly to their viewers.[80]

Iraq, which replaced Kuwaiti state television with its own network shortly after occupying the country, was quick to understand the growing political importance of CNN. Much like the US Pentagon, which consciously shaped media images on CNN and other networks during the war, Iraq publicized its own messages to the Middle East and broader world through those channels. In fact, Iraq was sufficiently successful that some conservative politicians in the United States accused CNN's Baghdad reporters of committing treason.[81]

The commercial potential of CNN was also clear to Arab businessmen and government leaders, who began to make plans to copy it. In December 1990, the Egyptian government, concerned that its view of Iraq's invasion had not received sufficient international attention, created the Egyptian Satellite Channel, the first satellite news service in the Arab world. This process included Egypt's launching its own satellite, since it had been excluded from ARABSAT because of its peace treaty with Israel. Other nations would soon follow Egypt's lead. Television in the Gulf and the wider Arab world would never be the same, but that did not become clear until after war. [82]

A New "Old" Order in the Gulf

Victory and the Postwar Order

Gulf Arabs naturally turned to CNN in January 1991 to watch Operation Desert Storm, the air and land campaign that dislodged Iraq's military from Kuwait. The commander of the US Central Command, General H. Norman Schwarzkopf, headed US, British, and French units. His Saudi counterpart, Lieutenant General Khalid ibn Sultan, commanded units from twenty-four non-Western countries, including 20,000 Saudis, 7,000 Kuwaitis, and 3,000 troops from other GCC countries.[83] States that did not participate directly in military operations contributed as well. For example, Oman's decision to allow the United States to utilize the prepositioned materials in the sultanate saved the US Air Force the equivalent of 1,800 airlift sorties to the region by C-141s.[84]

By April 1991, Saudi Arabia and the other Gulf governments could take a collective sigh of relief. The gamble they had taken by inviting the Americans into the region and then paying for their military operations had seemingly paid off handsomely. In a matter of weeks, US and allied forces defeated Iraq's formidable army, evicted it from Kuwait, and restored that nation's royal family to power. The strongly worded UN Security Council resolutions that had been passed in the months leading up to the war permitted future military action if Iraq sought to rearm or to attack Kuwait again. Iraq also would have to abide by a UN-defined border between itself and Kuwait and pay restitutions to Kuwait.[85]

The Gulf states now enjoyed their strongest strategic position since the early 1970s: US power was supreme, Iraq was beaten and out of the regional balance of power, and Iran was still recovering from its brutal eight-year war with Iraq. The collapse of the Soviet Union—and Russia's acquiescence to the war—heightened the Gulf victory by emphasizing US power globally and removing Iraq's principal international benefactor. Furthermore, the Oslo Peace Process, which was launched in 1993, promised to solve the Palestinian issue and the Arab-Israeli conflict, long one of the chief factors limiting close ties between the Gulf states and Washington. By the mid-1990s, two Gulf states, Oman and Qatar, did something that had long been seen as unimaginable: they publicly opened informal diplomatic links with Israel.[86]

"911 Emergency Calls Only Ring in Washington"

Recognizing the unique opportunities available to them after the war, the Gulf states swiftly moved to cement their alliances with Washington. Abandoning the "over the horizon" policies of the 1970s and 1980s, the Gulf states signed open agreements with the United States. Kuwait and Bahrain signed ten-year defense agreements with Washington in 1991, and Qatar and the UAE signed similar agreements with the United States in 1992. Saudi Arabia deepened its informal military partnership with Washington. All the Gulf states also agreed to pre-position US matériel (up to 110 tanks each) and permanently open air and naval facilities to US forces. In addition, most of the Gulf states had reached military access and defense agreements with a host of other nations, including Great Britain, France, Italy, Russia, Turkey, and China. The agreements with countries other than the United States were more for show, however, than for anything else. For example, France promised to deploy 85,000 troops, 130 combat aircraft, and one aircraft carrier battle group to the UAE if it were ever invaded, but this was ludicrous, since France had struggled to deploy only 15,000 soldiers to the Gulf in 1991.[87]

By the middle to late 1990s, various US facilities honeycombed the Gulf from Kuwait to the Suez Canal, and thirty-five US warships regularly sailed the region's waterways. A third of these forces were stationed in Saudi Arabia, and the rest in Kuwait, Bahrain, and the UAE.[88] US forces, which retained the ability to rapidly increase their levels to an additional 20,000 soldiers on short notice, conducted annual training exercises with the GCC states.[89] Although the arrangements for most of the US military bases were informal, the US Navy formally homeported the personnel and fifteen ships of the US Fifth Fleet at Bahrain's port of Mina Sulman.[90] The US Navy also maintained almost as large a temporary presence in Dubai's Jebel Ali port as well as in Omani and UAE ports that face the Indian Ocean or are near the Straits of Hormuz.[91] The US Air Force flew regular combat and supply missions from air bases throughout the region.

Just as they had done in the decades before Iraq's invasion of Kuwait, the Gulf states continued to make significant arms purchases after the war. Between 1993 and 2000, Saudi Arabia purchased $24.5 billion worth of foreign weapon systems; the UAE, $19 billion; Kuwait, $6 billion; Oman, $1.4 billion; and Bahrain, $100 million.[92] Washington continued to win a significant share of these sales—100 percent of Bahrain's, 66 percent of Saudi Arabia's, 50 percent of the UAE's, and 50 percent of Kuwait's—with the rest going to major Western European and Asian suppliers.[93] In 1998, the UAE acquired from Lockheed Martin eighty F-16s that were technically more advanced than the F-16s then in service with the US Air Force.[94] The initial cost of the purchase was $8 billion, but the real cost was far higher because the UAE signed long-term contracts with foreign companies to maintain the jets and to train its pilots.[95] These types of maintenance contracts were increasingly common in the Gulf in the 1990s and usually meant that the expenditures related to arms purchases were higher than the cost of the initial sale.

Those costs, however, were seemingly worth the investment to the Gulf states. US power had freed Kuwait and protected the regional states from a very real threat in 1991 as well as from Iraq and Iran in subsequent years. Iraq repeatedly challenged the sanctions and inspection regimes imposed on it after the Gulf War, along with the legality of its border with Kuwait. In October 1994, Iraq moved its Hammurabi and al-Nida Republican Guard divisions to positions within 20 miles of Kuwait before withdrawing after intense international pressure.[96] In 1996, Iraq again stationed its armed divisions sufficiently close to Kuwait to deploy in the country with as little as five hours notice.[97] Kuwait did not have the strategic military depth to wait for the international community to act if Iraq invaded. Only the threat of swift US military retaliation appeared to deter future Iraqi attacks.

In the southern end of the Gulf, Iran represented a similar threat. In 1992, Iran asserted full control over Abu Musa Island, carried out military exercises on and near the island, and deployed military forces there, including units of its elite Revolutionary Guard. For the UAE, a federation the size of the US state of Maine, Iran's sudden seizure of its territory and military deployments raised the possibility that the UAE, too, could be suddenly overrun as Kuwait had been in 1990. These fears were only heightened by Tehran's refusal to negotiate the status of the island with the UAE, which Iranian leaders labeled as a ploy to cement US power in the Gulf. Nor could Qatar and Bahrain discount possible Iranian seizures of their territories, for they had economic, territorial, and socioreligious disagreements with Iran. Close military ties with Washington were just as imperative for these three states as they were for Kuwait. A US diplomat in Abu Dhabi liked to say, "Everybody in the Gulf knows that 911 emergency calls only ring in Washington."[98]

Political Reform

The Need for Partners

However logical the GCC decision was to ally closely with the United States during and after the Gulf War, it contributed to a debate throughout the Gulf about basic questions of governmental legitimacy. The debates flowed from (1) the intense public conversations in the GCC societies about supporting US military action in 1991 and (2) the establishment of domestic consultative political institutions in several Gulf states to give their populations a greater voice in government. It is significant that changes in one Gulf state were closely related to changes in all the others. For example, when Kuwaitis fled to Saudi Arabia and other states, they interacted with other Gulf Arabs, whose traditions and views impacted how they looked at Kuwait and also how those others looked at their own nations. Furthermore, it was impossible for Kuwaitis and Saudis to avoid the television images of the war and its aftermath on their soil. In several states, citizens directly petitioned their governments for new institutions.

Although the new consultative mechanisms varied from appointed advisory commissions to parliaments with regular elections and constitutionally defined powers, they represented a desire of the GCC governments to bridge the clear gaps between state and society that were revealed by the war. These new institutions were also meant to reinvigorate local governance and to convince ordinary Gulf citizens to assume a far greater role in nation building than ever before. In general, the effort to empower citizens reflected the realization that the Gulf states, despite their tremendous reserves of oil, could not provide security or prosperity at home without a series of partners—be they Western military forces, a neighboring state, foreign investors, or ordinary citizens. At the same time, these consultative mechanisms were not between equals—that is, the governments worked to maintain a leading role in Gulf life, even if that meant using force with their own populations, thereby risking widespread social unrest.

Saudi Arabia

For the Saudi government, these challenges emerged even before the war began. In the first months of 1991, two groups addressed public letters and petitions to King Fahd, asking for reforms. The first letter, widely described as a "secular petition," won the support of forty-three prominent former cabinet officials, businesspeople, and university professors. The preamble to the letter voiced support for the Saudi royal family but called for the creation of a consultative council, municipal councils, modernization and independence of the judicial system, socioeconomic equality for all Saudis, greater media freedoms, and a reduction of the role of the religious police in Saudi life. (Municipal councils had briefly existed in the past and had garnered wide participation in local elections but had been discarded in the early 1960s.[99]) The petition called for greater participation of women in business and government. A significant point was that the secular petition reflected long-standing views of the Saudi professional class, but it was also a response to the public debates among *Kuwaitis* within Saudi Arabia, who, during the war, had demanded the reinstatement of Kuwait's suspended constituent assembly.[100]

The second major letter, the so-called religious petition, won the support of fifty-two prominent Islamist scholars and became the framework for the *Mudhakarat al-Nasiha* (Memorandum of Advice), which garnered the support of more than a hundred Islamists. Published outside of Saudi Arabia, the memorandum relentlessly criticized Saudi society, the government, and the socioeconomic system, in addition to calling for Muslim scholars to play a far more direct role in the daily affairs of the kingdom. Echoing the criticisms of al-Hawali's tape, the memorandum condemned the Saudi state for permitting Western social values to take hold, for failing to spend money on weapons wisely, for not seeking Muslim rather than US support to fight the Gulf War, and for providing insufficient funds for the social welfare, education, and health of ordinary Saudis. It also called for an independent judiciary and the creation of mechanisms to account for the spending of many governmental agencies and commissions. Throughout the text, there was an implicit criticism: Saudis had lost God's favor and brought on Iraq's invasion of Kuwait by distancing themselves from Islam and God's core teachings.[101]

A year and a half later, in the spring of 1992, the Saudi government responded to these twin challenges with three major reform programs: the Basic Law of Government, a consultative council, and a reorganization of Saudi regional government. Riyadh could not ignore public anger over the fact that its vast oil wealth had been of little use in defending the homeland in a crisis. Nor could it ignore the fact that Islamic and secular elements had effectively seized on this anger over the war to call for reform. The Basic Law established that Saudi Arabia was a sovereign Arab and Islamic state that was committed to promoting Arab-Islamic values, including Islamic human rights, equality before the law, and an independent judiciary. Although the Basic Law outlined the state's responsibility to provide employment, health care, and other social services, it also highlighted the patriarchal structure of the family as the core foundation of Saudi society.[102]

The Basic Law also created a sixty-member national consultative council, which was empowered to propose and interpret laws, as well as parallel councils on the regional level. It is striking that the regional councils were empowered to set development plans and initiate other regional reforms on their own, although the king had the power to appoint the members of these councils. In a move designed to win the supporters of the secular petition, the king appointed mostly Western-educated and secular technocrats to the national consultative council and few religiously trained officials.[103]

The Basic Law also defined the duties of the provincial governors and their relationship with the Saudi interior ministry. This reform, which signaled the first time that such relationships were defined in law, was an effort by the central government to address corruption at the local level, which was then a chronic problem.[104] In typical fashion, the Saudi government had heard complaints and responded to them with a solution that was meant to address the competing components of the kingdom's diverse society.

Bahrain

Bahraini intellectuals were similarly successful at first in pursuing limited democratic change through petitions. In 1992, two of the island's principal opposition groups, the Popular Front for the Liberation of Bahrain, which had a broad base among the island's working class, and the National Liberation Front, a secular group that cut across sectarian lines, presented a petition to the Bahraini emir signed by 350 prominent citizens. The petition called on the emir to restore Bahrain's constitution and elected assembly, both of which he had suspended in 1975 after members of the assembly challenged his budget, his ties with the United States, and his management of the island's common land.[105]

In response, the emir created a council analogous to Saudi Arabia's. The initial council included a broad cross section of Bahrainis, including equal numbers of Shia and Sunni Muslims. But the Speaker was a Shia Muslim, an apparent recognition of the numerical majority of the Shia population and the fact that the Sunnis dominated the other levels of government. Bahrain's diverse opposition groups seemingly had real reason for optimism for the first time in decades.[106]

The optimism was short lived, however. The new council lacked the powers of the old assembly and had a limited agenda—namely, building sewage treatment plants, passing antismoking ordinances, and debating the merits of breast-feeding babies versus giving them formula. The council could not address the bedrock issues of the kingdom, such as unemployment and sectarian divisions. By the summer of 1994, there were mass demonstrations and violence. When more than 20,000 Bahrainis signed a petition that called for the restoration of the parliament, an end to corruption, a reduction in unemployment, and a curtailment of expatriate labor, the government reacted harshly, arresting thousands of Shia, including leading clerics, and accused Shia Iran of fomenting violence.[107]

Under this pressure, the organizations and institutions that had long bridged divisions among Bahrainis began to collapse. Instead, Sunni and Shia Islamists thrived, finding a base among the impoverished masses who had been neglected by the Bahraini government. Mirroring the actions of the Muslim Brotherhood in Egypt and of Hezbollah in Lebanon, the Bahraini Islamists provided health care, education, and other social services through charities and civic organizations to disadvantaged Sunni and Shia Bahrainis. Among the Shia, the al-Wifaq emerged as the most important of these types of Islamist organizations. It included a host of political groups, such as Bahraini supporters of Hizb al-Da'wa, an important Shia Iraqi political party. For the rest of the 1990s, Bahrain experienced a level of ongoing violence and political instability that was unheard of in other states in the region until the US invasion of Iraq in 2003.[108]

Kuwait

Kuwait's assembly also reflected the desire of the emirate's population to regain democratic freedoms, which had been suspended several times in the past. Political activists were successful in the 1990s because of the confluence of three factors.

First, the Kuwaiti government desired to reestablish its domestic legitimacy, which had been badly damaged by its poor performance during the invasion. Ordinary Kuwaitis, on the other hand, made it clear in numerous forums that they wanted a return to democracy.[109]

Second, during the run-up to the Gulf War, there had been significant public debate in the United States over the wisdom of going to war to restore a monarchy. This debate had in part informed the Saudis' decision to establish a consultative council, but the debate had an even greater impact on Kuwait's leaders. Since they depended on US military power more than ever, they could not risk the chance that US public opinion would prevent the US government from protecting Kuwait in a future crisis. Thus, it was imperative that Kuwait at least *look* democratic.

Third, the Kuwaiti government could rest assured that its allies since the 1970s—the Islamists—would do well in postwar elections. During the war, the Samidun had won widespread recognition for their resistance to Iraqi rule. In late 1990, the Kuwaiti government established a Higher Advisory Committee charged with reviewing laws and making recommendations on how to ensure that these laws conformed to Islamic law.[110]

When the monarchy was restored in 1991, the government helped guarantee Islamist control of key financial, educational, and charitable institutions. The Kuwaiti government praised the role of Islamist activists, downplayed the role of women and other groups, and allowed the Islamists to define Iraq's invasion and occupation in terms of their own agenda. The Islamists, who were especially impressed with the piety of the Saudis whom they had met while in exile in Saudi Arabia, argued that the invasion and occupation of Kuwait signaled God's displeasure with Kuwaitis' lavish lifestyle. Only by returning to Islam could Kuwaitis realistically guard against further divine retribution. In October 1992, the Islamists overcame religious and tribal divisions in Kuwaiti society by winning nineteen out of fifty seats in the parliamentary elections, compared to the nine seats they had won in the previous Kuwaiti parliamentary election in 1986.[111]

Qatar and the UAE

In the southern Gulf, government leaders did not feel the pressure for change that their peers did in the rest of the region. The legitimacy of these governments was not seriously challenged by allying with Washington in response to Iraq's invasion of Kuwait. Nor was there significant public debate about the wisdom of postwar political and security arrangements with Washington, which were seen as a guarantee against future actions by Iran and Saudi Arabia as well as by Iraq. Both the UAE and Qatar had long-running territorial conflicts with Iran and Saudi Arabia and believed that Riyadh and Tehran did not fully recognize their independence.

It should therefore come as no surprise that the Qatari emir reacted harshly when fifty-four prominent Qataris presented a petition in 1992 that was similar to the 1991 "secular" petition in Saudi Arabia, calling for the creation of an elected national assembly. Although the emir had long promised to create an assembly, he ordered the telephones of the signatories to be tapped, confiscated their passports, barred some from leaving the country, and even arrested a few. After that, all the signatories faced government harassment and were strongly pressured to withdraw their signatures from the petition and to personally apologize to the emir, in whose hands power firmly remained, just as it had before Iraq's invasion of Kuwait.[112]

Nor did war bring significant change to the UAE, where there were no petitioners. In 1991 the federation re-ratified the provisional constitution, which had been in place since the federation's founding in 1971. The federation had two legislative bodies: the Supreme Council of Rulers and the Federal National Council. The first, composed of the rulers of the UAE emirates, was the higher legislative body; the second was a consultative council analogous to the one in Saudi Arabia. The rulers of the UAE saw little reason to change the federation's system of government.[113]

Oman

By contrast, Oman's consultative council, the Majlis al-Shura, emerged in a sociopolitical context that was very different from those of the other Gulf states. Founded in 1991, the council reflected the strategy of the ruler, Sultan Qaboos, to expand popular participation in government gradually instead of implementing a constitution and a parliament akin to those in Kuwait. Nine years after seizing power in 1970, Qaboos created the advisory Council of Agriculture, Industry, and Fisheries, which in 1981 became the State Consultative Council (SCC), a purely advisory body selected by the sultan. The SCC included ordinary Omanis, bureaucrats, and senior officials from Oman's five regions. The Majlis al-Shura differed little from the SCC, except that government officials could not serve, and women were not barred from serving.[114]

Qaboos also benefited from the fact that Iraq's invasion of Kuwait did not impact Oman in the same way that it did Kuwait and Saudi Arabia—both of which faced repeated attacks on their territories and the potential collapse of existing national governments. Although US and UK forces used Omani air facilities, Oman did not provide the same financial or military assistance to the war effort as did Kuwait, Saudi Arabia, and the UAE. Qaboos never faced the questions about the sultanate's role in the war and about the failure of government that one found in Kuwait and Saudi Arabia. This did not mean, however, that Qaboos was unaware of regional political sensitivities and how they might impact his foreign and domestic standing. His decision to announce the formation of the council in December 1990, weeks before Desert Storm started, suggested that he hoped to deflect criticism of his strong support for the US position.[115]

Qaboos had good reason to be careful. In 1994, his government uncovered a wide-ranging Islamist conspiracy that included an ambassador-designate to the United States, an undersecretary at the Ministry of Commerce and Industry, businessmen, members of the Omani Chamber of Commerce, school principals, and engineers. Qaboos reacted to the discovery with fury, arguing that the Islamists were in reality an opposition party dedicated to overthrowing his government. Subsequently, the Omani government carefully monitored the population for signs of further Islamist tendencies. Potential Islamist figures were isolated, retired, or given harmless executive positions.[116]

The Saudi Islamist Challenge

The Islamist Frame

As serious as the Islamist threat had been in Oman in 1994, it did not match the Islamist challenge in Saudi Arabia. Saudi Islamists represented a diverse segment of the kingdom's elites, which included university professors, judges, ambassadors, business leaders, bureaucrats, and religious scholars. Many were Western educated and spoke Western languages. They endorsed the ideas contained in the Saudi "religious" petition and supported Islamists in Oman and Kuwait. They saw the Saudi alliance with Washington as a dangerous step on a slippery slope that led to Western materialism, hedonism, and other social practices incompatible with Islamic values. Even before the Gulf War, Saudi Islamists were wary of the Islamic credentials of Saudi Arabia and its neighbors, whose governments they accused of suppressing basic human rights, squandering oil wealth on luxuries and foreign-made weapons, and serving Western interests at the expense of Muslims. They asked how governments that committed themselves to upholding Islamic values could permit foreign elements to enter Gulf society and promote female employees in their embassies abroad.[117]

Saudi Arabia's decision in August 1990 to ask the United States to defend the kingdom's northern border from Iraq only reinforced all of these arguments.[118] In a moment of crisis, Islamists argued, the Gulf governments should have turned to other Muslim governments for assistance or have utilized their own weapons first. Furthermore, they argued, the Gulf governments opened Islam's holiest lands to the US military and provided billions of dollars in subsidies. Saudi Arabia and its fellow GCC governments' actions after the war were almost as damning in the Islamist frame, because the Gulf states purchased new Western weapons systems, which was an astonishing decision, since the weapons they had bought before the war had failed so spectacularly in the Gulf War. The price tag of the weapons systems required the governments of the region to cut social spending or to go deeply into debt. Islamists repeatedly asked how Arab-Muslim monarchies could partner with the United States, which provided billions of dollars in aid every year to Israel, the principal enemy of the Palestinians.[119]

According to the Islamists, the answer to this question was *fasad* (corruption). In order to earn US protection, they asserted, the Gulf states protected Western interests and sold the region's wealth, values, and traditions at bargain prices. It mattered little, so went the Islamist argument, if these actions violated fundamental tenets of Gulf culture and Islamic law, so long as the corrupt rulers remained in power. The Gulf governments, Islamists contended, had forfeited their legitimacy and risked bringing God's wrath onto Gulf societies.[120]

Within this frame of thought, the way to restore justice was to sever the linkage between Washington and the Gulf states, abandon Western social practices, and re-Islamize society. Such a re-Islamization would go beyond mainstream interpretations of Islam and sharply curtail the rights then enjoyed by women and non-Muslims. But the Islamists' agenda did not yet include overthrowing existing governments; it was better, they felt, to reform them. Nor could Islamists realistically have overthrown existing governments, even if they had intended to do so. Their organizations were marginal, lacked prominent leaders, and contained dozens of members at most. There were hardly enough members to seize Mecca's Grand Mosque again, let alone challenge even the weakest of Gulf monarchies.

Many Gulf Arabs, they said, sympathized with Islamist arguments. The conservative Islamist social milieu promoted in the 1970s had produced a generation of activists and others who sympathized with the Islamist view. These people also distrusted Washington and were angry at the gap between their governments' rhetoric and reality. The widespread sympathy toward Islamist views explains why the Gulf governments imprisoned so many Islamists or forced them to live abroad. In the decade after the Gulf War, Islamist groups such as the Committee for the Defense of Legitimate Rights (CDLR) and the Movement for Islamic Reform in Arabia emerged as the most prominent opposition, at home and abroad, to the Gulf states. Most of all, they benefited from a unique nexus of technology and shrewd marketing to Western audiences.[121]

Islamists in London

The new generation of Islamists in London was not the first group of exiled opposition figures to challenge the legitimacy of the Gulf states or to use foreign media to do so. Arab nationalists and Nasserists in the 1950s and later Islamists in the 1980s had mirrored the beliefs of their adopted nations, especially Egypt and Iraq, and often won direct support from host governments. But the CDLR, Bahraini opposition groups, and others established a base of support in the 1990s in the West—an ironic choice, given their rhetorical attacks on Western power and the corrosive impact of Western culture.[122]

Rather than supporting Islamists, Western governments worked hard to deport them to third states or back to the Gulf states. In 1996, the British government, in response to heavy lobbying from the Saudi government, tried to deport the head of the CDLR, Muhammad al-Mas'ari, to Dominica.[123] Following the attacks of September 11, 2001, on Washington and New York, pressure on Islamists intensified even further. One could hardly imagine a less friendly environment than the United States or the United Kingdom from which to oppose Riyadh and the other Gulf states.[124]

But al-Mas'ari, the founder of the CDLR, the Saudi intellectual Saad al-Faqih, and other Islamists thrived in the West because they knew that it offered them three powerful tools to challenge the Gulf states.

First, the West offered Islamists open and virtually unregulated access to fax machines, electronic mail, the Internet, and electronic finance. From his base in London, al-Mas'ari could send his pamphlets about Islamic opposition in Saudi Arabia to a much broader audience than al-Hawali's tapes had reached in 1990 and without the fear of direct state retribution. The Internet, in particular, allowed adherents in the Gulf states to learn about Islamists' activities anonymously without taking the dangerous step of attending a meeting or interacting with opposition leaders and their associates.[125]

Second, al-Faqih and others could repackage themselves as prominent leaders with a following measured in hits to their websites instead of membership rolls.[126]

Third, London Islamists could utilize their media to raise funds for their organizations.[127]

Nevertheless, al-Mas'ari's principal audience was not just in the Gulf: it included the dozens of Arab and Western media outlets, nongovernmental organizations (NGOs), and reporters based in London and elsewhere, including CNN, Human Rights Watch, Amnesty International, and other NGOs. Few if any of the individuals who worked for such organizations, including Arab reporters, had expertise in the Gulf. Yet they understood that there was considerable global and Arab public interest in the Gulf after Iraq's invasion of Kuwait. Al-Mas'ari, who had a doctorate in chemistry from a German university, and other Gulf Islamists were well educated, fluent in multiple languages, and willing to appear on television. This was a perfect match for CNN, other satellite news channels, and NGOs that were interested in Saudi Arabia or the other Gulf states.[128]

The Islamists in London seized this opportunity, using free air time to establish their position as authentic political leaders. Al-Faqih was especially effective in forwarding this view on the PBS program *Frontline,* which is critically acclaimed in the United States for its balanced reporting and investigative journalism.[129] He appeared there as an academic who offered informed opinions on Saudi society, the life of Osama bin Laden, and the Saudi royal family. The program included a Saudi "opposition" video with commentary by al-Faqih, which questioned the assertions of Saudi Arabia's longtime ambassador to Washington, Prince Bandar bin Sultan. Al-Faqih asked hauntingly about Saudi Arabia, "Who can believe that a country pumping nine million barrels a day with a small population of between ten and twenty million peoples is two hundred billion dollars in debt?"[130] The answer was corruption.

Islamists also marketed themselves as indispensable sources for Western scholars and journalists who wrote on modern Islam, Islamic political and religious movements, and the threat of Islamic terrorism. Most of these Western scholars and journalists had spent little time in the Islamic world, did not know the languages spoken there, and did not have the time or the inclination to gain experience on their own. Instead of traveling to Afghanistan, Saudi Arabia, and other lands that Westerners saw as dangerous or too opaque to understand, they could go to London to talk with English-speaking Arab Gulf Islamists who had access to Islamists around the world. Islamists cultivated these Western contacts and both consciously and unconsciously presented themselves, their societies, and their political movements in terms that were understandable to westerners and consciously played to their biases.[131]

Bin Laden, Al-Qaida, and Terrorism

There was no individual whom Western journalists and scholars worked harder to talk to and learn more about than Osama bin Laden, the Saudi Islamist *par excellence*. Although Bin Laden did not live in London, his followers, including members of the Advice and Reform Committee (ARC), built close ties to al-Mas'ari and other Islamists. The scion of a wealthy family, Bin Laden had fought in Afghanistan against the Russians and previously had offered the services of his Afghan fighters to the Saudi government when Iraq seized Kuwait in 1990. When he publicly opposed the decision to invite US troops into Saudi Arabia, the Saudi government stripped him of his Saudi citizenship. He was first exiled to Sudan and then, under pressure from Riyadh and Washington, left Africa to settle in Afghanistan. By the late 1990s, he had supplanted the CDLR as the most strident public critic of the Saudi royal family, Israel, and the United States. In February 1998, Bin Laden and a select group of other Islamists announced the creation of the World Islamic Front against Jews and Crusaders, which shortly thereafter became Al-Qaida.[132]

Utilizing Western democratic theory blended with Islamist arguments, Bin Laden presented a coherent vision of a worldwide Islamic movement, its goals, and its enemies. He argued that the US people, because they elect their government, were responsible for its actions and those of Saudi Arabia and other US-supported governments.[133] He chastised Muslims for valuing materiality (*dunya*) over justice (*adal*) and for not upholding their dignity, especially that of women.[134] If Americans and other westerners did not heed his warnings, he predicted that they would suffer from ever-escalating attacks on Western targets and pro-Western governments, including Saudi Arabia and other Arab Gulf states. To make his point clear, he took responsibility on behalf of Al-Qaida for terrorist attacks against US targets in Saudi Arabia in 1996, Kenya and Tanzania in 1998, Yemen in 2000, and the United States itself in 2001. Furthermore, rumors of failed terrorist plots in the Gulf flooded the international media in the late 1990s and early 2000s.[135]

Bin Laden presented three unique challenges to the Arab Gulf states. First, he committed himself and his followers to overthrowing the Gulf governments, no matter what the cost, since he was comfortable using violence if negotiations and reforms did not meet his objectives.

Second, he had a far keener understanding of media and technology than any member of the CDLR. For example, he ruthlessly took advantage of the interest of Western reporters in his actions, using carefully choreographed interviews to emphasize his own importance. He and his followers also pioneered use of the Internet and other similar tools to recruit, train, and manage a burgeoning worldwide network of Islamic activists.[136] By 2006, Al-Qaida's own media company, al-Sahab, regularly produced videos and posted them to the Internet for global distribution.[137] These featured Bin Laden along with rising leaders in the organization, such as Abu Yahya al-Libi.[138]

Third, Bin Laden merged the use of modern technologies with traditional Muslim symbols of authority. To begin with, he assumed the title of shaikh (religious leader), acquired *fatwas* from senior religious leaders to justify his and his associates' actions, and always spoke in superb quranic Arabic. Furthermore, he always emphasized his austerity, piety, and personal sacrifice for justice. Bin Laden's personal image masterfully contrasted with the popular view among Saudis and other Muslims of the al-Saud: a royal family that was outwardly dedicated to upholding Islamic principles but that actually lived in opulent luxury. Even worse, the Saudi royal family had firmly allied itself with the United States, which attacked Iraq, a Muslim nation. The implied hypocrisy of the royal family was impossible to ignore and implicitly reinforced Western fears that the Saudi government would one day collapse in a revolution akin to the one that overthrew the shah of Iran in 1979.[139]

Satellite Broadcasting

Saudi Space

Bin Laden's already formidable position was enhanced still further by his ability to utilize and appear on a new factor in the politics of the Arab Gulf, satellite television. That one of Saudi Arabia's fiercest critics could take advantage of this new medium should come as no surprise, given that Saudi Arabian financiers were among the earliest individuals in the Gulf to realize the political and commercial potential of the medium after the emergence of CNN in 1990 and 1991.[140] These men understood that satellite television could serve Saudi national interests in much the same way that radio stations, terrestrial television stations, and pan-Arabic daily newspapers had helped to defend the sovereignty of Saudi Arabia against Fascist radio programs, Arab nationalists, and a host of other threats in the past.

Starting in 1991, a number of Saudi leaders, including King Fahd himself, created new satellite channels for the Arab world: the Middle East Broadcasting Corporation (MBC), Arab Radio and Television (ART), and Orbitz.[141] The new networks consciously modeled themselves on CNN, but by broadcasting in Arabic, were meant to be more accessible to Middle Eastern audiences than the US news channel. Based in Western Europe rather than Riyadh, the new networks hired educated Arabic-speaking professionals living in London, Rome, and other Western cities as anchors, writers, editors, and producers. But the Saudi ownership and purpose of these networks were clear for all to see. In 1997, the Saudi daily newspaper *al-Riyadh* observed in an opinion piece that "when talk in Arab media circles turns to Arab television news, the sentence 'space is Saudi' is often heard."[142] By *space* the author meant not only editorial control but the literal outer space—that is, the realm from which Arab satellite television is directed at earth.

Saudi space, however, faced a series of financial, legal, and market challenges. Saudis invested hundreds of millions of dollars in MBC, ART, and Orbitz for new staff and equipment. In fact, Orbitz alone may have cost $1 billion to put on the air.[143] Because these types of costs were significantly above advertising revenues, ART lost approximately $168 million per year in the late 1990s, and MBC lost $100 million just in 1997.[144] Equipment and satellite packages for viewers, initially priced in the neighborhood of $10,000 each, had to be cut by a quarter to win subscribers, whose numbers were thus far below expectations.[145] Also devastating to advertising revenues was the fact that Saudi religious elites convinced Riyadh to place severe limits on satellite dishes within the kingdom, the wealthiest media and entertainment market in the Middle East.[146] Similar bans were in effect in Bahrain and Qatar.[147] Although more Saudis and others gained access over time, the networks' inability to take advantage of the kingdom's market devastated their ad revenues.

Saudi satellite channels also faced other serious commercial and intellectual challenges. Not only did CNN, European, and Asian channels compete for the Arab and Middle East market, but by 1996 every Arab state except Iraq had either state-run satellite broadcasters or a significant private presence in regional satellite television, or both. In the UAE, which had an open-skies policy, individual emirates had their own satellite stations, and viewership reached 81 percent of UAE households by 1995.[148] The Kurds and other regional nonstate actors also started satellite channels.[149] It was impossible for Saudi satellite television stations to turn a profit, let alone stay on the air, without regular infusions of cash from the owners. By the late 1990s, MBC had fired more than a hundred staff members and severely curtailed its ambitious growth forecasts.[150]

Even though the costs of keeping satellite channels on the air were daunting, they paled in comparison with the intellectual challenges of creating "CNN in Arabic."[151] Although the networks promised to protect intellectual freedom and create an environment akin to that of a US newsroom, ART producers and journalists were expected to abide by guidelines similar to those of Saudi Arabia's restrictive 1982 press law. In fact, the networks regularly practiced self-censorship. For example, Orbitz's problems with the BBC are legendary. As part of its £100 million ten-year contract to provide an Arabic news service for the BBC, Orbitz promised not to interfere with the editorial content of the BBC's broadcasts.[152] But when BBC reporters covered Saudi Islamists or human rights in the kingdom, Orbitz broke off the transmission and terminated its contract early.[153] As a consequence, dozens of Arab journalists lost their jobs. Although Orbitz's decision may have protected the interests of the Saudi royal family and the kingdom's regional reputation, it demonstrated that the Saudis were not ready to produce an "Arab" version of CNN and would never dominate satellite television in the Arab world.

"Nothing but the Truth"

Al-Jazeera, a satellite service based in Saudi Arabia's neighbor, Qatar, eventually accomplished both of these objectives. Modeled as an editorially independent, public corporation akin to the BBC, al-Jazeera went on the air on November 1, 1996.[154] It followed Qatar's tradition—established with *al-Sakir* in the 1970s—as the launching pad for successful pan-Arab media. The network hired a number of the journalists who had been part of the BBC-Orbitz partnership, and these individuals helped to create a programming content and style that resembled CNN and was similarly provocative.[155] The network later broadened its mandate to include Western journalists, such as veteran ABC news correspondent Dave Marash, a Jewish American, and Josh Rushing, a former US Marine information officer, who was made famous by the movie *Control Room*.[156]

The network's chief benefactor, Qatari emir Hamd bin Khalifa al-Thani, had broached the idea of a private pan-Arabic network based in Qatar as early as 1994.[157] He saw it as central to the emirate's future and, like King Faysal in the 1960s, saw mass media as central to defending his state's sovereignty vis-à-vis its neighbors. After seizing power from his father in a bloodless coup in 1995, al-Thani established al-Jazeera. His motivation was to differentiate

Qatar from its neighbors by holding elections in which women participated, by promoting transparency and efficiency in government, and by establishing close ties with Israel, Iran, Hamas, and other entities traditionally shunned by members of the GCC.[158]

Qatar's new satellite network fit perfectly within al-Thani's vision by granting airtime to viewpoints that rarely appeared on Saudi-owned satellite television and by rigorously applying CNN's news model to Arab journalism. Al-Jazeera's initial annual operating budget was $137 million, but it had no trouble supplementing al-Thani's subsidy, since it found new revenue streams in advertising and the sale of news footage.[159] The network opened offices in key Muslim and Arab countries as well as in Western nations and Israel.[160] The network's decision to hire Arabic-speaking journalists, some of whom had been fired from the Orbitz-BBC partnership, set it apart from CNN and other Western news organizations in the Middle East, whose correspondents and producers rarely spoke local languages, depending instead on staffs of local translators and guides. It is significant that such individuals could easily be employed by governments, intelligence agencies, or political groups to promote specific viewpoints to Western journalists and to shape Western media reports about the region They could also steer Western news organizations away from potentially sensitive political issues, individuals, or geographic areas. In effect, local staff could limit what even the most intrepid Western journalist saw simply through translations or by warning that a particular neighborhood or individual area was unsafe. Thus, although Saudi Arabia and other Gulf nations frequently complained about biased news coverage of their politics in the West, it was an open secret among officials in the region that Western news organizations often produced exactly what the governments of those nations wanted.

Al-Jazeera's broadcast theme—*al-ray wa al-ray al-akhar* (a view and the other view)—permeated its lively discussion on call-in shows, which touched on a host of long taboo subjects in the Arab world, including family planning, religion, gender issues, and corruption. Producers consciously picked controversial guests and themes that would both clash and address Arab concerns not covered by CNN. Al-Jazeera also deployed correspondents to war zones, airing graphic images of Palestinian uprisings and US military actions in Iraq and Afghanistan. In a 1998 interview, the network's director, Muhammad Jassem al-Ali, stated al-Jazeera's philosophy: "We are not against any government. All we do is tell the truth and nothing but the truth."[161]

The network's philosophy and approach to covering news reflected the makeup of its staff as much as that of the Qatari government. Most of the network's correspondents, anchors, and other employees were not Qatari Arabs, which gave the network a pan-Arab rather than Qatari feel. Particularly noticeable were the women on air, many of whom dressed in Western fashions rarely worn by Qatari nationals. The network was much more of a mirror of the entire Arab world. One could not say that al-Jazeera had created "Qatari Space" in the same way that Saudi satellite channels had earlier created "Saudi Space."

Nonetheless, al-Jazeera rarely criticized Qatar and its foreign policy directly or through its guest speakers. Instead, it provided a platform, among other things, for Israelis, Americans, and Arab figures who criticized Qatar's Arab Gulf neighbors and other Arab states. For example, during coverage of Saddam Hussein's Army Day speech in 1999, al-Jazeera broadcast in unedited form his call to overthrow all Arab monarchs.[162] Also, the interviews and messages associated with Bin Laden, which al-Jazeera transmitted live to CNN and other networks around the world, transformed al-Jazeera into an international household name and put its host nation, Qatar, "on the map."[163]

A New Platform

The second Palestinian intifada, in 2000 and 2001, revealed al-Jazeera's power and its ability to deliver an Arab view of key events in the Middle East. Although CNN and other networks provided coverage within Israel and of acts of violence perpetrated against Israelis, al-Jazeera covered acts of violence against both Israelis *and* Palestinians. For example, the network gave prominent coverage to the death of a young boy who was caught for hours in the crossfire between Israeli soldiers and Palestinian gunmen, along with the grief of his father, who held him as he died.[164] This emotional footage became famous among Arab audiences and later appeared in Al-Qaida videos, including the infamous tape that appeared in the Middle East in the weeks leading up to the terrorist attacks of September 11, 2001.

Al-Jazeera's coverage of the September 11 terrorist attacks, the US invasion of Afghanistan in 2001 (when it was originally the sole international network in Afghanistan), and the US invasion of Iraq in 2003 further cemented the role of the network in the Arab world as a leading independent news organization.[165] A Gallup poll in April 2002 found that al-Jazeera was the most popular network for news in Kuwait and Saudi Arabia, earning 56 percent and 47 percent of viewers, respectively, with 54 percent of Kuwaitis regarding the network as objective.[166] (By comparison, only 11 percent of Kuwaitis and 2 percent of Saudis saw CNN as objective in the same study.[167]) A Gallup poll in November 2002 found similar results among Kuwaitis and Saudis, with 56 percent of the former and 47 percent of the latter turning to al-Jazeera first for their information on world affairs.[168] Nor was al-Jazeera limited to Gulf Arabs: the Gallup poll found that the network had a wide following in Lebanon, Morocco, and other Arab countries, not to mention hundreds of thousands of viewers in the United States and Europe.[169]

This popularity in part explains why al-Jazeera became required viewing for academics, government officials, and anyone else interested in the Middle East and the broader Islamic world. The network added to its viewership after it launched several spinoff channels in 2006, including a 24-hour news channel in English and an English-language website.[170] Although the English-language television channel failed to win wide distribution in the United States, al-Jazeera's English-language website received more than 3 million hits a week from within the United States by 2008.[171] Furthermore, in 2008 the Qatari network's videos were among the most popular of those featured on the video-sharing website YouTube.[172] In addition, US soldiers deployed in Afghanistan regularly watch the network at a North Atlantic Treaty Organization (NATO) base in Kabul.[173]

In the 1990s, al-Jazeera presented a political and security challenge to the Gulf states. It was a seemingly unregulated platform for broadcasting dissent in Arabic into homes throughout the region. Using language similar to the British agent in Kuwait in 1935, who hoped that Egyptian state radio would remain "under proper control," Arab and Western government leaders pressed the Qatari government to limit al-Jazeera's coverage of embarrassing or politically sensitive stories. Crown Prince Abdullah of Saudi Arabia reportedly informed the Qatari emir that the satellite network "encouraged terrorism, discredited the Gulf states, harmed the Arab royal families, and threatened Arab stability."[174] Other states used far more symbolic measures to signal their displeasure with al-Jazeera's actions by closing the network's offices within their borders, recalling their ambassadors to Qatar, suing in domestic courts, and rejecting the network's application for membership in the Arab States' Broadcasting Union.[175]

None of these actions, however, produced changes in Qatar's foreign policy or in al-Jazeera's programs. Because of the network's official independence and the absence of international satellite laws regulating the transmission of content, Qatari government officials could reject official pressure from international sources to modify stories and change programming. What counted for al-Jazeera was not political considerations but which stories or shows boosted its ratings. If that meant interviewing Bin Laden or covering anti–United States protests in Bahrain, the stories received airtime. It did not matter if the stories accused Saudi Arabia of abandoning the Palestinian cause or alleged that Kuwaitis had killed Palestinians and Iraqis with acid in 1991.

The strength of al-Jazeera's regional influence is perhaps best demonstrated by the fact that the Algerian government felt in 1999 that the only way it could prevent its citizens from seeing a particularly unflattering story was by cutting off electricity to its capital city, Algiers.[176] The option that had been employed in the past—jamming transmissions—was no longer possible for Algeria or any other government in the Arab world, including the Gulf states.

The Politics of Socioeconomic Limits

If al-Jazeera revealed the limits of the Gulf states to control the flow of information into and out of their societies, international energy markets made clear the socioeconomic limitations of economies and government budgets based almost exclusively on hydrocarbon production to build modern states. At a time when oil revenue as a percentage of GDP fell substantially in most states in the Gulf, oil revenue as a percentage of government income actually increased modestly in most Gulf states.[177] For example, the UAE's income from investments, which was at one time enough to rival its large oil revenues, dropped from 20 percent to 10 percent of GDP in the 1990s.[178] Kuwait's overseas investment funds, valued at $117 billion in the 1980s, were thought to be worth as little as $60 billion in the 1990s.[179]

Nevertheless, most Gulf states continued to spend substantial amounts on the social welfare programs they had started in the 1970s. In the UAE, domestic spending increased by 10 percent a year between 1992 and 1995 alone.[180] The most important factor driving the spending was population growth and the costs associated with it. Gulf families remained large, and women bore children at rates higher than those of many developing nations. These burgeoning new families required new infrastructures (especially schools, hospitals, and housing), and their sons and daughters could command higher salaries than the expatriate workers they were meant to replace in the workforce.

The population growth statistics for the Gulf in the 1990s are startling. In 1990, the collective population of the GCC states stood at 23,534,000.[181] A decade later, it had risen to 30,641,961.[182] Because 40 percent of the population of the GCC states in 2000 was below the age of fifteen, and only 2.5 percent was above the age of sixty-five, the Gulf's population was certain to rise at a rapid pace well into the future.[183] Kuwaiti electricity and water subsidies, which increased from 107 million Kuwaiti dinars in 1998 to 431 million dinars in 2004, provided a preview of what lay ahead for the Gulf states.[184]

These types of budget increases might have been potentially sustainable if the Gulf states had won foreign (or domestic) investments and if oil prices had remained high or moderately high for sustained periods. Nearly $700 billion of assets of Gulf individuals and governments flowed out of the GCC to safe havens in the 1990s, mostly to the United States, Europe, and Japan.[185] Restrictions on foreign ownership remained in most Gulf industries, which resulted in the region's attracting only 0.2 percent of the world's foreign direct investment and in its stock markets' underperforming other emerging markets in Asia, Eastern Europe, and Latin America.[186]

The global oil market only made things more problematic. Following the Gulf War, oil markets underwent their second collapse in as many decades. Although oil prices stabilized in the mid-1990s, they fell again in 1999, when they reached a low of $10 a barrel. Economic growth slowed and current account surpluses dropped. Between 1991 and 1997, the UAE's economic growth did not exceed 1.3 percent annually.[187] Saudi Arabia and several other GCC states recorded low current account surpluses in 1998, which were half of what they had achieved in 1995.[188] The Saudi American Bank found that 20 percent of Saudi men between the ages of twenty and twenty-nine had no paid work, and the rest of Saudi society was even worse off, with an unemployment rate of 25 percent.[189] Ordinary Omanis, Bahrainis, and Emiratis registered even higher rates.[190]

The Gulf states dealt with these declines in the same way they had done in the 1980s—that is, by incurring budget deficits and liquidating overseas assets. As a consequence, Gulf budget deficits skyrocketed: Qatar's deficit in 1995 and 1996 was equal to a third of its annual budget; Kuwait's deficit was equal to 36 percent of its budget between 1990 and 1996; the UAE's deficit in 1994 was 14.6 percent of the federation's GDP; and Saudi deficits were 19 percent of GDP in 1991.[191] Global financial institutions raised questions about how deep the official Gulf pockets—as opposed to the royal pockets—really were.

To make matters worse for the Gulf states, population and spending growth was not accompanied by a reduction in *expatriate* workers. Despite decades of programs aimed at increasing the percentage of nationals participating in GCC public and private workforces, the percentage of nationals in the Gulf workforce decreased, from 40.2 percent in 1975 to 27.9 percent in 2000.[192] Two of the poorest GCC States, Bahrain and Oman, witnessed especially steep declines in the percentage of their citizens working in their workforce: from approximately 60 percent in 1975 to 44.3 percent and 44.6 percent, respectively, in 2000.[193] Overseas workers had of course filled the gap.

The Gulf states had remarkably achieved the worst possible outcome in their labor policies in the 1990s. There were more expatriate workers—who sent most of their salaries out of the region—along with more indigenous workers—who depended on state assistance. The factors that led to these imbalances were not hard to find. Many Gulf nationals—particularly younger men—failed to find private-sector employment. Just like their parents in the 1970s, they lacked the necessary skills to enter the private sector or they could make higher and more secure salaries in the public sector. In 1995, the UAE created 50,000 jobs in the private sector; just 30 were taken by Emirati nationals.[194] (In all, 736 nationals worked in the workforce in 1995, 1.5 percent of the UAE labor force.[195]) In 1994, 16,259 Saudis graduated from Saudi universities, and only a third of them found jobs in the private sector.[196] Nor were the experiences of Saudi and Emirati nationals unusual. Expatriates made up 83 percent of the workforce in Qatar, 82 percent in Kuwait, and 60 percent in Bahrain.[197]

An equally important factor was that population growth—indigenous and expatriate—pressed the environment of the Gulf states, especially limited regional water supplies. Between 1980 and 2000, demand for water grew exponentially in the Gulf states, forcing them to use quantities of water hundreds or thousands of times more than domestic renewable resources of water. To make up this difference between demand and supply of water, Gulf states developed deep underground wells that, in turn, have depleted regional water tables. They also built large and expensive desalinization plants that provided water and electricity.[198] One plant—Saudi Arabia's Jubail—accounted for 50 percent of the country's drinking water.[199] What would happen if one of the plants were to malfunction or be destroyed in a military or terrorist attack was unclear. Even if a crisis never materialized, desalinization plants emit dangerous greenhouse gases and pollute waterways and coastal areas.[200] There was little question that it was a costly way of fulfilling two basic human needs in a desert environment: water and electricity.

The financial and environmental realities in the Gulf states, however, reflected far more than just a fall in oil prices; they signaled the emergence of new socioeconomic factors that threatened the longer viability of the cradle-to-grave security provided by GCC welfare states. Meeting the costs of building and running desalinization plants required millions of dollars in investments and thousands of barrels of petroleum. For Bahrain, Oman, Dubai, and Qatar, the latter requirement was especially daunting since it was clear in the 1990s that their petroleum reserves were decreasing rapidly. Although the UAE and Saudi Arabia produced approximately 2.5 million and 11 million barrels per day of oil, respectively, Bahrain's chief oil field, Awali, produced only 35,000 barrels per day throughout the 1990s.[201]

But the differences in production should not hide a larger factor: the rapid increase in population of GCC nationals has decreased the "societal" impact of petroleum income, because there are more people who can demand services funded by oil. This was a shift as important for the people of the Gulf as the collapse of the pearling industry had been in the 1930s and the subsequent discovery of oil supplies in the Gulf region. Whether the Gulf states could depend on oil supplies to maintain their way of life was no longer just a hypothetical question, and the answer clearly was that they could not.

Among the most visible examples of this problem was the largest oil producer, Saudi Arabia. Its per capita income from oil sales was $6,900 in 1996; it had been $19,800 in 1980.[202] The drop in Saudi income placed the kingdom below that of some developing nations and actually below the World Bank's rich-poor median line of $7,620.[203] The reality of the decline in national wealth emerged in a 2003 article and lengthy photo essay on Saudi Arabia in the US magazine *National Geographic*.[204] The article showed pictures of destitute Saudis and expatriates, some of whom lived in squalid conditions, along with extraordinarily wealthy Saudis. Though the story was banned in Saudi Arabia, its key arguments were no secret: rich and poor existed in Saudi Arabia, and there were large concentrations of wealth. Although the average Saudi income was $6,000 in 1999, the National Commercial Bank estimated that there were 120,000 millionaires (out of a population of 22 million), who controlled a combined fortune of more than $400 billion.[205]

Even in states where income was more evenly distributed and the decline in per capita oil income had been less dramatic, there were worrying signs that wealth had declined at the start of the twenty-first century. In the early 2000s beggars and various individuals were observed going door to door requesting money in Dubai and other Emirati cities. Dubai police arrested 1,381 beggars in 2004 and 992 beggars in 2005. Among those arrested were expatriates and nationals of both genders, sometimes from respectable families.[206]

Conclusion

The seeming paradox—poverty and stark deprivation in a land of enormous wealth—was impossible for either Gulf governments or their populations to ignore. It was a perfect foil for al-Mas'ari, Bin Laden, and others who worked to undermine the authority of Gulf states and could be easily televised by al-Jazeera and other international media. New media and communication technologies had transformed the politics of the Gulf, much as they had done in North America and other parts of the world in the 1990s. There was no religious, historical, or sociocultural shield to justify the poverty shown on television or that existed in cities, since it undermined two moral pillars of Gulf monarchial rule that preceded the rise of oil industry. First, the paradox showed that monarchies in the Gulf states could not or would not assist all of their populations in a time of need. They had reneged on their communal obligation, an obligation encapsulated by Ibn Saud's need to "pay, pay, pay" his people. Second, beggars and abject poverty undermined the picture Fahd had painted in his 1986 speech of a technologically advanced, educated, and wealthy Gulf society that remained true to its tribal and religious values.

A new path was clearly needed, but one that differentiated from the approach of the Gulf states of the past two decades, which had been to build enormous financial surpluses when oil prices were high, assume that downturns in oil markets were rare and infrequent, and use oil rents to postpone domestic and international security challenges. In particular, the downturns of the 1980s and 1990s had taught the Gulf states that oil prices—if they remained too high—could lead to sudden declines in oil prices, declines as swift and as devastating as that of pearls in the 1930s. The growth of domestic and expatriate populations meant that oil money, even when it returned to high levels, would not have the per capita impact that it had had as recently as 1980. Nor was an oil-based economy able to address environmental issues or protect against the political challenges posed by Islamist leaders and satellite news channels. Higher oil prices, which ironically led to economic growth, increases in population, and infrastructure projects, intensified such problems by putting greater strains on the environment and by creating further opportunities for opposition figures to point out official malfeasance and corruption.

To their credit, the Gulf states began to adopt a new set of policies to address their financial and economic difficulties in the late 1990s. From Kuwait to Oman, governments privatized such industries as power, cut basic subsidies, and actively courted foreign investment. Agriculture, education, tourism, health care, and manufacturing were opened to foreign investors, some of whom were allowed to buy 100 percent ownership without local partners for the first time. Governments also worked to "sell" a more palatable image of themselves to Western and other overseas audiences to compete with Islamists. In addition, Qatar made a massive investment and took out vast loans to build a new industry, liquefied natural gas (LNG). In 1999 LNG began to pay dividends, and it came to rival oil as Qatar's chief export. Finally, Dubai's service-oriented economy, which I will discuss in greater detail in Chapter 4, suggested the viability of a socioeconomic model not grounded in the export of oil but that nevertheless took advantage of the region's expatriate workforce and linkages to international commerce.

The reforms significantly coincided with the emergence of a new generation of Gulf leaders, many of whom had been educated in the West. They were more willing than their predecessors to adopt or at least seriously consider new approaches to governance and socioeconomic development. They benefited from a significant uptick in oil prices and new investment in the region at the turn of the twenty-first century that eased the financial problems of the 1980s and 1990s. Government surpluses swelled to levels not seen since the 1970s, scores of postponed infrastructure projects were funded, and financial markets rose quickly. At the same time, these leaders would face new challenges that would prove as vexing as anything their predecessors had faced in the 1980s or the 1990s: the US invasion and occupation of Iraq, the war on terrorism, the financial decline of the United States, and the emergence of Iran and other new powers in the Gulf.

Notes

1. "Address by Saudi King and Crown Prince to Hajj Pilgrims," Saudi Press Agency, July 10, 1986, reprinted in Alan de Lacy Rush, ed., *Records of the Hajj: A Documentary History of the Pilgrimage to Mecca*, vol. 8: *The Saudi Period (Since 1952)* (Cambridge: Cambridge University Press Archive Editions, 1993), 689.

2. Shaikh Zayid's advisers in the 1970s reportedly talked him out of building a dome over his capital, Abu Dhabi.

3. Fareed Mohamedi, "The Economy," in *Saudi Arabia: A Country Study*, ed.

Helen Metz, 119 (Washington, DC: Federal Research Division, Library of Congress, 1993).

4. "Address by Saudi King and Crown Prince," 689.

5. Anthony Cordesman, *Saudi Arabia Enters the Twenty-First Century* (New York: Praeger, 2003), 291–294; George Philip, *The Political Economy of International Oil* (Edinburgh, United Kingdom: Edinburgh University Press, 1994), 179–186.

6. Philip, *The Political Economy of International Oil,* 173–174.

7. Ibid.

8. Cordesman, *Saudi Arabia Enters the Twenty-First Century*, 244; Eric Hooglund and Anthony Toth, "United Arab Emirates," in *Persian Gulf States: Country Studies*, ed. Helen Metz, 216 (Washington, DC: Federal Research Division, Library of Congress, 1994).

9. Philip, *The Political Economy of International Oil,* 165.

10. Energy Information Administration, "Table 4.6: OECD Countries and World Petroleum (Oil) Demand, 1970–2007," *February 2009 International Petroleum Monthly*, March 10, 2009 (available at http://www.eia.doe.gov/).

11. Cited in Philip, *The Political Economy of International Oil,* 165–166.

12. Ibid., 164.

13. Ibid., 169.

14. The production of non-OPEC oil exporters was facilitated by the election of conservative governments in the United Kingdom and the United States. These governments were committed to deregulation, to opening new territories for oil exploration, and to allowing market forces to dictate prices. They had little interest in negotiating with OPEC and hoped that lower oil prices could weaken the strategic position of the Soviet Union, which depended on profits earned from exporting oil. Ibid., 162.

15. Energy Information Administration, "Table 4.6: OECD Countries and World Petroleum (Oil) Demand, 1970–2007."

16. Energy Information Administration, "Table 11.7: Crude Oil Prices by Selected Type, 1970–2008," *Annual Energy Review 2007* (Washington, DC: United States Government Printing Office), 351 (available at http://www.eia.doe.gov/).

17. Philip, *The Political Economy of International Oil,* 173–174.

18. Ibid.

19. Gary Sick, "The Coming Crisis," in *The Persian Gulf at the Millennium: Essays in Politics, Economy, Security, and Religion*, ed. Gary Sick and Lawrence Potter, 17 (New York: St. Martin's Press, 1997).

20. "Appendix," in *Persian Gulf States: Country Studies*, ed. Helen Metz, 385, 392, 398, 403, 407 (Washington, DC: Federal Research Division, Library of Congress, 1994); "Appendix," in *Saudi Arabia: A Country Study*, ed. Helen Metz, 293 (Washington, DC: Federal Research Division, Library of Congress, 1993).

21. Between January 1985 and January 1986, for instance, the dollar lost more than 25 percent of its value. Ghassan Salameh, "Hangover Time in the Gulf," *MERIP,* March–April 1986, 40.

22. Hooglund and Toth, "United Arab Emirates," 218.

23. Fawzi al-Sultan, *Averting Financial Crisis—Kuwait* (Washington, DC: World Bank, 1989), 33.

24. Kiren Chaudhry, *The Price of Wealth: Economies and Institutions in the Middle East* (Ithaca, NY: Cornell University Press, 1997), 35–37.

25. Sick, *The Coming Crisis,* 21.

26. For more on this issue, see Sean Foley, "Kuwait, Bahrain, Qatar, Oman, and the UAE," in *Guide to Islamist Movements,* ed. Barry Rubin (New York: M. E. Sharpe, 2010).

27. Madawi al-Rasheed, *A History of Saudi Arabia* (Cambridge: Cambridge University Press, 2002), 157; Michael Casey, *The History of Kuwait* (Westport, CT: Greenwood Press, 2007), 80–83.

28. Christopher Davidson, *The United Arab Emirates: A Study in Survival* (Boulder, CO: Lynne Rienner Publishers, 2005), 205–206; Joseph Kechichian, *Oman and the World: The Emergence of an Independent Foreign Policy* (Santa Monica, CA: Rand, 1995), 110–112.

29. Davidson, *The United Arab Emirates: A Study in Survival*, 205–206.

30. Jean Tartter, "Regional and National Security Considerations," in *Persian Gulf States: Country Studies*, ed. Helen Metz, 325–326 (Washington, DC: Federal Research Division, Library of Congress, 1994).

31. Ian Black, "Saudis Tried to Buy Off Iran in 1985," *Guardian*, August 5, 1987, reprinted in Rush, *Records of the Hajj: A Documentary History of the Pilgrimage to Mecca,* 8:706; Scherazade Daneshku and Ali Tehrani, "Mecca Battles Signal Breakdown in Tense Saudi-Iran Relationship," *Guardian,* August 6, 1987, reprinted in Rush, *Records of the Hajj: A Documentary History of the Pilgrimage to Mecca,* 8:708–709; David Hirst, "Massacre in Mecca Follows Iranian Mischief-Making," *Guardian,* August 2, 1987, reprinted in Rush, *Records of the Hajj: A Documentary History of the Pilgrimage to Mecca,* 8:704; "Saudis Ready for Head-on Confrontation with Iran After the Massacre at Mecca," *Guardian,* August 29, 1987, reprinted in Rush, *Records of the Hajj: A Documentary History of the Pilgrimage to Mecca,* 8:712; Liz Thurgood, "Iran Blames Saudis for Mecca Blast," *Guardian,* December 7, 1989, reprinted in Rush, *Records of the Hajj: A Documentary History of the Pilgrimage to Mecca,* 8:730–731; John Witherow, "Fahd Moves Missiles into First Line of Defence," *Sunday Times,* May 1, 1988, reprinted in Rush, *Records of the Hajj: A Documentary History of the Pilgrimage to Mecca,* 8:718–719.

32. Cordesman, *Saudi Arabia Enters the Twenty-First Century,* 122.

33. Anthony Cordesman, *Kuwait: Recovery and Security After the Gulf War* (Boulder, CO: Westview Press, 1997), 10.

34. United States Arms Control and Disarmament Agency, *World Military Expenditures and Arms Transfers 1997 Report* (Washington, DC: United States Government Printing Office, 1997), 59, 78, 85, 87, 89, 95 (available at http://dosfan.lib.uic.edu/).

35. Witherow, "Fahd Moves Missiles into First Line of Defence."

36. Cordesman, *Kuwait: Recovery and Security After the Gulf War,* 9; Anthony Cordesman, *Bahrain, Oman, Qatar, and the UAE: Challenges of Security* (Boulder, CO: Westview Press, 1997), 38, 126, 203, 225, 290, 300.

37. For more on Iraqi-US relations during this time period, see Zachary Karabell, "Backfire: U.S. Policy Towards Iraq, 1988–2 August, 1990," *Middle East Journal* 49, no. 1 (Winter 1995): 28–47.

38. Adel Darwish, "Saudis Court Iran and Tighten Haj Season Security," *Independent,* June 16, 1990, reprinted in Rush, *Records of the Hajj: A Documentary History of the Pilgrimage to Mecca,* 8:736.

39. Ahmed Rashid, "Islam's Political Pilgrims Seek Out the Saudis' Ear," *In-*

dependent, June 20, 1991, reprinted in Rush, *Records of the Hajj: A Documentary History of the Pilgrimage to Mecca,* 8:743.

40. "Hajj Rally," *Independent,* June 19, 1991, reprinted in Rush, *Records of the Hajj: A Documentary History of the Pilgrimage to Mecca,* 8:742.

41. Robert Litwack, *Regime Change: U.S. Strategy Through the Prism of 9/11* (Baltimore, MD: Johns Hopkins University Press, 2007), 204.

42. Phebe Marr, *The Modern History of Iraq*, 2nd ed. (Boulder, CO: Westview Press, 2004), 219–221; Anthony Cordesman and Ahmed S. Hashim, *Iraq: Sanctions and Beyond* (Boulder, CO: Westview Press, 1997), 185.

43. Marr, *The Modern History of Iraq,* 220–221.

44. Ibid.

45. Ibid., 221.

46. Ibid., 223–228.

47. Cordesman, *Kuwait: Recovery and Security After the Gulf War,* 86.

48. Mary Ann Tétreault, "A State of Two Minds: State Cultures, Women, and Politics in Kuwait," *International Journal of Middle East Studies* 33, no. 3 (May 2001): 211.

49. Ibid.

50. Jill Crystal, *Kuwait: The Transformation of an Oil State* (Boulder, CO: Westview Press, 1992), 159–161.

51. This process was aided by the fact that the National Bank of Kuwait had overseas facilities and kept a complete copy of its own records in duplicate abroad. Ibid., 159; Dilip Hiro, *The Second Gulf War: Desert Shield to Desert Storm* (New York: Universe, 2003), 113.

52. Marr, *The Modern History of Iraq,* 228–233; R. Stephen Humphreys, *Between Memory and Desire: The Middle East in a Troubled Age,* 2nd ed. (Berkeley: University of California Press, 2005), 105.

53. Humphreys, *Between Memory and Desire,* 109–110.

54. Marr, *The Modern History of Iraq,* 232.

55. Cordesman, *Saudi Arabia Enters the Twenty-First Century,* 39; Europa Publications, *Middle East and North Africa, 2003* (New York: Routledge, 2003), 1297.

56. However, Saudi Arabia actually had closer to 162,500 under arms if one includes the kingdom's large national guard. Al-Rasheed, *A History of Saudi Arabia,* 163. Robert Dorr, *Desert Shield: The Build-Up: The Complete Story* (Osceola, WI: Motorbooks International, 1991), 23.

57. Al-Rasheed, *A History of Saudi Arabia,* 163–168.

58. Steve Coll, *The Bin Ladens: An Arabian Family in the American Century* (New York: Penguin Press, 2008), 375–377.

59. Cordesman, *Bahrain, Oman, Qatar, and the UAE: Challenges of Security,* 39, 126, 225; Sean Foley, "What Wealth Cannot Buy," in *Crisis in the Contemporary Persian Gulf,* ed. Barry Rubin, 49 (London: Frank Cass, 2002); al-Rasheed, *A History of Saudi Arabia,* 163–164.

60. Al-Rasheed, *A History of Saudi Arabia,* 168

61. Ibid., 165–166.

62. Davidson, *The United Arab Emirates: A Study in Survival,* 206; Christopher Davidson, *Dubai: The Vulnerability of Success* (New York: Columbia University Press, 2008), 227–228.

63. Al-Rasheed, *A History of Saudi Arabia,* 166.

64. Mamoun Fandy, *Saudi Arabia and the Politics of Dissent* (London: Macmillan, 1997), 62–68.

65. Cordesman, *Kuwait: Recovery and Security After the Gulf War,* 18; Foley, "What Wealth Cannot Buy," 49; and United States Department of State, Bureau of Near Eastern Affairs, "Background Note: Saudi Arabia," January 2009 (available at http://www.state.gov/).

66. Cordesman, *Saudi Arabia Enters the Twenty-First Century,* 410.

67. Casey, *The History of Kuwait,* 78.

68. Cordesman, *Kuwait: Recovery and Security After the Gulf War,* 18.

69. Ibid., 48.

70. Fandy, *Saudi Arabia and the Politics of Dissent,* 67–87.

71. For more on this issue, see Chapter 5.

72. N. R. Kleinfeld, "Making News on the Chief Pay Off," *New York Times,* April 19, 1987.

73. Maureen Dowd, "Confrontation in the Gulf: Reporter's Notebook; For Speed Ball Bush, On to Helsinki," *New York Times*, September 8, 1990 (available at http://www.nytimes.com/).

74. Clifford Krauss, "Confrontation in the Gulf; Kuwaiti in U.S. Speaks of an Exile Leadership," August 16, 1990 (available at http://www.nytimes.com/).

75. Jon Alterman, *New Media, New Politics? From Satellite Television to the Internet in the Arab World* (Washington, DC: Washington Institute for Near East Policy, 1998), 16.

76. Ibid.

77. Naomi Sakr, *Satellite Realms: Transnational Television, Globalization, and the Middle East* (London: I. B. Tauris, 2001), 10–11.

78. Ibid., 10. These professional workers constituted a new class; for more on this topic, see Alterman, *New Media, New Politics?* 16–17.

79. Mike George, "A Background to Advertising in Bahrain," in *Doing Business with Bahrain,* ed. Philip Dew and Jonathan Wallace, 162–163 (New York: Wiley, 2002).

80. S. Abdallah Schleifer, "Media Explosion in the Arab World: The Pan-Arab Satellite Broadcasters," *TBS Journal* 1 (Fall 1998) (available at http://www.tbsjournal.com/); Mohamed Arafa, "Qatar," in *Mass Media in the Middle East*, ed. Yahya R. Kamalipour and Hamid Mowlana, 238–239 (Westwood, CT: Greenwood Press, 1994).

81. Peter Smith, *How CNN Fought the War: A View from the Inside* (Secaucus, NJ: Carol Publishing Group, 1991), 31–33.

82. William Rugh, *Arab Mass Media* (Westwood, CT: Greenwood, 2004), 221–222.

83. Casey, *The History of Kuwait,* 104.

84. Kechichian states that the United States and other coalition nations "could not have achieved their success in the liberation of Kuwait were it not for the prepositioned equipment in Oman." Kechichian, *Oman and the World,* 157–158.

85. Marr, *The Modern History of Iraq,* 239–241, 265–270.

86. Cordesman, *Bahrain, Oman, Qatar, and the UAE: Challenges of Security,* 133, 227.

87. Ibid., 39, 126, 225–226; Cordesman, *Kuwait: Recovery and Security After*

the Gulf War, 126; Sean Foley, "The UAE: Political Issues and Security Dilemmas," *Middle Eastern Review of International Affairs* 3, no. 1 (March 1999): 33–34 (available at http://meria.idc.ac.il/).

88. Anthony Cordesman, *US Forces in the Middle East* (Boulder, CO: Westview Press, 1997), 68–77.

89. Cordesman, *Bahrain, Oman, Qatar, and the UAE: Challenges of Security,* 117.

90. David Winkler, *Amirs, Admirals and Desert Sailors: Bahrain, the U.S. Navy, and the Gulf* (Annapolis, MD: US Naval Institute Press, 2007), 177.

91. Cordesman, *US Forces in the Middle East*, 76.

92. Richard Grimmett, *Conventional Arms Transfers to Developing Nations, 1993–2000* (Washington, DC: Congressional Research Service, 2001), 47 (available at http://www.fas.org/).

93. Ibid.

94. Richard Russell, *Weapons Proliferation in the Middle East* (New York: Routledge, 2005), 110.

95. Ibid.

96. Cordesman, *Iraq: Sanctions and Beyond,* 187.

97. Cordesman, *Kuwait: Recovery and Security After the Gulf War,* 128.

98. Foley, "What Wealth Cannot Buy," 44–47.

99. In the early 1960s, Saudi religious leaders deemed elections un-Islamic, and the councils were replaced by appointed municipal councils. Jafar al-Shayeb, "Saudi Arabia: Municipal Councils and Political Reform," *Arab Reform Bulletin,* November 2005 (available at http://www.carnegieendowment.org/).

100. Al-Rasheed, *A History of Saudi Arabia*, 168–169.

101. Ibid., 169–172.

102. Ibid., 172–173.

103. Ibid., 173.

104. Ibid., 174–175.

105. Munira Fakhro, "The Uprising in Bahrain: An Assessment," in *The Persian Gulf at the Millennium: Essays in Politics, Economy, Security, and Religion,* ed. Gary Sick and Lawrence Potter, 180 (New York: St. Martin's Press, 1997).

106. Ibid., 175.

107. Ibid., 181.

108. Foley, "Kuwait, Bahrain, Qatar, Oman, and the UAE."

109. Mary Ann Tétreault, *Stories of Democracy: Politics and Society in Contemporary Kuwait* (New York: Columbia University Press, 2000), 83–100.

110. Haya al-Mughni, *Women in Kuwait: The Politics of Gender* (London: Saqi Books, 2001), 156.

111. Tétreault, *Stories of Democracy,* 101–131.

112. Youssef Ibrahim, "54 Qatari Citizens Petition Emir for Free Elections," *New York Times,* May 13, 1992 (available at http://www.nytimes.com/).

113. Foley, "What Wealth Cannot Buy," 39–41.

114. Foley, "Kuwait, Bahrain, Qatar, Oman, and the UAE"; Kechichian, *Oman and the World,* 53–54; Fareed Mohamedi, "Oman," in *Persian Gulf States: Country Studies,* ed. Helen Metz, 310–312 (Washington, DC: Federal Research Division, Library of Congress, 1994).

115. Kechichian, *Oman and the World,* 112–113.

116. Foley, "Kuwait, Bahrain, Qatar, Oman, and the UAE."

117. Fandy, *Saudi Arabia and the Politics of Dissent,* 50–60.

118. The decision to invite US soldiers to defend Saudi Arabia was made after a meeting between King Fahd and senior US officials, including then secretary of defense Dick Cheney. Bob Woodward, *The Commanders* (New York: Simon and Schuster, 1991), 266–273.

119. Pascal Ménoret,.*The Saudi Enigma*, trans. Patrick Camiller (London: Zed Books, 2005), 123–124.

120. Al-Rasheed, *A History of Saudi Arabia,* 179–180.

121. Ibid., 177–187; Fandy, *Saudi Arabia and the Politics of Dissent,* 144.

122. Cordesman, *Bahrain, Oman, Qatar, and the UAE: Challenges of Security,* 43; Fandy, *Saudi Arabia and the Politics of Dissent,* 126–128.

123. Daryl Champion, "Saudi Arabia: Elements of Instability Within Stability," in *Crisis in the Contemporary Persian Gulf,* ed. Barry Rubin, 128 (London: Frank Cass, 2002).

124. Ibid.

125. Fandy, *Saudi Arabia and the Politics of Dissent,* 128–129.

126. Ibid., 131–135.

127. Ibid., 142.

128. Ibid., 122–144, 237.

129. Martin Smith and Lowell Bergman, "Looking for Answers" (includes interviews with Ahmed Sattar, Rifat El-Sayed, Fouad Allam, Edward Walker, Nabil Fahmy, Saad al-Faqih, Milt Bearden, Richard Armitage, Hassasn Turabi, Prince Bandar bin Sultan, and Shaikh Ali Chee), *Frontline*, PBS, October 11, 2001 (available at http://www.pbs.org/).

130. Ibid.

131. An excellent account of this process is Saïd K. Aburish's book, *The Rise, Corruption, and Coming Fall of the House of Saud* (London: Bloomsbury, 1994).

132. John Esposito, *Unholy War: Terror in the Name of Islam* (Oxford: Oxford University Press, 2002), 1–25; Coll, *The Bin Ladens,* 375–377.

133. Esposito, *Unholy War,* 24–25.

134. Sean Foley, "*The Naqshbandiyya-Khalidiyya,* Islamic Sainthood, and Religion in Modern Times," *Journal of World History* 19, no. 4 (December 2008): 541.

135. Mehron Kamrava, *The Making of the Modern Middle East: A Political History Since World War I* (Berkeley: University of California Press, 2005), 203.

136. Peter Bergen, *Holy War Inc.* (New York: A Touchstone Book/Simon and Schuster, 2002), 40–43.

137. Hassan Fattah, "Al Qaeda Increasingly Reliant on Media," *New York Times,* September 30, 2006.

138. Michael Moss and Souad Mekhennet, "Rising Leader for Next Phase of Al Qaeda's War," *New York Times,* April 4, 2008.

139. Cordesman, *Saudi Arabia Enters the Twenty-First Century,* 212; Michael Scheuer, *Imperial Hubris* (Dulles, VA: Potomac Books, 2004), 104.

140. Rugh, *Arab Mass Media,* 212.

141. Ibid., 211–214; Alterman, *New Media, New Politics?* 15–22.

142. Sakr, *Satellite Realms,* 32.

143. Ibid., 48.

144. Ibid., 45–46.

145. Ibid., 44.

146. Rugh, *Arab Mass Media,* 198.

147. Amos Thomas, *Imaginations and Borderless Television: Media, Culture, and Politics Across Asia* (New York: Sage, 2005), 96.
148. Sakr, *Satellite Realms,* 21.
149. Ibid., 61–64.
150. Rugh, *Arab Mass Media,* 213.
151. Sakr, *Satellite Realms,* 45.
152. Rugh, *Arab Mass Media,* 213.
153. Ibid.
154. Ibid., 215.
155. Ibid., 216.
156. Lorne Manly, "Translation: Is the Whole World Watching?" *New York Times,* March 26, 2006; Eric Pfanner and Doreen Carvajal, "The Selling of Al Jazeera TV to an International Market," *New York Times,* October 31, 2005.
157. Rugh, *Arab Mass Media,* 215.
158. Ibid.
159. Sakr, *Satellite Realms,* 57–58.
160. Rugh, *Arab Mass Media,* 216–218.
161. Sakr, *Satellite Realms,* 119.
162. Rugh, *Arab Mass Media,* 217.
163. Ibid.
164. Mark Lynch, *Voices of the New Arab Public: Iraq, al-Jazeera, and Middle East Politics Today* (New York: Columbia University Press, 2006), 42.
165. Mamoun Fandy, *(UN)civil War of Words* (Westport, CT: Greenwood, 2007), 47.
166. Lydia Saad, "Al-Jazeera: Arabs Rate Its Objectivity," *Gallup Polls,* April 23, 2002 (available at http://www.gallup.com/).
167. Ibid.
168. Richard Burkholder, "Arabs Favor Al-Jazeera over State-Run Channels for World News," *Gallup Polls,* November 12, 2002 (available at http://www.gallup.com/).
169. Ibid.
170. Eric Pfanner, "Al Jazeera English Tries to Extend Its Reach," *New York Times,* May 19, 2008.
171. Noam Cohen, "Few in U.S. See Jazeera's Coverage of Gaza War," *New York Times,* January 11, 2009; Susan Stamberg, "Washington Correspondent Departs Al Jazeera" (includes interview with Dave Marash), *Weekend Edition Saturday,* April 5, 2008.
172. Stamberg, "Washington Correspondent Departs."
173. Roger Cohen, "Bring the Real World Home," *New York Times,* November 12, 2007 (available at http://www.nytimes.com/).
174. Rugh, *Arab Mass Media,* 233.
175. Ibid., 232–234.
176. Ibid., 233.
177. Sick, *The Coming Crisis,* 17.
178. International Monetary Fund, "United Arab Emirates: Selected Issues and Statistical Appendix," IMF Country Report no. 03/67, March 2003, 29–30 (available at http://www.imf.org/).
179. Markus Bouillon and Ralph Stobwasser, "Kuwait," in *Worldmark Encyclo-*

pedia of National Economies, ed. Sarah Pendergast and Tom Pendergast, 301 (Detroit, MI: Gale Group, 2002).

180. International Monetary Fund, "United Arab Emirates: Recent Economic Developments," IMF Staff Country Report, no. 98/134, December 1998, 39, 78 (available at http://www.imf.org/).

181. The World Bank, *The Status and Progress of Women in the Middle East and North Africa* (Washington, DC: World Bank Press, 2007), 129, 135, 139, 140, 141, 144 (available at http://siteresources.worldbank.org/).

182. Ibid.

183. Indira Chand, "Young People Pose Challenge to Gulf States; Pressure Builds for Job Training," *Gulf Daily News,* December 22, 2001.

184. International Monetary Fund, "Kuwait: Statistical Abstract," Country Report no. 04/197, July 2004, 24 (available at http://www.imf.org/).

185. International Monetary Fund (IMF), *Balance of Payments Statistics Yearbook: Part 1: Country Tables* (Washington, DC: IMF, 1993), 53, 398, 519, 592; IMF, *Balance of Payments Statistics Yearbook: Part 1: Country Tables* (Washington, DC: IMF, 2000), 63, 477, 664; IMF, *Balance of Payments Statistics Yearbook: Part 1: Country Tables* (Washington, DC: IMF, 2006), 419, 736, 841; United Nations Conference on Trade and Development, "World Investment Report 2007: Country Fact Sheet Bahrain" (available at http://www.unctad.org/); United Nations Conference on Trade and Development, "World Investment Report 2007: Country Fact Sheet Kuwait" (available at http://www.unctad.org/); United Nations Conference on Trade and Development, "World Investment Report 2007: Country Fact Sheet Oman" (available at http://www.unctad.org/); United Nations Conference on Trade and Development, "World Investment Report 2007: Country Fact Sheet Qatar" (available at http://www.unctad.org/); United Nations Conference on Trade and Development, "World Investment Report 2007: Country Fact Sheet Saudi Arabia" (available at http://www.unctad.org/); and United Nations Conference on Trade and Development, "World Investment Report 2007: Country Fact Sheet UAE" (available at http://www.unctad.org/).

186. Sick, *The Coming Crisis,* 27.

187. Foley, "What Wealth Cannot Buy," 60.

188. International Monetary Fund, *International Financial Statistics Online,* "Bahrain, 1945–2003," "Kuwait, 1945–2003," "Oman, 1945–2003," "Qatar, 1945–2003," "Saudi Arabia, 1945–2003," and "UAE, 1945–2003" (available at https://login.library.lausys.georgetown.edu/).

189. John Mazor, "Saudi Arabia," in *Worldmark Encyclopedia of National Economies,* ed. Sarah Pendergast and Tom Pendergast, 502–503 (Detroit, MI: Gale Group, 2002).

190. Foley, "What Wealth Cannot Buy," 63; Ralph Stobwasser and Markus Bouillon, "Bahrain," in *Worldmark Encyclopedia of National Economies,* ed. Sarah Pendergast and Tom Pendergast, 38 (Detroit, MI: Gale Group, 2002); Salamander Davoudi, "Oman," *Worldmark Encyclopedia of National Economies,* ed. Sarah Pendergast and Tom Pendergast, 426 (Detroit, MI: Gale Group, 2002).

191. Ugo Fasano and Qing Wang, "Testing the Relationship Between Government Spending and Revenue: Evidence from the GCC Countries," IMF working paper, 2001, 3–12.

192. M. A. Ramady, *The Saudi Arabian Economy: Policies, Achievements, and Challenges* (New York: Springer Press, 2005), 448.

193. Ibid.

194. Sick, *The Coming Crisis,* 18.

195. Ibid.

196. Ibid., 17.

197. Ibid., 18.

198. Foley, "What Wealth Cannot Buy," 64.

199. Eric Schmitt, "War in the Gulf: Overview; U.S. Bombers Hit Iraqis' Air Bases and Supply Lines," *New York Times,* February 4, 1991 (available at http://www.nytimes.com/).

200. An important by-product of the desalinization process is that salt and toxins are released in concentrated forms directly into the ocean. Katherine Boyle, "Water: Resource Control, Pollution Problems Accompany Desalination—Report," Greenwire, February 5, 2009.

201. Environmental Information Administration, "Country Analysis Brief: UAE," "Country Analysis Brief: Saudi Arabia," and "Country Analysis Brief, Oil: Bahrain" (available at http://www.eia.doe.gov/).

202. Environmental Information Administration, "Country Analysis Brief: Saudi Arabia."

203. Sick, *The Coming Crisis,* 20.

204. Frank Viviano, "Kingdom on Edge: Saudi Arabia," *National Geographic* 204, no. 4 (October 2003): 3–41.

205. Mazor, "Saudi Arabia."

206. Ashfaq Ahmed, "VIP Beggars Hit UAE Streets," Financial Times Information, Global News Wire—Asia Africa Intelligence Wire, June 27, 2006; Bassma al-Jandaly, "Begging on the Rise as the Ramadan Spirit Sets In," Financial Times Information, Global News Wire—Asia Africa Intelligence Wire, October 25, 2004; Economist Intelligence Unit, *August 2004 UAE Country Report* (London: EIU, 2004), 13–14.

4

The Twenty-First-Century Gulf

The United States is neither feared nor respected.

—Rami Khouri, American University of Beirut, 2007

The best we can do is to search for ways to . . . co-exist as nationals with the expatriate majority.

—Jamal al-Suwaidi, director general,
Emirates Centre for Strategic Studies and Research, 2007

The peg to the U.S. dollar . . . prevented an effective response to the surge in inflation over the period 2003–2008.

—Dr. Nasser al-Saidi, chief economist,
Dubai's International Financial Centre Authority, 2008

In 2005, the International Monetary Fund (IMF) noted that the UAE's financial resources had grown so vast in the twenty-first century that the federation no longer needed to worry about a problem that had haunted it and its fellow GCC states for years—namely, how to employ the Gulf country's own citizens. Using conservative estimates of economic growth and population growth projections, IMF economists counseled that the UAE should ignore a generation of advice from international institutions and many Western experts, who had pressed the federation and other GCC states to educate their nationals and encourage their private companies to hire fewer expatriates. Instead, the IMF concluded that it would be much more efficient for the UAE to pay an "annuity to every entrant to the labor force, . . . either in the form of direct subsidies and transfers through the budget or in the form of increased (excess) government sector employment at the cost of increasing inefficiency in that sector."[1] Echoing World Bank and CIA predictions about the financial health of the UAE and Kuwait in the late 1970s, the IMF estimated that the UAE had enough wealth to continue the recommended process for at least another thirty years.

The central factor shaping the IMF's advice to the UAE was the price of oil, which skyrocketed during the first decade of the twenty-first century. Oil prices, which had been $20 a barrel in the late 1990s, surged to $145 a barrel in July 2008,[2] fueling an economic boom in the Gulf states that was reminiscent of the late 1970s. In January 2008, the head of Royal Dutch Shell predicted that demand for oil would outstrip supply by 2015.[3] Many industry observers considered it inevitable that prices would reach $200 or even $500 a barrel in the near future.[4] Experts argued that the new prices of oil reflected a host of factors, including continued high usage in the United States; rising demand in India, China, and other developing nations; ongoing political instability in the Gulf after the September 11, 2001, attacks; the US presence in Iraq; and tensions between Israel and the United States, on the one hand, and Iran, on the other.

But what goes up must come down. Starting in late July 2008, oil prices started a rapid descent: in December 2008, oil cost $38 a barrel—70 percent below the July peak.[5] Several attempts by Saudi Arabia and other oil-exporting countries to correct world oil markets failed because these countries could not compensate for the collapse in global demand thanks to the worst economic recession since the 1930s. For the first time since 1982, global oil demand declined in 2008.[6] Although Gulf governments had sought to shield themselves from the vagaries of the oil market by investing in non-oil industries and implementing state budgets based on oil at $50 a barrel, many faced the same financial questions that they had had when the last oil shock occurred in the 1980s.[7]

In this chapter, I explore the first decade of the twenty-first century in the Arab Gulf. During this time period, the Gulf states amassed unprecedented wealth, sought to transform their economies by using Dubai's post-oil model of development, and faced new financial and security challenges. Among the most important of these challenges was the declining position of the United States—which had guaranteed peace and stability in the Gulf for a generation. Throughout the decade, the GCC states have forged new relationships with many important global actors, but no state has expressed a desire to replace the US military role in the Gulf. Nor could the GCC states agree upon a way to replace their peg to the US dollar, whose deteriorating value (which accompanies falling US interest rates) facilitated an unprecedented boom in borrowing but left governments unable to check inflationary pressures. Despite a period of enormous prosperity and success at checking domestic political threats, the Gulf states faced many of the challenges that they had faced a generation earlier.

Finding a New Balance

Iraq and Iran

The twenty-first century effectively began in the Gulf in 2003, when US forces invaded Iraq and overthrew Saddam Hussein's government. No GCC state openly supported the overthrow of the Iraqi government, but there was no question that the GCC states assisted US and coalition partners' military operations in Iraq in a variety of ways. The UAE and Oman allowed overflight rights, and Bahrain, Oman, and Saudi Arabia allowed the stationing of thousands of sailors, soldiers, and combat aircraft within their national borders. The Gulf states cooperated with the United States because they recognized that it would have enormous influence over the region's politics and commerce after the fall of Saddam Hussein's government.

The invasion of Iraq seemingly ushered in a new balance of power in the Gulf region. For the first time in years, Iraq was not part of the regional balance, and a new force, the United States, was again—with its 100,000 army, navy, and air force personnel. At the same time, the US government used the invasion of Iraq to implement a fundamental shift in its military strategy in the Gulf, abandoning much of its network of airfields, army bases, and ports in GCC states and instead depending on a combination of force mobility, carrier battle groups, and limited overseas deployments to project power in the region.

Although this approach did not signal a return to the over-the-horizon policy of the 1980s, Washington's new approach addressed a key source of tension in Saudi Arabia in the 1990s. Shortly after Baghdad fell, Washington withdrew thousands of personnel from its bases in the GCC states. In Saudi Arabia alone, the US military presence dropped from more than 12,000 military personnel in March 2003 to just 385 in December 2003. During this same time period, the United States implemented similar reductions in other states in the Gulf. With large US bases in nearby Iraq, the GCC states seemingly no longer had to weigh the benefits of allying with Washington in order to guarantee their security against the dangers of housing thousands of US servicemen and women on their home soil.[8]

Handing Over Iraq

Whatever satisfaction the GCC governments might have attained from their new strategic position was tempered by the political, economic, and security challenges represented by Iraq and Iran. GCC leaders regularly voiced their disappointment with the political process in Iraq and their skepticism about the capabilities of the new government to secure and reinvigorate the country, especially after a Sunni insurgency killed thousands of Iraqis and brought the state to the verge of civil war. The GCC leaders were particularly worried about the growing influence of Iraq's one-time rival for power and influence in the Gulf, Iran.

Although there had been increased political contacts between the GCC states and Iran after the election of reformist Muhammad Khatami as president of Iran in 1997,[9] there were two issues that could not be resolved: Iran's desire to develop nuclear weapons and its relationship with Iraq. In the eyes of the GCC governments, these developments portended a sea change in Middle Eastern politics. First, Iran's desire to acquire nuclear weapons was regarded as an unacceptable first step toward Iranian domination of the Gulf. Second, the Shia government in Iraq allowed Tehran to realize a goal that it had failed to accomplish during the Iran-Iraq war—namely, a government in Baghdad committed to working with Tehran on regional affairs. Instead of competing with Tehran, Baghdad sought to harmonize its policies with its neighbor. Furthermore, Iraq's government could exercise considerable influence on Bahrain, Saudi Arabia, Kuwait, and other Gulf states that contain thousands of Arab Shia loyal to Iraqi Shia clerics. A Rand Corporation study in 2008 estimated that 70 to 80 percent of Saudi Shia follow the edicts of Iraq's most prominent Shia cleric, Grand Ayatollah al-Sistani.[10]

Perhaps most frustrating for the GCC governments was the growth of Iran's influence while Washington's influence in Iraq was at its height. This frustration and anger with US policies was voiced in September 2005 by Saudi foreign minister Prince Saud al-Faysal. In a speech to the Council on Foreign Relations in New York, he stated that he disagreed with President George W. Bush's contention that "tyrannical" governments in the Middle East were the source of Muslim extremism. In his eyes, the Arab-Israeli conflict was the root cause of Middle Eastern extremism and terrorism and the chief factor dividing the Muslim world from the United States. Referring to the Iran-Iraq war, in which Saudi Arabia and the United States supported Iraq against Iran in the 1980s, he observed, "We fought a war together to keep Iran out of Iraq. Now we are handing the whole country over to Iran without reason."[11]

The sense of apprehension and exasperation in Faysal's words raised three critical questions for the GCC states.

First, how serious a threat did instability in Iraq and the rising power of Iran (and of Shia Muslims in general) pose to the GCC states? GCC fears in part reflected Arab Sunni bigotry toward Shia Muslims and Iran. Yet the 2006 crisis in Lebanon brought these threats into far sharper view, compelling many GCC governments to alter their strategies for maintaining political stability in the region.

Second, how viable was the traditional alliance with the United States in light of stark policy differences with that country and its seemingly reduced regional influence? This question was important after 2006, when it became clear that US public opinion wished to withdraw US forces from Iraq and that the peg to the US dollar had contributed to high inflation in the Gulf states, which had created unrest among the expatriate workers. Nor could Gulf leaders ignore the fact that the United States—in the words of political scientist Rami Khouri—carried neither military nor moral weight among many people in the Middle East.[12]

Third, was it possible to recreate Dubai's "postpetroleum" economic model in the rest of the Gulf and integrate more Gulf nationals into the political and economic systems? Although many states in the region wished to free themselves of their dependence on petroleum exports and on expatriate workers, it turned out that creating non-oil industries and finding nationals with the skills to serve them was a very difficult task. Nearly a generation of programs had already failed. What is more, it remained unclear if there was sufficient global demand for many of the products and services produced by the Gulf's new nonpetroleum industries.

Kuwait

No government in the Middle East welcomed the end of Saddam Hussein's regime more than that of Kuwait. In 1990, Iraqi soldiers had invaded the Gulf state and then been driven out in 1991 by a broad military coalition led by the United States. In 2003, during the second Gulf War, Kuwait hosted thousands of US ground forces and was the only Arab state to receive hostile fire from Iraq. Following the US invasion, Kuwait continued to host thousands of US troops and signed long-term agreements with Washington for use of the Ali al-Salem airbase.[13] Furthermore, Kuwait's open political system, regular elections, and potent national legislature provided a good example for US officials, who sought to promote the benefits of democracy in the Middle East.

An excellent example of Kuwait's vigorous political system and the potential success of US-inspired models in the Gulf was the Orange Movement. The movement arose among male and female Kuwaiti students and recent university graduates in response to a series of political crises in Kuwait in 2006. Members of the movement adopted orange as their defining color and used blogs to determine strategy, organize mass demonstrations, support reformist political candidates in elections, and bypass Kuwait's mainstream media. The Orange Movement's success in the 2006 elections and the subsequent reduction of electoral districts from 25 to 5 showed the ability of technology to radically transform the politics of the Gulf—just as the cassette tape had done in Iran in 1979 and radio had done in the 1930s in the Gulf.[14] Although polls suggested that a large percentage of Kuwaitis acquired unfavorable views of the United States after 2003,[15] Kuwait's government maintained warm ties with Washington. Kuwaiti elites may not have liked US policies in the Middle East, but they believed that it was the one state that could guarantee their security. Kuwaitis knew that Iraq's claims to their state were decades old and widely accepted by Iraqis of all political backgrounds. They also had to factor in the possibility that Iraq would seek to protect Kuwait's Shia minority.[16]

Within this political environment, Kuwaitis were faced with daunting questions. To begin with, how long could they depend on the United States to defend the sovereignty and territorial integrity of Kuwait? Second, would the US military be able to defend Kuwait in a crisis after it left Iraq?[17] Third, would Washington take Kuwaiti interests into account in a US or Israeli confrontation with Iran, with whom Kuwait enjoys close military and political ties? Finally, would Washington defend Kuwait after it depegged its currency from the US dollar? The depegging action would be an economic decision made to address rising inflation in the Kuwaiti economy, but a highly symbolic act, given Kuwait's dependence on Washington for security guarantees.[18]

Yet another factor adding to Kuwaitis' sense of anxiety was the uncertain nature of the nation's oil reserves, which the government had long maintained were nearly 100 billion barrels.[19] In 2006, however, a Kuwaiti official leaked a series of documents to a US energy trade journal, which confirmed that Kuwait's reserves were half the official estimate.[20] For Kuwaitis, already concerned about their government's ability to respond to regional challenges, no news could have been more unsettling. A Kuwaiti vacationing in the Saudi resort city of Taif expressed his countrymen's views when he told a Saudi newspaper in 2006 that he had taken his children there so they could enjoy a better climate and a more stable society than in Kuwait.[21]

Central Gulf

Situated on the other side of the Arabian Peninsula from Taif, Qatar hosted the US Central Command Center at Camp al-Saliya as well as 5,000 US and UK troops during the first Gulf War. The US government upgraded the al-Udaid Airbase, which was an important center for US operations during the US invasion of Iraq in March 2003. By December 2003, the base had replaced Saudi Arabia's al-Dhahran Airbase as the center of US operations in the Gulf region, and by 2008 it was the largest US military base in the Middle East. Qatar agreed to permit US forces to use the al-Udaid facility on a long-term basis and to construct a permanent command center there.[22]

The government of Qatar coupled its close political alliance with the United States with a program of gradual political reform centered on a new constitution, an independent and powerful constitutional court, and the election of two-thirds of the forty-five seats in its national parliament, the Majlis al-Shura (Consultative Council). The constitution balances the executive, judicial, and legislative branches of government and offers "equal rights and duties" for all Qatari citizens. Qataris overwhelmingly ratified the constitution on April 30, 2003.[23]

As with Kuwait, Qatar's principal reasons for forging close ties with the

United States relate to a sense of strategic vulnerability and poor relations with a larger neighbor: Saudi Arabia. Saudi-Qatari relations had been tense ever since the coup in Doha in 1995, the launching of al-Jazeera in 1996, and that channel's airing of stories seen as unfavorable to the Saudi royal family. Throughout this period, Qatari officials publicly emphasized their official policy of noninterference in al-Jazeera's coverage while offering the Saudis a chance to "rein" in the network's newscasts in exchange for financial and political concessions. Qatari diplomacy paid off in 2007, when Riyadh supported a host of key Qatari initiatives, and al-Jazeera was awarded the exclusive right to broadcast the popular European soccer tournament in Saudi Arabia. From 2007 forward, al-Jazeera journalists complained to the *New York Times* that their stories about Saudi Arabia had to be approved by the network's senior managers and were repeatedly censored.[24]

Qatar has balanced its diplomacy with Washington and Riyadh with considerable charitable contributions to Hamas and investments in countries that are at odds with the United States, including Syria, Sudan, Iran, and Zimbabwe. It has also taken strong diplomatic stands against US and Israeli military and diplomatic initiatives. Qatar's emir has affirmed Iran's right to nuclear technology, but the statement also showed his desire to mitigate the consequences for Qatar, should it be caught in the middle of a conflict between Iran and the United States.[25] This balancing act reflected the fact that part of the North Gas Field, Qatar's largest natural gas depository, is in Iranian territorial waters and is shared with Iran. Reviewing Qatar's dizzying diplomacy in the early 2000s, a Qatari official noted: "The idea is to try to keep everybody happy—or if we can't, to keep everybody reasonably unhappy."[26]

By contrast, Bahrain has maintained a steady diplomacy in the twenty-first century: strong ties with Saudi Arabia, from which it receives subsidies, and warm relations with the United States. The tiny island state accommodated thousands of US sailors and will host the US Fifth Fleet's headquarters for the foreseeable future. The two nations signed a free-trade agreement in 2004, Bahrain's reward for half a century of cooperation with the United States. Still, the Bahraini government, fearing that Iran might use its influence among Bahraini Shia to undermine the country's stability, maintains close ties with Iran.[27]

Events in Iraq after 2003 disrupted this delicate balance because Bahraini Shia see their status as analogous to that of Iraq's Shia. Bahraini Shia, who have lacked their own senior religious figures for years, regularly seek guidance from Iraq's Shia scholars on both political and social issues.[28] Following the model pioneered by the Orange Movement in Kuwait, Shia activists have also utilized blogs and other web-based media tools to organize mass political rallies, influence elections, disseminate information, and voice far sharper criticisms of the government than possible in other venues.[29] Their success similarly points to the potential of new media to transform Gulf politics. Although

Shia activists have taken part in national elections, their relations with the central government remain problematic. For instance, in 2008, when Bahraini Shia met in Washington, DC, with a US congressional task force on religious freedom, Interior Minister Shaikh Abdullah al-Khalifa threatened to prosecute them for violating laws that prohibit the discussion of sensitive internal political matters overseas.[30]

The Southern Gulf

Much like the northern members of the GCC, the UAE was pleased to see the US war in Iraq end swiftly and prioritized its bilateral relations with the United States. Abu Dhabi's offer to facilitate the exile of Saddam Hussein raised the UAE's international profile and helped to deflect subsequent criticism regarding the federation's limited comments about the war once it actually started. Abu Dhabi's policies reflected the UAE's desire to balance its needs to use US power to counter the federation's neighbors while simultaneously recognizing domestic opposition to US policies in the Middle East generally. US domestic politics and inflationary pressures associated with the UAE's long-standing peg to the US dollar further complicated matters. In 2006, the US Congress rejected a bid of Dubai Ports World, a Dubai-owned company, to manage several US ports.[31] During the debate, US politicians and pundits portrayed the UAE as an ally of Al-Qaida and other Islamic terrorist groups. A year after the collapse of the Dubai Ports World bid, Emirati officials discussed dropping the peg to the US dollar as a way of addressing inflation within the UAE, which rose to more than 13 percent in 2007.[32]

Nevertheless, US-UAE ties have remained strong because of the importance of each country to the other's strategic calculations. The United States helps to guarantee the UAE's security and provides direct investment. In return, the UAE invests hundreds of millions of dollars in US properties and companies.[33] The UAE also allows the US Navy access to its port in Dubai, which, as I noted above, is the only one deep enough to berth an aircraft carrier. This privilege is significant for the United States as it reorganizes its force structure in the Gulf region in favor of aircraft carrier battle groups rather than land-based aircraft and ground forces. In addition, Washington welcomed the 2006 elections in the UAE's Federal National Council and labeled the federation "a model Muslim nation."[34]

Finally, in Oman, the fall of Saddam Hussein's government had no immediate or medium-term impact. As Oman had done in previous Western military actions in the Gulf region, it permitted US and UK forces to use its air bases during the 2003 war in Iraq. In that same year, Oman extended the franchise to all adult Omanis regardless of gender, although all power remains centralized in the sultan. The United States and Oman also reached a free-trade agreement in 2005. Although inflation reached double digits by 2008,[35] Oman maintained its peg to the US dollar.[36] Despite its close ties to Washington and London, Muscat has maintained close links to Tehran for many years, confident that it will not be affected greatly by whatever happens in Iraq or between Iran and the United States.[37]

Saudi Arabia

Saudi Arabia, unlike Oman, shares a long land border as well as tribal and religious ties with Iraq. Although the kingdom is geographically larger than the other GCC states, its government shares the sense of weakness and vulnerability to larger, stronger neighbors that is found in all of the other Gulf Arab states. Since the end of World War II, Riyadh has looked to Washington to shield it from external threats and ensure that Saudi oil reached world markets. Nearly a decade of terrorist attacks against US targets, culminating in those of September 11, 2001, has forced the Saudi government to admit that its traditional dependence on US security is potentially untenable. Two factors have reinforced Saudi perceptions of the United States. First, the majority of the terrorists involved in the September 11 attacks were Saudis. Second, Riyadh has been repulsed by Washington's ironclad support for Israeli actions in the West Bank, Gaza, and Lebanon.

Thus, the chief goal of Saudi foreign policy in recent times has been to overcome the kingdom's strategic vulnerabilities without a large amount of assistance from the United States. In this context, a US-led attack aimed at overthrowing Saddam Hussein's government in Iraq would give Washington a golden opportunity to withdraw the US aircraft and troops that had been stationed in Saudi Arabia since 1991. Before the US invasion of Iraq, Washington and Riyadh reached an understanding: the US military would use Saudi facilities to topple Saddam Hussein's government but would leave Saudi Arabia shortly after the end of hostilities. In fact, within months of the fall of the Iraqi government, virtually the entire US military contingent had withdrawn from the kingdom. Since the initial invasion was short, Riyadh appeared to have achieved a victory at relatively little cost.[38]

This apparent victory in foreign affairs, however, was quickly negated. In May 2003, terrorist attacks in Riyadh killed nearly thirty people and injured nearly 200, including ten Americans.[39] The attacks demonstrated that the hoped-for public relations windfall from the US military's withdrawal from the kingdom had not materialized. Other attacks of varying degrees of severity have been made subsequently on expatriates and key infrastructure facilities in the kingdom. Furthermore, scores of Saudis traveled to Iraq, joined the Sunni resistance, and helped to fund and carry out attacks there. To complicate matters for Riyadh, Washington also repeatedly threatened to use force to check Iranian nuclear and regional ambitions—setting the stage for a military confrontation in which Saudi Arabia would be vulnerable to an Iranian attack.

US support of Israel during the 2006 Lebanon crisis only added to Saudi frustrations. When asked at a news conference about US secretary of state Condoleezza Rice's assertion that the war in Lebanon was part of "the birth pangs of a new Middle East," Saudi foreign minister Faysal scoffed that Saudi Arabia wanted "to go back to the old Middle East," adding that the only thing he saw "from this new Middle East is more problems and more disasters." Riyadh's and Washington's positions could hardly have been farther apart.[40]

Security, Reform, and Succession

Faysal's rebuke of Rice reiterated a seemingly new course that Saudi officials and their counterparts in other GCC states had adopted—namely, their long-term security no longer rested solely on US military power and its ability to deter Iran and others from attacking Arab Gulf states. Although the GCC states would retain close ties with the United States, they understood that their future security also depended on their own ability to address domestic challenges. These challenges revolved around social and economic institutions, the environment, policies to address expatriate and Shia grievances, and groups committed to political violence. In considering these problems, the GCC states gave first priority to addressing political violence, since reform programs were impossible to consider when they could be easily disrupted by terrorist attacks. Confronting those organizations was difficult, given that many elements of GCC society, including religious and political elites, were sympathetic to the terrorists' objectives and worldview. This problem was most acute in Saudi Arabia.[41]

To its credit, since 2003, Riyadh has recognized the importance of confronting political violence despite its widespread earlier denial of the problem. The Saudi government has invested considerable resources in counterterrorism training and in improving its domestic intelligence capabilities. Saudi officials granted interviews to journalists in which they outlined their improved tactics, including house-to-house sweeps of both wealthy and poor areas of major cities.[42] Checkpoints, concrete barriers, and other similar structures have become increasingly common sights.[43] In 2008, US ambassador to Saudi Arabia Ford Fraker lauded the success of these policies, noting that "Saudi security services have shown themselves to be efficient, focused, and effective."[44]

Nevertheless, the Saudi government came to realize that apprehending a given terrorist cell would not matter in the long run if the Saudi royal family failed to win the hearts and minds of ordinary Saudis. Here, too, Riyadh took steps to address the political, social, and economic grievances of extremist groups and others. Among the most important of these reforms have been religious seminars for Saudis convicted of extremism and social programs to restart their lives after release, including employment counseling, housing assistance, transportation, familial reintegration, and marriage. Employment and marriage have been critical aspects of these postrelease programs because a number of Saudi extremists—much like many other young Saudi men—have lacked the resources to pay the *mahr,* the dowry paid by the groom to the bride. It is widely believed among Saudis that married men are unlikely to participate in extremism—a belief borne out by the success of these programs. According to a US State Department report in 2008, the recidivism rate has been very low among the nearly thousand individuals who have completed these programs and been released from jail.[45]

On a broader national level, Saudi reforms have included a human rights organization, the Human Rights Commission, headed by an official with ministerial rank. The commission, whose twenty-four-member board of directors is appointed by the king, has launched an official website and fielded more than a thousand complaints about misconduct in prisons and other government institutions.[46] The kingdom also held elections in 2005 in which both Sunnis and Shia participated. King Abdullah bolstered these reforms by making clear that the Saudi government would promote the interests of *all* Saudis, including Sunnis, Shia, Sufis, and Bedouins and other tribal populations who reside in remote regions.[47] In addition, he met with various religious leaders, emphasized national unity over regional identities, and promoted massive development programs throughout the kingdom.[48] In February 2009, King Abdullah appointed moderate and non-Hanbali Sunni Muslim scholars to the Grand Ulama Commission, an influential commission that issues official *fatwas.* For the first time, the commission will represent all branches of Sunni Islam.[49]

Although some question the sincerity of these reforms, there is evidence that the Saudi public accepts them and has sought to take advantage of the opportunities they present.[50] Shia and Sunni Arabs participated in the national elections, erecting tents for candidates, hosting nightly speakers, and distributing candidate lists through word of mouth and by text messaging to cell phones.[51] During the first public meeting of Riyadh's municipal council, residents asked the council members difficult questions about municipal and budgetary issues and also demanded improvements in public health, drainage pipes, security, and official transparency.[52] Even though the council members were unprepared to respond to all of the concerns, the meeting demonstrated that the residents of Riyadh had some insight into and acceptance of how a local democratic system might work in Saudi Arabia. Still, the most important barometer of public acceptance of King Abdullah's reform program may be his continued personal popularity among his subjects. The king is, in fact, thought to be more popular than any other Saudi leader since the reign of King Faysal, the most respected and beloved monarch in recent Saudi history.[53]

The centrality of Abdullah's position to the future of Saudi Arabia points to another key fact of life in the Gulf in the twenty-first century—that is, that political power remains tied to personal loyalty, tribal solidarity, and hierarchy, just as it always has in the Gulf. Within this framework, leadership and succession issues in royal families are paramount. Although the process of succession in the ruling families of the emirates of Abu Dhabi and Dubai occurred smoothly in 2004 and 2006, respectively, there was considerable uproar in Kuwait in 2006 after the death of Emir Shaikh Jabr al-Ahmad al-Jabr al-Sabah, and the ascension of his crown prince, Shaikh Sa'ad Abdullah al-Salem al-Sabah. Groups representing different wings of the Kuwaiti royal family—including the aforementioned Orange Movement—staged large demonstrations both for and against the new emir, who was in very poor health. To calm the situation, the Kuwaiti ruling family compelled Shaikh Sa'ad to step down. It then nominated another member of the royal family, Shaikh Sabah al-Ahmad al-Jabr al-Sabah, to become emir. Kuwait's assembly formally authorized the transfer of power shortly thereafter.[54]

The question of succession in both Saudi Arabia and Oman may become even more important in the long term. King Abdullah is an octogenarian and lacks a clear successor beyond his own elderly generation of Saudi princes, so it is unclear if his policies will remain in place after he dies. In Oman, Sultan Qaboos, who has no children, has left the matter of his successor to his family. If they cannot agree, the head of the sultanate's Defense Council will open a sealed letter from the sultan, naming his successor. Some speculate that Sultan Qaboos will transform the sultanate into a republic after his death.[55]

A New Boom and Its Consequences

The Dubai Model

Whoever succeeds the current group of GCC leaders will face the challenge of how best to address the Gulf's traditional dependence on hydrocarbon exports and on expatriate workers. As I have argued in Chapters 2 and 3, dependence on hydrocarbon exports has left the states of the GCC open to boom-and-bust cycles. Dependence on expatriate labor also presents vexing problems, since expatriates send much of their incomes home and foster a culture of complacency among many of the Gulf nationals, many of whom could easily find "work" in government. Ironically, the development programs that Gulf governments have pursued in the early twenty-first century to liberate themselves from their dependence on hydrocarbon exports have exacerbated their old dependence on expatriate workers—sometimes to levels that threaten the future viability of Arab Gulf society itself.

Nowhere has this been clearer than in the UAE, especially in Dubai. As Christopher Davidson notes in *Dubai: The Vulnerability of Success,* the leaders of the emirate faced the challenge of their rapidly declining oil revenues by building on their reputation as a regional commercial center.[56] Through the use of foreign direct investments, advanced infrastructures, and borrowing, Dubai's leaders built an economy that was dependent not on oil but on transportation, manufacturing, and services.[57] The emirate also created special self-contained free-trade zones and miniprincipalities that offered tax-free status, Western legal norms, and regulations that were liberal by Emirati or Gulf standards.[58] As I will detail in Chapter 6, Dubai also found a ready pool of labor in Asia, where the governments saw the emirate, and the Gulf in general, as places where their rapidly growing populations could find work that was unavailable at home while earning needed foreign exchange. In addition, by promoting both Islamic finance and encouraging women to go into business, Dubai became a business hub for hundreds of thousands of Arabs, Iranians, and South Asians.[59] Finally, since the 1970s, Dubai's relatively tolerant social climate has attracted wealthy individuals fleeing civil conflicts in the Middle East.

During the 1990s and the early years of the twenty-first century, Dubai's model reached new heights of success. The following examples illustrate the rapid growth of Dubai and the vision of its planners. Whereas the emirate lacked hotels, an airport, open beaches, and other tourist facilities in 1960, it was one of the chief transportation hubs and resort destinations in the world by the 1990s.[60] In 2006, the emirate boasted one of the most exclusive hotels in the world, the Burj Arab, and Dubai's international airport accommodated 146 million passengers annually—as many as London-Heathrow, Frankfurt, and Paris combined.[61] Even more impressive was the rise of Dubai's real estate industry. Although there was no property market in the city in the 1990s, Dubai was one of the most important real estate markets in the world by 2006, with more than $50 billion in committed property-related projects.[62] Dubai's *Gulf News* estimated in June 2008 that 24 percent of the world's construction cranes were in the emirate.[63]

Throughout its meteoric rise in the 1990s and 2000s, Dubai and its leaders marketed its success to the Gulf, Middle Eastern, and global communities. The city portrayed itself as a new financial powerhouse on a par with Hong Kong, Frankfurt, New York, and London. Dubai's leaders stressed the need to make Gulf economies competitive, end dependence on government assistance, privatize government entities, and adopt a mindset that, in the words of their emir, Shaikh Muhammad bin Rashid al-Maktum, "spurs creativity, innovation, dedication, and productivity."[64] By the mid-2000s, Dubai was not only an importer of capital but also a leading investor, owning New York's Chrysler Building, a nearly 50 percent share in NASDAQ OMX, a 20 percent share in the London Stock Exchange, and portions of Travelodge in Britain, Mauser in Germany, and Barney's and Loehmann's in New York.[65] In fact, Shaikh Muhammad argued in his autobiography, published in 2006 in English and Arabic, that Dubai's successes should serve as the model for development in all Arab states.[66]

Taking a Shaikh's Advice

By every indication, the GCC states accepted Shaikh Muhammad's recommendation with a vengeance, as Gulf governments joined the World Trade Organization, welcomed foreign investment, and directed billions of dollars to large projects meant to replicate Dubai's success. And they had good reason to adopt the approach. The Dubai model promised to transform the GCC states into diversified economies in which hydrocarbon exports were only one of a number of profitable sectors. Foreign direct investment, especially in computer and software companies, encouraged scholarship, research, and technology, all of which had been clearly deficient in the Gulf. The region appeared to have found an economic model that could end the boom-and-bust economic cycles that had plagued it for decades.

At first, the Dubai model appeared to be working perfectly, since it coincided with the largest and most sustained economic boom in the region since the 1970s. On average, the Gulf economies grew 8.0 percent in 2003, 9.5 percent in 2004, 7.4 percent in 2005, 6.8 percent in 2006, 7.3 percent in 2007, and 7.0 percent in 2008.[67] The UAE's economy more than doubled in size, from $71 billion in 2002 to $163 billion in 2006.[68] Between 2003 and 2006, the GCC countries used their new surpluses to reduce their public debt from 60 percent to 18 percent of GDP.[69] Saudi Arabia alone paid off $85 billion in debts.[70] By December 2008, the fiscal surpluses for the GCC states reached $600 billion.[71]

Unlike the boom in the 1970s and early 1980s, this boom was not fueled solely by petroleum. According to official IMF statistics, real UAE nonhydrocarbon GDP growth was 11 percent in 2005, whereas the real 2005 UAE oil sector grew by only 2.1 percent.[72] There was similar growth in the UAE between 2006 and 2008. Real nonhydrocarbon growth averaged 9 percent, whereas real hydrocarbon growth averaged only 4.5 percent. The *Middle East Economic Digest* estimated in the spring of 2006 that projects under way in the Gulf were worth $1 trillion. By May 2008, the number had doubled to $2 trillion.[73]

A key part of these new projects was a surge in foreign direct investment from Iran, India, China, Russia, Europe, and the United States.[74] The UAE, Qatar, and Bahrain attracted especially large amounts of such investments. In fact, the foreign direct investment in Bahrain in 2007 was double the value of the overseas investments held by Bahrainis.[75] US investment in the Gulf soared by 120 percent between 2001 and 2008.[76] This surge in US investment was facilitated by new bilateral free-trade agreements between the United States and the GCC states as well as by the decision to keep the region's currencies fully or partially pegged to the US dollar. Since the late 1970s, the dollar peg had helped to deliver price and monetary stability throughout the Gulf. The peg also symbolized the preeminent political position of the United States in the region and the decades-old financial ties between Gulf and US elites, especially in Saudi Arabia and the United States.

From the Arabian Sea to Kuwait, the United States and other clients participated in dozens of enormous nonpetroleum projects, which transformed the face of the Gulf region in a way not seen since the failure of pearling and the emergence of the petroleum industry in the 1930s and 1940s. Oman expanded its hospitality industry and established Innovation Valley, a technology hub modeled on Dubai's Internet City. Saudi Arabia established an $8 billion technology center at Hail and opened the kingdom to mass tourism for the first time, investing heavily in Red Sea resorts. Abu Dhabi spent $28 billion on a brand-new city with 150,000 people and twenty-nine hotels. It also formed a partnership with US firms Boeing and Lockheed Martin to repair aircraft and bought Manchester City Soccer Club, a member of England's premier league. Kuwait created an $86 billion transportation and industrial hub to serve Central Asia and the Middle East. Qatar invested in smelting and industrial hubs, transportation infrastructure, and the 985-acre Pearl Islands Complex—a hotel for the world's wealthiest tourists, which was meant to outclass any hotel in Dubai. Not to be outdone, Bahrain invested in smelting plants, its own stock market, and expensive hotels.[77]

At the same time, Gulf governments sought to improve on the Dubai model by using new investments to improve their existing cultural and educational facilities. Saudi Arabia spent $12.5 billion to build a new university modeled on the Massachusetts Institute of Technology (the King Abdullah University of Science and Technology), and Abu Dhabi invested hundreds of millions of dollars in partnerships with the Louvre and the Guggenheim to open branch museums, share exhibits, and develop tourism.[78] Abu Dhabi and Qatar formed partnerships with US research universities—Cornell, Northwestern, Georgetown, and New York University, among others—to run fully functional campuses in their states. Kuwait, Sharjah, and other Gulf communities have also welcomed the introduction of US universities modeled on long-standing US institutions of higher learning in Cairo and Beirut. These types of institutions not only offer unparalleled higher education to Gulf nationals but also have the added benefit of providing research and development opportunities to private Gulf firms.

"Sensible Working Hours"

Despite the benefits of the Dubai model, it was clear by 2007 that it had definite drawbacks. As the Federal Reserve reduced US interest rates, the US dollar peg provided an enormous monetary stimulus to Gulf economies on top of the stimulus from oil prices. Financial institutions and governments in the Gulf were rich in dollars, and the costs of borrowing declined steeply. Governments, private corporations, and individuals borrowed more than ever before to fund new projects based on the Dubai model.[79] Financial institutions often extended mortgages to buyers who put down as little as 5 percent on a property.[80] Inflation reached double-digit levels in many states, and the money supply grew by 20 percent annually in some Gulf states.[81] Gulf governments prudently raised the wages for nationals throughout the region.[82]

Nor were inflationary pressures the only drawback to the Dubai model. Gulf governments, in their rush to build postpetroleum economies, did not consider whether there was sufficient demand for what they were building. Could Oman or Saudi Arabia compete for foreign technology investment or tourism with Dubai or Qatar? In light of Kuwait's strategic vulnerabilities, consultative political system, and limited incentives for foreign direct investment, could any of its projects compete with safer and more business-friendly regions in the Gulf? Furthermore, proposed privatization programs had the potential to widen economic divisions and create opportunities for corruption. This issue is particularly problematical because many GCC states have long treated their budgets as virtual state secrets.

Even if there were sufficient demand for the projects and the issue of corruption could be addressed, it was not clear who was to work and live in the thousands of properties under construction in a region with a population of less than forty million people. Even with the new universities, it would take decades before there would be enough Gulf nationals to acquire the skills necessary for the new economies. The easiest answer to these questions was to use the region's chief source of labor for decades: expatriate workers. Their numbers have soared and contributed to population growth rates of 3 percent or higher in the UAE, Oman, and Kuwait.[83] By 2008, nine out of ten residents in Dubai were immigrants.[84]

As the new expatriates flooded into the Gulf, they altered traditional labor dynamics. With a greater demand for labor in the Gulf states, expatriate workers, especially those with skills, have commanded better salaries and working conditions. As a consequence, Saudi Arabia lost expatriate engineers to Dubai and Qatar,[85] and expatriates have left the UAE for Oman, where rents are generally lower.[86] As the US dollar has depreciated, Gulf currencies and incomes have declined relative to the value of the home currencies of many expatriate workers.[87] Therefore, for the first time, salaries and wages in India and other regions of Asia have been competitive with those in the Gulf.[88]

If these financial problems were not enough for the Gulf states, Western governments and international institutions linked the accession of Gulf governments into free-trade agreements and global trading bodies with improved labor standards for workers across the region.[89] Human Rights Watch, Western labor unions, the World Trade Organization, Western governments, and other organizations saw the treatment of expatriate workers in the Gulf as particularly barbaric and certainly falling far short of international norms.[90] In June 2007, the US State Department placed every GCC state on its blacklist for trafficking in people, accusing them of abusing and mistreating foreign workers.[91] Such reports shredded the appealing public images carefully crafted by the Gulf governments of conditions in their states, hampering their ability to reach larger national objectives.

Arab satellite channels also played a key role in exposing labor conditions for expatriates in the Gulf. For example, al-Jazeera ran an extensive series in English and Arabic entitled "Blood, Sweat, and Tears," which detailed the substandard working and living conditions of foreign workers in the UAE, Qatar, and other Gulf states. These reports included interviews with representatives of NGOs, government officials in the Gulf and Asia, and dozens of expatriate workers. The series also contained extensive secretly filmed footage of worksites and living areas—footage that clearly contradicted statements made on camera by government officials, demonstrating beyond a doubt their disrespect and callousness toward expatriate workers. The report implicated not only Gulf business and government leaders but also their partners in Asia, Europe, and the United States.[92]

Encouraged by the global support for them, expatriate workers in Dubai, Bahrain, Kuwait, and Qatar did the unthinkable: they went on strike and publicly demanded higher wages and improved working conditions.[93] Although strikes were illegal throughout much of the Gulf, tens of thousands of workers went out anyway. In Dubai alone, 40,000 workers participated in one strike. Arabtec and other companies in the Gulf saw construction of Burj Khalifa (Khalifa Tower) and other projects grind to a halt.[94] In February 2008, more than a thousand temporary foreign workers who were building an enormous luxury development on Bahrain's coast went on strike and won substantial pay raises.[95]

Even though Gulf governments repressed some of these demonstrations and expelled a limited number of individuals, expatriate workers as a whole achieved many of their demands.[96] Televised images on Arab and non-Arab satellite channels of defenseless Indians and other expatriates being abused and living in squalor were not what Gulf leaders wished to portray to foreign investors and governments. When reports surfaced in the media in 2008 of the widespread abuse of foreign workers in Kuwait, no less a figure than Crown Prince Shaikh Nawaf al-Ahmad al-Sabah urged immediate action, proclaiming, "Kuwait will never allow anything to tarnish its good image abroad."[97] Just as Islamic resistance movements had used al-Jazeera, CNN, and other satellite channels to impact Gulf politics in the 1990s, expatriates now utilized these same media outlets to forward their own agenda.

Throughout the Gulf, governments improved workplace conditions and safety, provided social services to expatriates, increased salaries by 20 percent, instituted minimum wages, and, in Bahrain, Oman, and Qatar, permitted some form of collective bargaining.[98] In 2007, employers in Bahrain were forced to apologize for beating workers.[99] Gulf parliaments, human rights commissions, and bureaucrats championed expatriate rights by redrawing labor contracts and vigorously enforcing labor laws.[100] Civic groups and local governments established anonymous hotlines to assist foreign workers, and they also opened temporary shelters for workers who were fleeing abusive employers.[101] In addition, GCC governments cooperated with Indian and other diplomats to serve expatriate workers better before and after they had come to the region.[102] In 2008, Gulf construction firms went so far as to discuss offering "sensible working hours" to their expatriate employees.[103]

The Costs of Sensible Hours

The changes described above carried enormous direct and indirect costs. To begin with, expatriates sent home $27 billion in remittances in 2005, $38 billion in 2006, and $72 billion in 2007.[104] On top of the remittances, expatriate workers also require far greater quantities of basic resources than GCC governments had previously provided, especially in the form of food, water, and electricity.

For food, Gulf Arabs had maintained their populations for many years by generously subsidizing their own farmers and importing what they lacked. But as their expatriate populations grew in the early years of the twenty-first century, these sources were no longer sufficient. Instead, Gulf Arabs were forced to subsidize, rent, and purchase millions of arable acres overseas, sometimes as distant from the Gulf as Indonesia.[105] Domestic water resources were also increasingly insufficient to meet the demands of rising Gulf populations. These gaps forced Gulf governments to fall back on the same strategies that I discussed in Chapter 3: ever larger and more expensive desalinization plants.

Equally striking is the fact that GCC states were compelled by soaring domestic energy demand (8 percent annually) to invest for the first time in nuclear, coal, and renewable energy—despite the fact that they had among the largest reserves of oil and gas in the world.[106] In 2008, some experts estimated that the UAE alone would need to spend an enormous sum, $10 billion, to meet its energy needs for just the next three years.[107] In that same year, Abu Dhabi signed partnerships with General Electric and the United Kingdom to build Masdar City, a centrally planned community that will utilize renewable power and develop renewable fuels.[108] King Abdullah Economic City, a Red Sea port community in Saudi Arabia, will also be powered by renewable resources. Qatar, Saudi Arabia, and Oman have announced plans to build wind, thermal, and solar power plants.[109] But these projects may take years to come on line, and it remains an open question in the twenty-first century whether GCC states can amass the human and natural resources necessary to make the Dubai model work.

The Downfall of the Dubai Model

The most dangerous drawback to the Dubai model did not appear until the end of 2008. Throughout Dubai's rise to prominence, the emirate's leaders regularly took out large loans to fund their commercial projects. Although economists warned as early as 2005 that a bubble had begun to form in Dubai and elsewhere in the GCC, no official action was taken until the credit crisis, decline in oil prices, and global economic slowdown in 2008 eviscerated stock prices and real estate values.[110] By then, it was already too late, and panic swept throughout Gulf economies. To prevent a banking crisis, Gulf governments were compelled to take the unprecedented step of safeguarding domestic bank deposits. The UAE alone had to inject more than $32 billion into its financial system.[111] These were financial problems beyond anything that had been seen in the region for years.

Formerly signature companies, such as Kuwait's Gulf Bank and Dubai's Amlak and Tamweel real estate brokers, collapsed, which necessitated enormous government bailouts and the immediate repatriation of overseas assets.[112] Emaar Properties saw its stock value plummet by 75 percent in 2008, and Emirates Airlines, Dubai's most well-known company, was nearly nationalized in January 2009.[113] Terrified by worsening economic conditions, Kuwaiti members of parliament blocked their government from signing a multi-billion-dollar partnership with the Dow Chemical Company to produce polyethylene.[114] Layoffs occurred throughout every sector of the Gulf economy, forcing thousands of expatriate workers to return home.[115]

A remarkable change occurred within the UAE when Abu Dhabi provided Dubai with billions of dollars to pay off its considerable debt obligations. By February 2009, Dubai's government owed $20 billion, and its state-owned companies owed an additional $70 billion. In November and December 2009, Dubai suspended debt payments; published media reports suggested that the emirate's debt had reached $100 billion, or $400,000 per capita.[116] Although Dubai's officials emphasized that they had enough assets to pay off their debts, the actions of the UAE federal government (prompted by Abu Dhabi) suggested otherwise. The federal constitution was quickly amended to bar the UAE's prime minister (Dubai's Shaikh Muhammad), all his deputies, and all federal ministers from holding any private-sector job and from carrying out business with federal or local governments. How Abu Dhabi could bar Shaikh Muhammad, a wealthy businessman in his own right, from carrying out private business with the government he headed was not clear, but the message of the changes was not hard to discern: Dubai's government had accumulated sufficient debt that it was no longer independent of Abu Dhabi financially or politically. Indeed, Dubai's economic model no longer appeared to work in Dubai itself.[117]

Anxiety and a New Path Forward

The staggering financial losses in Dubai and the rest of the Gulf are minor compared to the social consequences of another wave of expatriate laborers. For governments and societies already grappling with questions of political and social legitimacy, the additional influx of expatriate workers raises new questions and increases a host of long-felt existential fears on the part of the domestic populations in the Gulf. In particular, Gulf Arabs worry that international institutions, the prevalence of the English language, European conceptions of gender, and marriage to expatriates are so influential that they will compel everyone to conform to Western social norms and to abandon the traditions and social practices that defined Gulf life. Despite their wealth and their distance from military conflicts in the Middle East, Gulf Arabs often view themselves as unable to combat forces that are altering life in their societies.[118]

Jamal al-Suwaidi, who directs the Center for Emirates Studies, a top GCC policy institution in Abu Dhabi, articulated this angst in a series of articles published in the UAE media. His views are worth noting because he is a leading Emirati academic and adviser to Abu Dhabi's crown prince, Shaikh Muhammad bin Zayid al-Nahyan.[119] In 2006, he noted in *al-Itihad,* a major Arabic daily in the UAE, that he and his fellow Emiratis no longer existed socially or politically. "Our country," he lamented, is now "filled with various nationalities to such an extent that there is no longer any place left for us."[120] Although al-Suwaidi failed to define what the consequences of this situation might be, he implied that indigenous Emirati culture might soon vanish in a society comprising people who are neither Arabs nor Sunni Muslims.[121] The minister of labor of Bahrain, Majid al-Alawi, echoed al-Suwaidi's words in 2008, observing that the presence of 17 million South Asians and other foreigners was "a danger worse than the atomic bomb or an Israeli attack" to the future of the Gulf.[122]

What danger do the expatriates pose? Here al-Suwaidi provided a clear window into the views of some Emiratis and other Gulf Arabs. He told Dubai's *Gulf News* in an extended interview that during a trip in 2007 to a mall in Dubai he felt awkward, since everyone there was staring at him as if he were "from another planet." Why were they staring at him? His outfit, the *dishdasha* worn by Emiratis and other Gulf Arabs, set him apart from everyone else at the mall. Throughout the rest of the article, al-Suwaidi focused on how socioeconomic changes over the past quarter-century had robbed Emiratis of their identity, making them feel like strangers in their own land. Implying that the government deliberately understated the percentage of the population that is foreign, he claimed that it has done little to help Emiratis. The attitudes of senior leaders, he insisted, were similar to the laissez-faire economic ideas of the political philosopher Adam Smith.[123]

Notwithstanding al-Suwaidi's anxiety about the future of Emiratis and his anger at the government's inability or unwillingness to assist them, he did not call for a change in official policy or suggest that expatriates should be expelled. Nor did he call for greater implementation of programs by which Emiratis and other Gulf Arabs could replace expatriate workers, which is the chief policy response of Gulf governments to the demographic problems facing their societies. Instead, he admitted that there is no way to fix the demographic imbalances. Expatriates, he conceded, are the permanent majority, will have a say in how the Gulf states are administered, and cannot be dismissed as outsiders. Indeed, the best approach is for Gulf nationals to find ways to cooperate with foreigners and to stress areas of common concern and mutual interest.[124]

Conclusion

Al-Suwaidi's comments reflect the profound feeling of vulnerability among an important segment of GCC Arabs in the twenty-first century and the compromises that they feel they will have to make in order to prosper. GCC governments face a variety of challenges that appear to be beyond their immediate control or that of their partners. To their north, Iraq remains militarily and economically weak. The Shia-dominated central government of Iraq cannot realistically invade a GCC state or check the rise of Iran's influence from the Gulf to the Mediterranean. Yet the new government carries even greater social and political weight in the region than the government of Saddam Hussein or his Sunni predecessors did, because it is allied with Iraq's Shia clerical elite. It is significant that Iraqi Shia clerics are Arab and therefore carry an authority among Gulf Arab Shia that is unmatched by their Iranian colleagues. There are no senior-ranking Shia clerics in the GCC states, so many Gulf Arab Shia look to Iraqi clerics for guidance and political support. From the vantage point of the GCC governments, the rise of Shia political power has added a potentially dangerous wild card into their societies at a time when regional politics are in considerable flux. Such a wild card could hinder the difficult task of managing these diverse and rapidly changing societies.

A key factor that is reinforcing the vulnerability of the GCC governments has been the actions of the United States. Despite the presence of thousands of US soldiers in Iraq and the withdrawal of US forces from their own states, GCC officials believe that the Gulf and the wider Middle East are far more dangerous at this time than they were before the fall of Saddam Hussein's government. They are mystified that Washington seemingly abandoned Iraq to Shia Arabs, allowed Iranian power to grow regionally, and supported Israeli military actions with little regard for the views of even the most pro-US GCC states. This final point is important because Israeli actions have further alienated segments of the GCC population who were already furious at the situation in Iraq and therefore tempted to utilize force against their governments. This fact, along with the ongoing decline in the value of the US dollar and the growing cultural-political power of Iraqi Shia clerics, has led the GCC governments to come to a profound realization—namely, that their security can no longer rest chiefly on the ability of the US military to deter every domestic and foreign threat. In the future, the GCC governments will have to look for new mechanisms to maintain their security that do not begin and end with US power. This realization represents as profound a shift in the strategic thinking of the GCC states as what occurred when Great Britain withdrew from the region in the 1970s or when the shah's government fell in Iran in 1979.

However harrowing the transition may be for the GCC states in the short term, they may reap significant benefits in the long run. The new consultative institutions and the new emphasis on openness may serve as useful mechanisms to address social, cultural, and political grievances. Greater official transparency could also help to combat corruption and to compel Gulf Arabs to more honestly evaluate their challenges. Furthermore, the new emphasis on privatization and economic diversification introduces two additional checks on corruption: international investors and multilateral institutions.

As I will detail in Chapter 6, policies aimed at integrating expatriates in the Gulf could build on the region's long history of supporting diverse peoples by easing the social and cultural tensions described by al-Suwaidi and others. The new policies may also have the added benefit of convincing expatriates to spend more of their salaries in the GCC rather than sending most of their money back to their home countries.[125]

The GCC governments can rely on a host of foreign partners. For example, their relationship with Iraq is not a one-way street. Just as Shia clerics in Iraq can influence the domestic politics of Arab Gulf states, the GCC governments can shape the politics of Iraq. They can do this by utilizing existing tribal and religious networks and by funding political parties and religious institutions. The GCC states will be much freer to pursue these options after the withdrawal of US forces from Iraq.

Gulf Arabs already maintain a regional customs union and can live and work in any GCC state. Despite its many problems, the GCC is steadily evolving into an institution akin to the European Union. The GCC aims to establish a monetary union that will eventually have an independent central bank that is similar to the European Central Bank. That new bank will control a single Gulf currency, tentatively called the khaliji.[126] The new currency will be linked first to the dollar but eventually—like Kuwait's currency—to a basket of currencies in which the dollar will be just one of many. The new system could help to address many problems in the Gulf that are connected to inflation and monetary policy. It is worth noting, in this connection, that Nasser al-Saidi, the chief economist for Dubai's International Financial Centre Authority, noted that the peg to the US dollar had thwarted attempts in the Gulf to control surging inflation after 2003.[127]

The GCC states have found willing commercial and political partners in Europe, Asia, and the Middle East. Iran in particular has been one of the strongest markets for GCC goods—especially those from the UAE and Saudi Arabia—since 1995.[128] China represents an even larger market for GCC oil producers and a source of both investment and advanced weapons systems. Although oil prices declined substantially in 2008 in response to the world economic slowdown, many experts believe that these prices will rebound strongly when the global economy recovers.[129] (In fact, oil prices had already rebounded to between $70 and $80 a barrel by December 2009.[130]) In the long run, the increased income from oil will allow the Gulf states to further diversify their economies and to invest in alternative energy. On the other hand, there is no reason for the GCC states to jettison their mutually profitable financial relationship with the United States.

Although there is no guarantee that the GCC states will make better choices with new and more democratic institutions, broadening the decision-making process at least increases the probability that Gulf Arabs (and their expatriate populations) will not repeat their past mistakes. The capacity of the consultative institutions to produce beneficial policies for their societies rests on the goals of the leadership and the sociopolitical makeup of the Gulf Arab states. It is important to bear in mind that monarchs have been the driving force for reform in the Gulf and that personal and tribal ties remain highly significant. As Gulf societies have grown ever larger and more diverse, their leaders have sought to maintain the personal quality of politics through significant investments in government websites that feature strict quality control and that promise guaranteed prompt responses from officials.[131] These systems build on the long-held principle that government leaders should be directly accountable to their subjects—a principle that at one time prompted rulers in the Gulf to have their telephone numbers printed in the phone book and to hold regular meetings with their subjects.

If the GCC states can maintain stability at home and abroad, their reform programs will make gains that were scarcely imaginable only a few years ago. On the other hand, if there is either external or internal instability, the GCC governments will be unable to carry out bold socioeconomic reform programs. Standards of living—which have declined by more than half since 1980 in Saudi Arabia—could produce ever worse cycles of poverty, violence, and despair.

One should not forget that most of the challenges discussed above are decades old and predate the wars in Iraq, the terrorist attack of September 11, and even the start of Saudi Arabia's special relationship with the United States. Furthermore, many of the GCC states' responses to these challenges, including closer regional integration and finding new international partners, have worked well in Europe and other parts of the world. The fact that the GCC states are still thriving and have drawn foreign investment despite all these problems is a testament to the vast resources they still have at their disposal. These resources are not limitless, however. Failure to take advantage of recent opportunities presented at home and abroad could make the current instability in the region permanent, thereby needlessly wasting a host of resources.

Nowhere is this danger clearer than in the position of female nationals. They are the one segment of indigenous Gulf populations who have the skills and the desire to work in modern postpetroleum economies. How Gulf Arabs reconcile women's desire to fill leadership roles in politics and business with conservative social and religious traditions is the subject that I will address in the next chapter.

Notes

1. International Monetary Fund, "United Arab Emirates: Selected Issues and Statistical Appendix," Country Report 5/268, 29 (available at http://www.imf .org/).

2. Jad Mouawad, "Oil Demand Down; First Time Since '83," *New York Times,* December 11, 2008.

3. Carl Mortished, "Demand for Oil and Gas Will Outstrip Supply Within 7 Years, Says Shell Chief," *Times* (London), January 25, 2008.

4. Steven Mufson, "Skyrocketing Oil Prices Stump Experts," *Washington Post,* May 22, 2008; Mike Nizza, "The Lede Notes on News: Market Faces a Disturbing Forecast," *New York Times,* May 22, 2008 (available at http://thelede .blogs.nytimes.com/); Adam Shell, "Spiraling Oil Prices Could Skewer Stocks," *USA Today,* May 22, 2008 (available at http://www.usatoday.com/).

5. Mouawad, "Oil Demand Down; First Time Since '83."

6. Ibid.

7. Jad Mouawad, "OPEC Looks to Stem Fall in Oil Prices," *New York Times,* December 16, 2008; "Plunging Oil Prices May Hamstring Region's Bold Sustainability Plans," *Greenwire,* December 17, 2008. That said, it is estimated that GCC states could continue to make a profit on producing oil as long as the global price of oil was above $8 a barrel.

8. For more on these troop reductions, see United States Department of Defense, "Active Duty Military Personnel Strengths by Regional Area and by Country," 309A, March 31, 2003 (available at http://siadapp.dior.whs.mil/); United States Department of Defense, "Active Duty Military Personnel Strengths by Regional Area and by Country," 309A, June 30, 2003 (available at http:// siadapp.dior.whs.mil/); United States. Department of Defense, "Active Duty Military Personnel Strengths by Regional Area and by Country," 309A, December 31, 2003 (available at http://siadapp.dior.whs.mil/); United States Department of Defense, "Active Duty Military Personnel Strengths by Regional Area and by Country," 309A, June 30, 2004 (available at http://siadapp.dior.whs.mil/).

9. Iranian and GCC officials exchanged numerous visits after 1997, and both Khatami and his successor, Mahmoud Ahmadinejad, visited multiple GCC states.

"Iran, Bahrain Stress Closer Political, Economic Ties," Iran News Agency, August 31, 2004 (distributed by United Press International); "Iran and Oman Issue Joint Communiqué, Call for Restoration of Security in the Region," Financial Times Information, Global News Wire—Asia Africa Intelligence Wire, October 7, 2005; "Khatami Leaves the Kingdom," Saudi Press Agency, August 16, 2005 (distributed by United Press International); Economist Intelligence Unit, *June 2006 Oman Country Report* (London: EIU, 2006), 3, 8; "Iranian President Concludes Visit to Kuwait," BBC Monitoring Middle East—Political, February 27, 2006; "Iran's Ahmadinejad to Visit UAE, Oman," Agence France-Presse—English, May 7, 2007.

10. Frederic Wehrey, et al., *Saudi-Iranian Relations Since the Fall of Saddam: Rivalry, Cooperation, and Implications for U.S. Policy* (Santa Monica, CA: Rand Corporation, 2009), 30.

11. Claude Salahni, "Analysis: Fragmented Iraq: Saudi Challenge," United Press International, April 7, 2006; "U.S. Policy Handing Iraq Over to Iran," *Daily Times* (Lahore, Pakistan), September 9, 2005 (available at http://www.dailytimes.com/.pk).

12. Rami Khouri, "The US Is Neither Feared nor Respected Anymore," *Daily News Egypt,* April 25, 2007 (available at http://www.thedailynewsegypt.com/).

13. Jim Krane, "U.S. Air Bases in Persian Gulf to Eventually Replace Those in Iraq, Senior General Says," Associated Press, May 13, 2006.

14. Marc Lynch, "Blogging the New Arab Public," *Arab Media & Society I* (February 2007): 15–16 (available at http://www.arabmediasociety.com) and Eisa al-Nashmi, "Political Discussions in the Arab World: A Look at Online Forums from Kuwait, Saudi Arabia, Jordan, and Egypt" (Master's thesis, University of Florida, 2007), 87–89; and Jon Nordenson, "The Internet as a Public Sphere: A Case From Kuwait," paper presented at the annual meeting of the Middle East Studies Association (MESA), Boston, MA, November 2009.

15. Richard Burkholder, "Kuwaiti Impressions of U.S. Have Soured Since 2001: Just One-quarter or Less of Kuwaiti Citizens View U.S. as Friendly, Trustworthy," Gallup News Service, February 27, 2007 (available at http://www gallup.com/).

16. Sam Ghattas, "Tens of Thousands of Lebanese Shiites Protest Attack on Shrine in Iraq," Associated Press, February 24, 2006; Economic Intelligence Unit, *May 2006 Kuwait Country Report* (London: EIU, 2006), 19–20. Hundreds of Kuwaiti Shia reportedly protested the February 23, 2006, attack on a major Shia shrine in Iraq.

17. Economic Intelligence Unit, *May 2006 Kuwait Country Report,* 19–20.

18. Omar Hasan, "Kuwait Pegs Dinar to Basket of Currencies," Agence France-Presse—English, May 20, 2007.

19. For more on the "traditional" Kuwaiti position on its oil supplies, see Energy Information Administration (EIA), "Kuwait: Country Analysis Briefs," April 2009 (available at (http://www.eia.doe.gov/).

20. "Kuwaiti Oil Reserves in Doubt," *Middle East Oil and Gas News Wire,* April 15, 2006.

21. Abdulaziz Basleem and Mohammed al-Kinani, "Not So Cool in Taif," *Saudi Gazette,* July 20, 2006.

22. Economist Intelligence Unit, *April 2003 Qatar Country Report* (London: EIU, 2003), 15–18; N. Janardhan, "Politics—Qatar: Approval of Constitution

Seen as a Good First Step," Inter Press News Services, April 30, 2003; Faisal Batoot, "Qatar Gets First Woman Cabinet Minister," Agence France-Presse—English, May 8, 2003 (available at http://www.lexisnexis.com/).

23. Batoot, "Qatar Gets First Woman Cabinet Minister"; Economist Intelligence Unit, *April 2006 Qatar Country Report* (London: EIU, 2006), 7, 12, 14; Barbara Bibbo, "First Woman Elected to Qatar Chamber," Financial Times Information, Global News Wire—Asia Africa Intelligence Wire, May 18, 2006.

24. Robert Worth, "Al-Jazeera No Longer Nips at Saudis," *New York Times,* January 4, 2008.

25. "Peaceful Use of Nuclear Technology Iran's Right—Qatari Emir," Financial Times Information, Global News Wire—Asia Africa Intelligence Wire, May 2, 2006.

26. Quoted in Robert F. Worth, "Qatar, Playing All Sides, Is a Nonstop Mediator," *New York Times,* July 9, 2008.

27. Economist Intelligence Unit, *June 2006 Bahrain Country Report* (London: EIU, 2006), 8, 26.

28. Neil MacFarquhar, "In Tiny Arab State, Web Takes on the Ruling Elite," *New York Times,* January 15, 2006. Some Bahraini Shia have faxed messages to Iraqi Shia clerics asking if they should follow Bahrain's traffic laws, since they do not look at the Sunni ruling family as legitimate. Shaikh Ayatollah Ali al-Sistani reportedly responded that they had to abide by the laws.

29. Ibid. Among the most popular of these websites is www.bahrainonline.org.

30. "Bahrain: End Targeted Threats to Rights Activists," Targeted News Services, November 12, 2008.

31. "Dollar's Woes Eyed in Persian Gulf," *AFX International Focus,* May 21, 2007.

32. Ibid.; Ali Khalil, "Gulf States Should Aim to Narrow Inflation Gap: Report," Agence France-Presse—English, August 19, 2008.

33. Charles V. Bagli, "Dubai Royalty Plans to Restore a Times Sq. Landmark," *New York Times,* June 6, 2006 (available at http://www.lexisnexis.com); Ambrose Evans-Pritchard, "Middle East Trillion Dollar Gamble on Future of Gulf," *Daily Telegraph* (London), May 9, 2006.

34. "UAE Model Muslim Country: President Bush," Emirates News Agency/United Press International, January 13, 2008.

35. Inflation hovered between 15 percent and 16 percent in 2008. "Gulf Co-operation Council—Oil Fuels Ongoing GCC Boom—Healthy Oil Revenues Mean the Gulf Co-operation Council Countries Are Enjoying an Ongoing Boom and Even Concerns Over Inflation Cannot Shake the Optimism Surrounding the Region," *Banker,* September 1, 2008.

36. Omar Hasan, "Gulf States in a Fix over Tumbling Dollar," Agence France-Presse—English, March 17, 2008.

37. Economist Intelligence Unit, *May 2003 Oman Country Report* (London: EIU, 2003), 7–15; Paul Blustein, "Trade Deal Looks More Like a Distant Dream; Developing Nations Rise Up Against U.S. Insistence on Deep Tariff Cuts," *Washington Post,* July 4, 2006.

38. Sarah Kershaw, "US-Saudi Ties Frayed by Mideast Tensions," *New York Times,* April 30, 2003; Patrick Tyler, "The Saudi Exit: No Sure Cure for the Royals' Problems," *New York Times,* April 30, 2003; "US Moves Air Operations

Base from Saudi Arabia to Qatar," *World Market Research Limited,* April 30, 2003.

39. Glenn Kessler and Alan Sipress, "Bombings Kill 20 in Saudi Capital," *Washington Post,* April 13, 2003.

40. John King, "The War in Lebanon" (includes interview with correspondent Richard Roth), CNN, "This Week at War," August 5, 2007.

41. Michael Knights and Anna Solomon-Schwartz, "The Broader Threat from Sunni Islamists in the Gulf," *PolicyWatch* 883, July 19, 2004 (available at http://www.washingtoninstitute.org/).

42. Sabria S. Jawhar, "A Change in Security Force Tactics," *Saudi Gazette,* June 25, 2006.

43. Jad Mouawad, "Saudi Arabia Looks Past Oil; Enriched by Record Prices, the Nation Seeks to Diversify," *New York Times,* December 13, 2005.

44. Economist Intelligence Unit, *Country Report Saudi Arabia—Main Report* (London: EIU, 2008), 5.

45. Often these have included mass weddings that include dozens of couples. Michael Slackman, "Dreams Stifled; Egypt's Young Turn to Islamic Fervor," *New York Times,* February 17, 2008 (available at http://www.lexisnexis.com/; United States Department of State, *Country Reports on Terrorism 2007* (Washington, DC: United States Government Printing Office, 2008), 220 (available at http://www.state.gov/); Katherine Zopef, "Deprograming Jihadists," *New York Times,* November 9, 2008.

46. Michel Cousins, "Human Rights Team Holds Frank Talks with Saudi Officials," Middle East Newsfile, January 27, 2003; United States Department of State, Under Secretary for Democracy and Global Affairs, Bureau of Democracy, Human Rights, and Labor, *2006 Country Reports on Human Rights Practices,* "Saudi Arabia" (available at http://www.state.gov/); Turki al-Saheli, "Saudi Human Rights Commission Launches Website," Asharq Aawsat English, March 4, 2008 (available at http://www.aawsat.com/).

47. Frederic Wehrey et al., *Saudi-Iranian Relations Since the Fall of Saddam,* 27.

48. Faiza Saleh Ambah, "Saudi King Tiptoes Toward More Openness," *Christian Science Monitor,* October 6, 2006 (available at http://www.csmonitor.com/); Neil MacFarquhar, "Saudi Shiites, Long Kept Down, Look to Iraq and Assert Rights," *New York Times,* March 2, 2005; Kim Murphy, "Saudi Shias Take Hope from Changes Next Door," *Los Angeles Times,* May 8, 2003 (available at http://articles.latimes.com/); "Saudi King Attends Celebrations in the Eastern Kingdom," Financial Times Information, Global News Wire—Asia Africa Intelligence Wire, July 14, 2006.

49. Donna Abu-Nasr, "Saudi King Shakes Up Religious Establishment," Associated Press, February 13, 2009.

50. Toby Jones, "Violence and the Illusion of Reform," *MERIP,* November 13, 2003 (available at http://www.merip.org/); Gwenn Okruhlik, "The Irony of Islah (Reform)," *Washington Quarterly* 28, no. 4 (2005): 153–170.

51. For more on the elections, see International Crisis Group, "The Shia Question in Saudi Arabia," *Middle East Report,* no. 45, September 19, 2005, 7–9 (available at http://merln.ndu.edu/).

52. Mariam al-Hakeem, "Saudi Body Listens to Citizen Critique in First Open

Meeting," Financial Times Information, Global News Wire—Asia Africa Intelligence Wire, June 14, 2006; "Saudi Municipal Council Members Participate in First Public Meeting," Financial Times Information, Global News Wire—Asia Africa Intelligence Wire, July 4, 2006.

53. Max Rodenbeck, "All in the Family," *Economist,* January 7, 2006, 5–7.

54. Economist Intelligence Unit, *May 2006 Kuwait Country Report,* 12–16.

55. Economist Intelligence Unit, *May 2003 Oman Country Report,* 1–2.

56. Christopher Davidson, *Dubai: The Vulnerability of Success* (New York: Columbia University Press, 2008), 106–135.

57. Ibid.

58. Ibid.

59. John Arlidge, ""Sandstorm Hits Dubai's Dream; The Credit Crunch Has Left the Emirate Battling to Show Its Grand Plans Are More Than a Mirage," *Sunday Times* (London), June 21, 2009.

60. Davidson, *Dubai: The Vulnerability of Success,* 95, 120–121.

61. Evans-Pritchard, "Middle East Trillion Dollar Gamble."

62. Davidson, *Dubai: The Vulnerability of Success,* 128–134.

63. "Dubai, the City of Cranes," Associated Press, July 3, 2008.

64. "Emirates Leader: Fewer Foreign Workers," *AFX International Focus,* April 17, 2007.

65. Christopher Dickey, Vivian Salama, and Nick Summers, "Is Dubai's Party Over?" *Newsweek,* December 15, 2008; Chris Wright, "A Tremor in Blingopolis: The World's Glitziest City Faces an Unfamiliar Feeling: Worry," *Boston Globe,* August 3, 2008.

66. For more on his ideas, see Muhammad bin Rashid al-Maktum, *My Vision: Challenges in the Race to Excellence* (Beirut: Arab Institute for Research and Publication, 2006).

67. Economist Intelligence Unit, *April 2006 Qatar Country Report,* 5; Economist Intelligence Unit, *May 2006 Kuwait Country Report,* 5; Economist Intelligence Unit, *May 2006 Saudi Arabia Country Report* (London: EIU, 2006), 5; Economist Intelligence Unit, *May 2006 UAE Country Report* (London: EIU, 2006), 5; Economist Intelligence Union, *June 2006 Bahrain Country Report,* 5; Economist Intelligence Unit, *June 2006 Oman Country Report,* 5; Economist Intelligence Unit, *November 2008 Bahrain Country Report* (London: EIU, 2008), 5; Economist Intelligence Unit, *November 2008 Kuwait Country Report* (London: EIU, 2008), 7; Economist Intelligence Unit, *November 2008 Oman Country Report* (London: EIU, 2008), 5; Economist Intelligence Unit, *November 2008 Qatar Country Report* (London: EIU, 2008), 5; Economist Intelligence Unit, *November 2008 Saudi Arabia Country Report* (London: EIU), 6; Economist Intelligence Unit, *November 2008 UAE Country Report* (London: EIU, 2008), 5.

68. "Emirates Leader: Fewer Foreign Workers."

69. "GCC: Oil Revenue Bonanza Has Boosted Government Spending," *al-Bawaba,* 2007 (available at http://www.bilateralchamber.org/).

70. Ibid.

71. Nadim Kawach, "GCC Fiscal Surplus to Peak Due to Strong Crude Prices in 2008," *Emirates Business 24/7,* December 29, 2008 (available at http://zawya.com/).

72. International Monetary Fund, "IMF Executive Board Concludes 2006 Ar-

ticle IV Consultation with the United Arab Emirates: Public Information Notice No 06/76," July 12, 2006 (available at http://www.imf.org/).

73. "Value of Major Gulf Projects Exceeds $2 Trillion for First Time," *Middle East Economic Digest,* March 30, 2008.

74. International Monetary Fund, "United Arab Emirates: 2007 Article IV Consultation: IMF Country Report No. 07/347," October 2007, 42 (available at http://www.imf.org/).

75. Stanley Carvalho, "Foreign Direct Investment in the UAE Doubles," Financial Times Information, Global News Wire—Asia Africa Intelligence Wire, May 8, 2006; "Bahrain Major FDI Destination," *DubaiPhotoMedia,* August 13, 2007. Foreign direct investment in Bahrain was "double the value of overseas investments held by Bahrainis" in 2007.

76. "U.S. Secretary of the Treasury: UAE's Forward-looking Growth Model for GCC," Emirates News Agency, October 29, 2008.

77. Thanassis Cambanis, "Saudi King Tries to Grow Modern Ideas in Desert," *New York Times,* October 27, 2007; Evans-Pritchard, "Middle East Trillion Dollar Gamble"; Mariam al-Hakeem, "Saudi King Unveils Major Tourism Project in Taif," Financial Times Information, Global News Wire—Asia Africa Intelligence Wire, July 18, 2006; Mouawad, "Saudi Arabia Looks Past Oil"; David Parsley, "The Sheikh's Real Goal," *Sunday Times* (London), September 7, 2008; Seth Sherwood, "Is Qatar the Next Dubai?" *New York Times,* June 4, 2006; "Fully Booked," *Gulf Construction,* October 1, 2006; "Value of Major Gulf Projects Exceeds $2 Trillion for First Time."

78. Cambanis, "Saudi King Tries to Grow Modern Ideas in Desert"; Alan Riding, "The Louvre's Art: Priceless. The Louvre's Name: Expensive," *New York Times,* March 7, 2007.

79. "Plunging Oil Prices May Hamstring Region's Bold Sustainability Plans," *Greenwire,* December 17, 2008.

80. Ben Gilbert, "Dubai's Frenzied, Trillion-dollar Building Boom Falters," *Christian Science Monitor,* December 4, 2008 (available at http://www.csmonitor.com/).

81. Mohammad Fadhel, "Excess Cash, Peg to Weak Dollar Fuel Gulf Inflation," Agence France-Presse—English, March 23, 2008.

82. "UAE Salaries Rise by 10.7%—Study," Middle East Company Newswire, September 30, 2007.

83. "Kuwait's Population Reaches 3.4 million," Agence France-Presse—English, March 30, 2008; "Kuwait Population to Reach 5.63 Million by 2030," Middle East Financial News Wire, February 6, 2008; Central Intelligence Agency, World Fact Book, "Kuwait," "Oman," and "UAE" (available at https://www.cia.gov/).

84. Robert Worth, "Laid-Off Foreigners Flee as Dubai Spirals Downward," *New York Times,* February 11, 2009.

85. Joe Avanceña, "Sanctuary for Illegal Workers," *Saudi Gazette,* June 21, 2006.

86. Hassan Fattah, "In Dubai, an Outcry from Asians for Workplace Rights," *New York Times,* March 26, 2006; "Rents Rocket in Oman," Financial Times Information, Global News Wire—Asia Africa Intelligence Wire, April 22, 2006.

87. "Value of Indian Workers' Wages in Gulf May Fall Further," Indo-Asian News Service, April 2, 2008.

88. Habib Toumi, "Bahrain Minister Pushes for New Law," *Gulf News,* December 26, 2008 (available at http://www.gulfnews.ae/).

89. "World Briefing Middle East: United Arab Emirates: No Child Jockeys Left," *New York Times,* June 13, 2006.

90. Ibid.

91. Joel Brinkley, "U.S. Faults Allies over Human Trafficking," *New York Times,* June 4, 2005; "World Briefing: Middle East: U.S. Adds Gulf Allies to Trafficking Blacklist," *New York Times,* June 13, 2007; US Department of State, Under Secretary for Democracy and Global Affairs, Bureau of Democracy and Global Affairs, Office to Monitor and Combat Trafficking in Persons, "Trafficking in Persons: 2008 Report" (available at http://www.state.gov/); Robert F. Worth, "Voice for Abused Women Upsets Dubai Patriarchy," *New York Times,* March 23, 2008.

92. "Blood, Sweat and Tears," al-Jazeera English, August 22, 2007 (available at http://english.aljazeera.net/).

93. Barbara Surk, "Dubai's Workers Strike over Poor Conditions, Threatening City State's Building Boom," Associated Press, October 28, 2007; "Bahrain Firm Denies It Will Deport Striking Workers," Indo-Asian News Service, February 14, 2008; "Workers of Indian-managed Firm in Qatar on Strike," Indo-Asian News Service, September 3, 2008.

94. "40,000 Workers on Strike in UAE," Press Trust of India, November 9, 2007.

95. "1,300 Migrant Workers Strike in Bahrain over Pay," Agence France-Presse—English, February 10, 2008.

96. "Dubai to Deport Workers After Violent Strike," Deutsche Presse-Agentur, October 29, 2007; "Ninety Indians Charged for Violent Protests in Dubai," Press Trust of India, October 31, 2007; Barbara Surk, "Emirati Police Arrest Hundreds of South Asian Workers to End Violent Strike over Low Wages," Associated Press March 18, 2008.

97. "Kuwait Prince Calls for Protection of Expat Workers' Rights," Indo-Asian News Service, August 5, 2008.

98. "UAE to Become More Foreign Worker–Friendly," Indo-Asian News Service, March 26, 2007; Jason DeParle, "Fearful of Restive Foreign Labor, Dubai Eyes Reforms," *New York Times,* August 7, 2007; Barbara Surk, "Asian Workers' Strike Prompts Emirates to Start Considering Minimum Wage," Associated Press, November 5, 2007; "Dubai Laborers Get a 20 percent Hike," AME Info—ME Real Estate and Construction, November 17, 2007; "Bahrain Strike Called Off, Wages Raised," Press Trust of India, February 14, 2008; "Bahrain Workers to Get Pay Hike," Indo-Asian News Service, February 15, 2008; "Expat Workers Get Higher Pay, Strike Ends," United News of India, March 13, 2008.

99. "Bahrain Workers Call Off Strike After Employer Apologized," Press Trust of India, February 13, 2007.

100. "Bahrain Parliament to Discuss Indian Workers' Strike," Press Trust of India (available at http://www.lexisnexis.com); "Kuwait Prince Calls for Protection of Expat Workers' Rights," Indo-Asian News Service, August 5, 2008; "Kuwait Parliament to Hold Emergency Session on Labour Unrest," Agence

France-Presse—English, September 3, 2008; "Kuwait Parliament to Hold Emergency Session on Foreign Workers," Indo-Asian News Service, September 4, 2008.

101. Worth, "Voice for Abused Women Upsets Dubai Patriarchy"; "Labour Ministry Gathers Public Opinion on Revised UAE Labour," Emirates News Agency, February 5, 2007.

102. "India Pushes for a Minimum Wage for Its 5 Million Migrant Workers in the Gulf," Associated Press, March 26, 2008; "Indian Mission in Bahrain Settles Dispute Between Workers, Sponsors," Indo-Asian News Service, April 9, 2008; Omar Hasan, "Kuwait Mulls Change in Sponsor System After Labour Unrest," Agence France-Presse—English, September 10, 2008; "Kuwait Ambassador Meets Khaleda, Discusses Worker Issue," United News of Bangladesh, November 5, 2008.

103. "Gulf Construction Sector Faces Shortage of Workers," Indo-Asian News Service, February 25, 2008.

104. Stanley Carvalho, "Remittances Put Burden on Economy," *Gulf News,* March 19, 2005; "Gulf States $72 Billion Expatriates Remittances," InfoProd, April 30, 2008; "Gulf States: $413 Billion Expatriates Remittances," InfoProd, May 6, 2008.

105. Adam Schreck, "Booming Gulf Looks Overseas for Agriculture Needs," Associated Press, November 16, 2008.

106. Hassan Fattah, "Abu Dhabi Explores Energy Alternatives," *New York Times,* March 18, 2007; Lydia Georgi, "Nuclear Energy Best Option for Gulf States: Experts," Agence France-Presse—English, May 27, 2008; "GCC to Invest $120b in Power, Water Sectors," MENA English (Middle East and North Africa Financial Network), March 23, 2008; Mark Hibbs, "GCC Nuclear Vision Challenges Arab World's Technology Focus," *Nucleonics Week,* December 4, 2008.

107. "UAE Needs to Spend over $10 Billion to Address Demand for Power," *Tribune Regional News—The Middle East and North Africa Business Report,* August 3, 2008.

108. "GE, Abu Dhabi Governments Invest Co. Form $8B Commercial Finance Venture, Other Projects," Associated Press, July 22, 2008.

109. "Plunging Oil Prices May Hamstring Region's Bold Sustainability Plans," *Greenwire,* December 17, 2008; Hibbs, *GCC Nuclear Vision Challenges Arab World's Technology Focus;* "Alternative Energies Could Hold the Key," *Gulf Construction,* September 7, 2008.

110. Dickey, Salama, and Summers, "Is Dubai's Party Over?"

111. Ibid.

112. Margaret Coker and Chip Cummins, "Crisis Hits Gulf as Kuwait Rescues Bank," *Australian,* October 28, 2008; John Irish and Raissa Kasolowsky, "Dubai to Scale Back Lofty Ambitions; Bank Sector Rattled; $1 Trillion Worth of Projects Planned or in Progress," *National Post's Financial Post and FP Investing,* November 25, 2008.

113. Steve Creedy, "Emirates Ownership Changes," *Australian,* January 5, 2009; Gilbert, "Dubai's Frenzied, Trillion-dollar Building Boom Falters"; Dominic Rushe and Iain Dey, "Stake in Emirates Focus of Bailout," *Australian,* December 1, 2008.

114. David Jolly, "Kuwait Scuttles Venture With Dow Chemical," *New York Times,* December 28, 2008.

115. Gilbert, "Dubai's Frenzied, Trillion-dollar Building Boom Falters"; Ali Khalil, "Dubai Property Giant Sacks 500," Agence France-Presse—English, November 30, 2008; Ali Khalil, "Victims of Dubai Property Bust Face Series of Blows," Agence France-Presse—English, January 5, 2009.

116. Sabi Shah, "Dubai World Falling Victim to Global Economic Recession," *The News International* (Lahore, Pakistan), December 3, 2009 (available at http://www.thenews.com.pk/).

117. Dickey, Salama, and Summers, "Is Dubai's Party Over?"; Adam Schreck, "Dubai Government, Cash Injection, but at What Cost?" Associated Press, February 24, 2009.

118. Duraid al-Baik, "Divorce: A Raging Controversy," Financial Times Information, Global News Wire—Asia Africa Intelligence Wire, December 31, 2005; Mariam al-Hakeem, "Saudis Alarmed by Rising Rates of Divorce," Financial Times Information, Global News Wire—Asia Africa Intelligence Wire, May 7, 2006; Samir Salama, "Rights Body Opens Doors to Expatriates," Financial Times Information, Global News Wire—Asia Africa Intelligence Wire, March 25, 2006; EIU, *June 2006 Bahrain Country Report,* 15–16; "Bahrain Alcohol Clause Cause of Contention," Financial Times Information, Global News Wire—Asia Africa Intelligence Wire, July 11, 2006; Christopher Davidson, *The United Arab Emirates: A Study in Survival* (Boulder, CO: Lynne Rienner Publishers, 2005), 262–266.

119. Jamal al-Suawaidi's views and his position in UAE society are discussed at length in Abdullah Khalaq, "UAE's Demographic Imbalance," *Gulf News,* April 14, 2007 (available at http://archive.gulfnews.com/).

120. Cited in Abdelbari Atwan, "The Gulf's Momentous Challenges," *Mideast Mirror,* May 11, 2006.

121. Ibid.

122. "Bahrain Labour Minister Warns of Asian Tsunami," Agence France-Presse—English, January [illegible], 2008.

123. Mohammed al-Mezel, "Who Are We, That's the Question," *Gulf News,* March 21, 2007 (available at http://archive.gulfnews.com/).

124. Ibid.

125. Nora Boustany, "Barrier-Breaking Bahraini Masters Diplomatic Scene: Nonoo Is First Jewish Ambassador from an Arab Nation," *Washington Post,* December 19, 2008.

126. "GCC Central Bank to Be Independent Entity," *Global Banking News,* November 27, 2008 (available at http://www.lexisnexis.com); Issac John, "GCC Single Currency Should Track Basket, Say DIFC Economists," *Khaleej Times,* December 18, 2008 (available at http://www.khaleejtimes.com/); "Gulf Ministers Reach Accord on Monetary Union," Agence France-Presse—English, December 30, 2008.

127. John, "GCC Single Currency Should Track Basket, Say DIFC Economists."

128. International Monetary Fund, *Direction of Trade Statistics Quarterly: December 2004* (Washington, DC: IMF, 2004), 187; International Monetary Fund, *Direction of Trade Statistics Quarterly: June 2006* (Washington, DC: IMF, 2006), 191; "Saudi Arabia: Balanced Saudi-Iranian Trade," InfoProd, January 14, 2003;

International Monetary Fund, *Direction of Trade Statistics Quarterly: September 2008* (Washington, DC: IMF, 2008), 54, 217, 282, 304, 315, 377; Eric Lipton, "U.S. Alarmed as Some Exports Veer Off Course," *New York Times,* April 2, 2008.

129. Delphine Dechaux, "Oil Industry Sounds Alarm on Investment Threat," Agence France-Presse—English, March 18, 2009.

130. Tarek El-Tablawy, "Saudi Oil Minister: Oil Prices Perfect," Associated Press, December 5, 2009.

131. Davidson, *Dubai: The Vulnerability of Success,* 165.

5

When Only Women Will Work

Husa . . . tore the veil from her face, donned sword and trousers, and took command of the fort and the army.

—Raymond O'Shea, 1947

From whom and from what ties does the woman wish to be liberated?

—Juyaher al-Musa'ed, 1979

Young men are oppressed here [in Saudi Arabia]. . . . All I want is equality with girls.

—Muhammad Qarni, 2007

In January 2004, Lubna Olayan stepped up to the lectern to deliver a speech to the Jeddah Economic Summit. The Ivy League–educated mother of three was a natural choice to be the first woman to address the forum in the Saudi port city, because she headed one of Saudi Arabia's best-known conglomerates, the Olayan Financing Group. Lubna was a daughter of Sulayman Olayan, who had risen from humble circumstances to become one of Saudi Arabia's most successful businessmen. Yet, the organizers of the conference might have rethought their decision to let her speak had they known what she would say and the controversy it would spawn. Throughout her speech, entitled "A Saudi Vision for Growth," Olayan outlined a vision of a Saudi Arabia that was at odds with what the kingdom's religious elites sought (and still seek) to project to the outside world. For nearly twenty years, they had rigidly enforced social norms that aimed to exclude women from virtually all public settings and to create a workforce that was overwhelmingly male, even if that meant importing thousands of expatriate workers. Instead, Olayan argued that any Saudi, "irrespective of gender," who was serious about working should have the opportunity to "find a job in the field for which he or she is best qualified."[1]

The reaction of the audience, which was composed of Saudi and foreign men and women, was enthusiastic and electric. Bill Clinton, Queen Rania of Jordan, and many other notables gave Olayan sustained applause, and dozens of men and women praised her in subsequent speeches at the conference. Furthermore, she did not wear the full hijab and covering traditionally worn by women in Saudi Arabia in public settings. Pictures of her and other businesswomen, many of whom wore no veils and freely interacted with men in public, appeared on the front pages of Saudi newspapers. Olayan and her colleagues had broken social taboos and challenged the authority of Saudi religious elites.

It is not surprising that the reaction of these elites was one of profound shock and anger. The highest religious figure in the kingdom, Grand Mufti Shaikh Abdulaziz ibn Abdullah al-Shaikh, immediately released a statement in which he condemned the summit, especially the public mixing of men and women. He argued that such behavior was the "root" of every evil and catastrophe, along with the sins of decadence and adultery. He also expressed his bewilderment and sorrow that "such shameful behavior" could have ever taken place in Saudi Arabia. Although he did not mention Olayan or the conference organizers by name, he nonetheless made it clear that he felt that they should be reprimanded. The mixing of men and women, he said, "is highly punishable" and "prohibited for all."[2]

These were not idle threats. Fourteen years earlier, in November 1990, as mentioned in Chapter 3, the government had delivered swift retribution against forty-five elite educated women (many of them university professors) who deliberately dismissed their drivers and drove through the streets of Riyadh—an act legal under Saudi law but frowned upon by the religious establishment. The government immediately dismissed the women from their jobs, confiscated their passports, and sought to shame them and their families by labeling them infidels. Some were even forced into exile. It took years for the forty-five women to regain their rights and privileges in Saudi life. To make clear how seriously the government had taken the act, it formally outlawed women from driving in the kingdom. Those women who contemplated driving would now face the wrath of *both* the state and the religious authorities.[3]

Because Olayan had violated social taboos and challenged religious elites in the same way as the forty-five women drivers, one would have expected the grand mufti's words to bring a swift retribution against her. Quite the opposite occurred: the Saudi government did not take action against Olayan, who has continued to this day to advocate for women's rights and to appear at home and abroad without the traditional Saudi covering and hijab.

Only a year after Olayan's speech, *The Girls of Riyadh* appeared on the Saudi scene. The novel elicited blistering criticism from the grand mufti and other Saudi conservatives because it discusses premarital sex, socioethnic tensions in the kingdom, and normal interactions between unrelated men and women. Yet, the novel won quick approval for distribution from the Saudi government. Many members of the Saudi establishment supported the novel's author, Rajaa Alsanea, a young Saudi dental student. No less a figure endorsed the book and its message than Ghazi al-Gosaibi, the minister of labor and one of Saudi king Abdullah's closest advisers. Alsanea, who wears the hijab, continues to write on issues similar to those she covered in *The Girls of Riyadh* and has a goal of winning the Nobel Prize in Literature by 2015.[4]

In this chapter, I seek to explain how women in the Arab Gulf states have harnessed political, economic, and social changes to alter their standing at home and abroad. I contend that women are well positioned to take advantage of these changes, owing to their advanced educations, the ever higher social and financial costs of employing expatriate workers, and the inability of their male colleagues to fill either skilled or unskilled positions. As noted earlier, indigenous men prefer working in occupations, such as the military or family businesses, that do not require extensive education. It is ironic that as women gain a greater role in Gulf life in coming years, they will attain a position that will be much closer to that of their great-grandmothers and grandmothers in the 1920s than to that of their mothers in the 1970s and 1980s.

Gender, the West, and the Gulf

The patriarchal structures of Saudi Arabia and the other Arab Gulf states have received consistent attention over the years, with popular and scholarly accounts expressing both fascination and outrage at the status of women in the Gulf. These accounts have focused on the limitations that these societies have placed on women's scholastic and work opportunities, legal and political rights, and mobility in public. Scholars and critics in the West have argued that women are subordinate, second-class citizens in Saudi Arabia and the other Gulf states—victims of entrenched patriarchal structures that transcend state and religious authority. The governments, these observers say, reaffirm their religious credentials and cultural authenticity by controlling women. By contrast, these critics argue, regulating male behavior to a similarly uniform standard would be impossible because it would raise questions about a regime's commitment to core cultural and religious values.[5]

Although there is much evidence to support this widely held view of women in the Gulf, this approach overlooks three key points.

First, women in GCC societies have acquired ever greater socioeconomic power in recent years, since they are the only group besides expatriates who are able to fill the positions created by the private sector. Women have disproportionately benefited from investment by GCC governments in education and have overtaken men in every category of educational achievement. Since GCC girls are generally more literate and stay in school longer than their male counterparts, this gap will only widen in the future. This gap is not a minor issue, for most Gulf women still do not enter the workforce but instead become housewives, a potentially enormous social and financial loss.

Second, the position of women both within individual states and in the broader region is hardly uniform. There are enormous differences among the social status, rights, and economic opportunities of women, based on their nation of origin, class, ethnicity, religious affiliation, sociocultural setting, and communal history.

Third, questions of gender in the GCC states *are not limited to women.* Just as women are expected to dress and act according to established social norms and obligations, so men are also expected to adhere to social expectations. The *ghutra* or *isamah,* male headgear or turbans, are analogous to the veil, and the *thob* and *kandura,* caftanlike garments, are equivalent to the *chador.* Most states in the Gulf require their male nationals to wear these types of clothing in public. The importance of the regulations is clear to anyone who has flown to the Gulf and seen women and men quickly change from Western clothes to "local" dress just before a flight ends. Nor are the restrictions limited to clothing: Arab Gulf men, like women, face class, ethnic, religious, and familial barriers in education, employment, marriage, and sociopolitical freedoms. As I will note in Chapter 6, Shia and expatriates of both genders have substantially fewer rights than some Sunni women. Even some Arab Sunni men face barriers; a Saudi college student told the *Washington Post* in September 2007 that young Saudi men yearn to be equal with women and many face severe restrictions, including the right to dress as they please.[6]

Women in Gulf History Before 1930

To understand contemporary Saudi society and the gender relations that will shape it and its neighbors in the future, one must start in the period before the discovery of oil. During that time, as I described in Chapter 2, women, like men, lived in very poor societies, in which pearling was the chief means of livelihood. Within that milieu, the tribal, clan, or socioeconomic status of the women's husbands or male relatives defined their freedoms and horizons. In general, the female members of Gulf ruling families and the wives of leading merchants or clerics rarely appeared in public or interacted with individuals outside of their families. Since, as Haya al-Mughni notes, "it was considered shameful, or *aib*, to let women's voices be heard" and for women to be seen by men who were not their relatives, elite families in Kuwait built large walled compounds to provide maximum protection for their female members.[7] To fulfill their families' domestic chores, these women also had servants and slaves, mostly from East Africa, South Asia, or other regions of the Indian Ocean.

Yet the wives of wholesale or retail merchants from the Iranian side of the Gulf, where social mores regarding gender were more relaxed, did not face the same social restrictions and often received some education. The wives of pearl divers, fishermen, grocers, blacksmiths, carpenters, and other skilled trades had even more freedom. They bought and sold goods and worked as seamstresses and quranic instructors. There had been private schools and tutors, known as *mutawah,* for girls in some Gulf communities since the 1890s.[8] (The first public school for girls in the Gulf was established in Bahrain in 1892.[9]) Older women could be midwives or folk healers. By contrast, rural women worked in agriculture and animal husbandry. Bedouin women and girls wove clothing and produced small-scale craft goods. Many of them were the chief commercial agents for their tribes and managed tribal or family life for extended periods.[10]

Nonetheless, women had limited social freedoms everywhere in the Gulf. They could not choose their husbands and were generally expected to wear the veil and the long cloak (*abaya*). Significantly, the widespread use of the veil in coastal Arab Gulf communities reflected the presence of Iranian and South Asian merchants, both of whom saw the veil as a symbol of female decency and propriety.[11] (Veiling was far less common in rural and other areas of the Gulf, where these groups did not exist in large numbers.) Male relatives had considerable power over women and were allowed to use capital punishment if one sufficiently dishonored her family.[12] Dowries were modest and it was not unheard of for families to limit women's inheritances, thereby violating a chief tenet of Islamic law. Polygamy existed but was limited to very wealthy families. Nor was there any social stigma attached to women who worked when economic conditions warranted—a frequent occurrence. US missionaries noted in the 1930s that Gulf women were hard workers and made enormous sacrifices for their families.[13]

But patriarchal power had definite limits, just as it increasingly does today. Pearling, fishing, and commerce—the bedrocks of the old Gulf economy—all required men to spend long periods away from home—perhaps as much as half a year. Even when men were not away, women provided vital support to economic activity: they mended fishing nets, sorted products, and sold fish and other goods in the marketplaces. Wealthier women owned pearling ships and commercial caravans, invested in small businesses, and established retail shops of their own.

Women operated businesses not only in Dubai, Jeddah, and other coastal communities but also in urban communities and the heartland of what would become Saudi Arabia. As Soraya Altorki and Donald P. Cole show, women filled a variety of occupations in ‘Unayzah, a central Saudi city that has long been influenced by Wahhabi ideas. In that city, female merchants sold goods to men and women in the *souq* (market) and also staffed a *kuttab* for women (i.e., an elementary school that taught reading, writing, and the Quran). In the 1920s, the city was seen by King Ibn Saud as an admirable model for his new capital city, Riyadh. 'Unayzah's women still hold a remarkable variety of positions in government, education, finance, commerce, and even the media today.[14] Therefore, it should come as no surprise that Lubna Olayan, the daughter of one of the most commercially successful 'Unayzah natives of all time, Sulayman Olayan, is the most powerful businesswoman in Saudi Arabia today.[15]

The central role of women in the Gulf economy is well illustrated by the public reaction to a decision by the Dubai legislative council in 1931 to ban women from selling fish. Much to the surprise of the legislators, male fishermen, who presumably would have benefited the most from the new law, immediately called for it to be repealed.[16] Male fishermen argued that they could not simultaneously catch fish and sell their goods in markets—a clear indication of the importance of women in the local economic life. The law was quickly repealed, but as Fatima al-Sayegh notes, the fishermen's protests had little to do with time and everything to do with money, because women could sell fish at far higher prices than their male colleagues.[17] They simply had a better understanding of the market than did their husbands. Since fishermen would want to strive to get the best price for their fish, they understood that the best people for the job were their women.

Fishermen were hardly alone in their dependence on women. Bedouin life would not have been possible in Qatar and other regions of the Arabian Peninsula if women had not been capable of assuming direct responsibility for much of tribal and commercial affairs when their male relatives were away for long periods of hunting.[18] Bedouin women also produced textiles and other materials sold to supplement their tribe's income. Equally important, these women had few restrictions on their movement in urban, rural, or desert settings. There were no restrictions similar to those that exist today. Women could go wherever they wanted, whenever they wanted.

Furthermore, women worked to empower themselves and to address a host of social needs through Islamic and non-Islamic practices. These included a belief in mysticism, a realm of evil spirits (*jinn*) and witches, and various "sea" rituals that helped women to address the great uncertainties and isolation many of them felt. Out on the sea or off in the desert, it was not uncommon for men to die unexpectedly or to suffer debilitating injuries, both of which could be catastrophic for the livelihood of their women. Therefore, Gulf women routinely engaged in sea rites, such as setting palm trees or the seawater aflame while waiting on the beach for their male relatives to return from overseas commerce. The desperate position these women found themselves in is personified by the phrases of a Qatari women's song that called on the sea to bring their men home safely: "Enough, enough, oh sea! It's already been two months. . . . Don't you fear God? Bring them back, bring them back!"[19]

Even when Gulf women spent extended periods in the same physical space as men, religion provided opportunities for them to define a separate social space for themselves. By far the most important area of female religious life in the Gulf revolved around *zar,* a religious and healing tradition akin to voodoo. *Zar* took on its contemporary form in Ethiopia (although its name may be a variation on an Arabic word), spreading to the Middle East via Ethiopian and other East African migrants. *Zar* cults existed throughout the coastal and interior regions of the Arab Gulf states, including the heart of Saudi Arabia. A *zar* was thought to be a malicious spirit that possessed individuals, often women, and spoke a language only a shaikha or *mama* (a spiritual healer or mistress of *zar*) could understand. These women responded to the spirit's demands through special oil massages or through group exercises akin to Sufi *dhikr,* in which female participants fasted, danced, and played musical instruments.[20]

Although *zar* was used to address tuberculosis and other diseases, it could also address broader female social needs. *Zar* spirits demanded things directly or indirectly, often via dreams of the person whom the *zar* had infected. At times, the *zar* voiced demands through the dreams or mind of the shaikha. The items demanded by the *zar* were often ones that women desired but could never ask for directly from their husbands or fathers—such as expensive jewelry, clothing, and household goods. Women could demand things without having to assume responsibility for the demands. In effect, *zar* cults empowered Gulf Arab women to assume an enormous degree of social power. Because of the linkage of *zar* to *jinn,* men complied as best as they could with *zar* demands, lest they be on the wrong side of a vengeful spirit. Moreover, *zar* cults brought together women of different classes and backgrounds, creating a sense of community akin to that of a Sufi brotherhood, or *tariqa.*[21]

In addition, some women held political power in their own right and were highly influential figures in tribal and even international affairs. One example was Shaikha Husa bint al-Mur, (the wife of the ruler of Dubai, Shaikh Said), whom British officials compared to Catherine the Great of Russia (1729–1796) and the Celtic warrior-queen Boadicea (died ca. 60 C.E).[22] When Husa's husband and sons refused to fight a siege of Dubai in 1940, she took up arms, rallied the city's armed forces, and forced the enemy to withdraw.[23] (At the time, her son was far more interested in visiting gardens, collecting more wives, and smoking than in fighting for the city.) In addition to her military prowess, Husa owned land, engaged in trade, and was widely regarded as a shrewd and formidable businesswoman.[24] Husa also regularly held her own public *majlis,* which was open to men and women and was said to be "more attended than her husband's."[25]

Another example of a powerful woman was Shaikha Salamah (d. 1970), whose son, Shaikh Zayid, ruled Abu Dhabi from 1966 to 2004. She was a powerful figure in Abu Dhabi for decades, especially after she resolved a protracted and deadly political dispute in the 1920s in the Abu Dhabi royal family. Her influence was so great that Western oil companies treated her as a virtual ruler and sought her assistance, including paying royalties, to gain access to Abu Dhabi's oil reserves.[26] US diplomats told ARAMCO officials in 1958 that it was her visit to Buraimi that set off the extended conflict over the oasis.[27] Susan Hillyard, whose husband was a leading British Petroleum executive in the emirate, was even clearer in her memoirs about the extent of Salamah's power. "She was the power behind the throne," wrote Hillyard. "Not a move was made without her comment being sought. I doubt if a mouse moved without her knowing about it. Not to put it too bluntly, I would need only my fingers to count the people who were not scared of her."[28]

The First Oil Era

The emergence of petroleum production, along with the collapse of the Gulf's pearl industry, transformed the position of women in the Arab Gulf for the worse. As I noted in Chapter 2, the oil industry brought instant wealth and an unprecedented increase in state power, especially in the most conservative regime in the region, Saudi Arabia. The collapse of the pearl industry generated desolation and despair on an enormous scale. Almost overnight, the one source of foreign exchange dried up, export earnings plummeted, boats were laid ashore, and divers returned home permanently.

Within this environment, women often lost their savings, investments, businesses, and social status. Their male relatives were forced to look for work abroad, since there were few jobs in the Gulf communities in the 1930s. Even though women assumed greater authority over their families after their husbands and fathers had to be away for long periods, they were also responsible for more domestic chores. Elite and non-elite families alike asked women to take on the roles that slaves, servants, and men had filled in the past. A man's debts could extend to his entire family, so women were often responsible for their husbands' and brothers' debts. There are frequent reports that, to recoup lost debts, the wives of pearl divers were forced to become divers, too, after the deaths of their husbands.[29] Under these intense conditions, women retreated to the isolation and seclusion of their homes to a far greater degree than anything that had been seen before in the Gulf. In many communities, women all but vanished from public life.

The declining social status of women was reinforced by the emergence in 1932 of a new kingdom in the Arabian Peninsula: Saudi Arabia. One way that the kingdom's elites sought to govern over such a vast new area was by eliminating ethnic differences. They also imposed strict social, religious, and sartorial regimes on men *and* women. Saudi Arabia's first king, Abdul Aziz al-Saud, decreed in 1932 that all Saudi men serving in government must wear the Najdi Bedouin *thob* or *dishdasha* (a full-length, usually white, garment), which is the attire still seen widely in the kingdom and other regions of the Gulf today.[30] Old regional and far more colorful male dress disappeared. There grew to be such a close linkage of clothing in Saudi Arabia with the color white and government service that Greg Gause referred to a "*dishdasha* class" of workers there and in other Gulf states.[31]

Although the kingdom's women were not immediately forced to adopt Najdi female styles, they faced a government that was intent on implementing a strict Wahhabi interpretation of Hanbali Sunni Islam, which saw *zar* cults, Sufism, and any other possible vehicle for female religious expression as forbidden under Islamic law. Saudi government officials and religious paramilitary elites suppressed all of these modes of religious worship as un-Islamic and a threat to public morality. Over time, women's other freedoms were curtailed, and the *abaya* emerged as the national Saudi female equivalent of the *thob*.[32]

Although most other Gulf governments did not adopt socioreligious codes that were as conservative as Saudi Arabia's, the kingdom provided a model that implicitly shaped the treatment of women (and men) throughout the Gulf. Religious conservatives in Kuwait and other more liberal Gulf states, in which some women, including female government ministers, did not wear headscarves and veils, sought to impose Saudi dress and social codes. Even though these efforts failed, the Saudi *thob* and *abaya* emerged as de facto symbols of identity in the Gulf, despite the fact that Bahrainis and others in the region had little history of wearing either in the twentieth century.[33]

Besides the sheer size of Saudi Arabia vis-à-vis its neighbors, a significant factor in the kingdom's ability to shape the culture and politics of peoples beyond its borders was the discovery of oil deposits in the 1930s. As I noted in Chapter 2, this discovery brought immediate wealth into the kingdom, allowing the Saudi state to build a technologically advanced society while still adhering to conservative Muslim values. Flush with resources, the state came to dominate socioeconomic and political structures as never before via infrastructure projects, direct cash payments, and social services. Bahrain, Kuwait, Abu Dhabi, Dubai, Qatar, and eventually Oman adopted very similar strategies when petroleum was discovered within their boundaries.

The influx of oil revenues and investments brought some immediate tangible public benefits to women in various Gulf states. For example, in Qatar, the first primary school for girls (a small *kuttab*) opened in 1938 in Doha, and the first state school for girls opened in that city in 1956.[34] During the mid-1950s, Great Britain and various Arab states opened modern primary, secondary, and technical schools in the emirates, one of which was for girls. After Abu Dhabi and the other emirates began to earn tangible oil revenues in the mid-1960s, they established their own educational systems. Abu Dhabi funded six schools in 1964 with 528 students, 138 of whom were girls. Thirty-one schools existed in the other emirates, twelve of which were for girls.[35]

The progress of women in the emirates and Qatar, however, pales in comparison to the gains that women made in Kuwait and Bahrain, which were among the earliest states in the Gulf to benefit from petroleum sales. As I discuss in greater detail in Chapter 6, women studied in missionary schools in Bahrain and Kuwait from the 1890s to the 1960s. In the years after World War II, well-established Kuwaiti merchant families sent some of their daughters abroad for education, especially to universities in Arab states and Europe. These women found great inspiration in the ideas of female emancipation promoted by Qasim Amin, Taha Hussein, Georges Hana, and other leading secular Arab intellectuals. Kuwaiti women founded newspapers and women's and professional societies at home and abroad in the 1940s to rescue Gulf society from *rajiya* (backwardness) and to promote a vision of *nahda* (progress) consistent with Western modernity. These women focused on education, employment, and the veil. By the early 1960s, Kuwait's women's movement had two branches: the Cultural and Social Society (CSS) and the Arab Women's Development Society (AWDS). Although the organizations were briefly united, they ultimately pursued different agendas: the CSS focused on charity and social issues, and the AWDS advocated a Western feminist agenda.[36]

Even before the CSS and AWDS coalesced into viable organizations, educated Kuwaiti women pushed for open public discussion of gender issues and inspired a generation of female activists. By the 1950s, Kuwaiti newspapers were already featuring columns dedicated to issues of interest to girls and women. In 1951, there were six schools for girls in Kuwait City alone. A US missionary, who visited the Ayesha Girls' School in Kuwait's capital in that year, noted that it could have been like any school in the United States.[37] The school had air-conditioning, ceiling fans, florescent lights, hot and cold running water, and a basketball court.[38] Girls wore "plaid dresses" and studied Arabic, geography, math, history, science, cooking, and sewing.[39] Furthermore, in 1956, four young Kuwaiti women did the unthinkable: they took off their veils, burned them in a schoolyard, and went home barefaced. Although the incident generated enormous controversy, and the girls were forced to wear veils before they could return to school, Kuwaiti men were forced to take women's issues more seriously than ever before. In 1957, just a year after this protest, the Kuwaiti government issued new school uniforms to girls that, for the first time, did not include a head covering other than a red bow.[40]

Over the next decade, Kuwaiti women began to realize the secular, Westernized vision first promoted by the daughters of merchant families in the 1940s. Kuwait's constitution, issued when the emirate became independent from Great Britain in 1961, classified women and men as equal before the law and guaranteed equal access to education and employment regardless of gender. The establishment of Kuwait University in 1966 meant that women no longer had to travel abroad in order to earn a postsecondary degree. These women benefited from government policies that encouraged Kuwaitis to take positions previously held only by expatriates. By the early 1970s, ever fewer women were wearing the hijab, restrictions on the mixing of sexes were rarely being enforced, and limitations on women's employment and other public activities were receding. Female students studied alongside their male colleagues at Kuwait University, and Kuwait's legislature debated an equal rights amendment to the constitution, which would extend the vote to women. Moreover, Islamic and other conservative institutions that opposed the increasingly open position of women in public life were marginalized politically and socially.[41]

Bahraini women made similarly impressive progress in the 1950s and 1960s. The island nation had pioneered education for men and women at the start of the twentieth century. There were also Shia women who taught basic quranic lessons to young men and young boys.[42] When oil was discovered on the island in the 1930s, Bahrain used the proceeds to invest in education and to provide generous scholarships for Bahraini men and women of all classes and faiths to study abroad—including the daughters of converts to Protestant Christianity.[43] While these Bahraini women were in Cairo, Beirut, and other Arab capitals, they joined leftist, nationalist, or Communist groups dedicated to social change. Starting in the 1950s, women formed charity and volunteer societies, which became increasingly political.[44] Women readily joined political movements that demanded independence from Britain and popular participation in government. As May Seikaly notes, some Bahraini women signaled their commitment to Bahraini independence by removing their veils during public protests of Britain's continuing presence on the island.[45] Indeed, an ARAMCO employee who observed political rallies in Bahrain in November 1956 noted that they included "both men and women (with veils and without veils) demonstrating and shouting against the government."[46]

By the eve of Bahraini independence in 1971, women were constantly visible throughout the island. Younger, educated women drove cars, discarded the veil and the *abaya*, regularly associated with men, and could be found in the island's lively political salons. They also joined the island's workforce, taking advantage of Bahrain's booming economy and the government's desire to decrease the island nation's dependence on expatriate workers. Women also joined Bahrain's sports clubs and numerous professional associations. There was no law prohibiting them from driving, and they have been allowed to drive without a male escort ever since the 1950s.[47] Women were also well represented in the island's cornucopia of political organizations across the political spectrum. Despite their prominent role in politics, however, Bahrain's women won few personal and civil rights, and they were excluded from the island's short-lived constitutional democracy in the 1970s. Just because

Bahraini men welcomed women's participation in political movements did not mean that they were willing to share power with their female colleagues.

Women in areas of the Gulf outside of Bahrain generally had fewer rights and educational opportunities than their colleagues in Bahrain, especially if they were not wealthy. An important exception was the Hijaz region of Saudi Arabia, where women could attend any of several *kuttab* held in private homes and administered by Saudi and foreign women. A good example of this type of school was the al-Nasifiyah School, which was situated in an old family residence in the heart of Jeddah. The school was run for many years by the Indian-born wife of a famous Hijazi businessman and scholar, Shaikh Muhammad Nasif. In addition, daughters of prominent merchants and government officials often studied with private tutors. After graduating from a *kuttab,* the daughters of Jeddah's merchants usually attended a foreign school, including Egypt's prestigious Victoria (later Victory) College in Alexandria.[48]

Formal, state-funded female education in Saudi Arabia did not begin until the 1950s. The first Saudi school, Dar al-Hanan (House of Tenderness), aimed at producing better mothers and homemakers under the motto "The mother can be a school in herself if you prepare yourself well."[49] This motto reflected the fact that important constituencies in society and government were opposed to female education and worked to hinder women's progress in society. There were no domestic universities open to women, nor were there organizations equivalent to the CSS and Bahrain's professional associations. Instead, female students were prompted to join sewing and other "domestic" clubs in their schools or women's societies dedicated to charitable activities that were firmly under the control of a female member of a royal family.[50] In most communities, women did not drive or were severely limited in their opportunities to do so.

It is ironic that the chief advocates of women's education and female rights in Saudi Arabia were often young men. As the first generation of modern Western-educated men reached marriageable age in Saudi Arabia in the 1950s, they aggressively pressured the Saudi government to provide modern education to the kingdom's women. The reason is that they wanted to marry women—including non-Saudi women—who had, like them, received modern Western educations, to whom they could relate intellectually. By 1962, one Saudi researcher estimated that "for every Saudi marrying a Saudi girl, there is a Saudi marrying a foreigner."[51] The explanation for this pattern was clear to the researcher: Saudi men fervently believed that they could "know" and love foreign women far more easily than they could "know" and love Saudi women.[52]

These men had powerful advocates in Princess Iffat and her husband, Prince (later King) Faysal. In 1956, the princess supported the opening of a school for orphaned girls and other young women in Jeddah, the abovementioned Dar al-Hanan, which granted Saudi women opportunities to earn secondary and postsecondary degrees. The princess not only generously funded the school but also used her prestige to protect its reputation and autonomy.[53] At this time, there were already private schools for girls in Riyadh, one of which, al-Karimat (Nobility), was founded by then crown prince Saud bin Abdul Aziz, who sent his daughters to study there.[54] Riyadh also had a modern Western-style university, Riyadh University, which became King Saud University in 1982.

In 1960, over considerable opposition, Faysal and Iffat created various levels of state-funded primary and technical schools for girls[55] and allowed women to produce programs for the state radio network.[56] To deflect criticism from conservative Saudis, Faysal nominated a conservative cleric, Shaikh Muhammad ibn Ibrahim, to administer the General Presidency of the School of Girls, a new agency that was charged with running girls' schools.[57] In 1962, Riyadh University admitted its first four women.[58] An ARAMCO report on the status of Saudi women in 1962 remarkably found that those who worked earned "pay equal to that received by men for equal qualifications and service."[59]

Nevertheless, women's progress in Saudi Arabia should not be overstated. Official figures noted that only 2 percent of school-aged Saudi girls were enrolled in state schools for girls when these opened in 1960. Although these figures did not include students in *kuttab* schools, and the numbers of girls in all kinds of schools steadily increased in the 1960s, the educational standards, exams, and curricula for girls were significantly inferior to those for boys.[60] The introduction of government schools for girls and the creation of a directorate general for administering them ironically had the unintended consequence of significantly reducing educational standards in all but a few favored girls' schools in Saudi Arabia.[61] Governments and Western oil companies funded male and female students to study abroad, but few fellowships went to women. For example, in 1969, only ten of ARAMCO's sixty scholarships to study overseas went to women.[62] Furthermore, the rates of literacy among women remained low. An ARAMCO report concluded in 1970 that most female Saudi graduates were "poorly trained by Western standards" and lacked the skills to perform jobs traditionally held by women in most societies at the time (clerical work, teaching, nursing, and retail)—not to mention higher-skilled professional occupations such as medicine and engineering.[63]

The economic expansion in Saudi Arabia and many other Gulf states and the accompanying increase in state income meant that Gulf men earned regular salaries and could depend on generous state assistance. No longer having to rely on women's income, as they had in the past, they increasingly insisted that their female relatives, including those who had educations and were employed, stay at home. Adult illiteracy was nearly 99 percent in some Gulf communities as recently as 1970. Few non-elite and rural women attained university degrees, since no formal universities for women existed in the Gulf outside of Kuwait until the 1970s. Without university degrees, women could not aspire to positions much higher than menial office work.

The expansion of the state's role in daily life effectively checked the rights of both indigenous and foreign women. In 1970, the Saudi government issued an edict ordering foreign women, who had appeared in public in Western clothes for decades, to wear "modest dress" in public places.[64] Throughout the Gulf, governments portrayed their nations as an extended family under the leadership of the male head of the royal family. For example, Kuwait's government went so far as to encourage children to call the ruling emir "father." Gulf governments reinforced this concept of family by pledging to protect the most vulnerable members of the national family—namely, women and children.

Within this system, women came under both the definition and guardianship of their male kin. In every Gulf community, including Kuwait, they had no legal rights as individuals—only as members of families. State subsidies went to the male heads of household. Although men could pass citizenship to their children, regardless of the nationality of the children's mothers, a woman could not pass her citizenship to the children of a husband who was not already a citizen. Divorced or widowed women received welfare payments only if they had children and no intention of remarrying. At the same time, Gulf governments provided incentives for couples to have large families. They also encouraged women to prioritize their maternal role. It is not surprising that many women in the Gulf retreated still further into their homes and out of public view than ever before.

The Oil Boom and the Resurgence of Islam, 1970–1980

For the women of the Gulf, the events of the 1970s marked a transition as important as the disappearance of the pearling industry, decades earlier. When the international price of oil quadrupled in 1973, Saudi Arabia, Kuwait, and the newly independent states in the Gulf invested the proceeds from their newfound wealth in infrastructure, including education, and sought to build robust modern economies. Qatar, Bahrain, and others promulgated basic laws or constitutions in line with those in Kuwait and other parts of the world that promised equal rights and access to employment for men and women. Soon, vast modern, multiethnic, international cities took shape throughout the region, from the Gulf to the Red Sea.

Within this rapid social and economic transformation, women and their families took advantage of new homes, amenities, and social services. Movies, television, and other new information technologies exposed Gulf populations to Western conceptions of feminism, just as Islamist values were taking hold in other Arab states, Turkey, and South Asia. These technologies also introduced the rest of the world to the Gulf states, especially to the position of women. By the late 1970s, there were public discussions about the place of women in many Gulf states, and, in 1978, Naila al-Sowayel, a journalist, became the first Saudi woman to appear on television without a veil.[65]

Gulf women steadily gained access to every level of education in the new cities and began to surpass men in school enrollment, literacy, and even educational achievement. Yet they were also encouraged to have large families in order to swell the indigenous workforce—which was still tiny, compared to the expatriate workforces that were transforming the Gulf states into modern metropolises. The Gulf governments also sought to ward off leftist and Islamist challenges by supporting domestic Islamic groups and conservative social agendas. A key aspect of their strategy was to limit women's role in society and reverse whatever socioeconomic gains women had made in previous decades.[66]

Over time, Gulf states' development programs and the desire to boost female literacy and schooling created a contradictory situation. On the one hand, these states allowed women to attain greater educational achievement than ever before. They also built modern bureaucratic and economic systems, in which women could in theory put their educations to good use. Educated women were central to the development strategies, and education received substantial support. On the other hand, the same states fostered sociocultural climates that were hostile to women fulfilling the roles for which they were trained. Groups promoting a patriarchal vision in which women were objects to be controlled gained prominence and patronage. Gulf states invested in development programs in which women had a central role while simultaneously supporting groups and individuals that opposed the logical outcomes of those programs.

The root of these problems began with the investments that Gulf states made in the middle to late 1970s in education and social services. For instance, the education budget for Saudi Arabia between 1970 and 1975 was $2.5 billion but rose to $28 billion by 1980. The investment, however, paid enormous dividends. Across all levels, women's and girls' enrollment grew by 8.3 percent annually between 1975 and 2000, which was double the rate of boys. At the grammar school level, by 1989 nearly two-thirds of Saudi Arabia's 2.5 million schoolchildren were girls. The number of female secondary students grew from 1,674 in 1975 to 18,211 in 1988. Even as early as 1980, of the 40,000 students in Saudi universities, more than 9,000 were women. By 1984, women made up 50 percent of the student body at some Saudi universities and half of all Saudi students studying abroad. In 1990, as many women as men graduated from Saudi universities.[67]

Women made equally impressive educational progress in the UAE, Qatar, and Bahrain. In the 1970s, the UAE government, giving education an importance second only to defense in the national budget, opened 350 schools with

94,425 students.[68] Women made up 46 percent of the initial class at the UAE University at al-Ain in 1976 and more than 65 percent of the student body a decade later. The 1975 census in the UAE listed 3,005 females with an undergraduate university degree or its equivalent. By 1995, that number stood at 61,496.[69]

In Qatar, by the end of the 1970s, there were as many women as men in school at all levels, women performed better academically than their male counterparts, and more of them graduated.[70] The Qatari state also guaranteed economic equality between the sexes. When Qatar University opened in 1977, women represented 54 percent of the student body.[71] By the mid-1980s, they made up 62 percent of the university's enrollment.[72]

In Bahrain, despite official policies to maintain gender equality in higher education, women made far larger gains in enrollment than men, especially at the island's chief institution of higher education, the National University of Bahrain. In 1976, women had accounted for 30 percent of the college students in Bahrain; by 1986, they were 54 percent of the college population.[73]

Female students made the largest gains in Oman. Before the 1970s, there were only three primary schools and one religious institute in the entire sultanate, and those schools provided education to fewer than a thousand students.[74] In fact, the only school in the country that was not exclusively for boys was a US missionary school that served fifty nonnative girls. But Sultan Qaboos, when he seized power in 1971, identified women's education as a top priority of his government, seeing it as an easily identifiable mark of the modernization of Omani society. Thus, in 1975, there were 14,800 female Omanis in primary school, 200 in high school, and 57 in college. Although Oman's first comprehensive state university did not open until 1986, Omani girls and women continued to make educational progress. By 1990, there were 113,700 females in primary schools, 25,300 in high schools, and 9,689 in colleges and universities (which exceeded the number of men).[75]

Women's gains in access to education were reinforced by new female organizations and campaigns to eradicate illiteracy. For example, in 1973, Shaikha Fatima, wife of the UAE's first president, Shaikh Zayid, founded the Abu Dhabi Women's Association, whose priority, in the words of Fatima al-Sayegh, "was to help women emerge out of seclusion; use their leisure time to become literate, and to acquire knowledge about the modern world to enable them to raise their family's standard of living."[76] The organization soon inspired the creation of similar women's associations throughout the other UAE emirates and eventually the creation of a pan-UAE federation of women.

Although the UAE women's movement encouraged Emirati women to take a greater role in public life and to seek employment, the movement's greatest success lay in improving literacy. In 1970, female literacy in the UAE had stood at 37.7 percent. In 1980, it had risen to 59 percent; in 1990, to 70.6 percent; and in 2000, to 79.1 percent.[77] Thus, thanks to the efforts of Shaikha

Fatima and others, more than 18,000 women graduated from illiteracy eradication programs.[78]

Nor was the UAE alone in successfully promoting female literacy. Only 5.3 and 16.4 percent of Saudi and Omani women, respectively, were literate in 1970.[79] By 2000, those statistics stood at 65.4 and 69.6 percent, respectively.[80] Qatar, Bahrain, and Kuwait, which had rates of female literacy between 30 and 40 percent in the early 1970s, all increased female literacy to more than 80 percent by 2000.[81]

There were also impressive gains for women in other social categories, including poverty, life expectancy, maternal mortality during childbirth, and access to health care. Between 1960 and 2000, female participation in the Gulf workforce increased dramatically—as much as 691 percent in Saudi Arabia alone.[82] Whereas a woman living in the Gulf during the first half of the twentieth century might have had to travel weeks to get Western-style health care, her female descendants had access to high-quality health care right in their neighborhoods and could be certain that a physician would attend the birth of their children. Yet Gulf society in the late third of the twentieth century was even *more* socially conservative than it had been before World War II, and women had fewer opportunities to participate in the economy and in public life than ever before.

It is ironic that the same factors that helped women to improve their quality of life and level of education also spawned the conservative policies that limited their role in Gulf society. The influx of oil wealth in the 1970s meant that it was no longer financially necessary for thousands of Gulf women to work, since the governments now had the resources to turn what had been largely an ideal in the past—the separation and seclusion of women from men—into a tangible reality. Different facilities for men and women appeared in primary and secondary schools, university campuses, parks, homes, neighborhoods, and shopping malls. Nor were those facilities equal. For example, the men's library at King Abdulaziz University in Jeddah had 250,000 books, whereas the women's library had only 30,000 books.[83] In some Gulf countries, certain academic degrees were off-limits to women, such as in journalism, geology, and petroleum engineering. These types of social practices perpetuated the separation of the sexes in every aspect of daily life.

As women achieved higher levels of modern education, they often came under social pressure to abandon their jobs, especially after they married and had children. Social commentators admonished working women that they were selfish and were abandoning their national responsibilities as mothers and home builders to their "illiterate foreign nannies and housemaids."[84] Although virtually all Gulf governments publicly proclaimed a commitment to upholding the equality of all their citizens in the 1970s, they provided financial incentives for women to retire after marriage and limited women's access to both private and public employment.

Nor were there many opportunities for women who had not acquired a modern education or who were from modest circumstances. There were substantial differences between private and state secondary and postsecondary schools for women; in particular, public schools were plagued in the 1980s by shortages of female faculty. The occupations that had sustained working-class women for decades, such as housekeeping, tailoring, child care, education, and traditional medicine, were no longer open to them. Companies and families preferred working with expatriate laborers, who worked hard (for lower wages) and had significantly less negotiating leverage than did indigenous workers. Midwives literally ceased to exist in certain parts of the Gulf after the appearance of hospitals and medical clinics, where women now had their babies rather than at home. It should come as no surprise that fewer than 10 percent of the women of the UAE, Oman, and Saudi Arabia participated in the workforce in 1980.[85] The governments' and societies' message to Gulf women was clear and unambiguous: they had no public role outside of being mothers.

There is little question that attempts to control women's rights and public access were consistent with the conservative social mores that had governed Saudi Arabia and other Arab Gulf societies for years. But in the 1970s and 1980s, these attempts met with considerable success, since they addressed significant political challenges to the governments. As I discussed in Chapter 2, the Gulf governments sought for years, by distributing largesse and by forging political coalitions, to win support from merchants, Bedouins, religious minorities, poor indigenous populations, and even progressives. These measures were meant to prevent socialist, Marxist, religious, and Arab nationalist groups from influencing the indigenous national populations.[86]

The fear that such groups might gain influence was especially acute in Bahrain and Kuwait, where the national legislatures were the only elected representative bodies in the Gulf in the 1970s. As I discussed at length in Chapter 2, the Bahraini legislature at that time included groups that promoted Marxism, women's rights, the legalization of labor unions, and the promotion of the Shia majority. When those groups challenged the government's authority, however, the emir of Bahrain dissolved the legislature and won the support of Sunni Arab religious groups by promoting patriarchal social practices.

At around this same time, the Kuwaiti government feared that those of its legislators who were tied to leftists participating in Lebanon's civil war would ally themselves with the large expatriate Palestinian population to challenge the monarchy's hold on power. To check this potential challenge, the Kuwaiti government dissolved parliament in 1976 and allied itself with the one group that did not oppose this decision: Kuwait's largely apolitical Sunni Islamic societies. This alliance was sealed by the appointment of the head of Kuwait's Islam and Social Reform Society, Yusuf al-Hajji, as minister of pious endowments.[87]

A New Islamic Course

Al-Hajji and his fellow Islamic activists, who were working to Islamize Kuwaiti society, benefited from the surge in religious fervor in Kuwait and throughout the Arab world following Israel's victory over secular Arab regimes in the 1967 Arab-Israeli war. They also benefited from the events of the 1979 Islamic revolution in Iran, where the shah's secular government could not check a mass popular movement headed by a Muslim cleric, Ayatollah Khomeini. The seizure of the Grand Mosque in Mecca in November 1979, and the Soviet invasion of Afghanistan a month later, reinforced widespread concerns among Kuwaitis that their fellow Muslims were under assault and that Islam was indeed relevant to late-twentieth-century life.

Saudi Arabia was acutely aware of these various threats to orthodoxy and acted to counter them vigorously. At the heart of the Saudi program was a vision of a society that was technologically advanced but that rigidly upheld conservative Islamic values. This vision was without precedent in either Saudi history in particular or Islamic history in general. A critical benchmark for the success of this new society was the absence of women in public settings. Banning women from public places allowed the government to provide tangible proof that it was addressing the concerns of many conservative Saudis, including those who had stormed the Grand Mosque in the belief that the kingdom was no longer committed to upholding Wahhabi-Hanbali values. To reinforce its commitment to these values, the Saudi government gave wide latitude to the religious police to enforce Muslim morality regarding women in all public settings.[88]

Under this new arrangement, once gender-integrated institutions, such as buses, offices, and recreational areas, were rigidly segregated. A whole set of parallel buildings and sections of communities arose just for women. Pictures of Western women in newspapers and other publications, as well as on public signs, were edited to conform to Islamic norms. In 1982, the Saudi government curtailed opportunities for single Saudi women to study abroad.[89] The Saudi state also rigidly enforced the *mahram* regulation, by which women could not travel abroad without a close male relative. A royal decree in 1985 forbade women from working in all sectors of the economy outside of education and health. Nor could women manage businesses even if they owned them. In such cases, they had to prove that they had a male guardian or administrator. In addition, the Saudi ulama issued a *fatwa* announcing that a Saudi woman had to be accompanied by a male guardian to travel anywhere.[90]

Now confined to both private and gender-specific places, women focused on what the state saw as their two primary tasks: having very large families and helping to educate Saudis to replace foreign workers. Because salaries in the Gulf were far higher than those in India, Pakistan, the Philippines, and the other states that provided expatriate labor to the kingdom, Riyadh could easily keep those foreigners until its own population had produced enough educated technicians to run the kingdom's modern society on their own.

These changes in Saudi Arabia were especially important because they coincided with the creation of the Gulf Cooperation Council in 1981. This new organization, based in Riyadh, helped to create a new pan-Gulf social identity modeled on the social mores of the council's largest member state, Saudi Arabia. Personal status laws in various Gulf states began to mirror those of Saudi Arabia. Moreover, the tensions from the Iran-Iraq war in the 1980s, which pitted an Arab-Sunni government in Baghdad against a revolutionary Shia government in Tehran, further intensified conservative Sunni sensibilities throughout the Gulf. Many GCC states supported Iraq and used the war as an excuse to tighten controls over their Shia populations.

The example of Bahrain is instructive. Starting in the 1950s, Bahrainis of all ages began to wear Western clothing, and Bahraini men, as a Christian missionary noted at the time, "left the Arab gown" for "foreign clothes."[91] But when Bahrain joined the GCC in 1981, Bahraini men switched back, adopting the *thobs* worn by their fathers and grandfathers. It was now important for Bahrainis to look correct and to signal that they had joined the community of Gulf Arabs.[92]

Bahraini women were no exception to this trend. In the early 1980s, close to 95 percent of the female students at Bahrain's National University wore the veil, and those who chose not to were under constant pressure to do so.[93] Bahrain's government announced in the mid-1980s that it would regulate all aspects of women's work, a seeming retraction of the constitutional promise to promote gender equality. Furthermore, the island's government established a semiofficial policy of blocking the hiring and promotion of professional women, even if they were better qualified and had more experience than men or expatriate workers. The freedoms of the 1960s and 1970s were very much a thing of the past. Women were to stay at home, protect the nation's honor, and raise large families.[94]

Thanks in part to these policies, population growth was 7 percent in Bahrain in the 1980s and 3 percent in the other Gulf states—a far higher rate than in most other developing societies.[95] Saudi Arabia's population grew from 6.2 million inhabitants in 1970 to 24 million in 2003.[96] Saudi women took their roles as family educators very seriously. The number of Saudi females enrolled in university education climbed from 20,000 in 1983 to 47,000 in 1989.[97] But women usually married after graduation and either did not enter the labor force or left work as soon as they had children. Consequently, they comprised less than 14 percent of the GCC's total labor force in 1990, and only 18 percent in 2004.[98]

The Limits of the Islamic Facade

From the start, the Islamic facade had important and tangible limits. Wealthy Gulf Arabs of both genders often wore Western-style clothing behind closed doors at home or at embassies, and men and women mixed freely.[99] At the ARAMCO complex in Dhahran, Saudi women often worked side by side with Western women (and men) and wore Western-style clothing. Furthermore, they sometimes hosted cocktail parties with both men and women and served a homemade liquor called *sadeeki* (an Arabic word meaning "my friend").[100] Saudi women regularly drove on the compound as well (although without licenses), and the Saudi government issued official driver's licenses to both male and female drivers from Western nations. Furthermore, the female drivers on ARAMCO compounds were not the only women who drove in Saudi Arabia: Bedouin women drove trucks and other farm equipment. There were so many female Bedouin truck drivers in the 1970s that a Saudi prince, Bandar bin Sultan, half jokingly predicted to the *Washington Post* in 1978 that the "spearhead of the Saudi women's movement will come from the Bedouins of the desert."[101]

Even in conservative urban areas, women's opportunities expanded at the same time that they seemingly contracted. Although fewer women worked overall, a new generation of female writers appeared in wide-circulation newspapers and magazines, which featured women's columns and articles on "women's topics." Many of these new women writers reaffirmed conservative values while questioning the guiding assumptions of feminism and traditional Gulf society. A good example of this process is the emergence of a generation of female Saudi writers such as Juyaher al-Musa'ed. They have redefined male-female relations not in terms of antagonism but of discovery, in which a man is not only "a needed mate but also a victimized 'inmate.'"[102] These writers were sufficiently successful that male writers often used female pseudonyms when writing on issues of gender.[103]

The restrictions on unmarried Saudi women's traveling abroad for education arose at the same time that the Saudi government offered to pay the college tuition of any Saudi wife who married before she traveled abroad. Such incentives were meant, in part, to control the behavior of Saudi men abroad by encouraging them to marry Saudi women instead of foreigners. But the government would never have extended its tuition offer if officials did not believe (1) that many Saudi men wanted to marry educated women, (2) that many Saudi women wanted to be educated abroad, and (3) that many Saudi families viewed the higher education of their daughters as a viable reason for marriage.[104]

These insights take on greater importance when one bears in mind that Saudi society looks at marriage as a socioeconomic alliance between families or between tribes. Within this arrangement, brides have substantial say in marriages and wide latitude to reject potential spouses. Furthermore, when it comes to picking marital partners, families expect young men to defer to the judgment of others in their family, including their mothers and other female family members. The comparative weakness of Saudi men of all ages appears in al-Sanea's *Girls of Riyadh.* Throughout the novel, the male characters, including the most powerful and educated, cannot overcome their families' various objections to their desire to marry the Saudi and non-Saudi women they love. Commenting on the state of Saudi men, one female character notes that they are "passive and weak, . . . just pawns their families move around the chessboard."[105] Even in the most conservative of Gulf societies, Saudi Arabia, Islamic patriarchy clearly can have limits.[106]

Other states more directly exposed the limits of patriarchy and retained their commitment to Western notions of equality and female education. In Kuwait, for example, Islamists discovered that their influence had significant limits in the 1980s, especially in regard to women. An excellent example of this occurred in 1986, when Islamist deputies sought to establish an authority to enforce Islamic law in Kuwait, including severe restrictions on women's liberties. The government responded to this initiative first by indirectly hindering or ignoring it and then by dissolving the government. Although Islamists and liberal and secular groups often found common ground to oppose repeated government efforts to check parliamentary power, the two groups parted ways on many social and political issues. To divide the opposition, the Kuwaiti government sometimes forged alliances with secularists and at other times with Islamists.[107]

Just four years later, in August 1990, Kuwait became the centerpiece of a debate regarding women's rights in Saudi Arabia and the rest of the Gulf when Iraq invaded the tiny Gulf state. In response, the Saudi government invited the United States to deploy military forces to defend the kingdom and its strategic oil fields. Riyadh then expelled nearly a million Arab expatriates from Yemen and other countries that supported Iraq and also sought to free up Saudi men for military service. In September of that year, the Saudi government issued an edict that encouraged government agencies to accept female volunteers for social and medical positions. The significance of the edict was reinforced by the presence in Saudi Arabia of female US and Kuwaiti soldiers, many of whom drove their vehicles openly in public. In one widely told story, a member of the Saudi religious police used his stick to taunt a US female soldier, who had just driven her car to a store in the kingdom's Eastern Province. In response, she drew her pistol and forced him to flee for his life.[108]

The 1990 edict and the presence of armed foreign soldiers renewed the public debate about the role of women in Saudi life and may have prompted one of the most audacious challenges ever to the kingdom's separation of genders: the incident already alluded to, when forty-five women drove through the streets of Riyadh. No one in Saudi Arabia had ever seen anything quite like that, and the protest generated headlines around the world. Iraqi propagandists sought to frame this event, as well as the offer to allow women to volunteer in government agencies, as proof that the Saudi government was really an agent of the West and Israel.

For a government already worried about its Islamic credentials after it had invited tens of thousands of US soldiers into the kingdom, the only response was swift retribution.[109] Aside from losing their jobs and being publicly humiliated, some of these women received harassing phone calls, accusing them of sexual immorality and promoting Western vices and goals. The Saudi government then produced a children's television show to emphasize the point. Set to a chorus of singing children, the show contrasted correct Islamic behavior with the infidelity of women who wish to drive cars. Again and again, the girls sang, "I am a Saudi woman, and I don't drive a car."[110]

In Kuwait, as I noted in Chapter 3, the picture was quite different. Kuwaiti women's efforts in the war, both at home and abroad, were welcomed (at least until the war was over). During the occupation, Kuwaiti women outside the country mobilized support against Iraq, and some of them received military training at Fort Dix in the United States alongside their male Kuwaiti colleagues.[111] Women inside Kuwait launched the first mass public protests against the occupation, some of them paying for their actions with their lives. By the end of the Iraqi occupation in February 1991, women were such an important aspect of civil society in Kuwait that the country earned the nickname "the city-state of women."[112] Kuwait's women, who had a long history of activism, had seemingly come of age. Many expected that they would achieve full political rights after liberation.

But, as Mary Ann Tétreault has pointed out, their hopes were soon dashed. Wartime female activism had taken place within occupied Kuwait but faded from view shortly after the war. In the struggle for who would define the memory of the war between insiders and outsiders—that is, between those who had remained in Kuwait and those who had fled—the outsiders emerged victorious. In particular, Kuwait's Islamists framed the invasion and war to fit their own agenda, contending that the events signaled God's displeasure with the Kuwaitis' lavish lifestyle. Only by returning to Islam (including the control of women), they argued, could Kuwaitis guard against further divine retribution. This argument resonated with the people and won government support. Consequently, Kuwaiti Islamists performed well in parliamentary elections in the 1990s, successfully segregated Kuwait University by gender, and intimidated professors there who did not share their views.[113]

Socioeconomic Tensions in the 1990s

The success of the Islamists in the 1990s also significantly reflected technological and political changes in the Gulf. As I noted in Chapter 3, among the most important of these changes were the rise of Arab satellite news networks, the seemingly permanent deployment of Western military forces in the region, a steep decline in oil prices, the rise of opposition groups at home and abroad, and the erosion of the societal benefit from petroleum income due to population growth. All of these factors raised questions about the ability of governments and societies in the region to maintain their values and traditions. Within this transitional environment, women, like other elements in Gulf society, suddenly found new political and socioeconomic opportunities.

Among the earliest signs of the increasing tensions involving women in the Arab Gulf states were the large antigovernment protests in Bahrain, where the US military's presence was especially visible. Starting in 1994, violent street protests accompanied ever bolder religious and political challenges to the monarchy's authority. Women from both the Sunni minority and the Shia majority actively participated in all phases of these protests. They formed professional, charitable, and other organizations that forwarded the opposition's agenda and resisted government crackdowns. These women made up a quarter of the 25,000 signatories to a national charter, issued in October 1994, that outlined the chief demands of the opposition, particularly the restoration of democratic institutions on the island. The petition also demanded that women be integrated into Bahrain's political life and that the island reduce its dependence on expatriate workers.[114]

Yet the most cogent opposition to the status quo in the Gulf came in Saudi Arabia and from a very different direction. Two organizations were especially important in this. The first, Al-Qaida, was composed of former soldiers who had fought in Afghanistan under the leadership of Osama bin Laden, who framed his arguments in a Salafi tradition in which women's social role was to uphold the dignity of Muslim families.[115] This theme was central to an Al-Qaida-produced video that was widely distributed in the Middle East shortly before the terrorist attacks of September 11, 2001. Throughout the tape, graphic images of sickly children, demolished homes, battles, and soldiers beating elderly women are juxtaposed with calls to uphold male Arab-Muslim honor.[116]

The second organization, the Committee for Defense of Legitimate Rights, shared Al-Qaida's view of women and their place in society. The CDLR's founder, Muhammad al-Mas'ari, issued a statement in 1996 in which he argued that granting equal rights to women violated Islamic law and that his group opposed any diminution of laws that governed women's Islamic dress or lessened patriarchal power.[117]

As I noted in Chapter 3, one of the key factors contributing to the rise of opposition groups throughout the Gulf was Arab satellite television, especially al-Jazeera. Not only did unveiled female anchors and journalists appear on air, but religious scholars used the networks as platforms to present their views on issues long repressed in the Gulf and other parts of the Arab world, including gender.

Among the earliest religious scholars to take advantage of Arab satellite television was Shaikh Yousuf al-Qaradawi. His weekly telephone call-in show on al-Jazeera and his website transformed him into a household name in the Gulf and beyond. He was a former member of Egypt's Muslim Brotherhood and a graduate of al-Azhar, the most important Sunni seminary in the world, and had also authored a number of leading books on Islam. According to Barbara Stowasser, al-Qaradawi promoted a controversial vision of gender equality based on Muslim scripture in which women have the right to have an education, participate in political life, and hold senior positions in business and government. He has also used the Quran and other scripture to redefine or refute earlier interpretations of Islamic text, including those of leading contemporary scholars, that limit the opportunities available to Muslim women outside of the home. He has promoted progressive views within his own family. His daughters hold doctorates in the natural sciences from Western universities, and one teaches in the Physics Department at the University of Qatar. In addition, Qaradawi has a wide following among educated, professional women in the Islamic world.[118]

Women and their rights have come to define the career of the UAE-based Shaikh Ahmad al-Kubaisi, a rival to Qaradawi in the region. Al-Kubaisi, who regularly appears on Dubai Satellite Television, one of al-Jazeera's competitors, is a Sunni Iraqi. Like Qaradawi, he argues for a progressive interpretation of Islamic teachings, especially in regard to family status and women. At times, his views straddle a middle ground, drawing criticism from both conservative and liberal voices in UAE society. A good example of this was the reaction to his role in drafting a new UAE personal status law in 2005. Conservatives charged that he undermined traditional ways of interpreting Islam and encouraged a new school of Islamic thought. Liberal groups, by contrast, faulted him for imposing a universal norm of justice, rather than defending the rights of individuals to define themselves socially.[119]

Many conservative Muslim scholars have denounced both Qaradawi's and al-Kubaisi's interpretations of Islamic practices, labeling these as far too lax and too far removed from traditional Islamic practices. Scholars in Saudi Arabia have been among the harshest critics of these men, offering specific rebuttals to their positions on Islamic views of women's political rights and their right to work. In 1996, Shaikh bin Baz, a prominent Saudi cleric, penned a *fatwa* arguing that allowing women to work would lead to adultery and destroy the moral foundation of society—a direct challenge to Qaradawi's ideas. It should come as no surprise that Qaradawi's books have long been banned in Saudi Arabia.[120]

Setting the Agenda

Bin Baz's comments did not deter important elements of Saudi society, such as Crown Prince (later King) Abdullah, from listening to Qaradawi's arguments about the place of women in Islamic societies. In 1999, Abdullah asserted that "we will leave no door . . . closed to women . . . as long as it involves no violation of our religion and ethics."[121] Hinting at a possible future for Saudi women that was at odds with Bin Baz's vision, Abdullah added, "Issues like driving cars by women, and women [obtaining] ID cards are comparatively simple. The most important thing is their full participation in the life of the society."[122]

Just two years later, Saudi women were issued their own identification cards, so no longer would they be listed as dependents of their male relatives on family cards. The new identification cards for Saudi women included pictures of their uncovered faces.[123] In 2006, Saudi information minister Iyad Madani encouraged women to apply for driver's licenses when he observed that there was "nothing in the Saudi legislation that forbids Saudi women to apply for a driving license."[124] The minister's comments hinted that urban Saudi women could look forward to driving in much the same way that rural and Bedouin Saudi women had driven for years. And there was a financial logic to Madani's argument: women held half of all car loans in the kingdom, but females accounted for only 46 percent of the total population in 2004.[125] (As in the rest of the Gulf states, the percentage of females in Saudi Arabia is considerably less than half because the population figures include expatriates, the vast majority of whom are male.)

Other Gulf rulers were even bolder than those in Saudi Arabia. In 2002, Bahrain's emir drafted and helped win passage of a new constitution, which allowed women, who make up 43 percent of the total population, to vote and run for office in national elections.[126] The percentage of women in the Bahraini legislature is now higher than that of the US Congress. Qatar approved a new constitution in late April 2002 and held elections in 2007 for a Central Municipal Council, in which all Qataris—men and women—were allowed to vote.[127] In 2003, Oman's government extended the franchise to all Omanis, regardless of gender, including the 43 percent of the population who are female.[128] Kuwait permitted women to vote in 2006. Since the election in 2007 in the UAE, nine women have been serving in its forty-seat mixed (elected and appointed) Federal Legislature, a percentage of 23 percent, which is slightly lower than the percentage of females in the UAE's population (32 percent).[129]

This trend has already had an impact on politics in the Gulf. Although Kuwaiti Islamists opposed extending the franchise to women, their candidates courted female voters during the 2006 elections. They provided materials geared especially toward women, including cassette tapes of candidates' speeches for women unwilling to travel to public rallies or other campaign events. These materials and strategies were critical, given that more than 50 percent of the eligible Kuwaiti voters were women. The fact that Islamists polled well in the 2006 elections and won the firm support of many Kuwaiti women bodes well for their continued political success in future years.[130]

Since 2003, Oman, Qatar, Bahrain, Kuwait, the UAE, and, most recently, Saudi Arabia have appointed women to cabinet-level positions.[131] Among the most noteworthy of these new ministers is Lubna al-Qasimi, who founded Tejari.net, a successful UAE technology company; has regulated Emirati stock markets; and has regularly dined with such leading high-tech figures as Oracle's Larry Ellison and Hewlett-Packard's former chief executive officer (CEO), Carly Fiorina. In Qatar, Kuwait, and the UAE, women work as police and customs officers.[132] In Saudi Arabia, thousands of women serve as security guards in banks, hospitals, and female prisons.[133] Kuwaiti, Bahraini, and Qatari women have been senior diplomats. For example, in June 2006, Haya Rashed al-Khalifa, a Bahraini diplomat and attorney, became only the third woman in history to serve as the president of the General Assembly of the United Nations.[134] In 2008, Bahrain's government appointed a Jewish woman, Houda Nonoo, as ambassador to the United States. Nonoo was, in fact, the third woman to become a Bahraini ambassador, the others being Shaikha Haya al-Khalifa to France and Bibi Alawi to China.[135]

Women have also assumed leading roles in education and other cultural fields in the Gulf. Faiza al-Kharafi headed Kuwait University for many years, and Shaikha Abd Allah al-Misnad has served as president of Qatar University since 2003. The head of Qatar's College of Islamic Law, Aisha al-Mania, holds a Ph.D. in Islamic law from the oldest university in the world, al-Azhar University in Egypt.[136] Women also hold leadership positions in universities and educational systems throughout the Gulf as administrators, department chairs, and heads of research centers. Several Western-trained female members of Gulf ruling families have important social, religious, and cultural roles in the Gulf and represent their nations at international forums. These include Shaikha Moza of Qatar, a graduate of Texas A&M University; her daughter, Shaikha Mayassa, a graduate of Duke University; and Shaikha Latifa, the wife of the former Kuwaiti emir, who heads an official women's organization, the Islamic Care Society, and speaks frequently at global conferences related to women.[137]

In business, women's presence is even more pervasive. Here women have benefited from family connections, their own wealth (Saudi women own much of the real estate in Jeddah and Riyadh),[138] and a work environment that generally stresses merit and competence. For example, a prominent journalist for the leading English-language daily newspaper in Saudi Arabia, *Arab News,* is a woman, Ebithal Mubarak. Again, Lubna Olayan heads one of Saudi Arabia's largest businesses, the Olayan Group. Another Saudi,

Nahed Taher, directs Bahrain's Gulf One Investments, which has $10 billion in assets. (It is remarkable that all three are members of a society in which women are not supposed to work in any sector outside of education, health, and government.) Vidya Chabria overseas the Jumbo Group, a $2 billion Emirati multinational company that operates in fifty countries. Rajaa Easa Saleh al-Gurg manages the al-Gurg group, an Emirati conglomerate with twenty-nine manufacturing and trading companies and an annual revenue of $2 billion. Maha al-Ghunaim founded Global Investment House, a Kuwaiti investment firm with $7 billion of assets. Shaikha al-Bahar directs the Corporate Banking Arm of the National Bank of Kuwait. Lujaina Mohsin Haider Darwish holds senior management posts in more than half of the ten major trading houses in Oman.[139]

These women have won recognition at home and abroad in *Forbes, Forbes Arabia,* and other venues. Women now serve on chambers of commerce and corporate boards throughout the region. Olayan has appeared in *Time*'s "One Hundred Most Influential People" and *Forbes*'s "One Hundred Most Influential Women." Al-Ghunaim, Taher, Olayan, Chabria, al-Gurg, al-Bahar, and Darwish appeared in *Forbes Arabia*'s "Fifty Most Powerful Women in the Region."[140]

Even more impressive has been the ability of women to transform their prominence into a type of sociocultural power far more significant than either the right to vote or the right to drive. Olayan and her colleagues are increasingly setting the socioeconomic agenda for their societies, outshining figures who have long promoted religious and patriarchal worldviews. Despite the grand mufti's vocal protests against Olayan's Jeddah speech (itself a sign of his desire to make up for his diminished power), she has continued to promote her ideas at home and abroad, encouraged other women in her company to promote women's rights, and been photographed unveiled in public settings with men.

The author of *Girls of Riyadh,* Rajaa al-Sanea, openly promoted her book and won the endorsement of one of Saudi Arabia's most powerful men, the minister of labor, Ghazi al-Gosaibi. Rajaa Easa Saleh al-Gurg, head of the Easa Saleh al-Gurg Group in the United Arab Emirates, has similarly advocated women's rights. With the strong support of local royal families, Bahraini, Omani, and Emirati women have promoted greater female rights and formed regional associations of female elected officials. This type of advocacy has seeped into the movies as well: Saudi Arabia's first feature-length film, *Keif al-Hal?* (How's It Going?), treats the desire of some young women to have a career instead of marriage. Throughout much of the film, the lead character, Hind, and other women frequently appear unveiled, and Hind herself has multiple scenes in which she is driving—with her father's consent, no less.[141]

An Alliance

The power of Olayan, al-Ghunaim, and other women reflects a conscious decision on the part of Gulf decisionmakers to form an implicit alliance with educated Gulf women and to reduce the influence of groups that wish to preserve the patriarchal structures established in the 1970s and 1980s. As I discussed in Chapter 2, Gulf monarchies and their politics are interconnected sets of communities, federations, and coalitions that are constantly in motion. Although there is little doubt that King Abdullah and other Gulf leaders are idealistically committed to promoting equality between the genders, the decision to ally with women also serves the political and socioeconomic needs of Gulf rulers.

Women are a natural political base of support for regimes in their ongoing struggle with violent Islamic opposition groups, many of which voice their grievances in patriarchal terms, seeking to impose strict controls on women. Educated women in particular also provide the regimes with a more cosmopolitan, softer, and less austere vision of the Gulf to the outside world. This is not a minor issue for the Gulf states politically or economically. Osama bin Laden is a Saudi, and all but two of the hijackers who perpetrated the September 11, 2001, terrorist attacks were from the Gulf.[142] Citizens of Gulf states stand accused of financing and participating in extremist violence in Iraq, Afghanistan, and other areas around the world. Because of the close ties of Gulf governments to the international economy, and because of their desire to win foreign investment, these governments care more than ever about how investors in New York, London, Tokyo, and elsewhere *look* at their states. This explains, in part, why Nahed Taher was chosen in 2005 to lead a Saudi Arabian trade delegation to the United States to obtain more foreign investment in the kingdom.[143]

Because of critical changes in the economies and population dynamics of the Arab Gulf states, Taher and other educated women are positioned to solve two problems far greater than terrorism: expatriate labor and the dearth of qualified indigenous male workers. Both problems, as I have outlined in other chapters, originate in failed policies and in changes within the global economy. Despite decades of programs promoting male indigenous workers in every sector of the economy, such workers have been unable to obtain the skills necessary to compete with expatriate workers, who fill as much as 90 percent of the workforce in some sectors of the Gulf economy.

By contrast, indigenous Arab Gulf women offer an alternative solution that can fill the upcoming void of expatriate workers, especially those with skills. In Bahrain, Saudi Arabia, the UAE, Qatar, and Kuwait, female enrollment in higher education significantly exceeds that of men, sometimes by as much as 24 percent.[144] Women dominate a variety of disciplines in the liberal arts and journalism, in which they represent as much as 90 percent of the students.[145] Female students work far harder than their male counterparts and regularly outperform them in secondary and postsecondary institutions. In Kuwait, women's success at the college level is a political issue, with Islamist politicians claiming that it is unfair and demoralizing for Kuwaiti men to have to compete with female students.[146] In Bahrain, female high school students have a long tradition of outperforming their male counterparts. In 2007, for example, the girls graduated at a rate of 74.36 percent, compared to only 53.37 percent for the boys.[147]

Nor is this situation likely to change anytime soon. Even though, in 2007, equal numbers of girls and boys attended middle school in Bahrain, 828 girls achieved a score of at least 90 percent on their middle school exams, compared to the 263 boys who made the mark.[148] The World Bank reported in 2004 "that for every Qatari man aged 25 and graduating from university, there are two women graduates of the same age."[149] In Qatar and other Gulf states, the school dropout rate of males is double that of females.[150] The literacy rate of females between the ages of fifteen and twenty-four in the Gulf states has climbed since the 1970s, so that by 2007 it was consistent with that of women in developed nations.[151] This is an especially remarkable achievement when one remembers that there were *no* schools for women in some Gulf states as recently as 1970.

Are Women the Solution?

The question still remains: Can women dominate the professions and even the working classes of the Gulf states? In the UAE and Qatar, in particular, there are already reasons to believe this might occur. For example, in the UAE, women's share of the labor market jumped from just 9.6 percent in 1985 to 13.0 percent in 1995, and up to 22.4 percent in 2004.[152] In 2007, Emirati women became pilots for Bahrain-based Gulf Air and other regional carriers.[153] By that time, they had become as much as 60 percent of the employees of the government workforce in the UAE and Saudi Arabia.[154] In Qatar, it is commonly accepted among middle-class and even elite nationals that it is now an economic necessity for *both* spouses to work.[155] Qatari men have also largely accepted the fact that they may play the role of junior income earners.[156] Qatar is an important test case because it and Saudi Arabia are the only states in the world in which Wahhabism is the official interpretation of Islam and because Qatar is facing many of the same financial challenges as Saudi Arabia. An average middle-class woman in Saudi Arabia will pay nearly half her salary to a male driver (invariably an expatriate) to get her to and from work.[157]

At the same time, one must bear in mind that there are significant barriers to women's filling the future labor needs of the Gulf states. Although it is true that women dominate higher education, they are often not earning the types of technical degrees desired by employers—that is, in engineering, math, and various sciences. In part, this discrepancy reflects a broad preference among Gulf nationals of both genders to earn degrees in the humanities, religion, and social sciences. It is also indicative, however, of the scarcity of technical and vocational institutions and instructors for women in several of the Gulf states, especially Saudi Arabia, where the top jobs desired by employers in 2001 were in medicine and computer technology. Thus, in 2001, there were nearly 50,000 Saudi women looking for work; and in 2007, the Saudi government estimated that unemployment among Saudi women stood at 37 percent.[158]

Even those women who have the right sets of skills and experiences face two additional constraints. First, strong cultural and familial pressures for women to remain close to their families can limit their ability to travel to regions in which jobs are available or to assume positions for which they would otherwise be qualified. Second, Gulf employers do not necessarily perceive indigenous women as workers. A recent Saudi campaign to encourage indigenous women to work as housemaids, cooks, and babysitters—jobs traditionally held by expatriates—failed because most Saudis could not accept the idea of Saudi women working for other Saudis.[159]

In a similar case, when social critics repeatedly warned about the dangers to public morality from allowing expatriate males to work in lingerie stores, the Saudi government announced in April 2006 that it would ban expatriate men from working in those stores and that Saudi women would take their place by June. At that point, nearly 10,000 women applied for the new positions, forcing the Saudi government to announce, on June 1, 2006, that it would extend the deadline for changing over to female workers indefinitely.[160]

Religious leaders throughout the Gulf states have reinforced the barriers to women's working by pressing for limitations on their rights and opportunities to work. Kuwait's parliament passed legislation in 2007 that "prohibits women from working between 8:00 P.M. and 7:00 A.M. and in jobs that contravene with public morals and in all-men service places at any time."[161] How Kuwaiti female doctors, teachers, and government ministers, among others, could renounce their duties between 8:00 P.M. and 7:00 A.M. is far from clear, since these professions operate around the clock. Islamist politicians in Bahrain and Kuwait have also sought to pass revised family laws with strict provisions on the ability of women to pass along their inheritance rights and nationality to those of their children whose fathers are from overseas, including other Muslim nations.[162]

Another issue of importance to the Islamist groups is the "problem" of unmarried women, including unmarried professional women. For instance, in Saudi Arabia there were at least a million and a half unmarried women in 2002 and frequent calls to reduce the *mahr,* the dowry paid by the groom to the bride.[163] Abdulaziz al-Ansari, a preacher in neighboring Qatar, argues that the problem has reached crisis proportions. Although Qatar's male population is substantially larger than its female population, he contends that "there are 30 to 40 unmarried women, including widows and divorcees, for every two to three eligible bachelors." His solution: encourage polygamy, a social practice hardly compatible with the vision promoted by modern Gulf women. Al-Ansari frequently cites instances in which *women* made their marriage proposals conditional on the future husband marrying a second woman, usually a close friend or work colleague. In this way, "friends" could live happily under the same roof. Unfortunately, he fails to disclose how these women would work out the very real issues of polygamous marriage in the twenty-first century.[164]

Proposals in Qatar for polygamy have failed to win state support and have generated intense opposition from women's groups, which have called on al-Ansari to rescind his proposal and have requested that other religious leaders condemn it as inconsistent with twenty-first-century Islam.[165] Such activism is consistent with that of other women activists in the Gulf, who are building coalitions and seizing control of the public debate in ways that were unimaginable before 1990. Recognizing this reality, al-Ansari told the *Gulf News* newspaper in 2006 that men "prefer to marry employed girls" because of Qatar's high cost of living.[166]

Conclusion

Al-Ansari's views reflect how far the debate in the Gulf over whether women will work in large numbers has come in recent years. It is widely understood that maintaining the old system based on expatriate labor poses enormous financial, social, and cultural costs, which not even the wealthiest states in the region can sustain in the long term. Despite the Gulf states' massive investments in education, job training, and programs that favor indigenous male workers, Gulf men are in no better position to play a tangible role addressing the region's labor needs than they were in the 1970s. Nor is it likely that they ever will be. As I will detail in Chapter 7, the educational levels of Gulf men and women are analogous to those of their colleagues in the United States, where there were 2.6 million more women than men enrolled in colleges and universities in 2005.[167]

Women are and will remain the only cost-effective option to fill the Gulf states' future needs for skilled and unskilled labor. What is more, women are in a unique position to "rebrand" the conservative patriarchal image of Gulf states in the world community, to win needed foreign investment, and to forge new political alliances at home and abroad. Gulf governments have already begun to accommodate women's growing socioeconomic and political influence, promote their goals, and seek their support.

Popular culture is also preparing for a future in which women will have a foremost position. *Tash Ma Tash,* Saudi Arabia's most popular television program during the holy month of Ramadan, regularly shows women driving.[168] Despite religious *fatwas* written by senior clerics against watching the show and public demonstrations against the show in 2003, the show has remained on the air.[169] Another program, *Amsha bint Amash,* chronicles the life of a Saudi woman who is forced to work as a taxi driver. In an interview with the *New York Times,* Abdullah Samhan, the producer of *Tash Ma Tash,* explained why female characters are so often seen driving in his show. "A woman," he said, "cannot be separated from society, and women will be driving, whether it's now or fifty years from now."[170] These shows are already having a profound impact. As of 2006, nearly two-thirds of Saudis favor allowing women to drive and work.[171] Increasing numbers of Saudis also favor reducing the role of the religious police in public life, especially in regard to women.[172] In the Saudi Arabia of 2010, women drive tractors, water tankers, and cars in rural communities.[173] What's more, they are allowed to drive on the ARAMCO compound in the Eastern Province and the massive campus of King Abdullah University of Science and Technology.[174]

Despite Samhan's confidence in the inevitability of women's gaining the right to drive in Saudi Arabia, how women use their power in the future and engineer social changes remains to be seen. On the one hand, Olayan and a host of other well-placed professional women throughout government and business advocate a social vision that is consistent in many ways with Western social norms. In recent years, Olayan has linked the vision she outlined in Jeddah with a call for a society that is less dependent on expatriate workers. Her confidence in that vision is reflected by her personal choices. To begin with, she is married to a Greek American attorney, who was raised on the Upper East Side of Manhattan, John Xefos, and has three daughters with him. One doubts that she would have married Xefos and remained in the kingdom with him if she believed that her children would be treated as second-class citizens because their father was an American or because of their gender. Here it is worth noting that Olayan's mother, Mary, is a US citizen whose family hails from New England.[175]

Olayan's confidence is shared by the 1,100 women who delivered a petition in September 2007 to King Abdullah, demanding that women be given the right to drive—a petition that has received significant coverage at home and abroad.[176] To date, none of the signatories has faced any retribution, and one of them, Wajeha al-Huwaider, an educational analyst at ARAMCO, suffered no penalty when she posted a picture of herself on YouTube driving in Saudi Arabia to mark International Women's Day in March 2008.[177] In a similar incident, when Ruwaida al-Habis, a college student, drove her badly burned father and brothers to the hospital, her story appeared in one of the biggest Saudi newspapers, *al-Riyadh,* which called her actions "brave."[178] In addition, the Saudi media noted in June 2009 that approximately 3,000 foreign and Saudi women drive in ARAMCO's compounds and published interviews with some of these women, who emphasized their piety and how much their husbands and families benefited from their freedom to drive.[179]

On the other hand, there is evidence that not *all* women support the petitioners or Olayan's vision. More conservative women may lend their support to a vision consistent with the region's traditional patriarchal values. Islamic parties in Kuwait poll well among women, and young Gulf women have yet to abandon the hijab or other traditional symbols of patriarchal power. Muna Abdallah al-Damigh, the dean of one of the kingdom's teachers colleges, and other professional Saudi women have expressed views that are far more conservative than those of the male Saudi king. Al-Damigh noted in 1997 that Saudi women "do not need their alleged freedom, but we need to adhere to the law of God and the teachings of our Prophet Muhammad. . . . This is the real freedom, and this is the pure and chaste life."[180]

There is, of course, precedent for this type of conservatism among women in other parts of the world. Just as Margaret Thatcher, Angela Merkel, Nadia Yassine, Ann Coulter, and others have lent their considerable talents to conservative parties and causes, it is highly likely that conservative women activists will emerge in the Gulf. Conservative Sunni and Shia female activists have already played a key role in Bahrain's politics. Images of veiled women holding assault rifles were a powerful propaganda weapon for Ayatollah Khomeini in Iran's Islamic revolution in 1979.

It is ironic that women's place in the Gulf may evolve into something reminiscent of the nineteenth and early twentieth centuries. Al-Huwaider has already begun to argue that the past provides Gulf women with a possible future social model. "Our parents," she said, "had the right of movement; our grandparents had it too. . . . But we ladies of the cities lost the old ways and got nothing in their place."[181] In the past, as now, one can find women in positions of authority and power, even women leading men into battle. Women have been successful in commerce, medicine, education, and government. They have also been religious leaders, who received both social and cultural respect for their knowledge and power.

Future generations of women in the Gulf will most likely live in societies that resemble those of al-Huwaider's parents' and grandparents' generations far more than they do the Gulf states of the last quarter-century or even the 1990s. Women will be integrated into virtually every aspect of public and private life at home and abroad and will have an increasing say in how their societies are managed. Once this happens, earlier female experience will be reinterpreted and reevaluated. American songwriter Cole Porter made a point that applies strongly to women of the Gulf: "If you want a future, darling, why don't you get a past?"[182]

Notes

1. "Saudi Arabia's Top Cleric Condemns Calls for Women's Rights," *New York Times,* January 22, 2004.

2. Robin Gedye, "Unveiled Women Are Root of All Evil, Says Saudi Cleric," *Daily Telegraph* (London), January 22, 2004.

3. The women drove for at least an hour before they were stopped by the Saudi police. Donna Abu-Nasr, "Stunning Saudi Car Ride Celebrated 18 Years Later," Associated Press, November 14, 2008.

4. Omar El Okeily, "Asharq al-Awsat Interviews 'The Girls of Riyadh' Author Rajaa al-Sanea," *Asharq al-Awsat,* January 25, 2006 (available at http://www.aawsat.com/); Sophia Tareen, "Author Rajaa Alsanea Explores Tradition and the Muslim Woman's Search for Love," Associated Press, July 2, 2007 (available at http://www.lexisnexis.com/); "Rajaa Alsanea, the Author of Girls of Riyadh, Speaks Out" (available at http://www.marieclaire.co.uk/).

5. For more on these arguments, see Eleanor Doumato, *Women, Islam, and Healing in Saudi Arabia and the Gulf* (New York: Columbia University Press, 2000).

6. Faiza Saleh Ambah, "Bored Young Saudis Find Outlet in Graffiti," *Washington Post,* October 31, 2007.

7. Haya al-Mughni, *Women in Kuwait: The Politics of Gender* (London: Saqi Books, 2001), 45.

8. Louay Bahry and Phebe Marr, "Qatari Women: A New Generation of Leaders," *Middle East Policy* 12, no. 2 (2005): 104–105; Ahmad Suba'i, *My Days in Mecca,* trans. and ed. Deborah Akers and Abubaker Bagader (Boulder, CO: First Forum Press, 2009), 35.

9. Gawdat Bahgat, "Education in the Gulf Monarchies: Retrospect and Prospect," *International Review of Education/Internationale Zeitschrift für Erziehungswissenschaft/Revue Internationale de l'éducation* 45, no. 2 (March 1999): 129.

10. Abeer Abu Said, *Qatari Women: Past and Present* (London: Longman Group Limited, 1984), 24–25.

11. Fatima al-Sayegh, "Women and Economic Changes in the Gulf: The Case of the United Arab Emirates," *Domes* 10, no. 2 (2001): 3.

12. Al-Mughni, *Women in Kuwait,* 46.

13. Al-Sayegh, "Women and Economic Changes," 5.

14. For more on these issues, see Soraya Altorki and Donald P. Cole, *Arabian Oasis City: The Transformation of 'Unayzah* (Austin: University of Texas Press, 1989).

15. "Who's Who in the Arab World 1981–1982," n.d., William Mulligan Papers, Georgetown University Library Special Collections, Box 1, Folder 42.

16. Al-Sayegh, "Women and Economic Changes," 5–6.

17. Ibid.

18. Said, *Qatari Women,* 24–25.

19. Ibid., 29.

20 Doumato, *Women, Islam, and Healing,* 170–184.

21. Ibid.

22. Raymond O'Shea, *The Sand Kings: The Experiences of an RAF Officer in the Little-Known Regions of Trucial Oman, Arabia* (London: Methuen and Co., 1947), 64.

23. Ibid.; Peter Lienhardt, *Sheikhdoms of Eastern Arabia,* ed. Ahmed al-Shahi (New York: Palgrave, 2001), 171.

24. O'Shea, *The Sand Kings,* 62–63.

25. Ibid.

26. Al-Sayegh, "Women and Economic Changes," 4; Mulligan, "Confidential Memorandum: Conversation with Dhahran Consul W. K. Schwinn," November 22, 1958.

27. Mulligan, "Confidential Memorandum: Conversation with Dhahran Consul W. K. Schwinn," November 22, 1958.

28. Susan Hillyard, *Before the Oil: A Personal Memoir of Abu Dhabi, 1954–1958* (Bakewell, Derbyshire, UK: Ashridge Press, 2002), 62.

29. Al-Sayegh, "Women and Economic Changes," 6.

30. Mai Yamani, "Changing the Habits of a Lifetime: The Adaptation of Hejazi Dress to the New Social Order" in *Languages of Dress in the Middle East,* ed. Nancy Lindisfarne-Tapper and Bruce Ingham, 57–58 (Richmond, UK: Curzon Press, 1997).

31. Gregory Gause, *Oil Monarchies: Domestic and Security Challenges in the Arab Gulf States* (New York: Council on Foreign Relations, 1994), 71.

32. Doumato, *Women, Islam, and Healing,* 176, 182–183.

33. For more on this issue, see Bruce Ingham, "Men's Dress in the Arabian Peninsula: Historical and Present Perspectives," in *Languages of Dress in the Middle East,* ed. Nancy Lindisfarne-Tapper and Bruce Ingham, 40–54 (Richmond, UK: Curzon Press, 1997).

34. Bahry and Marr, "A New Generation of Leaders," 105.

35. Al-Sayegh, "Women and Economic Changes," 7.

36. Al-Mughni, *Women in Kuwait,* 67–73.

37. Madeline A. Holmes, "Kuwait, Ancient and Modern," *Arabia Calling* 237 (Autumn 1954): 9–11. The missionary also noted that the government paid for all books and paper and provided uniforms gratis (green jackets and gray trousers for the boys and plaid dresses for the girls).

38. Ibid.

39. Ibid.

40. Al-Mughni, *Women in Kuwait,* 58–60.

41. Ibid., 67–94.

42. Cornelia Dalenberg, "Unforgettable Patients," *Neglected Arabia* 217 (Summer 1949): 14–15. Dalenberg discussed one of these women at length: "Hajjia Fatimah is an elderly woman with twinkling brown eyes and wavy hair colored with henna to within about a half inch of the middle parting where the hair is white. She has made the long pilgrimage to Mecca two times and the shorter pilgrimage to Kerbela and Nejef at least twelve times. Many Bahraini women have been to Mecca, but very few are called Hajjia. Fatimah rates this title perhaps because she is a 'Mulaya,' a Koran reader. Every day of the week she goes out from house to house with her Koran, here to read over a sick baby, there to read a bad spirit out of a girl, then to a house of mourning for a Tazaia and then perhaps to the Matim for a public reading. She is also called 'Muallima' (Teacher). The first part of her mornings before she goes out to read, she has a Koran class for about twelve to fifteen small boys and girls. They sit on the ground or on flat date baskets with their Koran stands, made of two crossed pieces of wood, in front of them, all reading aloud in high-pitched voices. Hajjia sits on a mat near them with her

Nargileh in front of her, and has a puff at the pipe every few minutes while she listens to them. Some of the children stay with her long enough to learn the whole Koran, but most of them stay for few months only, ('Dalil' as she calls this preparatory period) and then go on to the public schools."

43. Rose Nykerk, "Mirage for Muneera," special women's edition, *Arabia Calling* 224 (Summer 1951): 17.

44. May Seikaly, "Women and Social Change in Bahrain," *International Journal for Middle East Studies* 26, no. 3 (August 1994): 418–419.

45. Ibid., 419. British diplomat Sir R. Hay noted in 1950: "The veil is still rigorously observed by all Arab ladies, though I have heard the opinion expressed in Bahrain that it will not be long before they begin to discard it." Hay to Bevin, "Social and Political Effects of the Development of the Oil Industry in the Persian Gulf," no. 34, EA 10110/2, Bahrain, April 24, 1950, reprinted in *British Documents on Foreign Affairs: Reports and Papers from the Foreign Office Confidential Print,* ed. Paul Preston and Michael Partridge, pt. 4: *From 1946 Through 1950,* Series B: *Near and Middle East, 1950,* ed. Malcolm Yapp, vol. 10: *Israel, Syria, Arabia, General, Jordan and Arab Palestine and the Lebanon 1950, January 1950–December 1950* (Bethesda, MD: University Publications of America, 1999), 203–204.

46. Salman Sau'd Halib (F. S. Vidal edited), "Events in Bahrain," November 5, 1956, William Mulligan Papers, Georgetown University Library Special Collections, Box 2, Folder 54.

47. Seikaly, "Women and Social Change in Bahrain," 420–422.

48. Phebe Marr, "Girls' Schools—The Hijaz," April 8, 1961, William Mulligan Papers, Georgetown University Library Special Collections, Box 3, Folder 6.

49. Mai Yamani, "Health, Education, Gender, and Security in the Gulf in the Twenty-First Century," in *Gulf Security in the Twenty-First Century,* ed. Christian Koch and David Long (Abu Dhabi, United Arab Emirates: Emirates Center for Strategic Studies and Research, 1997), 275.

50. Phebe Marr, "Instructions for Girls' Schools," April 3, 1961, William Mulligan Papers, Georgetown University Library Special Collections, Box 3, Folder 6, 1; Helen Metz, "Current Status of Women in Saudi Arabia," May 6, 1964, William Mulligan Papers, Georgetown University Library Special Collections, Box 3, Folder 21.

51. A. H. Kamal, "Memorandum to the Files: The Veil, a Talk by Mahmud 'Isa Mashadi, August 1, 1962," August 4, 1962, William Mulligan Papers, Georgetown University Library Special Collections, Box 3, Folder 14.

52. Ibid.

53. Marr, "Girls' Schools—The Hijaz," 3.

54. Fahda bint Saud bin Abdul Aziz, "The Concerns of Saudi Women," *al-Hayat,* February 19, 2007.

55. Opposition was so strong in Buraidah that Faysal had to send in the Saudi National Guard to open a girls' school there. 'Ulema in other communities, such as Hofuf, made clear their displeasure with the girls' schools. Metz, "Current Status of Women in Saudi Arabia," 1; William Mulligan to J. V. Knight, "Local Government Relations," March 28, 1961, William Mulligan Papers, Georgetown University Library Special Collections, Box 2, Folder 25.

56. A good example is Laila Yamani, who wrote scripts for a twenty-minute weekly women's program, *Rukn al-Marah* (Women's Corner), on Saudi Ara-

bia's Radio Mecca. The show provided advice on child care, food preparation, and biographies of outstanding women in Islamic history. Phebe Marr, "Memorandum to File: Visit of Dr. and Mrs. Ahmad Zaki Yamani," April 2, 1960, William Mulligan Papers, Georgetown University Library Special Collections, Box 2, Folder 64.

57. Phebe Marr, "Girls' Schools—Year-End Summary," September 18, 1961, William Mulligan Papers, Georgetown University Library Special Collections, Box 3, Folder 9.

58. These women did not attend formal classes at the university and took exams at the homes of faculty. Metz, "Current Status of Women in Saudi Arabia."

59. Phebe Marr, "Status of Women in Saudi Arabia," June 20, 1962, William Mulligan Papers, Georgetown University Library Special Collections, Box 3, Folder 13.

60. As Phebe Marr noted in her 1961 report on girls' schools in Saudi Arabia, the difference in the standard levels between boys and girls emerges clearly from a comparison of their respective examinations. The boys' exam was not only an hour longer than the girls' exam but also included significantly more questions devoted to arithmetic, geometry, geography, history, and science. Such differences reflected the curricula of the two systems of schools: girls' schools emphasized religion and domestic skills, whereas boys' schools had a curriculum far more consistent with European and American schools. Marr, "Girls' Schools—Year-End Summary," 2.

61. Marr, "Girls' Schools—The Hijaz," 6.

62. "Women in Saudi Arabia," February 1970, William Mulligan Papers, Georgetown University Library Special Collections, Box 3, Folder 34, 3.

63. Ibid.

64. "Ministry of Interior Announcement on Standards of Dress in Saudi Arabia (Radio Riyadh Broadcast of 8 June 1970)," June 8, 1970, William Mulligan Papers, Georgetown University Library Special Collections, Box 3, Folder 35.

65. Eleanor Doumato, "Women and the Stability of Saudi Arabia," *Middle East Report* 171 (July–August 1991): 35.

66. Doumato, *Women, Islam, and Healing,* 176, 182–183.

67. Ira Lapidus, *A History of Islamic Societies,* 2nd ed. (Cambridge: Cambridge University Press, 2002), 573; Eleanor Doumato, "Saudi Arabia: The Society and Its Environment," in *Saudi Arabia: A Country Study,* ed. Helen Metz, 96–104 (Washington, DC: Library of Congress Federal Research Division, 1993).

68. Al-Sayegh, "Women and Economic Changes," 7.

69. Ibid., 9.

70. Bahry and Marr, "Qatari Women: A New Generation of Leaders," 105–106.

71. Ibid., 105; al-Sayegh, "Women and Economic Changes," 7.

72. "Appendix: Table 19: Qatar: Enrollment in Government Schools by Education Level and Gender, Selected Academic Years, 1975–76 to 1988–1989," in *Persian Gulf States: Country Studies,* ed. Helen Metz, 396 (Washington, DC: Library of Congress Federal Research Division, 1994).

73. "Appendix: Table 13: Bahrain: Enrollment by Education Level and Gender, Selected Academic Years, 1977–78 to 1991–1992," in *Persian Gulf States: Country Studies,* ed. Helen Metz, 391 (Washington, DC: Library of Congress Federal Research Division, 1994).

74. Calvin H. Allen, *Oman: Modernization of the Sultanate* (Boulder, CO:

Westview Press, 1987), 101; Fareed Mohamedi, "Oman," in *Persian Gulf States: Country Studies,* ed. Helen Metz, 265–266 (Washington, DC: Library of Congress Federal Research Division, 1994).

75. "Appendix: Table: Oman Enrollment in Government Schools by Education Level and Gender, Selected Academic Years, 1975–76 to 1987–1991," in *Persian Gulf States: Country Studies,* ed. Helen Metz, 406 (Washington, DC: Library of Congress Federal Research Division, 1994).

76. Al-Sayegh, "Women and Economic Changes," 8.

77. Ibid.

78. Ibid.

79. World Bank, *Women in the Middle East and North Africa: Women in the Public Sphere* (Washington, DC: World Bank Press, 2004), 153.

80. World Bank, *The Status and Progress of Women in the Middle East and North Africa* (Washington, DC: World Bank Press, 2007), 139, 141 (available at http://siteresources.worldbank.org/); World Bank, *Women in the Middle East and North Africa,* 153.

81. World Bank, *Women in the Middle East and North Africa,* 153.

82. Ibid., 59.

83. Louay Bahry, "The New Saudi Woman: Modernizing in an Islamic Framework," *Middle East Journal* 36, no. 4 (Autumn 1982): 502–515.

84. Al-Sayegh, "Women and Economic Changes," 8.

85. The World Bank, *Women in the Middle East and North Africa,* 153.

86. Shafeeq N. Ghabra, "Balancing State and Society: The Islamic Movement in Kuwait," in *Revolutionaries and Reformers: Contemporary Islamist Movements in the Middle East,* ed. Barry Rubin, 106–108 (Binghamton: State University of New York Press, 2003).

87. Ibid., 106.

88. Eleanor Doumato, "Gender, Monarchy, and National Identity in Saudi Arabia," *British Journal of Middle Eastern Studies* 19, no. 1 (1992): 34–39; Eleanor Doumato, "The Saudis and the Gulf War: Gender, Power, and Revival of the Religious Right," in *Change and Development in the Gulf,* ed. Abbas Abdelkarim, 184–210 (New York: Palgrave Macmillan, 1999).

89. Doumato, "Gender, Monarchy, and National Identity," 41.

90. Munira Fakhro, "Gulf Women and Islamic Law," in *Feminism and Islam, Legal and Literary Perspectives,* ed. Mai Yamani, 257 (New York: New York University Press, 1996).

91. Ida Patterson Storm, "Bahrain," *Arabia Calling* 244 (Autumn 1956): 10.

92. Ingham, "Men's Dress in the Arabian Peninsula: Historical and Present Perspectives," 40–54.

93. May Seikaly, "Women and Religion in Bahrain: An Emerging Identity," in *Islam, Gender, and Social Change,* ed. Yvonne Haddad and John Esposito, 178 (New York: Oxford University Press, 1997).

94. For more on these issues, see Munira Fakhro, *Women at Work in the Gulf: A Case Study of Bahrain* (London: Kegan Paul International, 1990).

95. Economist Intelligence Unit, *2003 Bahrain Country Profile* (London: EIU, 2003), 16.

96. Frank Viviano, "Kingdom on Edge: Saudi Arabia," *National Geographic* 204, no. 4 (October 2003): 16–17.

97. Doumato, *Country Study: Saudi Arabia,* 101.

98. World Bank, *Women in the Middle East and North Africa,* 153.

99. "Women in Saudi Arabia."

100. Richard Harwood, "Change Is Slow for Saudi Women," *Washington Post,* February 12, 1978 (available at http://proquest.umi.com/).

101. Ibid. Bandar added that Bedouin women "had started driving trucks" in the desert and emphasized the seriousness (and veracity) of the observation by adding "and I'm not kidding."

102. Saddeka Arebi, *Women and Words in Saudi Arabia* (New York: Columbia University Press, 1984), 271–272.

103. Ibid., 254–255.

104. Doumato, *Country Study: Saudi Arabia,* 103.

105. Rajaa al-Sanea, *Girls of Riyadh,* trans. Rajaa al-Sanea and Marilyn Booth (New York: Penguin Press, 2007), 270. Booth has subsequently raised questions about the Penguin translation and how it deviated from the original text in Arabic: Marilyn Booth, "Translator v. Author: Girls of Riyadh Goes to New York," *Translation Studies* 1, no. 2 (July 2008): 197–211.

106. For its part, the Saudi state recognized these limitations and sought to encourage women—at least indirectly. In 1989, it awarded its highest award, the King Faisal Award in Islamic Studies, to the Egyptian scholar, Shaikh Muhammad al-Ghazali, who had taken a strong stand that year in an article in a Saudi daily newspaper on allowing women to earn an education and work. Youssef M. Ibrahim, "Saudi Women Quietly Win Some Battles," *New York Times,* April 26, 1989, A6 (*Historical New York Times*).

107. Ghabra, "Balancing State and Society," 107–108.

108. Youssef Ibrahim, "Amid Crisis, West Meets Mideast in Saudi Arabia," *New York Times,* August 25, 1990, 1 (*Historical New York Times*).

109. Doumato, "Women and the Stability of Saudi Arabia," 37.

110. Doumato, "Gender, Monarchy, and National Identity in Saudi Arabia," 32.

111. Mary Ann Tétreault, "A State of Two Minds: State Cultures, Women, and Politics in Kuwait, *International Journal of Middle East Studies* 33, no. 3 (May 2001): 211.

112. Ibid.

113. Mary Ann Tétreault, *Stories of Democracy: Politics and Society in Contemporary Kuwait* (New York: Columbia University Press, 2000), 110–131.

114. Munira A. Fakhro, "The Uprising in Bahrain: An Assessment," in *The Persian Gulf at the Millennium: Essays in Politics, Economy, Security, and Religion,* ed. Gary G. Sick and Lawrence G. Potter, 181 (New York: St. Martin's Press, 1997).

115. The Salafi tradition or Salafism ("pious ancestors") is a reform movement first led by Jamal al-Din al-Afghani and Muhammad Abdu in the late nineteenth century that was enormously influential in the twentieth century. For more on the Salafi tradition, see *The Oxford Dictionary of Islam,* 1st ed., ed. John L. Esposito (Oxford: Oxford University Press, 2003), s.v. "Salafi."

116. Sean Foley, "The Naqshbandiyya-Khalidiyya, Islamic Sainthood, and Religion in Modern Times," *Journal of World History* 19, no. 4 (December 2008), 535.

117. Eleanor Doumato, "Women and Work in Saudi Arabia: How Flexible Are Islamic Margins?" *The Middle East Journal* 53, no. 4 (Autumn 1999): 577.

118. Barbara Stowasser, "Old Shaykhs, Young Women, and the Internet: The

Rewriting of Women's Political Rights in Islam," *The Muslim World* 91 (2001): 99–119.

119. Duraid al-Baik, "Divorce a Raging Controversy," *Gulf News,* December 31, 2005.

120. Doumato, "Women and Work," 577–579; Stowasser, "Old Shaykhs," 101–102.

121. Hamad bin Hamid al-Salimi, "Where Is the Saudi Woman?" *Al-Jazirah* (Riyadh), May 3, 1999.

122. Ibid.

123. Kathy Sheridan, "They Mean Business: How Saudi Women Are Making a Breakthrough," *Irish Times,* February 18, 2006.

124. Christian Chaise, "Saudi Arabia Discreetly Presses Ahead with Reform," Agence France-Presse—English, March 1, 2006.

125. Donna Abu-Nasser, "Women Can Now Sell Cars in Saudi Arabia, but the Ban on Female Driving Remains," Associated Press, December 3, 2006; "Women Received 1,848 Auto Loans," IPR Strategic Business Information Database, December 26, 2006; "Saudi Women Receive 11% of Total Credit," Global News Wire—Asia Africa Intelligence Wire, December 26, 2006.

126. For more on women's role in politics,see Sean Foley, "The Gulf Arabs and the New Iraq: The Most to Gain and the Most to Lose," *Middle Eastern Review of International Affairs* 7, no. 2 (2003): 34.

127. Ibid.

128. Sean Foley, "The Gulf Arabs and the New Iraq: The Most to Gain, the Most to Lose," in *After the Dictator: The Rebirth of Iraq,* ed. Barry Rubin (New York: M. E. Sharpe, 2010).

129. "Woman Wins Seat in First UAE Poll," Financial Times Information Limited, December 17, 2006; "Chosen People of the UAE," Financial Times Information Limited, October 23, 2007.

130. For more on this issue, see Sean Foley, "Kuwait, Bahrain, Qatar, Oman, and the UAE," in *Guide to Islamist Movements,* ed. Barry Rubin (New York: M. E. Sharpe, 2010).

131. Sobhi Rakha, "New Woman Minister Cracks Saudi Glass Ceiling," Agence France-Presse—English, February 15, 2009.

132. Bahry and Marr, "Qatari Women: A New Generation of Leaders," 110.

133. "Saudi Women Brave Stares to Carve a Niche," Financial Times Information Limited, April 17, 2007.

134. "Bahraini Woman Takes Over UN General Assembly," Deutsche Presse-Agentur, September 12, 2006.

135. "Bahrain Names Jewish Ambassador," BBC (available at http://news.bbc.co.uk); "Bahrain Names Jewish Woman as Ambassador to US," Agence France-Presse—English, June 8, 2008.

136. Bahry and Marr, "Qatari Women: A New Generation of Leaders," 110.

137. Al-Mughni, *Women in Kuwait,* 104–111, 164–165.

138. John Esposito, *Unholy War: Terror in the Name of Islam* (Oxford: Oxford University Press, 2002), 130.

139. Information taken from the following sources: Greg Levine and Zina Moukheiber, "Al-Olayan Leads Forbes' Top Arab Businesswomen List," *Forbes Magazine,* March 28, 2006 (available at http://www.forbes.com/); Elizabeth MacDonald and Meghan Bahree, "The World's Most Powerful Women: Muslim

Women in Charge," *Forbes Magazine,* August 30, 2007 (available at http://www.forbes.com/); Elizabeth MacDonald and Chana R. Schoenberger, "Special Report: The 100 Most Powerful Women," *Forbes Magazine,* August 30, 2007 (available at http://www.forbes.com/); Elizabeth MacDonald and Chana R. Schoenberger, "The 100 Most Powerful Women," *Forbes Magazine,* August 31, 2006 (available at http://www.forbes.com/); Hassna'a Mokhtar, "Women's Empowerment a Must," *Arab News,* March 20, 2007 (available at http://www.arabnews.com/); "Special Issue: The Time 100," *Time,* April 10, 2005 (available at http://www.time.com/).

140. Information taken from the following sources: Greg Levine and Zina Moukheiber, "Al-Olayan Leads Forbes' Top Arab Businesswomen List," *Forbes,* March 28, 2006 (available at http://www.forbes.com/); Elizabeth MacDonald and Meghan Bahree, "The World's Most Powerful Women: Muslim Women In Charge," *Forbes,* August 30, 2007; Elizabeth MacDonald and Chana R. Schoenberger, "Special Report: The 100 Most Powerful Women," *Forbes,* August 30, 2007; Elizabeth MacDonald and Chana R. Schoenberger, "The 100 Most Powerful Women," *Forbes,* August 31, 2006; Hassna'a Mokhtar, "Women's Empowerment a Must," *Arab News,* March 20, 2007 (available at http://www.arabnews.com/); "Special Issue: The Time 100," *Time,* April 10, 2005 (available at http://www.time.com/); "The Top 20 Most Powerful Women in Oman," *The Oman Economic Review Online,* October 2008 (available at http://www.oeronline.com/php/2008_oct/cover.php).

141. Hassan Fattah, "Riyadh Journal: Daring to Use the Silver Screen to Reflect Saudi Society," *New York Times,* April 28, 2006 (available at http://www.lexisnexis.com/); Hassan Fattah, "Saudi Arabia Begins to Face Hidden AIDS Problem," *New York Times,* August 8, 2006).

142. The exceptions were Muhammad Atta, who was from Egypt, and Ziad al-Jarrah, who was from Lebanon.

143. "Saudi Arabia: From Banking to Racing," *Saudi-US Relations Information Service Newsletter,* February 12–18, 2006 (available at http://www.saudi-us-relations.org/).

144. World Bank, *Status and Progress of Women,* 129, 135, 139, 140, 141, 144.

145. "Bahraini Women Fail to Make It to the Upper Echelons of Journalism," Financial Times Information Limited, July 6, 2007.

146. Tétreault, *Stories of Democracy,* 160–164.

147. "Girls Outshine Boys in Graduation Exams," Financial Times Information Limited, June 13, 2007.

148. Ibid.

149. Barbara Bibbo', "Qatari Women Find Key to Greater Emancipation," *Gulf News,* March 24, 2007 (available at http://archive.gulfnews.com/); World Bank, *Women in the Middle East and North Africa,* 31–33.

150. World Bank, *Women in the Middle East and North Africa,* 31–33..

151. World Bank, *Status and Progress of Women,* 10.

152. Bahgat, "Education in the Gulf Monarchies," 134; al-Sayegh, "Women and Economic Changes," 9; World Bank, *Status and Progress of Women,* 144.

153. "UAE's First Female Pilot," United Press International, June 17, 2007 (available at http://www.lexisnexis.com/); "First Bahraini Lady Pilot Gains Her Wings with Gulf Air," *al-Bawaba,* February 5, 2007.

154. Al-Sayegh, "Women and Economic Changes," 9.

155. Bahry and Marr, "Qatari Women: A New Generation of Leaders," 112.

156. Ibid., 109.

157. Hassan Fattah, "Saudis Rethink Taboo About Women Behind the Wheel," *New York Times,* September 28, 2007.

158. For more on employment issues, see John R. Calvert and Abdullah S. al-Shetaiwi, "Exploring the Mismatch Between Skills and Jobs for Women in Saudi Arabia in Technical and Vocational Areas: The Views of Saudi Arabian Private Sector Business Managers," *International Journal of Training and Development* 6, no. 2 (2002): 112–124; "Saudi Arabia: Fewer Women Employed in Private Sector," Financial Times Information Limited, May 17, 2007 (available at http://www.lexisnexis.com/); "Women Rising in the Ranks in Middle East Job Market," Middle East Newswire, April 30, 2007.

159. "Families Will Refuse to Hire a Saudi Housekeeper," *Gulf News,* June 27, 2007.

160. "10,000 Chase KSA lingerie jobs," AME Info FZ, LLC—Middle East Retail and Leisure News Wire, April 22, 2006; "Saudi Suspends Lingerie Plans," AME Info FZ, LLC—Middle East Retail and Leisure News Wire, May 15, 2006; Alexandra Pironti, "Saudi Women Obliged to Discuss Underwear Size with Men," Deutsche Presse-Agentur, May 31, 2006. It is surprising that Qatar considered a similar ban in 2007. "Qatar Lingerie Ban for Men," Middle East Retail and Leisure News Wire, April 4, 2007.

161. "Kuwait Bars Women from Night Jobs," Agence France-Presse—English, June 7, 2007.

162. "Bahraini Activists Seek Scholars' Support for New Family Law," Financial Times Limited, May 28, 2007.

163. Pascal Ménoret, *The Saudi Enigma: A History,* trans. Patrick Camiller (London: Zed Books, 2005), 187.

164. "Spinsterhood in Qatar up as Men Shy Away from Marriage," *Gulf Times,* July 11, 2006.

165. "Qatari Women Outraged as Qatari Activist Backs Polygamy," Financial Times Limited, October 2, 2006.

166. "Spinsterhood in Qatar."

167. Michael Thurmond, "Georgia Men Hit Hardest by the Recession, December 2007 to May 2009," Georgia Department of Labor: White Paper on Georgia's Workforce, July 2009 (available at http://www.dol.state.ga.us/), 8.

168. The name Tash Ma Tash comes from a game played by children in the 1960s where they would "pop" the tops off soda bottles by shaking them hard. It roughly translates as "you either get it or you don't" or "make or break it." Neil MacFarquhar, "Riyadh Journal; Seeing the Funny Side of Islamic Law, and Not Seeing It," *New York Times,* November 24, 2003; Pascal Ménoret, "'State Television Has Guarded Us Against 'Cretins': Saudi TV's Dangerous Hit," *Le Monde diplomatique,* English edition, September 16, 2004 (available at http://mondediplo.com/).

169. Ménoret, "State Television Has Guarded Us."

170. Fattah, "Saudis Rethink Taboo."

171. Sheridan, "They Mean Business."

172. Donna Abu-Nasr, "Excesses of Saudi Religious Police Begin to Stir a Backlash," Associated Press, July 2, 2007.

173. Donna Abu-Nasr, "Saudi Ban on Women Drivers May Be Eroding," Associated Press, August 22, 2008.

174. Thanassis Cambanis, "Saudi King Tries to Grow Modern Ideas in the Desert," *New York Times,* October 27, 2007.

175. Steven Flax, "Sweet Equity, Saudi Style," *Forbes* 128 (July 6, 1981), 72; Ari L. Goldman, "Suliman S. Olayan, 83, Dies; One of the World's Wealthiest," *New York Times,* July 6, 2002; William G. Shepherd Jr., "Investor: Suliman S. Olayan: A Saudi's Stake in U.S. Banking," *New York Times,* October 19, 1980 F8 (Historical New York Times).

176. Faiza Ambah, "Saudi Women Petition for Right to Drive; Challenge Poses Risks in Sole Country Where Only Men May Take the Wheel," *Washington Post,* September 24, 2007.

177. For more on the right to drive and al-Huwaidar's other protests, see Betsy Hiel, "Dhahran Women Push the Veil Aside," *Pittsburgh Tribune Review,* May 13, 2007 (available at http://www.pittsburghlive.com/); Donna Abu-Nasr, "Saudi Ban"; and "Saudi Woman Defies Driving Ban to Mark Women's Day," Agence France-Presse—English, March 9, 2008.

178. Abu-Nassr, "Saudi Ban."

179. "Aramco Women Espouse Virtues of Driving," *Saudi Gazette,* June 3, 2009 (available at http://www.saudigazette.com/).

180. Eleanor Doumato, "Between Breadwinner and Domestic Icon?" in *Women and Power in the Middle East,* ed. Suad Joseph and Susan Slyomovics, 171 (Philadelphia: University of Pennsylvania Press, 2001).

181. Fattah, "Saudis Rethink Taboo."

182. Cole Porter, "Let's Misbehave," Paris, in *The Complete Lyrics of Cole Porter,* ed. Robert Kimball (New York: Vintage Books, 1984), 104.

6

Inclusion, Tolerance, and Accommodation

No two religions will coexist in the Arabian peninsula.

—the Prophet Muhammad, 632

In taming the untamable, medical missionaries are sometimes useful instruments [for British officials].

—Rev. Paul W. Harrison, Bahrain, 1940

The Jews had lived for generations in Najran [Saudi Arabia] on terms of perfect amity. . . . The Arabs could not dispense with their valuable services to the community for . . . they were the only gunsmiths and armourers in the district.

—H. St. J. B. Philby, *Arabian Highlands,* 1952

On November 11, 1967, Rev. Roman Benjamin Ament reached an important milestone and crisis in his life when he turned sixty years old. During those six decades, the native of Merrill, Wisconsin, had excelled as a student and later as a teacher in Catholic schools, had joined the Catholic Order of Friars Minor Capuchin, had become an ordained priest, had served among Nicaraguan Indians as a missionary, and, since November 1956, had ministered to ARAMCO's Catholic employees in six cities in Saudi Arabia: Dhahran, Ras Tanura, Abqaiq, Udhailiyah, Riyadh, and Jeddah.[1] He gave three masses a day on Thursdays and Fridays every week in Dhahran alone. During his eleven years in Saudi Arabia, Ament built a successful Catholic parish (Our Lady of Fatima) as well as a library and chapel in Dhahran with a six-foot-tall wooden cross on which was mounted a four-foot-tall carved wooden figure of Jesus.[2]

Although some of his US parishioners in Saudi Arabia disliked his demeanor ("He treated all his parishioners like the Nicaraguan Indians," one later remembered), Ament won a wide following among other Catholics there, especially Goans.[3] Senior-level ARAMCO managers appreciated his work.[4] Nor was he the only or the first priest or minister in Saudi Arabia. Catholic and Protestant clergy had visited the US airbase at Dhahran and ARAMCO facilities since the mid-1940s.[5] Although Ament and the other US and European clergy were formally classified by ARAMCO and the Saudi government as "teachers," there was no doubt what their role really was to Saudis and non-Saudis.[6] Furthermore, Christian missionaries had been known in the Gulf for decades by the term *teacher,* and an Arabic word for teacher (*mu'allim*) shared the same root as the Arabic word for religious scholar or cleric (*'ālim*).[7] Ultimately, Ament and the other Christian religious counselors for the employees of ARAMCO worked in a nation that was committed to defending the hajj pilgrimage and to upholding the prophetic tradition that no religion other than Islam would exist in Arabia.

Despite Ament's success in his ministry, ARAMCO officials informed him in March 1967 that they would terminate his position shortly after he reached the mandatory age of retirement for ARAMCO employees, which was sixty. He would then have to find employment elsewhere. Reacting with horror, Ament wrote a letter of appeal to ARAMCO's vice president of operations, William Sullivan, arguing that he was not an ARAMCO employee and that the company's decision greatly surprised and hurt him:

> I am not an employee of ARAMCO; I do not receive a salary; I am expressly excluded from retirements, disability benefits, group life insurance plan, medical payment plan. According to all contracts, agreements, arrangements made by me and my superiors with ARAMCO, nothing was ever mentioned about mandatory retirement. This rule of company employees had no part in my life, in my plans from 1955 until March 1967. Then it came out of the clear without warning, without prior notice of any kind, as a sudden, cataclysmic disruption in my life—causing irreparable damage and injury, as payment for 11 years of service for ARAMCO and its good people.[8]

In Ament's eyes, the company's actions were sufficiently deleterious to have represented a breach of contract that justified legal action on his part (and that of the Catholic Church) against the company. He loved his position in Saudi Arabia, he said, earned a higher salary there than he would have elsewhere, and was intent on keeping his position as long as possible.[9]

Nevertheless, Ament lost his appeal and left Saudi Arabia by May 1968, replaced by Rev. Joseph Doefler, also an American and a member of the Order of Friars Minor Capuchin.[10] In a series of letters to Ament, ARAMCO officials explained that they respected Ament's work and were willing to compensate him for his lost income. But they noted that although he was not paid by

ARAMCO, his status in Saudi Arabia was identical to that of a company employee.

Ament's status reflected a set of public and private arrangements by which Saudi Arabia's government publicly maintained that it only upheld a conservative vision of Islam within the kingdom while simultaneously permitting a significant degree of religious freedom. In the case of ARAMCO, the Saudi government and the company's president, Floyd Ohliger, had reached an understanding in 1950 that superseded a recently imposed formal prohibition on the entry of missionaries, priests, ministers, and other clergymen into Saudi Arabia. According to this private agreement, Catholic and Protestant clergy could visit company facilities in the kingdom, so long as there was no proselytizing or outward display of Christianity. Four years later, Ohliger reached a private oral agreement with King Saud himself that allowed Christian clergymen, such as Ament, to reside in Saudi Arabia, provided they were classified as teachers and treated exactly the same way as other ARAMCO employees.[11]

Although the understandings between Saud and Ohliger were nearly scuttled in 1955, after Reuters reported the appointment of a Catholic priest to serve in Saudi Arabia, the agreements endured for decades, surviving the nationalization of ARAMCO in 1980. Elements of them still survive today.[12] Other companies, military forces, and institutions followed ARAMCO's lead. For example, King Fahd University of Petroleum and Minerals in Dhahran hired a US Jesuit priest, Robert Sullivan, as a professor of English.[13]

ARAMCO's arrangement with Saudi Arabia was not unusual in the Gulf or simply a matter of pragmatism or convenience, as some have suggested.[14] Building on ties that stretched back to the nineteenth century, Christian communities built public presences in Kuwait, Bahrain, the UAE, and Oman. By the middle of the twentieth century, there were two Catholic vicarates in the Gulf, one for Kuwait and the other for the rest of the Gulf. The latter's letterhead featured a symbol of the Virgin Mary flanked by a palm tree and an oil well.[15]

The controversy over Ament's status and the King Saud–Ohliger agreement is indicative of the long, complicated relationship among Sunni Gulf Arabs, their governments, and a host of peoples who have found employment in the Gulf states. For centuries, these "foreign" individuals have filled important socioeconomic and political positions throughout the Gulf and played an integral, although often unheralded, role in the life of the Arab Gulf States. Building on centuries-old networks linking the Gulf to South Asia and other parts of the world, expatriates have provided needed technical skills, aided state formation, and facilitated socioeconomic development throughout the region. Without their contributions, areas as diverse as commerce, education, health care, and transportation would not be nearly as developed as they are today.

Nevertheless, scholars who study the Gulf have been hard pressed to understand the position of these Shia and expatriate populations within a conservative region that is outwardly hostile to non-Arabs and non-Sunni Muslims. Although these peoples fill vital socioeconomic roles, they are rarely part of formal political structures as decisionmakers or voters. They maintain a status as outsiders, who are tied, fairly or not, to foreign states and institutions that have their own interests in the Gulf (e.g., the Catholic Church and the oil companies). There is little reliable demographic data on these populations, which are rarely taxed or included in censuses and very often lack legal working status in the Gulf. These types of problems have been heightened since the 1970s, when thousands of migrants from Asia flooded into the region. For the UAE, the issue has become so sensitive that it stopped taking official census data in the 1980s and treats demographic issues as a state secret.[16]

In this chapter, I highlight the role of expatriate workers in the political and socioeconomic narrative that I laid out in the first five chapters of this book. In particular, I focus on the contributions of South Asians, Shia Muslims, Christians, and Jews from the late nineteenth century to the present day. Critical to my argument will be the impact of the hajj, the arrival of Western missionaries, the decline of the pearling industry, the rise of the Arab-Israeli conflict, the sudden infusion of oil wealth in the 1950s and 1970s, and the revolutionary events of the period between 1973 and 2010.

At the Dawn of the Twentieth Century

Ellis Island and Angel Island on the Red Sea

In the first third of the twentieth century, the Arab Gulf was an impoverished part of the British Empire, closely tied to many other regions of Africa and Asia. The hajj drew tens of thousands of pilgrims, students, merchants, bureaucrats, and others to Jeddah every year. Although most visitors were Muslim, there were also many Greek sailors and merchants, Catholic sailors from Goa, Jewish traders, European civil servants, and even journalists.[17] For example, Reuters maintained a full-time correspondent in Jeddah.[18] Jenny de Mayer, a US Protestant missionary and nurse who was aligned with the Reformed Church of America, ran a successful pharmacy and medical practice in Jeddah from 1908 until 1914.[19] Although Protestant, she built on the tradition of the Catholic Church, which had periodically sent priests and others to the city to proselytize and to minister to Catholics there.[20]

As H. St. John B. Philby, one of King Ibn Saud's senior advisers, noted to US diplomats in 1940, Hijazi toleration even extended to language and accents. Hijazis and other Gulf Arabs, he said, accepted "the variety of Arabic dialects, pronunciations, and mispronunciations" produced by the many visitors to the region, seeking to find the basic grasp of the subject matter, above all else.[21]

This toleration reflected not only the cosmopolitan and international nature of the Hijaz but also the fact that Greek, Italian, Russian, and other mariners were critical to the hajj, since they piloted the steamers that regularly transported Muslim pilgrims from around the world to Jeddah, as well as the goods that fueled the region's economy.[22] It was impossible in those days for merchants or pilgrims from most of the large Muslim communities in South and Southeast Asia to reach the Hijaz *except* by steamer.[23] It was also impossible for the Hijaz to keep itself properly provisioned without these steamers.[24]

European civil servants were also important to the region, since most of the steamers were European owned and thousands of the hajj pilgrims came from territories in Europe's Asian and African colonies. Virtually all of those pilgrims also had to pass through one of two British-administered quarantine stations before arriving in Jeddah: either al-Tur (in the Sinai Peninsula) or Kamarān (a Red Sea island).[25] For many decades, the threat of cholera and other diseases offered Europeans, especially Britons, a mechanism for asserting influence over what was in theory a wholly Muslim institution, the annual hajj pilgrimage.[26] Although Britain's attempts to have its doctors serve in the Hijaz failed, that nation nonetheless effectively wielded a veto power over much of the hajj, thanks to its quarantine stations and vast naval power. Britain also wielded influence over the International Medical Commission, founded in 1926, which issued reports on the hajj and was empowered to regulate it.[27] Thus, in both form and substance, the stations at al-Tur and Kamarān determined who entered the Hijaz in very much the same way that the immigration stations at Angel Island and Ellis Island controlled who entered the United States in the first half of the twentieth century.[28]

The infringement of national sovereignty inherent in British and European concerns over health was clear, and Ottoman and Arab officials sought many ways to circumvent it. For example, the Ottoman government intended the Hijaz railway, built at the turn of the twentieth century, to serve in part as an alternative route to the Hijaz that would avoid British quarantine stations, and that would not take as long as traditional land routes to Mecca. Istanbul built its own quarantine stations in the Hijaz and the Red Sea and explored ways, including raising money from India and building a permanent tent city for pilgrims, to preserve public health and resist further European infringement.[29] Following World War I and the dissolution of the Ottoman Empire, the new Hashemite government in the Hijaz built its own quarantine station in Jeddah and Western medical facilities in Mecca and Medina.[30] Yet these measures were never good enough for the British and other Europeans, compelling the Hashemite king Hussein to tell a traveler to Jeddah in 1920: "Let them come and see how well we can disinfect and how we can care for the health of the pilgrims. . . . Can't we fumigate as well as the English?"[31]

No Religion Other Than Islam in Arabia?

Despite the resentment of European military power, non-Muslims were sufficiently integrated into Hijazi economic life and society that it was not unusual in the nineteenth century for them to spend significant time in the region and even to visit the holy cities of Mecca and Medina. The famous Muslim tradition that the Prophet Muhammad had ordered no religion other than Islam to be allowed on the Arabian Peninsula had little effect on ordinary Muslims, their leaders, and most non-Muslims in the Hijaz or any other area of the Arabian Peninsula during the first half of the twentieth century.[32] Rather than being an exceptional port city, Jeddah was akin to other port communities in the region—Alexandria, Izmir, Muscat, Salonika, Dubai, and Manama—all of which had heterogeneous populations and commercial ties to Muslim and non-Muslims states. After visiting the Hijaz in 1918, Rev. Samuel Marinus Zwemer, who pioneered US missionary work in the Gulf, marveling at the veritable cornucopia of modern goods available in Jeddah, predicted that "before the end of the century, a visit to Mecca will not be more difficult than a trip to Hebron."[33]

Several examples illustrate the depth of local toleration for non-Muslims in the Hijaz and help to explain why Zwemer was so confident about the area's future. In 1916, during World War I, the new ruler of the Hijaz, King Hussein, invited British officers, who were facilitating the hajj, to visit Mecca. After the war, Hussein called on Syrian Christians in the United States to settle in the Hijaz, promising that they would "continue to trade and be happy" in the territory.[34] King Ibn Saud, who drove Hussein's family out of the Hijaz in the 1920s, similarly tolerated non-Muslim populations in the Hijaz and the rest of Arabia. Christians and Jews lived in places as diverse as Asir, Jeddah, al-Hasa, Najran, and other Saudi communities after the creation of Saudi Arabia in 1930.[35] They had their own rabbis—Najran's was Iraqi—and were, according to Philby, a "very valuable element of the population" of Najran since they were the sole producers of weapons and the only silversmiths in the town.[36]

Jews and Christians in Saudi Arabia were required to pay the *jiziya* (head tax) instead of *zhakat* (tithe), just as they did in other regions of the Middle East and had done for centuries under other Muslim regimes in the Arabian Peninsula.[37] Ibn Saud even boasted that "we Muslims love the Christians; why, we accept them as wives; that is perfectly allowable."[38] In addition, foreign Jews lived in the kingdom. For example, two out of the four diplomats assigned to the Soviet agency in Jeddah in the 1920s were Jews.[39]

Saudi and Arabian toleration of non-Muslims was not an accident or fluke. It reflected the practices of some past Wahhabi states and the jurisprudence and teaching of the intellectual father of Saudi Arabia's religious tradition, the eighteenth-century Hanbali Muslim scholar, Muhammad Ibn abd al-Wahhab.[40] As Natana DeLong-Bas notes in *Wahhabi Islam*, Wahhab left a significant record of scholarship on how proper Muslims should interact with non-Muslim tribes as well as with Christians and Jews, whom he referred to as *ahl al-Kitab* (people of the Book) and *dhimmi* (protected people).[41] He also counseled his followers to seek treaty relationships and nonviolent means of interacting with Christians and Jews.[42] Muslim men were to treat Christian and Jewish women with no less deference than they afforded to Muslim women, even if they did not wear the veil.[43] The same principles applied to non-Muslim property. So long as Christians and Jews paid the *jiziya* and acknowledged Muslim sovereignty, Muslim governments were expected to uphold their security and rights.[44]

One can also see Wahhab's teachings in the attitude of Saudi Arabia's founder, Ibn Saud, toward Christians and Jews. As I noted earlier, he confided to his famous British companion, Philby, that he would have no objection to marrying a Christian or Jewish woman and that she would be allowed to practice her faith openly.[45] He praised both Christians and Jews to Philby and used the quranic argument for official religious tolerance of Christianity and Judaism—namely, that adherents to the two faiths were people of the Book, just like Sunni Muslims.[46] There was nothing in what would evolve into Saudi citizenship laws under Ibn Saud that prohibited non-Muslims from becoming Saudis or specified that Saudis *had* to be Muslims. In reality, the opposite was true: former citizens of the Ottoman Empire, some of whom were Christians or Jews, could become Saudis, along with anyone else born inside the kingdom's boundaries, including those whose parents were not Saudis.[47] In fact, Ibn Saud held that Christians and Jews were superior to Shia Muslims, who, in his eyes, practiced *shirk* (polytheism). Although he periodically negotiated agreements with local Shia religious figures, he sanctioned discrimination toward the Shia in the Hijaz (near Medina), the Najd, Najran, and the Eastern Province. Shia were barred from worshiping in their own mosques, and attempts to restart the seminary at Qatif were ruthlessly suppressed. Structures in Mecca that were sacred to Shia were also destroyed, and Shia went without local religious leadership for extended periods, often depending on Iraqi Shia for their religious needs. Ibn Saud reinforced anti-Shia discrimination by disseminating two patently false myths: first, that the founder of Shiism was a Jew; second, that Shia religious leaders and the Iranian government had hindered Saudi Arabia from unifying Muslims against European imperialists in the 1930s. The message was clear: Shia were at best suspect members of Saudi society, and any demands they made for a separate religious or cultural identity would face harsh punishment.[48]

Neither Persian nor Arabian

Nor was Saudi Arabia unusual for its tolerance of non-Muslim populations. Thousands of Muslims and non-Muslims arrived in the Gulf on trade routes that traversed the region, participating in the pearling industry and in regional trade. The crews of the pearling ships that harvested the pearl beds in the Gulf, from Oman to Abu Dhabi to Kuwait, included people of various nationalities. An American visiting Doha in 1916 commented that a crew of pearling ships could include anyone: "They form a most curious and heterogeneous crowd. Many of them are Negroes, some of them runaways and other manumitted, but hailing from everywhere. One finds also men from India, Beluchistan, Persia, Oman, and not infrequently Bedouins from the interior of Arabia. I have even met natives of Zanzibar."[49]

The buyers of pearls were equally diverse. European Christian and Jewish merchants annually visited Bahrain, which was the undisputed center of the Gulf pearling industry, as well as smaller Gulf pearling centers, to purchase pearls for the finest boutiques in Paris, Bombay, and other major cities.[50] In the 1920s, Jewish businessman Victor Rosenthal and his family annually bought £1 million sterling worth of pearls in Bahrain[51] and gave generously to the US missionary hospital there.[52] Algerian and Iraqi Jews also participated in the pearling economy and helped their fellow Jews in the Gulf by funding schools for Jewish children.[53]

Significantly, Jewish pearl merchants in Bahrain formed part of a small but critical network of Jewish merchants throughout the Gulf. For example, in Bahrain, the Yadgars were wealthy textile traders, the Khedouris were the leading importers of tablecloths and bed linens, and the Nonoos were wealthy bankers, who also served on the Bahraini Municipal Council (as did Isaac Sweiry and Meir Dahoud Rouben).[54] Between 600 and 1,500 Jews lived in Bahrain during the first half of the twentieth century, and there were so many Jewish owned businesses along Manama's al-Mutanabi Road that it was informally called "Jews' Street," and its shops closed for the Jewish Sabbath. The community had its own cemetery and its own synagogue.[55]

In Oman, Jews worked alongside Catholic Christians for many years in various industries, including silver ornaments, banking, and the production of alcoholic beverages. Oman was also the home of Ishaq bin Yahuda, a famous Jewish merchant sailor, who traveled to China in the ninth century.[56]

In Kuwait, there were eighty Jewish families, who had their own synagogue, school, and substantial financial interests. Many of them were originally from Iraq and returned there when Emir Faysal, who had warm relations with Jews, became king of Iraq in the 1920s.[57]

None of these activities escaped the attention of British officials, who used many of the same tactics in the Gulf as they did in the Hijaz to gain influence.[58] Through the implementation of quarantine regulations and political and commercial treaties, they won leading roles in a number of pearling communities, and administered Oman, Kuwait, and especially Bahrain as extensions of the British Empire. After visiting the island of Bahrain in 1930, Ameen Rihani observed that the Gulf archipelago, situated thousands of miles away from South Asia, was part of Britain's vast empire in India. Britain's power was seemingly so strong within the island kingdom and the rest of the Gulf that there was no need to debate the centuries-old question of whether the Gulf belonged to Iran or to the Arabs. As Rihani observed, the Gulf "is neither Persian nor Arabian: it is British."[59]

The Lotus and the Lion

As powerful as Great Britain appeared to the outside world, British power in the Gulf, as I have argued earlier, had tangible limits in the nineteenth century and the first third of the twentieth century. For example, as Paul Harrison, a US missionary doctor, said about Dubai, it successfully resisted "pressure of steamship companies and of quarantine regulations" as well as "kept out political agents."[60] No British official set foot on the Trucial Coast for extended periods until World War II. Until the rise of air conditioning in the 1930s, hardly any British officials were ever stationed in the Gulf, which forced London to depend on others to maintain its informal and formal empire in the region.

One group was paramount in this process—South Asians, especially Hindus, whose ancient symbol is the lotus flower. Indians frequently operated in areas that did not fall wholly under British control, such as Dubai, and maintained an identity and networks that were linked to but also separate from the British government.[61] Although the British lion may have outwardly dominated the Gulf for Rihani and others, its presence there would not have been possible without considerable assistance from Indians.

Among the scholars who have done considerable recent work on this partnership is James Onley. His groundbreaking work, *The Arabian Frontier of the British Raj,* charts how Indian merchants operating in the Gulf often had British-Indian passports and served as commercial agents for the British government.[62] This status entitled them to fly the British flag in front of their homes, to be exempt from taxation, and, most important, to receive the support of the British government in commercial disputes with Gulf Arabs. There were many instances in which a British official sided with Indian merchants in such disputes.[63]

Yet the presence of Indians in the Gulf did not rest on British protection. Instead, that presence stretched back centuries before the British arrived in the region—six centuries in Bahrain alone.[64] During that time, Indians provided Gulf societies with commercial services, cheap labor from Asia and Africa, and access to global economic networks.[65] Indians were responsible for the greater part of the foreign trade of Kuwait, Bahrain, and Muscat and dominated banking and commerce in many communities.[66] Furthermore, Indians facilitated Gulf Arabs' procurement of goods and arms from Western nations, the export of dates to markets as far away as the United States, and the import of much of their food.[67]

At the turn of the twentieth century, there may have been as many as 200,000 Indians in the Indian Ocean diaspora. Indian networks were especially strong within the Gulf, both in regions under British control and in those that resisted British and Western power. In Bahrain, for example, which was under British control, the Hindu community numbered more than 300 families.[68] Between the 1890s and 1923, Bahrain's rulers farmed out the collection of taxes on goods entering and leaving the island to Indian merchants.[69]

In Oman, Khojas and Gujarati merchants dominated commerce, tying the country's interior with coastal communities via trade routes.[70] These merchants dined with Omani monarchs in Muscat and were often exempt from paying the *jiziya*.[71] Hindu and Sikh merchants in Oman publicly celebrated their religious holidays, had multiple temples (one of which is now several hundred years old), kept cows to meet their dairy needs, and faced minimal interference in their residential compounds.[72]

Indian merchants and mariners freely practiced their faiths in Abu Dhabi, Dubai, and other communities along the Trucial Coast. In Abu Dhabi, Indians owned and operated nearly all of the shops in the city's market and most of the pearling ships.[73] In Dubai, Sindhi Hindus dominated the textile trade, and Gujarati Hindus ran the lucrative gold market. Indians in Dubai also maintained a temple, a community association, and a cremation ground as well as their own herd of cows to meet their dairy needs.[74]

"We Are in Arabia to Make Men and Women Christians"

Whenever the owners of those Indian cows needed medical attention for their animals or themselves, they turned to Christian missionary doctors for care. Those doctors, many of whom were trained at top medical schools in the United States, ran an extensive system of hospitals and schools throughout the Gulf and the whole Middle East. The best known of these schools is the top Western university in the Middle East, the American University of Beirut. For Gulf Arabs, who equated modern medicine and European schools with invasive quarantines and imperialism, US Christian doctors provided a potential way of accessing Western medicine and education without losing more of their sovereignty.

In this way, an outside group in the Gulf capitalized on its proximity to but perceived distance from British officials to establish a firm base in the region. US Christian missionaries respected (often to the point of lionizing) British accomplishments in the Gulf and formed close social bonds with British officials in the region. Through a series of informal arrangements, British officials served as virtual US diplomats, authorized to renew US passports and issue birth certificates and other official documents. Before traveling on medical trips throughout the Trucial Coast and other Gulf areas outside of direct British influence, the US missionaries always consulted British diplomats, and when they returned, they provided British officials with valuable information on slavery, tribal politics, and local customs and traditions. Paul Harrison encapsulated this relationship when he noted in 1940 that British officials in the Gulf strongly encouraged him to visit Dubai and other areas of the Gulf where British power had failed to tame local populations.[75]

Those US Christian missionaries at the same time consciously differentiated themselves in a number of ways from British officials. For one thing, they maintained close ties to the United States, advised US oil companies,[76] and provided US officials with intelligence on British officials and on politics in the Gulf.[77] In particular, the US Christian missionaries worked to take advantage of the implied link between medicine and quarantines, on the one hand, and British power, on the other. They also sought to counter the perception among Gulf Arabs that, in Paul Harrison's words, "just behind the [US] missionary . . . [one] could discern the form of the British Political Agent."[78] The dangers of such perceptions were real, and it was imperative, in Harrison's eyes, for Christian missionaries "to avoid identifying . . . [with] the never resting advance of Western imperialism."[79]

Harrison's comment reflects the fact that he and his fellow missionary doctors in the Gulf depended on the fees paid by their patients and by charitable donations from wealthy Gulf Arabs to cover their expenses. Britain was always disturbed by the financial and potential ideological component of the Christian missions, and this concern exploded into a diplomatic row between Washington and London as early as the 1880s. At that time, to quell Bahraini opposition to the opening of a US Christian mission in Manama, Great Britain expelled several US missionaries from the island. In response, US secretary of state Richard Olney demanded that Britain reverse its decision, famously linking the US "Open Door" commercial doctrine to its missionaries. "We ask no greater privileges for missionaries than for merchants," he said, "but at the same time we insist that they shall have no less."[80] Facing this type of pressure, London backed down, permitting the opening of US Christian hospitals and schools in the Gulf.[81]

Although the US missionaries knew that they had little chance of converting many people in the Gulf to Protestant Christianity, they lobbied hard to gain access to every community they could possibly serve. If that meant enduring long trips into the desert and standing up to hostile Muslim activists, so be it. As their magazine, *Neglected Arabia,* stated on its cover in 1926, the Arabian mission's chief goal, from its inception, was to establish a base on the coast of Arabia and to "occupy the interior."[82] A decade later, one of these missionary doctors, Wells Thomas, noted, after visiting Saudi Arabia, that if US Christian missionaries chose to act "as much like Christ as we possibly can," then Arabia will be penetrated by "the pure light of Christ's religion" and "won to Christ by love."[83]

It is significant that Thomas and other US Christian missionaries did not aim to control the heartland of Arabia politically or militarily. They were interested only in saving the lives and the souls of Arab Muslims. From the late nineteenth century until the 1920s, US Christian missionaries started this process by building churches in Kuwait, Bahrain, and Oman and regularly holding church services in Arabic. In *Doctor in Arabia,* Paul Harrison proclaimed: "We are in Arabia to make men and women Christians."[84] He also made clear who he thought would ultimately win the trust of Arabia's Muslims and convert them: the missionary doctors.[85]

The Operations of the Reformed Church of America in the Gulf

By the late 1920s, the Reformed Church of America had established a vast medical and social services network to facilitate Harrison's vision of service and conversion. Not only were there male missionary doctors, but there were also dozens of women missionaries, who were teachers, nurses, and doctors as well.

In 1928, there were eight Sunday schools, seven Christian hospitals and dispensaries, four day schools for boys, two day schools for girls, and one boarding school for boys in the Gulf.[86] There were also discussions about sending US Christian doctors to the Eastern Province of Saudi Arabia.[87] Throughout the Gulf, there were often as many as thirty-five missionaries active at one time, along with their dependents and dozens of local and Indian assistants; the latter were collectively called "native assistants" in US Christian records.[88]

Missionary doctors and their assistants saw ever more patients in the 1920s and 1930s. For instance, in 1928, these doctors and their staff treated 77,000 patients out of a regional population numbering some 5 million.[89] Despite the onset of the Great Depression and the collapse of the pearling industry in the early 1930s, these missionary doctors served nearly 90,000 patients in 1933.[90] In the late 1930s, missionary doctors in Kuwait had as many patient visits as there were people in the whole country.[91]

The missionary doctors also took full advantage of the emergence of the automobile and the airplane in the Gulf, regularly using cars to travel in Bahrain and Saudi Arabia and planes to answer emergency calls. Emergency medicines that had once taken more than a month to arrive could be acquired in a matter of days, thanks to air travel. When Iran closed Britain's military and civilian air bases in 1930, the British transferred those bases to the Arab side of the Gulf, which brought US missionary stations in Bahrain and Oman into regular air mail contact with Europe and India. The US missionary doctors also utilized cars and planes to centralize their operations across the region and publicize their activities to potential donors in the United States and Europe. One can get an idea of the importance of air travel to the Reformed Church of America from its annual report in 1937, in which the Reverend

Dykstra used the images of an imaginary airplane flying from Baghdad to Oman to describe the organization's various activities in the Gulf to US contributors.[92]

The missionary hospital in Bahrain, Mason Memorial, was the first in the region to utilize x-ray machines and to offer dental care.[93] Along with the other US Christian hospitals, Mason Memorial in Bahrain drew male and female patients from the local community and many other areas: Linga and Bushehr in Iran; Qatif, al-Hasa, and Riyadh in Saudi Arabia; and Dubai, Oman, Muharraq, Hudd, and Sitra along the Trucial Coast.[94] Doctors at Mason Memorial also made thousands of house calls, driving thousands of miles every year within an island kingdom of only 239 square miles.[95]

Missionary medical tours into the interior of Arabia and Oman could last for months, during which more than 10,000 patients might be treated and hundreds of surgical operations performed. These tours also afforded the missionary doctors opportunities to distribute religious materials. For example, Stanley Mylrea sold hundreds of Bibles during a tour of the Trucial Coast in 1908. In one particularly grueling trip in 1924, US missionary doctors treated 6,552 patients while performing 214 minor and 128 major surgeries in just four months.[96]

The US missionaries also ran a system of schools, which served nearly a thousand students of various faiths, ethnicities, and classes. These schools, which opened in the first two decades of the twentieth century, competed with state schools and quranic teachers for students. Among the most successful of the US Christian schools was the girls' school in Bahrain, which catered to Arab, Iranian, African, Indian, Shia Muslim, Sunni Muslim, Jewish, and Protestant Christian students.[97] In 1929, 26 of the 107 students at the school were Jewish, and 76 were Muslim.[98] The school also had a few Jewish teachers.[99] In 1932, 33 of the 111 students were Jewish, 8 were Christian, and many spoke little or no Arabic.[100] A year later, there were even more Jews: 35 in a class of 110.[101] The boys' school was also diverse. In 1932, out of a class of 151 students, it had 112 Muslims, 33 Jews, 4 Hindus, and 2 Christians.[102] The statistics are especially notable when one considers that Bahrain's census in 1941 concluded that only 2 percent of the population was non-Muslim.[103]

By the late 1930s, multiple generations of students had attended the US missionary schools, whose doctors annually saw tens of thousands of people of various ages and backgrounds. Grand openings of US Christian facilities were major events in the Gulf, drawing British officials and members of ruling families.[104]

Perhaps most remarkable was the amount of service that US missionaries provided to Saudi Arabia, which had a population of a little more than 3.5 million in 1925.[105] Although the Reformed Church of America never built a mission in the kingdom, its doctors saw 275,000 patients in temporary clinics between 1914 and 1955 and visited 17,500 private homes, including those of leading merchants and politicians.[106] Paul Armerding, the lone scholar to write on the Reformed Church of America's mission in Saudi Arabia, estimates that US missionary doctors conducted 3,500 major and 14,000 minor surgical procedures during this period.[107]

Although it is important to keep these large numbers in context (missionary doctors saw on average fewer than 7,000 patients annually—or less than 2 percent of the Saudi population), they were highly valued by the Saudi elite and remained one of the options for modern healthcare well into the twentieth century. As late as 1951, 200 merchants in the eastern Saudi city of al-Hasa circulated a petition requesting that the local emir permit the Reformed Church of America to build a permanent hospital in their town.[108] In fact, the Reformed Church of America missionaries were sufficiently important to King Ibn Saud that he permitted them to hold a private Christian service in his capital, Riyadh, in 1935.[109]

Overall, US missionary doctors stimulated awareness in the Arab Gulf about modern public-health issues and laid the foundation for the rise of state-funded medical facilities and schools in Saudi Arabia, Bahrain, Kuwait, and other Gulf states. Impressed by the success of the Reformed Church of America, the rulers of the Trucial States allowed Sarah Hosman, a one-legged unmarried US woman missionary, to establish a permanent medical center in Sharjah at Bayt Sarkil in 1941.[110] That facility served as a major medical center for many years, and many of today's prominent Sharjans were born there. Hoping to similarly benefit from missionary doctors, Shaikh Shakbut of Abu Dhabi invited two Anglican missionaries, Pat and Marion Kennedy, to establish a church-funded hospital in the Buraimi oasis, his family's ancestral home, in the 1960s.

Insiders as Outsiders: The Shia of the Gulf

The relative success of the integration of Hindus and Christians into the socioeconomic fabric of the Arab Gulf contrasts markedly with the failure of the Arab and Iranian Shia Muslims to find a permanent place in society. Throughout the region, Sunni governments looked at their Shia populations with suspicion that they might support Iranian or Iraqi Shia. As a consequence, few Shia participated in the political process or were granted citizenship. Even those Shia who forged viable relationships with ruling families had to contend with the ire of mainstream Sunni society, which often saw the Shia as key supporters of imperial regimes and dictatorial monarchies and a critical factor in the prevention of more consultative government in the Gulf. The Shia regularly found themselves caught between their governments and the rest of Gulf society—hardly an enviable position.

To understand this dynamic, one should start out with the diversity of Shia in the Gulf. Within Kuwait, there were three separate strands of Shia. Two were Arab—the Hasawi and the Bahrana—with ties to Saudi Arabia, Bahrain, Iraq, and the Arab areas of Iran. The third group, the Ajam, were Iranians who had lived as merchants in the emirate for decades. Even among the three groups, there were key distinctions between old and new settlers. But Kuwait's Shia all enjoyed freedoms that were unimaginable in neighboring Saudi Arabia. They could maintain their mosques or community centers (*husayniyat*), observe Shia rituals and holidays publicly, and teach their children Shiism. The community's commercial class, especially the Ajam, allied closely with the al-Sabah ruling family, which it supported in the 1930s when the family came under great political pressure from Sunni clans and merchants.[111] Although the Shia constituted more than half of the total population of Kuwait in the 1930s, they were barred from participating in the country's first legislative assembly in 1938.[112]

In Oman and along the Trucial Coast, society accommodated both Arab and non-Arab Shia. In Oman, Indian Shia were merchants, lived in an exclusive area in the city of Matrah, and maintained their own schools and court system. In Dubai, Shia and non-Shia Iranians found a welcome escape from drought in Iran as well as from the increasing tariffs there and the central government's control of Iran's southern ports. Building on Dubai's sheltered creek, the city's rulers actively promoted international commerce, eliminated the city's customs duties, provided land to merchants, and permitted Iranian immigrants to settle permanently. The emir even gave land to an Iranian pearl merchant to construct a school specifically for Iranians.[113] Iranian merchants, in turn, used dhows to ship goods to Iran. The result of these policies was a commercial boom, exceeded in the region only by those in Kuwait and Bahrain. On a visit to the city in 1922, a US Christian missionary observed:

> Half or more of Debai's [*sic*] imports are said to be goods for Persian ports. Persia charges enormous import duties. In some cases they are said to run as high as 100 percent. A clerk who had worked in the Persian customs told me that in the year and more that he was there, not a case of tea entered the harbor and paid customs, in that particular port, although the Persians are notorious tea-drinkers, and during that period the shops in the Bazaar were always full of tea. Like most other things it was brought to Debai where there is no tariff, and from there shipped in Arab or Persian sail boats to its Persian port and landed. If necessary, it is easy to placate subordinate customs officials. The methods of doing that have been well worked out.[114]

Nor did the Iranians just bring their resources and time-tested methods for importing goods into Iran and avoiding paying import duties. As Christopher Davidson observes, Iranian merchants transferred their vast trading networks with Asia and Africa from Iran to Dubai. They also introduced Dubai to a very useful technology in a hot desert climate: wind towers, an early form of air conditioning that captures air from several stories up and redistributes it to lower-level rooms in a home. Today, wind towers are a symbol of "original" Emirati culture and ingenuity and are a standard part of promotional material and heritage sites in the UAE.[115]

By contrast, the Shia in Qatar and Bahrain faced far harsher conditions. In Qatar, the several hundred indigenous Shia Arabs and migrant Iranian Shia worked as boatbuilders, artisans, laborers, and merchants. They were an indispensable part of Doha's population (some even amassing considerable wealth through trade), but a distinct social and political minority in this peninsula nation. By the early 1930s, the ruling family allied with Saudi Arabia and upheld Wahhabism and doctrines about Shiism that were prevalent there. Within this framework, Shia Muslims were believed to be polytheists and not true Muslims, beyond any hope of social or political integration into Qatari life.

Although Wahhabism had little sway in Bahrain, most Shia Muslims were often not better off there than they were in Qatar. Since the eighteenth century, many Shia Arabs had steadily lost their legal rights and land to Sunni Arabs.[116] Sunni Muslims and their allies dominated Bahrain's politics and economics and deliberately imported Sunni Arab tribal populations from neighboring Saudi Arabia to erode the Arab Shia demographic majority on the island. These policies had their intended effect: Bahrain's census in 1941 reported that the two populations were roughly equal: 46,354 Shia to 41,944 Sunni.[117]

Ironically, a critical aspect of this discriminatory process was the alliance between the Bahraini ruling family and Iranian Shia merchants (known as the Ajam), who saw Bahrain, much like Dubai, as a haven from the troubles in their homeland. Iranian Shia, many of whom came from one district of Bushehr, rapidly intermarried into the local Arab population while still maintaining close ties to Iran.[118] (The community imported Islamic Shia scholars from Iran and maintained an Iranian government-sponsored school in Manama.[119]) They also took advantage of relatively unrestrictive immigration laws to settle thousands of Iranians on the island before the 1940s. Furthermore, Iranian Shia (and other) merchants lent a significant portion of the profits they made in Bahrain to the Bahraini ruling family in exchange for land and trade concessions. This exchange, Nelida Fuccaro observes, "effectively secured the coercive apparatus of government established by the al-Khalifas [Bahrain's royal family]" in the rural districts of Bahrain.[120]

These oppressive anti-Shia conditions only began to improve after a massive Shia uprising in 1928, the imposition of tight British administration, and the guidance of the controversial British adviser, Charles Belgrave, who dominated the island's political system from the late 1920s until the late 1950s. He pushed Bahrain's emir to open the first schools for Shia in Manama in 1928. Arab Shia, who valued education and performed well in the island's schools, took advantage of the modern civil service system promoted by Belgrave, in which promotion was based on merit rather than sect. In short order, Shia Bahrainis made tremendous social and economic advances.[121]

Oil and Decolonization

A key factor in the advances of Bahrain's Shia was the appearance of an industry that would come to define the Gulf: oil. Petroleum brought new wealth and power, especially to the ruling families. That sudden influx of wealth coincided with decolonization—a process that ended Britain's global empire in India and saw the emergence of the United States as a global power. These different factors had important consequences for non-Sunnis and non-Arabs, altering the makeup of expatriate peoples in the Gulf. In particular, the US Christian missionaries and the Jewish merchants, who had once held a central position in Gulf life, began to fade in importance or to leave the region altogether.

Continuity and Change

By the late 1950s, the once prominent Christian and Jewish populations in the Gulf were all but erased from popular and scholarly memory in the region. These populations were replaced over time by a new cadre of expatriates and non-Sunni Muslims, many of whom had Western educations. Doctors, engineers, teachers, managers, secretaries, oil workers, clerks, craftsmen, technicians, Catholic priests, Protestant pastors, and day laborers arrived in the Gulf in the mid-twentieth century, taking on roles as central as those played before 1930 by US Christian missionaries, Iranian émigrés, and Hindu Indian merchants. Just as previous generations of migrants were tolerated and given wide latitude to maintain their cultural or religious identities, the new expatriate workers, who lived in their own neighborhoods and residential compounds, enjoyed broad social freedoms. In this sense, the company camps and later compounds for oil company workers were parallel to the Shia and Hindu communities in Oman and the Trucial Coast. In addition, oil companies provided the linkages to the global economy that had once been provided by European and Indian merchants.

For all these continuities with the past, there were also key changes, which were related to the rise of nationalism and the disappearance of the British Empire. The Gulf rulers and their indigenous populations sought to define themselves as nations, distinct from—and sometimes superior to—the expatriate peoples who had long lived in the Gulf. Indians and others, who had once benefited from their affiliations with European empires, found that new independent governments in New Delhi and elsewhere guaranteed them little more than second-class citizenship in the Gulf. The days of the mighty Indian merchants were over in the Gulf.

Oil and the Transformation of the Reformed Church of America

Although many of the new arrivals were devout Christians, they had little interest in spreading the gospel or providing essential social services to Gulf Arabs in the way the US Christian missionaries had done. Instead, they were intent on finding one thing: oil. They benefited from the Great Depression, the collapse of the pearl industry, and the decline in the numbers of hajj pilgrims, all of which had left the Gulf's rulers scrambling to find new sources of income. This opened the way for westerners to search for oil—first in Bahrain in the 1930s, and later in other Gulf States. These oilmen found petroleum in commercial quantities, connected the region to worldwide oil distribution networks, and built the foundations for the Gulf's modern economy.

For the Reformed Church of America and its missionaries, the oil industry created two hazards. First, British officials, fearful of losing oil concessions to US companies, limited the scope and length of the Christian medical missions, whose doctors they suspected of being agents for US oil companies. Between the mid-1930s and 1945, US Christian missionaries were prohibited outright from visiting the Trucial Coast. The British government also began to compete directly for influence with the missionaries by dispatching permanent political representatives to areas of the Gulf where there previously had been no formal British presence and by investing in free medical facilities in Oman and the Trucial States.

Second, Bahrain, Kuwait, and other oil-producing states in the Gulf began to build their own hospitals and schools, some of which were considerably more advanced than those administered by the Reformed Church of America. This was the reverse of what had been the case for decades, when US missionary facilities had set the standard for the entire region.

As early as 1939, a Christian missionary doctor lauded the Bahraini government's use of its new proceeds from oil sales to establish male and female hospitals, conduct antimalarial campaigns, and build village dispensaries. But the doctor also wondered what this meant for the future of one of the main Christian hospitals in the Gulf. "We all rejoice in this forward step," he said, "because it is just what any government should do as its resources increase. One asks, however, where does old Mason Memorial stand now after nearly forty years of service?"[122]

By the 1950s, state hospitals in the region were so superior to the missionary hospitals that they prompted the leadership of the Reformed Church of America to discuss closing its facilities throughout the Gulf. Although the church's main hospital in Kuwait had seventy-five beds in the late 1950s, the government's nine hospitals had 3,000 beds and far more advanced equipment than was available in the missionary facilities.[123] In 1956, Marilyn Tanis, a nurse working at Bahrain's Mason Memorial Hospital, questioned if it was feasible for the hospital to continue operating "in the light of what was becoming a more sophisticated standard" in state hospitals in the Gulf. "No amount of face-lifting," she added, "will rejuvenate it. Only its rebirth into a new up-to-date air conditioned plant will enable it to function efficiently in Bahrain today."[124]

Since Mason Memorial's problems were not unique, and there were no apparent sources of funding to modernize it or other missionary facilities, the end of the Reformed Church of America's missions in the Gulf appeared to be only a matter of time. During the 1960s and 1970s, other missionary facilities in the Gulf were either shut down or fully incorporated into the national health-care systems. By 1980, only Mason Memorial remained as a testament to a system that had once been the backbone of the region's health-care system.[125]

"You Would Never Know That You Were in Arabia"

From the start of the oil industry in the region in the 1930s, the governments in the Gulf lacked the technical expertise to build an oil industry on their own, and there were nowhere near enough local skilled, technical, or even ordinary laborers to build one. It was consequently necessary for the Gulf's rulers to attract foreign expertise and labor, no matter what the social or financial costs were. Although Western governments and oil companies competed intensely at first for influence in Saudi Arabia and other Gulf states, they understood the Gulf rulers' weak positions.

During the 1930s and 1940s, British and US oil companies developed common strategies for dealing with political leaders and labor practices in the Gulf. Most of the laborers for the companies were local, generally Shia Arabs, along with thousands of South Asian and other workers from the British Empire. (Sunni Arab tribesmen had little interest in oil work.) Another important source of labor, especially in Saudi Arabia, was Italian craftsmen from former Italian colonies in Africa. Many of them had been held as prisoners of war during World War II on islands off Jeddah. Although there was significant Saudi resistance to using Italian workmen after the Italian air force bombed Dhahran in 1940, British officials convinced Riyadh to accept these men because skilled workers were unavailable from elsewhere.[126]

But the most senior executives were Americans or British nationals, many of whom had already served overseas in military, business, or diplomatic positions. As Robert Vitalis notes in *America's Kingdom,* oil company executives adopted nineteenth-century labor models for oil and mineral extraction that had been developed in the Americas after 1860; these models were characterized by rigid racial and social hierarchies.[127] Americans and Britons occupied the top tiers and relegated everyone else, including Italians, to a second-class position or worse. Ordinary workers endured often brutal living and working conditions and, with the exception of the Italians, were barred from negotiating for improvements.[128] Housing, dining, and medical facilities—even for the Italians—lacked air conditioning, clean water, indoor plumbing, and modern construction materials. Temperatures were sufficiently high in the infirmaries that glass containers routinely exploded. To add insult to injury, Arab and Italian workers earned significantly less than Americans or Britons did for the same types of labor. It is ironic that some of the Italians' work, especially woodwork, was of such high quality that ARAMCO officials viewed owning Italian-made desks and cabinets as symbols of status and power.[129]

By contrast, Americans and Britons of all ranks lived in settlements—al-Ahmadi in Kuwait, Dhahran in Saudi Arabia, and Awali in Bahrain—that were similar in appearance to North American suburban communities. They had row upon row of large modern homes with two-car garages, air conditioning, swimming pools, indoor plumbing, and modern furniture and appliances. But there was one thing that separated the settlements from suburban communities in the United States. They had no visible class differences—no rich and no poor—much like US diplomatic and military housing, then and now, in Panama, the Philippines, Korea, and other regions of the world. Everyone earned high salaries, and it was nearly impossible to spend one's salary in a location so isolated from Europe and North America. Dana Schmidt, a foreign affairs reporter for the *New York Times,* observed about these settlements that "housing and the circumstances of life make all live about the same."[130]

One can get a good idea of the early milieu of Dhahran and similar communities from letters that Clarence J. McIntosh, a US diplomat stationed in Saudi Arabia in the mid-1940s, sent to his family. He called Dhahran "a small America," marveling that it had all the accoutrements of a modern US city: multistory air-conditioned buildings, electrical appliances, a telephone system, paved streets, streetlights, schools, sidewalks, tennis courts, swimming pools, softball fields, a hospital, social clubs, a bar, and a movie theater.[131] Budweiser beer, Hershey chocolates, cinnamon buns, ham, and other staples of US life were easily available. "Everything," he wrote, "is direct from the U.S."[132] Christmas, Halloween, and other Western holidays were celebrated just as they were in the United States, complete with trees, special food, and decorations.[133] Some holidays included adult games between men and women.[134] By 1947, Dhahran even had its own Christian cemetery.[135] Muslim holidays were not respected, and McIntosh complained about the surliness of servant staff in Dhahran during Ramadan. Still, unless you "looked out of the window and saw the endless sand," McIntosh added, "you would never know that you were in Arabia."[136]

McIntosh subsequently visited Bahrain and spent the night at BAPCO's facility in Awali, where he noted that the place shared many things in common with Dhahran and ARAMCO's other large residential compounds in Saudi Arabia. Awali was, in fact, a replica of a modern US city with air-conditioning, paved streets, and well-manicured lawns along with a nightclub. He observed in 1944:

> [Awali has] paved streets, electric lights, buses, houses, trees, grass, and everything. All the houses are air conditioned, even the room I drew for the night. The mess hall was a delightful place, air conditioned, and with service and food deluxe. An open air cinema was enjoyed that evening, and I visited their swanky club with multicolored lights and a large open pavilion.[137]

McIntosh added that Awali was little different from Dhahran except in size and climate. "It was a model little city, and a delightful one," he concluded.[138]

McIntosh's comments were confirmed by Dana Schmidt, the *New York Times* reporter, who visited Dhahran in the 1950s and described the community as a US town "set down in the Arabian desert complete with week-end gardeners, women's clubs, Parent-Teacher Associations and television." The residents of the town were "recognizable as genuine suburbanites," who lived in nearly identical air-conditioned ranch homes with their own yards and hedges, situated on virtually identical streets. A quarter of the residents played the quintessential middle-class US pastime: bowling.[139] Children were "equipped with usual American toys and means of locomotion from scooters to hot rods." [140] The aerial picture of Dhahran that was included with the article could have easily been mistaken for Levittown, Pennsylvania.[141]

Peter Lienhardt, a British scholar, found similar conditions in company camps in Kuwait in the 1950s, which he compared to British military housing. The Kuwait Oil Company's facility at Ahmadi was a British township in all but name—"a well-appointed foreign enclave"—with modern streets laid out on a grid system akin to a "crossword puzzle."[142] Its homes were filled with furniture straight out of the "*Daily Mail* Ideal Home exhibitions."[143] Ahmadi's layout and buildings were sufficiently uniform that when doctors were called out on emergencies, they had to ask callers "to leave the patient and meet them at some recognizable crossroads." [144] Even individuals who had lived in Ahmadi and other oil compounds in the Gulf "found it difficult to tell one street from another"—a feeling many people still have today when they visit US suburban developments or military bases.[145]

The oil company executives believed that it was critical to pay their employees (especially Americans) well (as much as 40 percent above domestic US wages) and to keep them as comfortable as possible. Their philosophy was that "you can take the boy out of the country, but not the country out of the boy."[146] To ensure that this vision was a reality, in 1948 ARAMCO established a special division, ARAMCO Overseas Company (AOC), which was responsible for finding the right foods and transport workers, providing a host of scholarships to Saudis and other Arabs, and attending to the needs of Arab workers.[147] During its first six years, AOC purchased goods in countries from

Western Europe to Southeast Asia and saw its annual budget grow from $4 million to $25 million.[148] In addition, AOC provided important contracts to what would become Saudi Arabia's leading families, the Olayans and the Bin Ladens.

A Not So Delightful Situation

What appeared to be a delightful living arrangement to McIntosh and a profitable business opportunity for the Bin Ladens generated enormous unease among other people in the Gulf. Starting in the 1930s, there was deep unrest among Sunni and Shia oil workers, Sunni religious leaders, and ruling families regarding Western social mores, the oil companies' use of Indian workers, and Anglo-American political ties to Jewish communities in the Palestinian mandate.[149] As early as 1937, the Bahraini government imposed a nationality law on the Ajam, forcing them to choose between abandoning their Iranian nationality and becoming Bahrainis, at the risk of losing their properties to Bahraini citizens.[150] The Muslim staff about whom McIntosh complained certainly had friends and family *outside* of Dhahran, who told others of their experiences there. This unease exploded into anger in 1948 with the rise of the Arab-Israeli conflict and ultimately the founding of the state of Israel. Thanks to radio broadcasts, Gulf Arabs were exposed to the broader Arab world and the new secular and modern ideas emanating from Cairo, Damascus, Baghdad, and elsewhere.

Gulf Arab leaders got the point. Virtually overnight, the pronouncements of most Gulf rulers hardened toward Jews. In conversations with US and UK officials during the 1940s, Ibn Saud publicly reversed many of the positive statements that he had made earlier about Jews.[151] Instead, he insisted that Muslims had never gotten along with Jews, and he claimed that Jews had never lived in Saudi Arabia.[152] Ibn Saud's son, Crown Prince Saud, noted in 1950 in Cairo that it was now a religious duty for Muslims and Christians to cooperate in order to prevent Jews from introducing communism into the Middle East before it was too late.[153] To underscore the seriousness of the partnership, Saudi officials emphasized that their kingdom "welcomed all Palestinian refugees, including Christians."[154] Saudi officials also made clear to US officials that Jews, along with Hindus and Shia, were not permitted to enter the kingdom.[155]

Within this context, US support for Jewish claims to the Palestinian mandate and Washington's recognition of Israel emerged as potentially fatal developments. Official and unofficial Americans and Britons received stern lectures and sometimes unmitigated hostility regarding Israel and the plight of the Palestinians. To dramatize the seriousness of their anger at the Israeli-Palestinian dispute, Saudi officials barred major US companies such as Ford, which had business ties with Israel, from selling their products in Saudi Arabia and also hinted that Western oil companies might lose their concessions due to their governments' ties with Israel.[156] Even as early as 1944, Saudi officials reminded Americans who held ultimate sovereignty over Dhahran when they barred the US consulate from erecting a flagpole, contending that it was a symbol of US "ownership" of Saudi land.[157] In addition, governments in the Gulf refused to issue visas to Jewish visitors, with Saudi Arabia specifically demanding that US consulates in the Middle East certify that their nationals in the country were either members of a Christian denomination or "not Jewish."[158]

Nor were Jews the only ones barred from the kingdom: some Shia Muslims and all Christian missionaries and priests were refused visas. Sikhs, Zoroastrians, Hindus, and Baha'is were also excluded.[159] Despite intense US pressure to lift these restrictions on Jews and others, Riyadh held firm publicly to its position. It also provided support to Palestinian causes and insisted that ARAMCO hire Palestinian refugees as employees in its facilities instead of the Italians. Shortly thereafter, those Italians all but disappeared from ARAMCO.[160] They were soon followed out of the kingdom by the US missionary doctors, whose medical trips to Saudi Arabia declined in the early 1950s and were terminated altogether in 1956.[161]

By that time, Saudi Arabia and some of its neighbors were doing all they could to wipe out the memory of the Hindus, Jews, and Christians who had once been integral to the economic life of the Gulf. Instead, they sought to emphasize that they were homogeneous Arab Muslim societies that were politically linked to events in the Arab-Israeli conflict and the rest of the Middle East. In Saudi Arabia in particular, Judaism was seemingly not tolerated at all under any circumstances. In fact, it was widely accepted that the Jews had not been present in the Gulf since the lifetime of the Prophet Muhammad and that Western positions in the region remained tenuous. Western companies and governments now depended more than ever on medieval monarchies, which controlled societies that were seen at once as unchanging and intolerant but also Vesuvian, ready to explode in the same way that Iraq had in 1958.

"He Will Soon Be on His Way"

In reality, Gulf societies in the years after World War II were neither as stagnant nor as combustible as they may have appeared, and Western oil companies were able to solidify their position in the Gulf. Although there are a number of factors that contributed to the stability of the Gulf states, including the Cold War, the rise of the global demand for oil, the historical legitimacy of the rulers, and the 50-50 oil profit–sharing principle, another factor was central to this: Gulf Arabs' tradition of tolerance of and openness to the needs of non-Arabs and non-Muslims. This tradition helped the Gulf rulers to win widespread acceptance for the continued presence of the thousands of foreign workers necessary for the oil industry's phenomenal growth in the postwar years. In this context, Americans and Europeans were simply filling the roles once held by Indians or Jews. Rulers who consciously maintained an image of religious conservatism and fundamentalism were, in reality, flexible enough to accommodate a significant amount of diversity—even if that meant building ties to Catholics or fundamentalist Protestants.

At the same time, the Gulf rulers made an important promise to their own people regarding the foreign presence, making it clear that this presence was temporary. Once the local populations had grown and there were sufficient numbers of indigenous educated workers, so went the theory, local Arabs would assume jobs now held by Indians, missionary doctors, and non-Sunni Arabs. Peter Lienhardt observed in Kuwait in 1950:

> Most Kuwaitis I talked to about the immigrants . . . certainly supposed that they would soon be on their way. The laborers would have to return home once the construction was finished, while young Kuwaitis now at school or in universities abroad would soon be able to take over the work of the better educated. . . . It would not be many years before the population would again consist of Kuwaitis.[162]

Lienhardt further noted that Kuwaitis did not consider the possibility that the workers could be permanent. They justified the growing problems and expenses linked to expatriate workers by citing a proverb: *La ta'ti al-gharib al-'adha: huwa ra'ih* (Give the stranger something better than everyday treatment, and he will soon be on his way).[163] It was only a matter of time before Kuwaitis would live in a "normal" state in which they were the dominant segment of the population.

Yet it was clear to Lienhardt that these assertions were little more than hopeful thinking and had little basis in fact in Kuwait or anywhere else in the Gulf. There were few educated nationals in the emirate, and they were far more interested in asserting their superiority to expatriates by wearing traditional Arab Gulf dress than by actually taking their jobs. Lienhardt noted that "Kuwait was the place where one could meet Arabs from almost anywhere else except Kuwait."[164] How to accommodate the desire of Gulf Arabs to run their own modern societies, while hiring untold numbers of expatriate workers, would continue to haunt Gulf Arabs and expatriates for decades.

Jews in the Gulf and Arabia

Although Jews had lost much of their commercial role in the region after the collapse of the pearling industry, there is no evidence that rhetoric against Israel or Jews affected Jews' position in Saudi Arabia or elsewhere in the Gulf.[165]

In Bahrain, despite anti-Semitic incidents there in the 1920s and the Arab nationalist sentiments of a significant portion of the population,[166] nearly 300 Jews lived on the island in 1950.[167] A number who left for Great Britain and the United States after 1948 actually returned, became prosperous merchants, and retained close ties to the royal family.[168] Abrahim Baig started a prosperous record label, recording leading singers such as Muhammad Zouwayed, Abdullah Fadhalah, Yousif Foney, and many others.[169] Starting in 1958, the Ruben family held the dealerships for Sharp, Rolex, Longines, and Westinghouse in the country. Although the Jewish community's synagogue was damaged in anti-Israeli riots in 1948, Jews continued to practice and adhere to their traditions.[170] Once a year, they sent for a mohel from India to perform circumcisions on all the Jewish boys born during the previous year.[171]

In Saudi Arabia, after the founding of Israel in 1948, one did not see the same mass expulsions of Jews and confiscations of Jewish property that occurred in several other Arab states in the Gulf, outside of Iraq. Jewish passengers were even allowed to travel through Jeddah's international airport in 1949.[172] In 1950, Jews in Najran and elsewhere in Saudi Arabia left voluntarily for Yemen to participate in the airlift from that southern Arabian country to Israel. Although Najran's officials may have facilitated the departure of the city's Jews, the Saudi central government played no role at all. It is striking that after Ibn Saud learned of the Jews' arrival in Yemen, he demanded that Yemen's rulers promptly return "his subjects" to their native country. The Yemeni government, which had poor relations with Riyadh, saw no reason to comply and in fact robbed and pillaged the Saudi Jews, leaving them near starvation. They only survived the ordeal because of the help of Israeli and British officials.[173]

Jewish Americans filled various military and civilian positions in the Gulf, although sometimes under ridiculous circumstances. One case remembered among the Jewish community in Nashville, Tennessee, involved a Jewish American officer who worked in Saudi Arabia. After his arrival in the kingdom, he received fundraising requests from his former synagogue through a postal system monitored by the Saudi government. Anyone reading the letter, including those who did not know English, would have had no trouble determining its Jewish origins, because the synagogue's letterhead had several Hebrew words in it. Frustrated by what he viewed as harassment by his former synagogue, the officer sent a donation to the synagogue in the form of a 100 riyal note. Only then did the fundraising letters stop arriving. The officer served out the rest of his tour of duty without further incident—a striking development in a kingdom that publicly and proudly upheld a prohibition against granting visas to Jews, including those from the United States.[174]

Christianity on the Gulf Coast and Oman

Christians faced even fewer restrictions in Bahrain, Kuwait, Oman, and the Trucial Coast than Jews and other non-Muslims after 1948. They had their own clergy, established permanent places of worship, and even maintained their own burial grounds—perhaps the greatest signal of a community's acceptance. Not only did Protestant communities continue to flourish in the Gulf, but Catholics, Eastern Orthodox Christians, Chaldeans, and other Middle Easterners and South Asians also found a place in the Gulf. Although European and US Christians, such as Clarence McIntosh, who came from a devout Catholic family, made up a large percentage of the Christian population, there were also many Indian Christians, most of whom were Catholics, who constituted perhaps 30 percent of the total.[175]

Christian South Asians received significant benefits from the onset of decolonization. First, Gulf governments and many Arab Sunni Gulf nationals saw Shia Muslims, Hindus, Sikhs, and Baha'is as polytheists or apostates. Consequently, visa requirements were far tougher for them than for Christians and Sunni Muslims. Second, decolonization and the rise of India and other nation-states in former British colonies disrupted the social and political status of Sikhs, Hindus, and others in the Gulf states. They were no longer "British" nationals living in a region of the British Empire. Instead, they were "foreign" nationals living abroad and linked to India and other relatively weak governments with few representatives in the Gulf. Many chose to return home, creating new opportunities for the Christian expatriates.

Just as US Christian missionaries in the pre-oil era built close ties to Gulf rulers, new populations of Christians and their leaders forged close ties to Gulf ruling families. The rulers regularly donated land for churches, attended openings of new churches and church-related schools, and, most important, were significant financial patrons of Catholic and Protestant churches in the Gulf. Even though Gulf governments continued to promise their indigenous populations that Christians and other expatriates were temporary aspects of Gulf life, their investment in Christian places of worship, their authorization of Christian-only burial grounds, and their links with church leaders suggest that the opposite was true. Without saying so publicly, Gulf rulers recognized that a new reality was tied to the oil boom: Christian expatriates were now permanent members of Gulf society and had effectively become subjects.

This process began in Bahrain in the 1930s with the rise of the oil industry. Father Irzio Luigi Magliacani, a Catholic priest from Italy, settled in Bahrain at the time and, with the assistance of the emir, built the Sacred Heart Church in Manama in 1939. The emir also paid a quarter of the construction cost of a US evangelical church and permitted the construction of an Anglican church. Furthermore, the emir allowed the Catholics and Anglicans to build their own schools, Sacred Heart (Catholic) and St. Christopher's (Anglican), which together had more than a thousand students. Along with the remaining Reformed Church of America schools, these two became the island's elite centers of education. Even members of the royal family attended St. Christopher's. By the 1970s, Christians accounted for close to 2 percent of the island's population.[176]

Although Christians only constituted half of 1 percent of the population of Kuwait, they built a larger public role for themselves there than they did in Bahrain.[177] The Reformed Church of America had been in Kuwait since the early twentieth century, whereas the Catholic Church did not send its first permanent priest there until 1941. Nevertheless, Catholicism experienced rapid success, growing so fast that, in 1950, Rome designated Kuwait a separate vicarate with its own bishop. Six years later, Our Lady of Arabia Church opened in Awali, and Holy Family Cathedral opened in Kuwait City in 1961. Kuwait's emir, Shaikh Abdullah, provided the land for the cathedral and an interest-free loan of $150,000 to pay for its construction. In appreciation, Pope Pius XII designated Abdullah a knight commander of the Order of Pius and awarded him the Grand Cross of the Order of Saint Sylvester—both of which are prestigious papal honors reserved for active Catholic laymen. In addition, Anglicans and various Indian, Eastern, and Orthodox denominations of Christianity found an equally tolerant attitude. Several had their own schools and churches or shared space with other denominations. Consequently, Christian populations in Kuwait grew to 40,000 by the 1970s, about half of whom (19,500) were Catholic.[178]

Rulers in the Trucial Coast were equally tolerant and generous to Christians, who made up 3.87 percent of Abu Dhabi's population and 3.25 percent of Dubai's population by the 1970s.[179] Abu Dhabi granted land to the Anglican Church and the Roman Catholic Church to build places of worship in 1965 along the Corniche, the posh seaside boulevard in Abu Dhabi City.[180] Both facilities had large public crosses that were spotlighted at night. The Catholic church covered 6,000 square feet and had a chapel, a parish house, and a school. When the church building was dedicated in February 1965, Shaikh Shakbut, Abu Dhabi's ruler, became its formal patron and protector during a ceremony that had a twenty-one-gun salute. Nor were Anglicans and Catholics the only Christians in the area. There was also a substantial presence of Indian and Arab churches in Abu Dhabi, Sharjah, and Dubai.[181]

Finally, Sultan Qaboos donated land to the Catholic and Protestant churches in Muscat in the 1970s. As a symbol of the continuity of Oman's Christian community, a stone from the ruins of a sixteenth-century Franciscan monastery in the sultanate was inserted into the foundation of the Catholic church. Although the church could accommodate a thousand parishioners, and was located a significant distance from the center of Muscat, it could not hold the 3,000 people who arrived to see it for its first mass in May 1978.[182]

Christianity in Qatar and Saudi Arabia

The Christians who resided in Qatar and Saudi Arabia lived under circumstances that were both different from and similar to those in the rest of the Arab Gulf. In Qatar, Christians represented close to 4 percent of the population in the 1970s, but could not publicly practice their faith.[183] Requests by the one priest (a Catholic Capuchin) to build a church were refused by the Qatari government.[184] There were perhaps a handful of active congregations in Qatar, but most Arab Christians there sought to pass as Muslims.

In Saudi Arabia, Christians faced similar public restrictions and hostility from the government, which presented itself as a champion of Islam and the protector of the religion's two holy cities, from which non-Muslims were prohibited. There, the Prophet's command not to permit any religion other than Islam to exist in Arabia was taken far more strictly than anywhere else in the region, including Qatar. Any suggestion to the contrary met with swift official denials from Riyadh.

But the reality of religious life in Saudi Arabia was far more complicated than its visa regulations or the draconian statements about the kingdom that appeared in either newspaper or scholarly accounts from the time. Saudis, as I noted earlier, had a long scholarly tradition that justified peaceful coexistence and cooperation with non-Muslims. The Saudi government also worked with non-Muslims, including missionaries, when that served its interests. For example, when dealing with the US military or ARAMCO's US staff, who were overwhelmingly Christian, Saudi officials displayed flexibility by permitting, if only secretly, one of the largest expatriate Catholic and Protestant Christian populations in the Gulf to reside within its borders. That population enjoyed a degree of religious autonomy that rivaled the religious autonomy of more open states both in the Gulf and the rest of the Arab world. Indeed, US diplomat Parker Hart pointed out in 1953 that, in Saudi Arabia, "all persons, including the King, were equal before the law."[185]

The Christians in Saudi Arabia and the institutional structures associated with them arose in the late 1930s as the kingdom's relationship with the US military and the oil industry boomed. In 1939, Christian clergy based in Bahrain started visiting ARAMCO's facilities in Dhahran once a month to hold services there quietly and unofficially. Sixteen different Catholic and Protestant chaplains served at the US base at Dhahran's Character Guidance Center from 1945 until 1962.[186] Services were regularly held on the base, and in at least one instance in 1950 were attended by two Arab Muslim Saudis.[187]

Although ARAMCO formally requested the Saudi government to permit Protestant ministers and Catholic priests to visit the country in 1948, it was not until 1950 that the company president, Floyd Ohliger, negotiated an arrangement by which Christian clergy could regularly visit ARAMCO's facilities. He promised that they would not proselytize or practice Christianity in public, would be classified as teachers rather than missionaries or priests, and would not wear clerical garb in public. Ohliger also won approval for congregations without pastors to have the official status of "morale groups." These included Christian Scientists, Unitarians, Mormons, and others.[188] By 1965, ARAMCO had won approval for the construction of a Christian cemetery in al-Khobar, close to Dhahran.[189]

With these various agreements, Saudi Arabia formally adhered to its visa regulations that prohibited priests from entering the kingdom while simultaneously permitting ARAMCO's employees to practice their faith. From the start, the arrangements were confidential, unofficial, and subject to immediate change. Ohliger understood that the government would not ask and would never expect to be told about clergy and their activities. Riyadh could therefore maintain a facade that it was not aware of the Christian presence. Nor did Saudi officials seek to influence the content of masses and sermons as they did the weekly *khutbas* in the kingdom's thousands of mosques. Nonetheless, Saudi security forces made clear to US diplomats and to ARAMCO that they monitored Christian clergy, their congregations, and their activities in the kingdom. There were boundaries that could not be crossed.[190]

For their part, Ohliger and his colleagues worked to make the priests, pastors, and congregations as inconspicuous as possible in the kingdom. Although individual congregations or religious institutions selected their clergymen and paid their salaries, ARAMCO arranged their assignments, paid them an additional monthly stipend of $340, provided their benefit package, and determined their US tax status to blend them seamlessly into ongoing operations.[191] (The stipend was folded into household rent, which is why Ament argued that he was not an ARAMCO employee.[192]) By 1954, there were Protestant and Catholic clergymen in Dhahran. (They lived at a specific cul-de-sac that came to be called Preacher's Circle.[193])

Catholicism

Of the various denominations with clergymen, the Catholics quickly grew to be the largest. By the early 1970s, at least 9,000 parishioners were attending mass weekly in ARAMCO compounds in Riyadh, Jeddah, and communities near Ras Tanura.[194] William Mulligan and other Catholics who were long-term company executives helped to found a Catholic parish in Saudi Arabia, Our Lady of Fatima, which had multiple priests in ARAMCO facilities in Abaiq, Ras Tanura, Riyadh, Jeddah, and Dhahran.[195] There was also a Catholic chapel in Dhahran (later referred to as a "little cathedral"), which was attached to the priest's residence.[196] It sported statues, candles, an altar, and an enormous hand-carved Italian cross and figure of Jesus.[197]

Although Catholics in Saudi Arabia did not enjoy the relationships with government officials that Catholics did in Kuwait, their institutions were equally vibrant. Weekly collections at masses, which were donated to the Catholic Near East Welfare Association, were usually as high as $15,000 to $20,000—an astonishing figure. Rome recognized the Catholic community's vitality by publicly bestowing honors to Catholic laymen there. Many received honorary knighthoods, and John Kelberer, the president of ARAMCO from 1978 to 1988, received the Order of St. Gregory, the highest award a layman can receive from the Catholic Church.[198]

By the late 1960s, Catholics in Saudi Arabia administered a library, juvenile and young adult programs, religious classes, women's associations, singles groups, and other organizations that cut across racial and ethnic divisions among the expatriate community in the kingdom. The annual Christmas decoration contest included public displays, such as the North Pole scenes in Dhahran's Seventh Street cul-de-sac, which was sufficiently impressive to give the location the nickname Snowman Circle. At the baseball field, there was a Christmas pageant as well as camels, sheep, goats, and Saudi Bedouin tending them. According to a former ARAMCO official, "On Christmas eve, there would be the reading of the Christmas story and singing the traditional religious Christmas hymns around the manger."[199] ARAMCO's radio station also played carols during the Christmas season. In addition, in the center of Dhahran, there was an enormous Christmas tree, which was memorialized in a photograph that was used in 1973 on the Christmas card for the United Nations Relief and Works Agency, which provides services to the Palestinian people.[200]

A "Non-Muslim" Tribe and Its Impact

The existence of large public Christmas displays and trees in Saudi Arabia is indicative of the level of toleration that Saudi officials afforded to foreign workers in their midst. It also shows the respect that Saudis held, above all, for private property, including the private property of non-Muslims. Although it is certainly true that ARAMCO's living arrangements mirrored those of European compounds in Asia and Africa in an earlier era, it is worth noting that the compounds also fell within Saudi jurisprudence and Wahhabi tradition of how Muslims should conduct business with friendly non-Muslim tribes. Again, as DeLong-Bas notes, Ibn Wahhab argued that Muslims cannot even enter the territory of non-Muslim tribes friendly to Muslims except during jihads with the permission of their imam. And even then Muslims could not take more than a fifth of the non-Muslim tribe's property. Throughout his writings, Ibn Wahhab made clear "the Muslim's responsibility for the preservation and protection of both property and innocent life, whether human, plant or animal."[201]

Within this context, all Western facilities, including ARAMCO's, effectively became non-Muslim "tribal property" and were afforded rights and privileges in line with Ibn Wahhab's teachings on non-Muslim tribes. The locations were nearly fully autonomous areas, in which Gulf Arab rules did not fully apply. For example, women faced few of the restrictions present in mainstream Saudi life. Foreign and Saudi men and women regularly socialized together, a practice adopted by elites in Riyadh in the 1950s, including members of the royal family. Saudis and non-Saudis of both genders also worked in the compounds, wore Western clothing, and, as I noted above, drank alcohol. Indeed, drinking was so pervasive in the compounds that Catholics had their own Alcoholics Anonymous groups.[202]

When considering this social milieu, it is useful to take a look at ARAMCO's recommendations for US women living in Saudi Arabia in the 1950s and 1960s. These recommendations did not discuss any severe restrictions on what women could wear or imply that women would have to veil. Instead, it was suggested that they bring a varied supply of clothes to build up morale "for the whole camp as well as for yourself." Women were also asked to bring several bathing suits and were assured that shorts were fine for tennis and other sports.[203]

Nor were Western men and women seriously constricted in their movements in company compounds or beyond. There were no formal restrictions against women driving, and US women frequently drove in both oil compounds and in Jeddah in the 1950s. Dana Schmidt, who visited Jeddah in 1958, observed that frequently "foreign women, wives of American pilots flying for the Saudi Arabian airline, or wives of diplomats . . . drive their own cars."[204] The Saudi government routinely issued driver's licenses to male and female expatriates, and ARAMCO's company files include incident reports about accidents that involved non-Saudi female drivers.[205] The right to drive was important, given the sheer size of ARAMCO's facilities, some of which covered hundreds of square miles. As rules were formally strengthened in the 1970s to prohibit women from driving in the kingdom, foreign and Saudi women were still permitted to drive on private roads, including those in compounds.

The Law and Expatriates

Expatriate men and women in Saudi Arabia, as in other Arab Gulf states, benefited from government services, which included free or subsidized utilities, medicines, and pensions. What is surprising is that they could also take advantage of the Islamic court system. A court case in Jeddah in 1969 provides a window into this process and the workings of Saudi attitudes toward Christians in the kingdom. Given the centrality of Jeddah to Saudi life and political affairs, the city's chief judge, or qadi, was in general an august jurist with close connections to the kingdom's elites. His views certainly reflected mainstream Wahhabi legal doctrine, because the city was far too important for the Saudi government to appoint a person as qadi who did not have its complete trust or who would pioneer new interpretations of Islamic law. Consequently, the qadi's decision to validate the common-law marriage of two US Christians living in Jeddah is especially significant.[206]

The legal case began in March 1969, when a US couple formally petitioned the Jeddah Islamic court to legally validate their marriage. The chief qadi then met with the two Americans and requested to see Arabic translations of the divorce decrees from their previous marriages and proof that they were Christians. Once he was fully satisfied that they were eligible to marry and were Christians, the qadi ordered his staff to draw up a marriage contract for the two Americans. By doing so, he faced a quandary: it was illegal for a woman in Saudi Arabia—and in the Hanbali religious tradition practiced there—to marry without the consent of her legal guardian, and this woman's immediate family was not in Saudi Arabia.[207]

The qadi resolved the dispute by effectively having the Saudi court assume the status of guardian to the bride. By choosing this approach, he adhered to the teachings of Muhammad Ibn al-Wahhab, who argued that it was allowable for a senior religious or political figure to serve as a woman's guardian if another guardian or option were unavailable.[208] Before the marriage ceremony, the qadi lectured the bride and groom extensively about their rights and obligations under Islamic law. In particular, the qadi insisted that the bride understand her rights—in particular, that the groom was legally bound to pay her a dowry, treat her according to the principles of the Quran, and not be away from her for more than four months at a time without her consent. If the groom failed to fulfill his obligations, the qadi warned, the Islamic court could compel him to divorce her. After the bride demonstrated that she understood her rights, the qadi permitted her and the groom to sign the marriage contract. The US Embassy in Jeddah later validated the document as a valid marriage contract.[209]

Although the qadi's insistence that the bride demonstrate her understanding of her rights under Islamic law reflected a concern for women's welfare in a society in which female illiteracy was common, it illustrated two additional important principles. First, the Saudi state did not see religion as a barrier to its jurisdiction or to extending its protection to men and women in need. Christian expatriates in Saudi Arabia were now effectively under the jurisdiction and protection of the state—much as they had been in the 1930s. Henceforth, they could call upon it to protect their rights, seek redress if their rights were violated, or face sanctions if they themselves acted contrary to Islamic law. This relationship of patron and protector resembled that in Kuwait, Qatar, Bahrain, and Oman.

Second, the qadi's actions pointed to the religious diversity in Saudi Arabia's past—as evidenced by the aforementioned work of Ibn Wahhab—and demonstrated that Saudi courts had enough experience dealing with non-Muslim individuals to marry a Christian couple from the United States without giving it a second thought.[210]

Oil and the Shia: A Mixed Blessing

The close relationship between Gulf leaders and their expatriate Christian populations during the oil boom stood in stark contrast to the relationship to the Shia populations. Although some Shia were still barred from worshiping in their own mosques or directly benefiting from the economic boom, others seized opportunities to grow wealthy, integrate themselves economically, and gain new political voices and opportunities for political action. Thus, from Kuwait to the emirates, oil was very much a mixed blessing for the Shia. It altered their material condition but did little to reduce the social barriers, discrimination, and questions of loyalty that had dogged them in the Arab Gulf states for years.

Nowhere was this dichotomy clearer than for the Shia in Saudi Arabia, whose homes were at the epicenter of the kingdom's new oil industry. This quirk of geography brought renewed scrutiny to them but also a variety of new socioeconomic opportunities for a community that had been politically defeated and economically decimated by the collapse of the pearling industry. It is significant that US managers, who sympathized with the outsider status of Shia workers, did not always share the negative view of them held by Wahhabi clerics. Because Sunni Arab tribesmen refused to work on oil rigs, Shia came to constitute a third of the workers in ARAMCO, jobs that represented an improvement over their previous work as fishermen, craftsmen, and laborers for large Sunni landowners.[211]

The jobs at ARAMCO gave Shia Saudis the confidence to attempt to gain political leverage over both the Saudi government and ARAMCO. They staged strikes in 1944, 1953, 1956, and 1967, aligned themselves with Arab nationalism, and appealed directly to the Saudi government for their own mosques and court system, akin to the ones for Shia in Iraq or Bahrain.[212] In one particularly audacious episode in 1967, a delegation of leading Shia figures took their demands to King Faysal. One member of the delegation, Isa al-Bishr, told the Saudi monarch: "Enough injustice has fallen upon the Shia because they are not [considered] equal to others."[213] Faysal rejected the group's requests and Bishr's allegations. "Our country," he said, "is the country of the Muslims, and you are all the same. There is no discrimination between Sunnis and Shias. There are law courts open to all for litigation, and there are mosques for all to pray in."[214]

Faysal then dismissed the group and ordered that Bishr be immediately arrested. The Saudi state proceeded to ruthlessly suppress Shia political activity, and there were no more strikes or demands for improved conditions until the end of the 1970s.

By contrast, in neighboring Kuwait, local workers were guaranteed the right to unionize and were able to press the Kuwaiti Oil Company for better working conditions and a tangible reduction in the numbers of expatriate workers. The Shia in Kuwait benefited the most from the rise of the oil industry. Many of the Shia commercial families used their decades-old ties with the monarchy to win a portion of the economic boom associated with the oil industry. Ajam Shia, in particular, maintained their firm ties to the regime and opposed Arab nationalism. Although such support of the monarchy secured the Shia the right to vote in Kuwaiti elections and gave them a degree of religious toleration unimaginable elsewhere in the Gulf, it did little to reverse lingering questions about their possible loyalty to their fellow Shia in Iraq and Iran. Essentially, Shia support of the ruling family earned them the enmity of progressive Kuwaitis and of Sunni supporters of Arab nationalism, who saw the Shia as facilitators of the undemocratic tendencies of the Kuwaiti ruling family.[215]

Finally, the Shia in Bahrain benefited from the appearance of the oil industry, using it as a springboard to gain better employment and socioeconomic power. Like their brethren in Saudi Arabia, they staged strikes, starting in the mid-1940s, and were highly sympathetic to Arab nationalism, especially after the Suez Canal crisis of 1956. They looked at expatriate workers, BAPCO, the British government, and long-term British adviser Charles Belgrave as impediments to their legitimate aspirations. In making these arguments, the Bahraini Shia found common cause with Sunnis, women, and members of the Bahraini royal family. In 1956, political associations in Bahrain adopted a nonsectarian tone, and Sunni and Shia cooperated to oust Belgrave. When the island state became independent from Britain in 1971, these groups secured a constitution and a democratically elected legislature.[216]

Nationalization, Revolution, and the Lessons of Iraq

The promises of the early 1970s for Bahraini Shia collapsed shortly after independence and were totally gone by the end of the decade. Just as the discovery of oil marked a key turning point in the status of Gulf Shia and the composition of expatriate populations, independence and the nationalization of oil companies in the 1970s produced rapid changes in the socioeconomic structures and demographic realities of the Gulf states.

New Conservative Trends

Within this new environment, Gulf governments pressed hard to limit Shia activism, women's rights, and any vestiges of Iranian or Anglo-American influence in the Gulf—influence that did not conform to the nationalistic goals of wealthy and newly independent states or to the conservative Sunni impulses that were prevalent in the Arab world after the 1967 Arab-Israeli war. The accommodations that had marked much of the early period of oil production in the Gulf seemingly disappeared.

To begin with, what had been foreign property came under government control, especially as Gulf governments bought ARAMCO and other regional oil companies. Gradually, Arabs began to work and live in foreign compounds as never before, and social and other privileges associated with compound life gradually disappeared. In Kuwait, the KOC closed the schools, restaurants, and social clubs it had maintained for its US and British expatriate workers.[217] The company also faced increasing pressure to hire more Kuwaitis.[218] In Saudi Arabia, female Americans, including diplomats, were required to dress modestly in public and were officially barred from driving on public roads. Saudi religious police also regularly broke up Christian religious services, harassed congregants, and both jailed and expelled Christian clergy.[219]

When US ambassador John West raised the issue of the increasing harassment of Christians with the Saudi Arabian government in 1977, the minister of the interior, Prince Nayif, told West that Christian services could continue. But he warned that they were being closely monitored, should no longer expand, and must remain firmly out of sight. Nayif's message was clear: Christians had little room for error and could lose their right to attend services, even in private, if they did not strictly abide by the kingdom's rules.[220]

In response, Christians throughout Saudi Arabia—and throughout the Gulf, for that matter—became more low key and private in their religious observances. Although the Catholic Church still sent priests to work as "teachers" for ARAMCO after Riyadh nationalized the company in 1980, the services were smaller, held in private settings, and subject to direct regulation by the Saudi state.[221] Public Christmas pageants ceased, and Christmas carols were no longer heard on ARAMCO's radio station. The six-foot-tall wooden cross in Dhahran, a symbol of the Catholic community in Saudi Arabia since the 1950s, was now too dangerous to display, even in private settings.[222] It was hidden in the garage of an ARAMCO executive, who took it back with him to the United States when he retired.[223]

In 1985, Saudi Arabia announced that it had asked the last Catholic priest to leave the country. At the time, the Saudi government justified this action—a reversal of decades of informal Saudi policy—by arguing that it was necessary to bring it into line with the Prophet's injunction that no religion other than Islam could exist in the Arabian Peninsula.[224] Even when US forces were stationed in the country for the Gulf War in 1990, they were under strict orders neither to wear religious symbols in public nor to sing carols except nonreligious ones like "Jingle Bells."[225] Clearly, the Christmas displays of the old ARAMCO days were gone.

Like the Christians, the Shia throughout the region—as I noted in Chapters 2 and 3—felt intense pressure, especially after the Iranian revolution and the onset of the Iran-Iraq war. Shia were automatically suspect solely because of their religious identity. It mattered little how loyal they were or how fervent their opposition was to Iran and its fundamentalist government. In Bahrain, the

1980s became known as the "lost" decade for Shia Arabs, a feeling that was shared by many Shia in Saudi Arabia. This view was epitomized in the words of an anonymous Saudi Shia poet:

> We are Arabs, but
> Our land has become desolated
> and we who live on it have become
> [a people] without identity. . . .
> O God, give us American nationality
> So that we can live with dignity
> in the Arab countries.[226]

The only hope for Gulf Shia had nothing to do with their home societies or even Iran. It was to become an American and to live somewhere in the Arab world outside of the Gulf, where they would be respected and could live in dignity.

Limits to Social Change

The repression of Christians and Shia was not unlimited, and in some ways these minorities even prospered. During the 1980s and 1990s, the Saudis invested heavily in the Shia of the Eastern Province in part to keep their loyalty. In Kuwait the Shia maintained their communal institutions and commercial role.[227] The Shia in the UAE had little trouble with their own government and traded with Iran with few problems.[228] Thousands of Americans and other foreigners continued to work for ARAMCO, which remained structurally unchanged for nearly a decade after it was nationalized. As the Saudi government had done in the past, it issued driver's licenses to male and female ARAMCO employees and their spouses. Women were only formally restricted from driving on public roads, and those prohibitions were not finalized until the 1990s. As I noted in Chapter 5, Kuwaiti and US women were permitted to drive cars and jeeps in the early 1990s.

An important symbol of US culture that arrived with ARAMCO in the 1940s—Little League baseball—continued to be played in Western residential compounds. A team from Dhahran has regularly won its division title and has traveled to the Little League World Series in Williamsport, Pennsylvania, since 1980. An advertisement in *Newsweek* for ARAMCO in November 1980 emphasized the company's US ties with Little League baseball by featuring a picture of a smiling blond Little Leaguer flanked by two of his teammates above the caption "Jeffrey of Arabia."[229]

Since the 1980s, Saudi Arabia has permitted Catholics, Protestants, Mormons, and others to hold religious services, sometimes for as many as 800 people. Bill Casey, the head of the Central Intelligence Agency at the time, won the right to hold an Easter service in Riyadh in the early 1980s.[230] Despite the Saudi announcement alluded to earlier, Catholic priests have still operated discreetly in the kingdom and had places of worship with altars and small crucifixes. During these services, Saudi police officers have reportedly stood watch to maintain a list of worshipers and to "protect the service from being disrupted by the less disciplined morals police."[231]

The Dubai Model

In part, the limits of the conservative trends, even in Saudi Arabia, reflected the new social realities in the Gulf in the 1970s: the dramatic increase in the region's population, especially in people from India, Pakistan, and other parts of Asia. Even though the Gulf's population had always been highly diverse religiously and ethnically, the rate of growth in the 1970s and beyond was unprecedented. There were so many Indians arriving in Saudi Arabia that Indian diplomats were unable to keep track of them or brief their government ministers about them. When India's petroleum minister, Triguna Sen, visited Dhahran in 1975, he observed that he "never thought that there were so many Indians in Saudi Arabia."[232]

As I noted in Chapter 2, this flow of people emerged into the *kafala* system of labor, in which every foreigner from outside the GCC was required to demonstrate that he or she had a legal guarantor (or *kafel*). Few in the Gulf were better at seizing the advantages of the *kafala* system as a tool for development than the ruling family of Dubai, the al-Maktum. Lacking the massive hydrocarbon assets of other Gulf governments, they clearly understood that it would only be a matter of time before their oil reserves ran out. After defeating an attempt by Abu Dhabi to nationalize the UAE's oil assets in 1970—including Dubai's limited oil reserves—they set out to build independent economic institutions and implement an economic model that was not built on oil. Dubai's new model borrowed from Singapore's rapid growth and export-oriented models along with those of the developed nations of Western Europe and North America, which employed foreigners for positions ranging from seasonal farm workers to advanced scientists. In all of these contexts, Asian workers were often critical to keeping non-oil-exporting industries competitive in the world economy.[233]

The al-Maktum recognized that Asian workers represented a seemingly inexhaustible source of labor to construct scores of nonpetroleum industries, from simple manufacturing to media, tourism, banking, and other advanced services. Asian workers could be useful tools to protect Dubai's businesses from the inflationary pressures and wage increases that usually accompanied increasing oil prices in the Gulf and other commodity-exporting regions. As prices for other goods rose in inflationary conditions, Dubai's businesses could count on steady prices for labor, since expatriate workers had no legal or political means, such as unions or political parties, to demand higher wages and better working conditions. Nor were they likely to engage in strikes and other illegal activities, since that could jeopardize their jobs. After all, their wages were significantly better than anything available at home, and there were countless other Asians ready to replace them.

But the al-Maktum's success was not solely grounded in their access to cheap labor under the *kafala* system. The ruling family also had several institutional structures to support their wealth. Most important, they controlled land holdings that were perfect for development, and they maintained a series of profitable public-private corporations. As Lebanon collapsed into civil war in the 1970s and 1980s, Dubai promoted itself as the alternative to Beirut as the central service, transportation, and manufacturing hub for the Middle East, Asia, and Africa.[234]

Thanks to the *kafala* system, Dubai's leaders had the skilled and unskilled workers necessary to construct the Jebel Ali port, free-trade zones, and scores of other industrial and infrastructure projects. By the early 1990s, the al-Maktum had established a viable "postpetroleum" economic system—what I call in Chapter 4, the "Dubai model" of development. The system made the family rich, won the respect of the world financial and commercial communities, and earned the awe of their peers in the Gulf and the rest of the Arab and Islamic world.

Dubai's rulers had an equally significant understanding that the *kafala* system and the massive influx of foreigners meant that they had to accommodate at least some needs of their workers—just as they had done with Iranian immigrants in the 1930s. Expatriate clubs, schools, and community associations, some of which dated to the pre-oil era, flourished. Pakistanis, Indians, Filipinos, and others had active civic and cultural linkages to their home countries, from which they hosted politicians, sports figures, and singers. Christian churches and schools expanded in Dubai, Bahrain, and other Gulf states, fueled by Filipino and Korean workers who were eager to retain their religious traditions.

Nonetheless, no amount of tolerance could hide the fact that the Gulf states presided over a system in which thousands of individuals were compelled to work in conditions just short of complete slavery. For many Western scholars of the region, the *kafala* system appeared to be a modernized version of the labor systems that had existed in the Gulf before the discovery of oil, whereby slaves and indentured servants played a leading role in the pearling and other industries. Gulf Arabs were simply following the lead of their ancestors by actively exploiting Africans, South Asians, Filipinos, and others for profit.

Who Is Exploiting Whom?

Gulf Arabs could not maintain the *kafala* system without the support of the populations in the nations from which their labor forces were drawn. This system survives to the present day. Although most of the foreign populations never set foot in the Gulf, they are just as invested in the *kafala* system as the members of the al-Maktum family—or any other Gulf Arab family, for that matter. They manage the patron-client networks throughout Asia, which recruit and train the thousands of workers who come to Dubai and other Gulf communities every year.

These networks originate in rural areas, where brokers—usually village heads, local businessmen, religious figures, or other notables—provide both contacts and loans for workers to travel to often distant cities to sign up with human resource companies. In turn, these companies pay off the brokers and train the workers for jobs in the Gulf (as well as in Europe, Asia, and North America). The companies lend workers the money necessary for the cost of transportation and to gain visas and bureaucratic requirements. They also impose illegal recruitment fees, often thousands of dollars. The loans, interest, and recruitment fees are extraordinarily high and difficult for the workers to repay.

This extensive system has roots in ancient social structures and explosive population growth in the Asian countryside. The local managers of the networks often derive their authority and the workers' trust from what James Scott terms the "moral economy."[235] In this system, local notables have the right to exploit peasants or other workers with the understanding that they will provide for their relatives back home in the event of a calamity, such as a flood or famine. When the Gulf states started to import thousands of workers in the 1960s and 1970s, these brokers had access to ample supplies of workers, since the populations of many large and rural Asian states—especially India, Pakistan, Thailand, and the Philippines—nearly doubled from 1950 to 1975.[236]

These population increases have been especially difficult for rural societies to cope with, since they have not been accompanied by corresponding increases in cultivable land. It is not surprising that millions of people who cannot find employment in agriculture have to find work elsewhere. Climate change and other factors have only made the pressures worse in recent years.

The Gulf's need for workers presents a perfect opportunity for the governments of Asian states to export the problems created by their population growth: unemployment, rural unrest, and other vexing social issues. The Gulf is also a valuable source of much needed foreign capital from remittances. Many governments even maintain specific departments or ministries to manage and promote their overseas populations.

As this process originally unfolded, India and Pakistan moved especially quickly to meet the needs of the Gulf. They had, after all, provided labor to Arab Gulf oil producers as early as the 1930s and had commercial contacts in the region stretching back centuries.

Government officials in Asia increasingly looked the other way as the new system of labor took hold and integrated itself into a world system that Kevin Bales describes as a new form of global slavery. In this system, individuals caught in various forms of involuntary work fall victim to temporary work contracts and to a member of their community who preys on their deprivation and gullibility.[237] When the power of "persuasion" is not enough, brokers have two additional factors favoring the recruitment and retention of their workers.

First, wages in the Gulf have generally been far higher than in most of Asia. For educated workers, the ratio can be as much as twenty times higher. Second, brokers have a terrifying hold on expatriate workers in the Gulf: the ability to harm their family or friends, financially or physically. When workers commit suicide (as they do on a fairly regular basis), their families are expected to pay off their debts, regardless of the cost. As Shannon McNulty correctly observes, the real exploiters in the Gulf States are often "not local Arabs, as one might expect," but people of the "same or similar nationalities exploiting each other."[238]

The True Nature of Labor Power

The *kafala* system's exploitation of foreigners was designed to reassure Gulf citizens that they still controlled their own societies, which were growing exponentially in size and ethnic diversity. But it became increasingly clear that Asians had a powerful role in the *kafala* system, especially when the Gulf states expelled millions of Palestinian and other Arab workers for security reasons after the Gulf War in 1991. This power only became apparent when oil prices declined in the 1990s, and states throughout the Gulf sought to reduce their use of foreign workers. These governments face resistance not only from their own citizens and business communities but also from another source: the suppliers of expatriate laborers.

These people, who had little interest in the Gulf region's long-term vitality, proved to be so powerful that the numbers of expatriate workers and their importance to the Gulf's economic life continued to grow rapidly, regardless of economic circumstances in the Gulf.

Overseas remittances provided billions of dollars for impoverished rural communities, from the Arabian Sea to the Pacific, making up for inadequate development initiatives. In Pakistan, remittances from abroad represented the largest source of export earnings, of which those from the Gulf alone represented half in 2007.[239] Approximately $13 billion—or 50 percent—of all of

India's migrant earnings came from the Gulf in 2007.[240] Filipino remittances kept the Philippines financially solvent in the 1990s, provided for the livelihood of roughly half the nation's households, and often exceeded the value of the country's agricultural sector.[241] Today, nearly 3 million Filipinos work in the Gulf states, with Saudi Arabia alone boasting the second-largest Filipino expatriate population in the world, after the United States.[242] This dynamic resembles those that developed during the same time period between the United States and Mexico and between Western Europe and its southern and eastern neighbors.

The independent and wealthy Gulf states ironically found themselves in the 1980s and 1990s no less able to control the economic networks that provided their labor than they had been in 1900, when they were poor and completely dependent on networks managed by subjects of Britain's empire in Asia and Africa. The sun may have set on the British Empire, but, from the perspective of Gulf nationals, the power dynamics of the economic networks of the British Raj had hardly changed.

The Lessons of Iraq

By the early twenty-first century, the realities of the Gulf's expatriate labor system and its potential long-term implications were impossible to ignore. Not only did the system threaten the financial viability of the Gulf states whenever the price of oil declined, it also raised the specter that Gulf citizens would become aliens in their own states, which would lose their Arabic and Islamic characteristics. The number of foreigners in the region and the seemingly permanent nature of their presence made the *kafala* system look ever less attractive.

Furthermore, expatriate workers proved as adept as Bin Laden at using satellite television, the Internet, and pressure from abroad to compel Gulf governments and companies to change their discriminatory policies. Not only have expatriates continued to stream into the Gulf in the 2000s, but Gulf leaders have made unprecedented assurances to pay these workers higher wages and to protect their social and labor rights. In 2007, Ali bin Abdulla al-Kaabi, the minister of labor in the UAE, admitted to the *New York Times* that if "something happens between us and India [and all the Indians go home], our airports would shut down, our streets, [our] construction."[243]

The implications of these labor arrangements for Gulf Arabs were illustrated by the experiences of Sunni Arabs in Iraq, who governed an oil-rich country with a large Shia population for decades. Despite Iraq's large Kurdish population and the country's physical proximity to Shia Iran, Iraqi Sunnis kept the nation firmly aligned with the Sunni Arab world. Yet within months of the US invasion of Iraq in 2003, Iraqi Sunnis had lost control of the nation's government and economy. Thousands of Sunnis were expelled from their homes and lost their livelihoods. There is little chance that they will ever regain the power they once had. Although it is unlikely that the United States will ever topple a GCC regime, Iraq proved how quickly political power can be taken from Sunni Arabs in the Gulf, some of whom live in states in which they constitute a smaller percentage of the population than Sunni Arabs did in Iraq.

An Impossible Choice

As threatened as Sunni Gulf Arabs feel by the presence of foreigners in their societies, Shia Gulf Arabs feel even more threatened by the Sunnis. On the one hand, Shia in the Gulf made significant political strides in the 2000s and are increasingly integrated even into Saudi Arabia's political system. On the other hand, they still feel under siege. For instance, in April 2008, the Shia Saudi blogger Ahmed al-Omran wrote about his shock at finding a job application form for Saudi hospitals in al-Hassa that specifically asked for an applicant's religious sect:

> When I was a young student, I was taught in school that all citizens of Saudi Arabia are Muslims, period. That's why none of the official forms and papers used for Saudis here contain an item for religion. If you are a Saudi, you are automatically . . . a Muslim. Or at least this is what I thought until I stumbled upon this form.[244]

Al-Omran went to great lengths to prove that the form was legitimate, railing against such discrimination in his kingdom, especially with sectarian tensions in Iraq and elsewhere running so high. He found this bias hard to reconcile with the public commitment of leading Saudis to religious dialogue and toleration of Shia in Saudi Arabia.

Al-Omran's frustrations can also be found among Shia in Kuwait. Although they regularly serve as ministers in the government, several Shia Kuwaiti leaders were arrested and ruthlessly interrogated after they attended a rally to honor the death of Imad Mughnieh, a Hezbollah leader who was assassinated in Damascus in February 2008.[245] Weeks after the authorities found that the Shia leaders were not members of Hezbollah and released them, Sunni politicians in Kuwait continued to publicly challenge their loyalty and the loyalty of Shia in general.[246] One Islamist politician threatened to boycott the swearing-in of a new national government in which a Shia would serve as minister of public works.[247] In response, Abdulhameed Dashti, a Shia Kuwaiti, noted sarcastically in *al-Nahar,* a Kuwaiti newspaper, that Shia Kuwaitis could be considered loyal if they swore five times a day that they hated Iran and supported Israel.[248]

These concerns and attitudes are even more striking when one bears in mind that Shia and Sunnis in the Gulf speak the same languages and have similar religious and cultural traditions. If Sunni Arabs cannot successfully integrate Shia Arabs into existing Gulf institutions, is it likely that they will ever accept non-Arabs and non-Muslims?

A Two-Way Relationship

Although expatriates in the Gulf would surely prefer to live in a socioeconomic system in which they had more rights and better working conditions, that is a far cry from wishing to destroy Gulf societies and their economies. Gulf economies have always been built on the assumption that everyone who lives in the region benefits (or at least dreams of benefiting) enough to maintain the economic system. This has been especially true in Dubai, which has drawn expatriate workers from Saudi Arabia and other conservative Gulf states with the promise of greater social freedoms.

It is worth noting that expatriates in the Gulf have strong communal organizations that give them opportunities for political and social activism, both domestically and in relation to their home countries. An excellent example of the latter was the role of expatriate Filipino workers in the 2004 Filipino presidential election. The incumbent, Gloria Macapagal-Arroyo, owed her ultimate victory in part to the thousands of votes she received from Filipinos in Saudi Arabia. Another prominent example would be Abdul Nabi Bangash, a businessman based in Dubai, who, in March 2009, became the first expatriate from the emirate to serve in Pakistan's Senate, where he will represent the country's Northwest Frontier Province.[249] It is conceivable that participation by expatriates in elections in their native lands will become a mechanism for defusing the political discontents of those expatriates, thereby reducing their tensions with the Gulf Arabs.

The sociopolitical activities of expatriates vis-à-vis their homelands have certainly not gone unnoticed by Gulf nationals, and it is reasonable to assume that future civil institutions in the GCC states may not only include Indians, Pakistanis, and Filipinos but also look more like the civil institutions in India, Pakistan, and the Philippines. Although it is easy to dismiss such linkages owing to Gulf Arabs' well-known bigotry toward Asian expatriate workers, Saudis and Filipinos do share at least one common denominator: close cultural, political, and economic ties with the United States. One sees similar ties between a host of South Asian and Gulf communities that were both once in the British Empire. Indian parliamentarians, for instance, now train Bahrainis on how to administer a democratically elected parliament on the British model.[250]

Sports may be an even more important venue than politics for positive interactions between Gulf nationals and their expatriate populations. Over the last ten years, every Gulf state has created a national cricket team and federation, many of which are run by South Asians and play against teams from South Asia. The official statement on the Kuwait Cricket Federation's website notes that the organization was founded by Kuwaitis who had been inspired by the thousands of expatriate cricket players in the emirate.[251] How Gulf Arabs and their foreign populations use these linkages and other communal institutions to address common problems will play a large role in determining the future economic and political health of the Gulf.

Conclusion

On March 17, 2008, a new signature building emerged on the crowded skyline of Doha, the home of the al-Jazeera satellite television network and the capital of Qatar, one of the only two states in the world in which Wahhabism is the state religion. Donors from throughout the Arabian Peninsula helped to pay the $15 million required to construct the new building—an enterprise that was important enough that Qatar's emir, Hamad al-Thani, set aside land for it from his personal holdings. The building was also seen as a crucial component of Qatar's bid to one day host the Olympics.[252]

Although the new structure can accommodate almost 3,000 people, it is not one of the modern apartment complexes, office buildings, hotels, or campuses of Western universities that have defined Doha since the late 1990s. Nor is it a stadium or any other component of the city's infrastructure that would be necessary for the Olympics. In fact, it is Our Lady of the Rosary, a Catholic church that is the centerpiece of a new 7,000-home neighborhood for foreigners.

During the first mass at the church, Ivan Cardinal Dias, envoy of Pope Benedict XVI and the prefect of the Congregation for the Evangelization of Peoples, conveyed special greetings to al-Thani. "Without his precious gift of land to the Catholic community," he said, "we would not be here today."[253] In keeping with requests from the Qatari government, however, the building's exterior has none of the accoutrements normally found on a Catholic church's exterior, such as crosses, steeples, and bells. The interior is equally restrained, containing only a few crucifixes and ambiguous biblical imagery. The Qatari government also asked the worshipers to celebrate the new church in as low-key a manner as possible. Even though the Catholic church can openly preach to the expatriates in Qatar, it is forbidden from evangelizing to Qatari nationals, who face capital punishment if they convert from Islam to Christianity.[254]

The Qatari government had reason for its caution. Although the church serves close to 10 percent of Qatar's population and has cemented Doha's diplomatic ties with the Vatican, a number of Qataris have voiced their vehement displeasure in the media over the idea that non-Muslims have the right to express their faith in such a public setting. They characterized the government's decision as contrary to Islamic tradition, which they believe prohibits

Qatar and all other states on the Arabian Peninsula from permitting any non-Muslim religious structures within their boundaries. In a society as conservative as Qatar's, this was a serious challenge. Although several leading Islamic scholars supported the government's decision by asserting that the tradition only applied to the Hijaz region of Saudi Arabia and not to the other areas of the peninsula, the controversy was sufficiently intense that the government deployed armed guards to protect Our Lady of the Rosary and its immediate surroundings.[255]

The tension surrounding the decision to build a Catholic church in Doha illustrates the difficult decision that Gulf governments will have to make in future years to balance the needs of their expatriate workers with the growing fears of their conservative citizens and most senior officials. These governments are in no position to expel foreigners, as some citizens would prefer. Today's rulers in the Gulf, much like their forefathers at the start of the twentieth century, depend on foreigners from a host of nations to maintain their way of life and their position in the global economy. The enormity and vitality of the various socioeconomic labor networks in Asia would also hinder attempts to wean states in the Gulf from their expatriate workers. On the other hand, most Gulf rulers would face serious resistance and possibly even violence from their citizens if they chose to fully integrate foreigners into Gulf life. The intense public reaction to the reform of US immigration laws in 2006, the opening of a new large mosque in Birmingham (England) in 2009, and other public issues tied to foreigners in the West suggests that any future initiatives dealing with expatriates will test the skills of even the most astute rulers in the Gulf.

One way to deal with these challenges in the Gulf would be to have nationals, especially women, adopt some of the positions otherwise held today by expatriates. Another future option may be to outsource journalism, health care, education, and other services to South Asia whenever possible. But these are only partial solutions at best. There may never be enough nationals to come close to filling the jobs presently held by expatriates, especially as men fall further behind women in educational achievement. Nationals have long been a small minority of the workforce in Qatar and Kuwait, whereas expatriates have made up an ever increasing percentage of the workforce in other Gulf states.

A more durable solution than the two suggested above may lie in the Gulf's past, when the region's leaders forged mutually profitable business and social relationships with a host of non-Muslim and non-Arab peoples. Although many of these partnerships from the first third of the twentieth century are rarely acknowledged today, they have hardly been forgotten. In a remarkable post to a website dedicated to disseminating information about Jewish refugees around the world, an anonymous Saudi wrote a post in September 2007 noting that Jews had lived for many years in peace in Najran until they left for Israel in the 1950s. Indeed, many of their homes still existed in Najran.[256]

In a subsequent message, the same Saudi asked for information on Najran's Jews and how he or she could find more information about this Jewish community and their descendants in Israel. The website's editors, expressing profound surprise at the request, provided information on Yemeni and other similar Jewish Arab refugee organizations in Israel. (Najran had been part of Yemen until the 1930s, and Najran's Jews later fled from Saudi Arabia via Yemen.) Whether the anonymous Saudi followed up on the information and contacted these organizations is not known. What is clear, however, is that half a century after Najran's Jews left Saudi Arabia for Israel, the community's presence is still important enough to be remembered and to compel an individual to seek out information on them.

Nor are Najran's Jews the only non-Sunni Muslim community remembered in this manner in Saudi Arabia or other parts of the Gulf. In the UAE, Sunni Arab women still sing songs that they were first taught by Protestant US missionaries decades ago.[257] Promotional materials for Sharjah's art center prominently mention that it was a former missionary hospital and the birthplace of many of the emirate's leading residents.[258] There are stone tablets, burial grounds, and ruins of Jewish and Christian communities from Oman to Kuwait. At the same time that the Saudi government was supposedly expelling the "last" priest from the kingdom in the 1980s, ruins of churches and cemeteries from the fifth to the ninth centuries were being uncovered in the Eastern Province cities of Jubail and Thaj. The ages of the churches are especially important because they suggest that Christian communities flourished in Arabia far beyond the rise of Islam—a fact that contradicts one of the justifications for Saudi Arabia's ban on permitting Christians to build houses of worship in the kingdom, the Prophet's injunction against two religions existing in Arabia.

These ruins and the history of non-Sunni Arabs in the region may help to provide a framework to include ever more peoples in Gulf society. One already sees this process under way in Bahrain. There the government has extended a host of labor and civil rights to foreigners, appointing Christians, Hindus, and Jews to advisory commissions and granting their children government scholarships to study abroad. In 2007, the island kingdom's Jews penned a history of their community and its accomplishments, *From Our Beginning to Our Present Day,* which they dedicated to Bahrain's ruling family. A year later, Bahrain's government took the unprecedented step of appointing a Jewish woman, Houda Nonoo, to serve as its ambassador to the United States, one of the most important and prestigious postings for a Bahraini diplomat anywhere in the world.[259] Although many in the Western media had difficulty in 2008 seeing beyond Ambassador's Nonoo's gender and religion, it is now clear that Bahraini subjects need not necessarily be Muslims and that non-Muslims can aspire to high positions in the government.

Bahrain's experience ultimately holds out hope that the resolution of the decades-old existential questions about foreigners and work in the Gulf may not be a complicated strategy of exclusion, quotas, and replacements but one based on the region's long-standing tradition of inclusion, accommodation, and toleration.

Notes

1. Patrick McSherry, ed., "Necrology: Book of Remembrance [January]" (available at http://www.capcomm.org/).
2. William Mulligan, "Notes on the Church in Saudi Arabia," January 18, 1966, William Mulligan Papers, Georgetown University Library Special Collections, Box 7, Folder 21; "The Church in Arabia," 1975, William Mulligan Papers, Georgetown University Library Special Collections, Box 7, Folder 21; "Our Lady of Fatima Parish Information Sheet," Dhahran, September 1969, William Mulligan Papers, Georgetown University Library Special Collections, Box 7, Folder 21; "Our Lady of Fatima Parish Bulletin," Dhahran, July 28, 1978, William Mulligan Papers, Georgetown University Library Special Collections, Box 7, Folder 21; "Our Lady of Fatima Parish Bulletin," Dhahran, September 22, 1978, William Mulligan Papers, Georgetown University Library Special Collections, Box 7, Folder 21; and William Mulligan to Mary Norton, February 11, 1992, William Mulligan Papers, Georgetown University Library Special Collections, Box 7, Folder 21.
3. Mulligan to Norton, February 11, 1992.
4. D. K. Wallace to Father Roman Ament, November 4, 1967, William Mulligan Papers, Georgetown University Library Special Collections, Box 7, Folder 21.
5. William Mulligan, "Catholic Priests in Arabia," n.d., William Mulligan Papers, Box 8, Folder 2; William Mulligan, "Resident Catholic Priests Stationed in Saudi Arabia," n.d., William Mulligan Papers, Georgetown University Library Special Collections, Box 8, Folder 2.
6. Thomas Lippman, *Inside the Mirage: America's Fragile Partnership with Saudi Arabia* (Boulder, CO: Westview Press, 2004), 204.
7. K. C. Fisher, "Minutes of Meeting on Religious Services Held on Monday, October 30, 1950," November 27, 1950, William Mulligan Papers, Georgetown University Library Special Collections, Box 7, Folder 21.
8. Roman Ament to William Sullivan, November 18, 1967, William Mulligan Papers, Georgetown University Library Special Collections, Box 7, Folder 21.
9. Ibid.
10. Mulligan, "Resident Catholic Priests Stationed in Saudi Arabia."
11. Wallace to Ament, November 4, 1967.
12. Mulligan, "Notes on the Church in Saudi Arabia."
13. Mulligan, "Resident Catholic Priests Stationed in Saudi Arabia."
14. Lippman, *Inside the Mirage*, 205.
15. The Vicariate Apostolic of Arabia was founded in 1888, and a separate vicariate for Kuwait was created in 1954. Victor Sanmiguel, *Christians in Kuwait* (Beirut: Beirut Press, 1970), 66; Mulligan, "Notes on the Church in Saudi Arabia."

16. Rima Sabban, "United Arab Emirates: Migrant Women in the United Arab Emirates: The Case of Female Domestic Workers," GENPROM Working Paper no. 10, Gender Promotion Program, International Labor Office Geneva, 2006, 7 (available at http://www.ilo.org/).

17. David Hogarth notes in *Hejaz Before World War I* that the population of Jeddah included Indians, Greeks, and Jews and that non-Muslims were permitted to live within the city's walls. David Hogarth, *Hejaz Before World War I: A Handbook* (Oxford: Falcon-Oleander, 1978; first published in 1917 by Arab Bureau, Cairo), 29. Citation is to the 1978 edition.

18. Ameen Rihani, *Around the Coasts of Arabia* (Boston: Houghton Mifflin, 1930), 98–99.

19. Jenny De Mayer, "Reminiscences of Pioneer Work at Jidda," *Neglected Arabia* 114 (July–August–September 1920): 3–9.

20. S. M. Zwemer, "Three Visits to Jeddah," *Neglected Arabia* 106 (July–August–September 1918): 5.

21. Bert Fish, Consul, US Legation Cairo to Secretary of State, "Remarks of Mr. St. John Philby at Jeddah," no. 2019, March 9, 1940, reprinted in United States Department of State, *Records of the Department of State Relating to Internal Affairs of Saudi Arabia, 1930–1944* (Washington, DC: National Archives, National Records and Archives Service, General Services Administration, 1974), Reel 3.

22. David Hogarth notes in *Hejaz Before World War I* that steamship and mail companies from Great Britain, Holland, France, Austria, and India visited the city regularly. Hogarth, *Hejaz Before World War I,* 79 (citation is to 1978 edition); Rihani, *Around the Coasts of Arabia,* 11–13, 174.

23. For more on the business of hajj transportation and on European ship transport in particular during this time period, see Michael B. Miller, "Pilgrims' Progress: The Business of the Hajj," *Past and Present* 191, no. 1 (May 2006): 189–228.

24. Ralph Chesbrough, US Legation Beirut, "The Economic Resources and Commercial Activities of the Kingdom of the Hedjaz, Nejd, and Dependencies," no. 16, June 30, 1930, reprinted in United States Department of State, *Records of the Department of State Relating to Internal Affairs of Saudi Arabia, 1930–1944* (Washington, DC: National Archives, National Records and Archives Service, General Services Administration, 1974), Reel 1; Wallace Murray, Division of Near Eastern Affairs, to the Secretary of State, "Economic Situation in the Hejaz and Nejd and Its Dependencies," January 27, 1931, reprinted in United States Department of State, *Records of the Department of State Relating to Internal Affairs of Saudi Arabia, 1930–1944* (Washington, DC: National Archives, National Records and Archives Service, General Services Administration, 1974), Reel 1.

25. Great Britain seized Kamarān in 1915 and held it until 1967. Before that time, the Ottoman Empire maintained a quarantine station on Kamarān to monitor pilgrims going to Mecca.

26. Rihani, *Around the Coasts of Arabia,* 80–83.

27. Ibid., 81. For more on Great Britain's and Europe's role in the hajj before the rise of Saudi Arabia, see the recent work of Birsen Bulmuş, "The Plague in the Ottoman Empire, 1300–1838" (Ph.D. dissertation, Georgetown University, 2008); Michael Low, "Empire and the Hajj: Pilgrims, Plagues, and Pan-Islam Under British Surveillance, 1865–1908," *International Journal of Middle East Studies* 40, no. 2 (May 2008): 269–290.

28. Rihani, *Around the Coasts of Arabia,* 77.

29. Ibid., 80–81.

30. Ibid., 98–99.

31. Ibid., 79.

32. It is worth noting that Jews and Christians lived in Arabia well after the rise of Islam, and early Muslim caliphs hired Christian engineers and architects to control flooding in Medina. C. D. Matthews, "Exclusions of Non-Muslims from Mecca and Medina," William Mulligan Papers, Georgetown University Library Special Collections, Box 7, Folder 21.

33. Zwemer, "Three Visits to Jeddah," 6.

34. Ibid., 20.

35. Ibid., 123; Alexei Vassiliev, *The History of Saudi Arabia* (London: Saqi Books, 1998), 305.

36. H. St. J. B. Philby, *Arabian Highlands* (Ithaca, NY: Cornell University Press for the Middle East Institute, 1952), 278.

37. Muhammad Mughairibi Futaih al-Madani, *Al-Nahdhat al-Haditha fi Jazzirat al-Arab fil Malaka al-Arabiya al-Sadiya* (Cairo: Dar Ahya al-Kutub al-Arabiyya, 1952), 42–43.

38. Louis Dame, "A Trip to Central Arabia," *Neglected Arabia* 167 (January–March, 1934): 19.

39. The two Jews were Naum Markovich and Moses Axelrod. Axelrod was an aide to Kerim Khakimov, the head of the Soviet mission in the 1920s and early 1930s. Bullard to Chamberlain, E3518/2442/91, May 18, 1925, reprinted in *British Documents on Foreign Affairs: Reports and Papers from the Foreign Office Confidential Print,* ed. Kenneth Bourne and D. Cameron Watt, pt. 2: *From the First to the Second World War,* Series B: *Turkey, Iran, and the Middle East, 1918–1939,* ed. Robin Bidwell, vol. 4: *The Expansion of Ibn Saud, 1922–1925* (Bethesda, MD: University Publications of America, 1985), 287–289; Stonehewer-Bird to Chamberlain, no. 49, E3363/332/91, April 9, 1928, reprinted in, *British Documents on Foreign Affairs: Reports and Papers from the Foreign Office Confidential Print,* ed. Kenneth Bourne and D. Cameron Watt, pt. 2: *From the First to the Second World War,* Series B: Turkey, *Iran, and the Middle East, 1918–1939,* ed. Robin Bidwell, vol. 6: *Eastern Affairs, January 1928–June 1930* (Bethesda, MD: University Publications of America, 1985), 35–36.

40. Saudi-Wahhabi tolerance was not unusual in Arabia. Another leading Arabian political family, the Rashids, was similarly tolerant. R. Bayly Winder, *Saudi Arabia in the Nineteenth Century* (New York: St. Martin's Press, 1965), 240–241.

41. Natana DeLong-Bas, *Wahhabi Islam: From Revival and Reform to Global Islam* (Oxford: Oxford University Press, 2004), 239.

42. Ibid., 98.

43. Ibid., 155.

44. Ibid., 209–211.

45. Yitzhak Nakash, *Reaching for Power: The Shi'a in the Modern Arab World* (Princeton, NJ: Princeton University Press, 2006), 44.

46. Ibid.

47. For example, Nora Johnson notes in *You Can Go Home Again* that her first daughter, who was born in Dhahran in the 1950s, "not only was a Catholic, but could, if she liked, choose Saudi citizenship at age eighteen." Nora Johnson, *You Can Go Home Again* (New York: Doubleday Books, 1982), 64. Even today, Saudi

Arabia's citizenship law defines Saudis as those who "acquired Ottoman nationality in 1914" and who were born in what is today Saudi Arabia. Ottoman nationality in 1914 included Muslims, Jews, or Christians (available at http://www.moi.gov.sa/).

48. Nakash, *Reaching for Power: The Shi'a in the Modern Arab World,* 45–48.

49. D. Dykstra, "Arab Life at Close Quarters," *Neglected Arabia* 128 (January–February–March 1924): 5–6.

50. According to British reports on pearling in the Gulf, the largest merchants in the 1920s were Haji Muhammad Ali Zinal, Victor Rosenthal (French), Muhammad Faruq, Dr. David (French), and Abdul Rahman Qusaibi (Bahraini). A. A. Russell, "Summary of News from the Arab States for the Month of September, 1928," no. 7, 1928, reprinted in *Political Diaries of the Persian Gulf,* vol. 8: *1928–1929,* 161 (Cambridge: Archive Editions, 1990).

51. Hans Nadelhoffer, *Cartier* (New York: Chronicle Books, 2007), 125; A. A. Russell, "The Political Agency Bahrain—16 to 31 October 1930," no. 20 of 1930, November 1, 1930, reprinted in *Political Diaries of the Persian Gulf,* vol. 9: *1930–1931* (Cambridge: Archive Editions, 1990), 317–318.

52. Alfred DeWitt Mason and Frederick J. Barny, *History of the Arabian Mission* (New York: Board of Foreign Missions, Reformed Church of America, 1926), 194; "Report for 1925," *Neglected Arabia* 137 (April–May–June 1926): 5.

53. Among those who participated were Mr. S. Pack from Paris, D. Bienefeld from Switzerland, and Joseph Simon (secretary to D. Bienefeld), an Algerian Jew. A. A. Russell, "Summary of News from the Arab States for the Month of June 1929," no. 6, 1929 reprinted in *Political Diaries of the Persian Gulf,* vol. 8: *1928–1929* (Cambridge: Archive Editions, 1990), 405; F. J. Barny, "Annual Report of the Arabian Mission for the Year 1933," *Neglected Arabia* 168 (April–May–June 1934): 12–13; Sugata Bose, *A Hundred Horizons: The Indian Ocean in the Age of Global Empire* (Cambridge, MA: Harvard University Press, 2006), 86.

54. Nancy Khedouri, *From Our Beginning to Present Day* (Manama, Bahrain: al-Manar Press, 2007), 35–43. I thank the Bahraini Embassy in Washington, DC, for providing me with a copy of this book.

55. Ibid., 11–18.

56. Richard Hall, *Empires of the Monsoon* (New York: Harper Collins, 1996), 9–11.

57. Faisal Alkanderi, "Jews in Kuwait," *Islam and Christian-Muslim Relations* 17, no. 4 (October 2006): 445–456; Edwin Calverley, "Education in Kuwait," *Neglected Arabia* 142 (July–August–September 1927): 12; Rihani, *Around the Coasts of Arabia,* 234.

58. British officials closely monitored the comings and goings of US missionaries, including them in official reports. For example, A.A. Russell, "Summary of News from the Arab States for the Month of September, 1928," 156; Frederick William Johnston, "Summary of the News from the Arab States for the Month of December 1928," no. 10, 1928, reprinted in *Political Diaries of the Persian Gulf,* vol. 8: *1928–1929* (Cambridge: Archive Editions, 1990), 226.

59. Rihani, *Around the Coasts of Arabia,* 300.

60. Paul Harrison, "The Outlook in Oman," *Neglected Arabia* 147 (October–November–December 1928): 5.

61. Nurah al-Qasimi, *Al-Wujud al-Hindi fi al-Khalij al-Arabi, 1820–1947* (Al-Shariqa: Da'irat al-Thaqafa wa-al-I'lam, 1996), 118–123, 217–240.

62. James Onley, *The Arabian Frontier of the British Raj: Merchants, British, and Rulers in the Nineteenth-Century Gulf* (Oxford: Oxford University Press, 2007), 1–20.

63. James Onley, "Britain's Native Agents in Arabia in the Nineteenth Century," *Comparative Studies of South Asia, Africa, and the Middle East* 24, no. 1 (2004): 131–132.

64. C. Kondapi, *Indians Overseas, 1838–1949* (New Delhi: Indian Council of World Affairs, 1951), 201.

65. Al-Qasimi, *Al-Wujud al-Hindi fi al-Khalij al-Arabi, 1820–1947,* 89–158.

66. Kondapi, *Indians Overseas,* 359.

67. Calvin H. Allen, "The Indian Merchant Community of Masqat," *Bulletin School of Oriental and African Studies* 44, no. 1 (1981): 42.

68. Omar Khalidi, "The Lotus and the Crescent: Hindus in the Islamic Lands," *Journal of the Institute of Muslim Minority Affairs* 14, no. 1 (January 1993): 89; Kondapi, *Indians Overseas,* 527–528.

69. Nelida Fuccaro, "Mapping the Transnational Community: Persians and the Space of the City in Bahrain, c. 1869–1937," in *Transnational Connections and the Arab Gulf,* ed. Madawi al-Rasheed (New York: Routledge, 2005), 43

70. Khalidi, "The Lotus and the Crescent: Hindus in the Islamic Lands," 89.

71. Ibid.

72. Allen, "The Indian Merchant Community of Masqat," 39–55; Khalidi, "The Lotus and the Crescent: Hindus in the Islamic Lands," 89.

73. Christopher Davidson, *The United Arab Emirates: A Study in Survival* (Boulder, CO: Lynne Rienner Publishers, 2005), 13.

74. Khalidi, "The Lotus and the Crescent: Hindus in the Islamic Lands," 89; Harrison, "The Outlook in Oman," 4; Paul Harrison, *Doctor in Arabia* (New York: John Day, 1940), 273.

75. Harrison, *Doctor in Arabia,* 274. For more on the close ties between US missionaries and British officials, see Rosemarie Zahlan, "Anglo-American Rivalry in Bahrain, 1918–1947," in *Bahrain Through the Ages,* ed. Shaikh Abdullah bin Khalid al-Khalifa and Michael Rice (London: Keğan Paul International, 1993), 568.

76. Ray Fox, American Counsul, Aden to Secretary of State, "Oil Concession for the al-Hassa Area of Saudi Arabia," no. 19, June 24, 1933, reprinted in United States Department of State, *Records of the Department of State Relating to Internal Affairs of Saudi Arabia, 1930–1944,* Reel 2.

77. Alexander Sloan, US Legation in Baghdad to Washington, Diplomatic Series no. 120, February 6, 1932, reprinted in United States Department of State, *Records of the Department of State Relating to Internal Affairs of Saudi Arabia, 1930–1944,* Reel 1; Parker Hart, American Vice Consul, Jeddah to Washington, "Recent Visitor to Dhahran," no. 32, December 27, 1941, reprinted in United States Department of State, *Records of the Department of State Relating to Internal Affairs of Saudi Arabia, 1930–1944,* Reel 3; Alexander Sloan, US Legation in Baghdad to Washington, "British Officials' Conferences with King Ibn Saud Persian Gulf," no. 151, March 12, 1932, reprinted in United States Department of State, *Records of the Department of State Relating to Internal Affairs of Saudi Arabia, 1930–1944,* Reel 1.

78. Harrison, "The Outlook in Oman," 5.

79. Ibid.; Harrison, *Doctor in Arabia,* 272–273.

80. T. H. Mackenzie, "The Log of the Barala," *Neglected Arabia* 117 (April–May–June 1921): 18.

81. Ibid.

82. *Neglected Arabia* 137 (April–May–June, 1926): 1. The original statement of the missionary founders was "Our ultimate object is to occupy the interior [of Arabia]."

83. Wells Thomas, "From a Doctor's Journal," *Neglected Arabia* 180 (October–November–December 1937): 13.

84. Harrison, *Doctor in Arabia,* 294.

85. Louis Dame, "Objectives in Arabia," *Muslim World* 20, no. 2 (1930): 180.

86. Louis Dame, "1928 Annual Report: The King's Business," *Neglected Arabia* 148 (January– February–March 1929): 10, 15.

87. Louis Dame, "Touring Inland Arabia," *Neglected Arabia* 130 (July–August–September 1924): 6; Cornelia Dalenberg, "Forward to Hasa," *Arabia Calling* 232 (Summer 1953): 3–5.

88. For example, see *Neglected Arabia* 139 (October–November–December 1926): 2; *Neglected Arabia* 150 (July–August–September 1929): 2; Barny, "Annual Report of the Arabian Mission for the Year 1933," 4–15.

89. Dame, "1928 Annual Report: The King's Business," 14.

90. George Gosselink, "Annual Report for the Arabian Mission for the Year 1934," *Neglected Arabia* 170 (January–February–March 1935): 3–15.

91. Harold Storm, "Annual Report of the Arabian Mission for the Year 1938," *Neglected Arabia* 185 (April–May–June 1939): 9.

92. D. Dykstra, "Wings over Arabia: Annual Report of the Arabian Mission for 1937," *Neglected Arabia* 181 (January–June 1938): 10.

93. Henry Cobb, "Annual Report for the Arabian Mission for the Year 1936," *Neglected Arabia* 178 (January–February–March 1937): 18; Angela Clarke, *Through the Changing Scenes of Life 1893–1993: The American Mission Hospital Bahrain* (Bahrain: American Mission Hospital Society, 1993), 37–38.

94. Louis Dame, "Arabs Met at Bahrain Hospital," *Neglected Arabia* 125 (April–May–June 1923): 9.

95. Cornelia Dalenberg, "Bahrain's Little Traveler," *Neglected Arabia* 134 (July–August–September 1925): 6–9.

96. Louis Dame, "Entering New Territory," *Neglected Arabia* 131 (October–November–December 1924): 4.

97. US missionaries were especially proud of their ability to teach Arab, Christian, and Jewish children. In 1945, the cover of *Neglected Arabia* featured a picture of four girls with the caption "Solving the Racial Problem in Arabia: Arab, Christian, and Jewish Girls in School." "Solving the Racial Problem in Arabia," *Neglected Arabia* 207 (October–November–December 1945): 1.

98. "Annual Report of the Arabian Mission, 1929–1930," *Neglected Arabia* 156 (January–Februray–March 1931), 7.

99. Ruth Jackson, "Our Girls' Club in Bahrain," *Neglected Arabia* 204 (October–November–December 1945): 6–8; Ruth Jackson, "Of Girls in Bahrain," *Neglected Arabia* 229 (Autumn 1952): 10; Khedouri, *From Our Beginning to Present Day,* 31. In 1952, four of the teachers in the mission school in Bahrain were Jewish, one of whom was Lebanese.

100. Ruth Jackson, "Annual Report of the Arabian Mission for the Year 1932," *Neglected Arabia* 164 (January–June 1933): 11.

101. Barny, "Annual Report of the Arabian Mission for the Year 1933," 12.

102. Jackson, "Annual Report of the Arabian Mission for the Year 1932," 11.

103. According to the 1941 census (results from it were included in the 1950 census), there were 1,672 non-Muslims and 88,298 Muslims on the island in 1941. Government of Bahrain, "Bahrain Census: 1950," William Mulligan Papers, Georgetown University Library Special Collection, Box 7, Folder 14.

104. A good example was the opening of the Olcott Memorial Hospital in Kuwait in 1939. Dr. Mylrea, "The Opening of the Olcott Memorial Hospital," *Neglected Arabia* 186 (July–August–September 1939): 3–7.

105. "Report for 1925," 1.

106. Paul L. Armerding, *Doctors for the Kingdom: The Work of the American Mission Hospitals in the Kingdom of Saudi Arabia* (Grand Rapids, MI: William B. Erdmans Publishing Company, 2003), 14.

107. Ibid.

108. Armerding, *Doctors for the Kingdom;* Dalenberg, "Forward to Hassa," 4–5; Anna Harrison, "Annual Report: Heritage and Vision," *Neglected Arabia* 231 (Spring 1953): 14.

109. W. H. Storm, "Pan Arabia Tour," *Neglected Arabia* 176 (July–August–September 1936): 3. Another person who remembered this time period was Evadna Burba, the wife of an ARAMCO employee. She notes in her memoir, published in 1981, that US missionary medical staff "were under great demand by the local population" in Saudi Arabia in the 1940s and 1950s. Evadna Burba, *Seasoned with Sand: An American Housewife in Saudi Arabia, 1948–1966* (New York: Adne Press, 1981).

110. Fatima al-Sayegh, "Women and Economic Changes in the Gulf: The Case of the United Arab Emirates," *Domes* 10, no. 2 (2001): 7; William E. Mulligan, "Arabian Affairs Division: Sarah Hosman," March 8, 1961, William Mulligan Papers, Georgetown University Library Special Collections, Box 3, Folder 6.

111. Graham Fuller and Rend Francke, *The Arab Shi'a: The Forgotten Muslims* (New York: Macmillan, 2001), 161.

112 Ibid.

113. Cyril Charles Johnson Barrett, "Summary of News from the Arab States for the Month of November 1929," no. 11, 1929, reprinted in *Political Diaries of the Persian Gulf,* vol. 8: *1928–1929* (Cambridge: Archive Editions, 1990), 562–563.

114. P. W. Harrison, "The Appeal of Oman," *Neglected Arabia* 120 (January–February–March 1922): 15.

115. Davidson, *The United Arab Emirates: A Study in Survival,* 5–63.

116. Nakash, *Reaching for Power: The Shi'a in the Modern Arab World,* 59.

117. Government of Bahrain, "Bahrain Census: 1950."

118. Fuccaro, "Mapping the Transnational Community: Persians and the Space of the City in Bahrain," 45–48.

119. Ibid., 52–53.

120. Ibid., 43.

121. Nakash, *Reaching for Power: The Shi'a in the Modern Arab World,* 62–63; Mahdi al-Tajir, *Bahrain, 1920–1945: Britain, the Shaykh, and the Administration* (New York: Routledge and Kegan Paul, 1987), 135–161.

122. Reformed Church in America, Reformed Protestant Dutch Church (US), General Synod, *Acts and Proceedings of the Regular Session of the General Synod: 1939* (New York: Board of Publication and Bible-school Work, 1939), 31.

123. Clarke, *Through the Changing Scenes of Life, 1893–1993: The American Mission Hospital Bahrain,* 211–212.

124. Marilyn Tanis, "Bahrain," *Arabia Calling* 245 (Winter–Spring 1956–1957): 10.

125. Clarke, *Through the Changing Scenes of Life, 1893–1993: The American Mission Hospital Bahrain,* 211–215.

126. Ian J. Seccombe, "A Disgrace to American Enterprise: Italian Labour and the Arabian American Oil Company in Saudi Arabia, 1944–1954," *Immigrants and Minorities* 5, no. 3 (November 1986): 240–246.

127. Robert Vitalis, *America's Kingdom: Mythmaking on the Saudi Oil Frontier* (Stanford, CA: Stanford University Press, 2007), 31–61.

128. W. A. Eddy to Gordon Merriam, Chief of Near Eastern Affairs, Department of State, June 17, 1944, reprinted in United States Department of State, *Records of the Department of State Relating to Internal Affairs of Saudi Arabia, 1930–1944* (Washington, DC: National Archives, National Records and Archives Service, General Services Administration, 1974), Reel 5.

129. William Mulligan, "Pasta and Packing Crates, ARAMCO's Italian Craftsmen," *Al-Ayyam al-Jamilla* (Spring 1992), William Mulligan Papers, Georgetown University Library Special Collections, Box 8, Folder 8; Seccombe, "A Disgrace to American Enterprise," 246–252.

130. Dana Adams Schmidt, "Arabian Town Is Like a U.S. Suburb," *New York Times,* November 23, 1959, 3 (*Historical New York Times*).

131. Clarence J. McIntosh to McIntosh Family, August 16, 1944, Clarence J. McIntosh Papers, Georgetown University Library Special Collections, Box 2, Folder 24, Letter 27.

132. Ibid.

133. Clarence J. McIntosh to McIntosh Family, December 27, 1944, Clarence J. McIntosh Papers, Georgetown University Library Special Collections, Box 2, Folder 40, Letter 44.

134. Clarence J. McIntosh to McIntosh Family, October 13, 1945, Clarence J. McIntosh Papers, Georgetown University Library Special Collections, Box 3, Folder 39, Letter 40.

135. "5 Killed in Saudi Arabia," *New York Times,* July 3, 1947, 6 (*Historical New York Times*).

136. McIntosh to McIntosh Family, August 16, 1944, 4.

137. Ibid., 3.

138. Ibid.

139. "Bowling Heaven? It's in the Oil Lands of Arabia," *New York Times,* July 10, 1957, 37 (*Historical New York Times*).

140. Raymond Daniel, "By Flying Carpet to Arabia's Oil Fields: Ibn Sa'ud's Primitive Kingdom Already Feels the Impact of American Enterprise and Ideas," *New York Times,* January 18, 1948, SM8 (*Historical New York Times*); Schmidt, "Arabian Town Is Like a U.S. Suburb."

141. Daniel, "By Flying Carpet to Arabia's Oil Fields"; Schmidt, "Arabian Town Is Like a U.S. Suburb."

142. Peter Lienhardt, *Disorientations: A Society in Flux: Kuwait in the 1950s*, ed. Ahmed al-Shahi (Reading, UK: Ithaca Press, 1993), 31.
143. Ibid.
144. Ibid.
145. Ibid.
146. Alfred R. Zipser, "Arabian Miracle: Yankee Victuals; ARAMCO Subsidiary Scours Half the World for Food for American Workers," *New York Times*, October 31, 1954, F1 (*Historical New York Times*).
147. Ibid.
148. Ibid.
149. Bullard to Halifax, no. 116, E3791/10/31, Jeddah, June 6, 1938, reprinted in *British Documents on Foreign Affairs: Reports and Papers from the Foreign Office Confidential Print*, ed. Kenneth Bourne and D. Cameron Watt, pt. 2: *From the First to the Second World War*, Series B: *Turkey, Iran, and the Middle East, 1918–1939*, ed. Robin Bidwell, vol. 13: *Eastern Affairs, December 1937–September 1939* (Bethesda, MD: University Publications of America, 1986), 40–44; Bullard to Halifax, no. 164, E6860/1/31, Jeddah, November 16, 1938, reprinted in *British Documents on Foreign Affairs: Reports and Papers from the Foreign Office Confidential Print*, ed. Kenneth Bourne and D. Cameron Watt, pt. 2: *From the First to the Second World War*, Series B: *Turkey, Iran, and the Middle East, 1918–1939*, ed. Robin Bidwell, vol. 13: *Eastern Affairs, December 1937–September 1939* (Bethesda, MD: University Publications of America, 1986), 200; Bullard to Halifax, no. 174, E7036/1/31, November 24, 1938, reprinted in *British Documents on Foreign Affairs: Reports and Papers from the Foreign Office Confidential Print*, ed. Kenneth Bourne and D. Cameron Watt, pt. 2: *From the First to the Second World War*, Series B: *Turkey, Iran, and the Middle East, 1918–1939*, ed. Robin Bidwell, vol. 13: *Eastern Affairs, December 1937–September 1939* (Bethesda, MD: University Publications of America, 1986), 206–207.
150. Fuccaro, "Mapping the Transnational Community: Persians and the Space of the City in Bahrain," 52–53.
151. William Eddy, US Legation to Jeddah, "Remarks About Jews Made by King Abdul Aziz al-Saud," no. 30, October 30, 1944, reprinted in United States Department of State, *Records of the Department of State Relating to Internal Affairs of Saudi Arabia, 1930–1944*, Reel 3.
152. Niles Lind, Attaché of US Legation to Jeddah, "Memorandum: King Abdul Aziz-Saud's Remarks About Jews," October 30, 1944, reprinted in United States Department of State, *Records of the Department of State Relating to Internal Affairs of Saudi Arabia, 1930–1944*, Reel 3 enclosed within William Eddy, US Legation to Jeddah, "Remarks About Jews Made by King Abdul Aziz al-Saud," no. 30, October 30, 1944, reprinted in United States Department of State, *Records of the Department of State Relating to Internal Affairs of Saudi Arabia, 1930–1944*, Reel 3.
153. Ibn Saud's son argued that it was a religious obligation for Muslims and Christians to forgo their points of disagreement and to emphasize their points of contact in a common struggle against atheism and communism. "Islam-Christian Base Against Reds Urged," *New York Times*, March 19, 1950, 31 (*Historical New York Times*).
154. George Weller, "Saudi Arabia Reported Ousting Arab Refugees," Chicago Daily News Foreign Service, January 26, 1956.

155. Raymond Hare, US Legation Cairo to Secretary of State, "Labor Conditions in Saudi Arabia: Builders and Contractors at Jedda," no. 2025, March 18, 1940, reprinted in United States Department of State, *Records of the Department of State Relating to Internal Affairs of Saudi Arabia, 1930–1944,* Reel 5.

156. "Saudis' Boycott Said to Widen," *New York Times,* March 8, 1956, 4 (*Historical New York Times*).

157. Clarence J. McIntosh to McIntosh Family, November 21, 1944, Clarence J. McIntosh Papers, Georgetown University Library Special Collections, Box 2, Folder 35, Letter 39; Clarence J. McIntosh to McIntosh Family, December 6, 1944, Clarence J. McIntosh Collection, Georgetown University Library Special Collections, Box 2, Folder 37, Letter 41.

158. "Saudi Arabia Renews Biased Visa Terms," *New York Times,* March 23, 1950, 19 (*Historical New York Times*); "U.S. Criticized on Arabian Pact," *New York Times,* June 18, 1956, 2 (*Historical New York Times*); Irving Spiegel, "End of U.S. Pact with Saud Urged," *New York Times,* May 15, 1957, 4 (*Historical New York Times*).

159. RIH, "Memorandum," March 22, 1972, William Mulligan Papers, Georgetown University Library Special Collections, Box 7, Folder 21.

160. Seccombe, "A Disgrace to American Enterprise," 252–254.

161. Ethel Thomas, "The Story of the Year," *Neglected Arabia* 245 (Winter–Spring 1956–1957): 10. Thomas noted that the "outreach work in Hasa was closed down for want of permission from the ruler of Arabia to continue." See also Armerding, *Doctors for the Kingdom,* 138.

162. Lienhardt, *Disorientations: A Society in Flux,* 50.

163. Ibid.

164. Ibid., 43.

165. Parker T. Hart, US Consulate Dhahran, "General Observations Regarding Dhahran, Bahrain," no. 51, December 20, 1944, William Mulligan Papers, Georgetown University Library Special Collections, Box 7, Folder 6.

166. For example, when an Iraqi assaulted a Jew in a bazaar in Manama in September 1929, the matter was quickly smoothed over by community leaders, who offered and accepted formal apologies. Cyril Charles Johnson Barrett, "Summary of News from the Arab States for the Month of September 1929," no. 9, 1929, reprinted in *Political Diaries of the Persian Gulf, vol. 8: 1928–1929* (Cambridge, Archive Editions, 1990), 499; Norman Horner, "Present-Day Christians in the Gulf States of the Arabian Peninsula," *Occasional Bulletin of Missionary Research* (April 1978): 55–56, William Mulligan Papers, Georgetown University Library Special Collections, Box 7, Folder 21.

167. Government of Bahrain, "Bahrain's 1950 Census."

168. Khedouri, *From Our Beginning to Present Day,* 21–22.

169. Ibid., 59–60.

170. Charles Belgrave, *Personal Column* (London: Hutchinson, 1960), 148–150.

171. Michael Rosenbloom, "Island Girl," *Congregation Ohav Shalom Tales of Survival,* March 2002 (available at http://www.ohav.org/).

172. Trott to Younger, "The Pilgrimage to the Hejaz During 1949," no. 45, ES 1718/15, June 22, 1950, reprinted in *British Documents on Foreign Affairs: Reports and Papers from the Foreign Office Confidential Print,* ed. Paul Preston and

Michael Partridge, pt. 4: *From 1946 Through 1950,* Series B: *Near and Middle East, 1950,* ed. Malcolm Yapp, vol. 10: *Israel, Syria, Arabia, the Middle East (General), Jordan and Arab Palestine and the Lebanon, January 1950–December 1950* (Bethesda, MD: University Publications of America, 1999), 223–224.

173. Tudor Parfitt, *The Road to Redemption* (Leiden: E. J. Brill, 1996), 247–248; Ya'akov Meron, "Expulsion of Jews from Arab Countries: The Palestinians' Attitudes Towards It and Their Claims," in *The Forgotten Millions,* ed. Malka Hillel Shulewitz (London: Cassell Press, 1999), 86; Reuben Ahroni, *Jewish Immigration from the Yemen: Carpet Without Magic* (Richmond, Surrey, UK: Curzon, 2001), 27–28. It is also worth noting that at least eighteen Israeli citizens between 1949 and 1956 told the Israeli Registrar of Foreign Claims that they had lost property in Saudi Arabia. Michael Fischbach, *Jewish Property Claims Against Arab Countries* (New York: Columbia University Press, 2008), 132–133 and 294–295.

174. Mike Mehlman, discussion with the author, March 2008.

175. Horner, "Present-Day Christians in the Gulf States of the Arabian Peninsula," 55–56.

176. Ibid.

177. Ibid., 54–55.

178. Ibid.; Sanmiguel, *Christians in Kuwait,* 66–81.

179. Horner, "Present-Day Christians in the Gulf States of the Arabian Peninsula," 57.

180. Ibid.

181. "Abu Dhabi: Booming Oil State in the Arabian Gulf," *New York Herald Tribune,* May 23, 1965, William Mulligan Papers, Georgetown University Library Special Collections, Box 7, Folder 21.

182. "Bishop Administers Sacrament," *Gulf Mirror,* May 5, 1978, William Mulligan Papers, Georgetown University Library Special Collections, Box 7, Folder 21; Horner, "Present-Day Christians in the Gulf States of the Arabian Peninsula," 58–59.

183. Horner, "Present-Day Christians in the Gulf States of the Arabian Peninsula," 56–57.

184. Ibid.

185. Parker Hart, "Application of Hanbalite and Decree Law to Foreigners in Saudi Arabia," *George Washington Law Review* 22, no. 65 (1953): 165.

186. Wallace to Ament, November 4, 1967; Mulligan, "Resident Catholic Priests Stationed in Saudi Arabia."

187. Mulligan, "Notes on the Church in Saudi Arabia."

188. William Mulligan, "Employee Directed Morale Groups," Dhahran, September 21, 1960, William Mulligan Papers, Georgetown University Library Special Collections, Box 7, Folder 21; W. B. Murphy, "Review of Morale Groups," January 13, 1962, William Mulligan Papers, Georgetown University Library Special Collections, Box 7, Folder 21.

189. Mulligan, "Notes on the Church in Saudi Arabia."

190. US Embassy Riyadh, "Draft Memcon on Ambassador West's Meeting with HRH Prince Nayyif bin Aziz, Minister of Interior, at His Palace in Jidda, Nov. 29, 1977, 2 PM," William Mulligan Papers, Georgetown University Library Special Collections, Box 7, Folder 21.

191. Mulligan, "Employee Directed Morale Groups."

192. Ibid.

193. This was the same street as Christmas Tree Circle, or the Seventh Street cul-de-sac. Former ARAMCO employee, conversation with author, July 2008; William Mulligan, "Ghosts of Christmas Past," *Arabian Sun,* December 19, 1973, William Mulligan Papers, Georgetown University Library Special Collections, Box 16, Folder 7.

194. Father Costello, "R. C. Group of Dhahran with Reflections on Our Capuchin Services in Abqaiq and Ras Tanura," June 1979, William Mulligan Papers, Georgetown University Library Special Collections, Box 7, Folder 21.

195. Ibid.

196. "Our Lady of Fatima Parish Bulletin," January 16, 1976, William Mulligan Papers, Georgetown University Library Special Collections, Box 7, Folder 21.

197. Mary Norton to William Mulligan, February 7, 1992, William Mulligan Papers, Georgetown University Library Special Collections, Box 7, Folder 21; William Mulligan to Mary Norton, February 11, 1992; "Our Lady of Fatima Parish Bulletin," January 16, 1976.

198. Former ARAMCO employee, conversation with the author, June 2008.

199. John Cuddeback, "Italian Crucifix at St. John Neumann," e-mail communication to author, June 5, 2008.

200. Cuddeback, "Italian Crucifix at St. John Neumann"; Mulligan, "Ghosts of Christmas Past."

201. DeLong-Bas, *Wahhabi Islam,* 210–211.

202. Lippman, *Inside the Mirage,* 204.

203. ARAMCO, "Suggested Personal and Household Items for Women in Saudi Arabia," May 1949, William Mulligan Papers, Georgetown University Library Special Collections, Box 7, Folder 9.

204. Dana Schmidt, "Traditions of Islam Are Guarded in Jidda, on the Road to Mecca," *New York Times,* November 15, 1959, 37 (*Historical New York Times*).

205. Former ARAMCO employee, conversation with author, July 2008. A good example of this practice is detailed in "The 'X' Case (a Woman Driver)," in "Liquor Cases (Category II)," n.d., William Mulligan Papers, Georgetown University Library Special Collections, Box 5, Folder 13.

206. "First Certificate of Witness to Marriage Shar'ia Law Nuptials Ellis Howard (age 53) and Alma M. Bowman (age 40)," March 30, 1969, William Mulligan Papers, Georgetown University Library Special Collections, Box 7, Folder 21; John R. Jones, "Memorandum to the File," April 5, 1969, William Mulligan Papers, Georgetown University Library Special Collections, Box 7, Folder 21; George M. Baroody, "Christian Marriages in Saudi Arabia," June 21, 1969, William Mulligan Papers, Georgetown University Library Special Collections, Box 7, Folder 21.

207. "First Certificate of Witness to Marriage"; Jones, "Memorandum to the File," April 5, 1969.

208. DeLong-Bas, *Wahhabi Islam,* 142.

209. Jones, "Memorandum to the File," April 5, 1969.

210. Ibid.

211. Nakash, *Reaching for Power: The Shi'a in the Modern Arab World,* 47–48.

212. Ibid., 48.

213. William Mulligan, "Shiah Request to HH King Faysal," Dhahran, March 13, 1967, William Mulligan Papers, Georgetown University Library Special Collections, Box 3, Folder 28.

214. Ibid.

215. Fuller and Francke, *The Arab Sh'ia: The Forgotten Muslims,* 161–163.

216. Nakash, *Reaching for Power: The Shi'a in the Modern Arab World,* 261–265.

217. J. A. Mahon, "Report on Visit to Kuwait Oil Company Ltd., August 1970," Joseph A. Mahon Papers, Georgetown University Library Special Collections, Box 1, Folder 7, 2–5; John Jones, "Notes on Kuwait Oil Company Relations," June 23, 1965, William Mulligan Papers, Georgetown University Library Special Collections, Box 3, Folder 24; Phebe Marr, "Memorandum for the Files: Labor Unions in Kuwait," December 3, 1961, William Mulligan Papers, Georgetown University Library Special Collections, Box 3, Folder 10.

218. John Jones, "Notes on Kuwait Oil Company Relations," June 23, 1965, William Mulligan Papers, Georgetown University Library Special Collections, Box 3, Folder 24.

219. Father Andre to William Mulligan, November 28, 1979, William Mulligan Papers, Georgetown University Library Special Collections, Box 7, Folder 21; Reverend Pascal Siles to William Mulligan, October 9, 1985, William Mulligan Papers, Georgetown University Library Special Collections, Box 7, Folder 21; Father Watrin to William Mulligan, February 11, 1980, William Mulligan Papers, Georgetown University Library Special Collections, Box 7, Folder 21; Mulligan to Norton, February 11, 1992; Norton to Mulligan, February 7, 1992.

220. US Embassy Riyadh, "Draft Memcon on Ambassador West's Meeting with HRH Prince Nayyif bin Aziz."

221. Norton to Mulligan, February 7, 1992; Mulligan to Norton, February 11, 1992.

222. Mulligan to Norton, February 11, 1992.

223. Norton to Mulligan, February 7, 1992; Mulligan to Norton, February 11, 1992; Cuddeback, "Italian Crucifix at St. John Neumann."

224. Mulligan, "Resident Catholic Priests Stationed in Saudi Arabia."

225. Philip Shenon, "Out of Saudi View, U.S. Force Allows Religious Their Rites," *New York Times,* December 22, 1990, 1 (*Historical New York Times*).

226. Poem extracted from *al-Thawra al-Islamiyya* 88 (July 1987): 1, in Nakash, *Reaching for Power: The Sh'ia in the Modern Arab World,* 43.

227. Joseph A. Kechichian, *Succession in Saudi Arabia* (New York: Palgrave Macmillan, 2001), 99.

228. Fuller and Francke, *The Arab Shi'a: The Forgotten Muslims,* 25, 40.

229. "Jeffrey of Arabia," *Newsweek* 96, no. 19, November 10, 1980, 1.

230. Steve Coll, *Ghost Wars* (New York: Penguin Books, 2004), 93.

231. Elaine Sciolino, "For Outsiders in Saudi Arabia, Worship Comes with a Risk," *New York Times,* February 12, 2002.

232. Sharif Mukaddam, "Spotlight on Indians in Arab World: Indians Active in Saudi Arabian Cultural Life," *Clarity,* November 1, 1975, William Mulligan Papers, Georgetown University Library Special Collections, Box 10, Folder 1.

233. Abdullah Taryam, *The Establishment of the United Arab Emirates,*

1950–85 (London: Croom Helm, 1987), 242–248; Frauke Heard-Bey, *From Trucial States to United Arab Emirates: A Society in Transition* (London: Longman, 1981), 371, 389; Christopher Davidson, *Dubai: The Vulnerability of Success* (New York: Columbia University Press, 2008), 99–113.

234. Davidson, *Dubai: The Vulnerability of Success*, 88.

235. James Scott, *The Moral Economy of the Peasant* (New Haven: Yale University Press, 1976), 3–7.

236. United Nations Department of Economic and Social Affairs, Population Division, *United Nations' World Population Prospects* (available at http://esa.un.org/).

237. Kevin Bales, *Disposable People: New Slavery in the Global Economy* (Berkeley: University of California Press, 2004), 12–29.

238. Shannon McNulty, "A Lifetime of Servitude? Low-wage Labor in the Arabian Gulf" (Master's thesis, Georgetown University, 2004), iii.

239. "Pakistan Receives Record $21 Billion Remittances from GCC States," Pakistan Newswire, June 2, 2007.

240. "Flow of Migrant Earnings to Developing Nations Won't Be Counted as Foreign Aid," Inter Press Service, January 28, 2008.

241. KAKAMMPI [Association of Filipino Migrant Families and Returnees], "Philippine Overseas Migration Amidst the Asian Crisis," paper presented to Southeast Asian Regional Conference on Migrant Workers and the Asian Economic Crises: Towards a Trade Union Position, Bangkok, Thailand, November 5–6, 1998 (available at http://www.philsol.nl/).

242. "Kuwait Court Upholds Filipina's Death Sentence," Agence France-Presse—English, April 1, 2008); Michael Caber, "More Filipinos Signing Up for Saudi's Repatriation Program," *Manila Standard,* June 12, 2007.

243. Jason DeParle, "Fearful of Restive Foreign Labor, Dubai Eyes Reforms," *New York Times,* August 6, 2007.

244. Ahmed al-Omran, "Form for the Other Saudis," *Saudi Jeans,* April 14, 2008 (available at http://saudijeans.org/).

245. "Kuwait Grills Shiite Ex-MPs over Hezbollah Links," Agence France-Presse—English, March 25, 2008.

246. Ibid.

247. "New Kuwait Cabinet to Meet Amid Islamist Anger," Deutsche Presse-Agentur, May 29, 2008.

248. Omar Hasan, "Shiite Crackdown Fuels Sectarian Tensions in Kuwait," Agence France-Presse—English, March 13, 2008.

249. Ashfaq Ahmed, "Abdul Nabi Bangash Appointed Pakistan Senator," *Gulf News,* March 7, 2009 (available at http://www.gulfnews.com/).

250. "India to Train Bahrain Parliament Staff," Press Trust of India, October 1, 2006.

251. Kuwait Cricket Federation, "Kuwait Cricket," 2009 (available at http://www.cricketkuwait.com/).

252. Sonia Verma, "The Invisible Church Prays for a Quiet Easter in the Emirate of Qatar," *Globe and Mail,* March 21, 2008.

253. "First Roman Catholic Church Opens in Qatar," *USA Today,* March 26, 2008 (available at http://www.usatoday.com/).

254. Shabina S. Khatri, "Qatar Opens First Church, Quietly," al-Jazerra.net, March 13, 2008 (available at http://english.aljazerra.net/).

255. Verma, "The Invisible Church."

256. "Where Can I Find Information on the Jews of Najran?" September 23, 2007 (available at http://jewishrefugees.blogspot.com/).

257. Fatima al-Sayegh, "American Missionaries in the UAE Region in the Twentieth Century," *Middle Eastern Studies* 32, no. 1 (1996): 135.

258. These materials are available at http://www.sharjahtourism.ae/en/.

259. Nora Boustany, "Barrier-Breaking Bahraini Masters Diplomatic Scene: Nonoo Is First Jewish Ambassador from an Arab Nation," *Washington Post,* December 19, 2008.

7

Beyond Oil and Islam

The center of life is no longer the mosque but the oil derrick.
—Dr. Paul Harrison, *Doctor in Arabia,* 1940

There is no technology on the horizon that can completely replace oil.
—Saudi prince Turki al-Faisal, *Foreign Policy,* 2009

In March 2007, David Lesar, the CEO and president of Halliburton, announced that the company would open a new corporate headquarters in Dubai. Although Halliburton would maintain its existing corporate headquarters in Houston, Lesar, a US citizen, would move permanently to Dubai. Because Halliburton retained its legal incorporation in the United States, however, it would still be subject to US laws and regulations.[1]

The move generated considerable public surprise in the United States. Congressman Henry Waxman, chairman of the US House of Representatives' Oversight and Reform Committee, called for immediate hearings on the move, citing legal, financial, and security concerns.[2] The company, which had been headed by future vice president Richard Cheney from 1995 to 2000, was the bête noire of US progressives because of its close ties to the George W. Bush administration and allegations that it had profited from US operations in Iraq.[3] Liberal pundits were especially suspicious of Lesar's move to the UAE because it occurred while his company's operations in Iraq, Kuwait, and Nigeria were under investigation for fraud by both the Justice Department and the Securities and Exchange Commission.[4] Furthermore, Halliburton was already paying billions of dollars in settlements for asbestos litigation. It was an open question whether Lesar hoped that his move to Dubai would shield him from future litigation, since the UAE lacks an extradition treaty with the United States.[5]

Halliburton announced that the decision to move Lesar was part of a company strategy, begun in 2006, to concentrate its efforts in the Middle East, where state-owned oil companies represented a growing source of business.[6] It made far more sense, the company contended, for Lesar to be based in Dubai rather than Houston, which was seventeen hours by plane from where most of Halliburton's current and future customers were located. Dubai was also far closer geographically than Houston to the booming economies of Asia, especially India and China, which had long been seen as the future of the oil industry. Melissa Norcross, a spokesperson for Halliburton, explained that moving Lesar to Dubai "makes good business sense, as it is the center of our Eastern Hemisphere operations and a global business hub."[7]

Whatever the reasons for moving Lesar to Dubai, the decision to move him allows us to revisit the four themes that are at the heart of this book. First, the GCC states are normal states that face many of the same political and socioeconomic problems that other states do. Second, many of the challenges that Gulf states face in the twenty-first century predate the rise of the region's oil industry in the 1930s. Third, we cannot understand either the past or contemporary realities in the Gulf states unless we come to terms with their diversity and look at the roles of non-Arabs and women. Fourth, technological change has had an important effect on life and on politics in the Gulf.

To begin with, Lesar's move to Dubai showed that the socioeconomic and cultural differences between Houston and Dubai were not large enough to justify keeping the chief executive of a major US corporation physically based in the United States. Dubai, a metropolis situated in a socially conservative Arab Muslim monarchy, could now serve as the home for an American who had been born and educated in Wisconsin, had ties to senior US politicians, and had lived in Houston for years.[8] Indeed, the Gulf city's culture and society now largely mirror those of large metropolitan regions in North America and other parts of the world.

Equally important, Lesar's move was part of a long tradition, whereby thousands of Americans and other non-Arabs and non-Muslims have gone to the Gulf and made important contributions to the region. Both before and after the rise of the oil industry in the 1930s, individuals as disparate as Italian Catholic priests, US Protestant missionaries, Greek mariners, European geologists, and Indian and Jewish merchants have played important roles in the region. Gulf Arabs in the early twenty-first century have often depended on workers from the same Indian Ocean labor networks as their forefathers had done prior to the discovery of oil in the 1930s, when Great Britain ruled supreme in the Gulf and on the world stage. Despite the enormous changes in the world and the Middle East during the twentieth century, the role of foreign workers and of Indian Ocean labor networks lives on in the Gulf.

By employing foreigners in vast numbers and facilitating their basic socioreligious needs, the Gulf states have also utilized an economic strategy akin to those used by governments from North America to Asia. All of these states allow their companies to employ migrants fleeing their homelands in search of better social and economic opportunities. Two keys to this process of migration are the existence of Indian Ocean and other socioeconomic labor networks and the fact that television programs, movies, and other mass media have convinced millions of people that anyone can strike it rich abroad and realize the local equivalent of the so-called American dream. It is worth noting that Dubai's impact on Asian and Middle Eastern societies is analogous to that of Chicago today on the midwestern states, which annually lose thousands of their top university graduates to the Windy City because of its economic promise and social freedoms.[9]

The benefits of attracting Asians, Europeans, non-Gulf Arabs, and others to the Gulf may have been strained by the post-2008 global economic recession, however. The current global downturn, the worst since the Great Depression, could bring sweeping technical change to the Gulf and, with that, economic and political changes. The downturn of the 1930s not only decimated what had been for years the foundations of the Gulf's economy (pearling, transit trade, and pilgrimage) but also allowed the United States to overtake Great Britain as the dominant regional power and paved the way for the rise of the new petroleum industry in the region. The changes were so startling that Paul Harrison noted in 1940 that oil had superseded every other aspect of Gulf society, including Islam.[10]

Although the current downturn has yet to devastate the Gulf petroleum industry in the same way that the Great Depression decimated pearling and pilgrimage, there are signs that it may accelerate social and technological trends that will reduce the petroleum industry's importance to the Gulf and to the world economy in general. The United States, Germany, China, and Great Britain have all introduced legislation meant to stimulate their economies by investing in technologies that will decrease their use of oil, promote reusable energy sources, and reduce carbon emissions.[11] These policies reflect the success of environmental activists, especially in the United States, where both the Democratic and the Republican nominees for president in 2008 committed themselves to tackling global warming.[12] In the long run, these new investments could have as significant an impact on the demand for and price of oil as the reduction of coal use did in the United States and Europe in the 1950s and 1960s—although in the opposite direction.

As sobering as these socioeconomic trends are, their threat to the future of the Gulf states may be dwarfed by two other factors. First, even as OPEC has cut supplies to the world oil markets, it has found that economic conditions are sufficiently weak that oil prices will not soon return to the highs of 2008.[13]

For Gulf governments that had planned to earn far higher profits on their oil, the price decline will certainly lead to dangerous budget shortfalls.

Second, those shortfalls have been aggravated by the fact that they occurred when the Gulf states' sovereign wealth funds were substantially reduced by declining stock markets and other investments around the world. In the past, these funds provided a useful tool for Gulf governments to survive sustained declines in the global oil market. Gulf leaders do not appear to have that option at this time. By March 2009, these funds had already lost at least $800 billion, or 40 percent of their value six months earlier.[14] In November 2009, Dubai shocked global financial markets when it announced that its sovereign wealth fund, Dubai World, would suspend payments on all or part of its $59 billion debt for at least six months.[15] Nor were sovereign wealth funds alone in facing severe financial problems: family conglomerates based in the Gulf had an equally difficult time servicing their debt, with two Saudi firms alone reportedly unable to pay at least $20 billion in debt in November 2009.[16]

Within this financial environment, the Gulf Arabs have an opportunity to reshape their societies fundamentally and realize an economic model more in line with that of Mexico, where petroleum is important but not, to paraphrase Paul Harrison's words, the center of daily life. While Dubai's financial challenges may remain serious for some time to come, the emirate's past success compelled Gulf governments to make a host of investments in manufacturing, alternative energy, services, and knowledge industries. These investments will serve the region long after the Dubai model is forgotten and will provide a base for socioeconomic transformation. Here again, technology is playing a key role. Already one can see this type of change in the use of the Internet, which the Saudi novelist Rajaa al-Sanea told a conference in Dubai in 2009 has greatly widened the opportunities for writers to express their views freely without fear of government retribution.[17]

Potentially, an even larger engine of change than the Internet may be the new universities built in the region after the 1990s, especially those schools that are partnered with existing elite research universities in the United States, Australia, and Europe.[18] These institutions will enhance the skills of Gulf nationals and the region's workforce. Because they are more research intensive than older Gulf universities, the new schools could form the types of public-private partnerships and technology transfers that have worked well in Europe, Asia, and North America. One already sees this type of linkage in alternative energy research, which has the added benefit of addressing energy use and global warming, key issues for Gulf Arabs, who have already faced energy shortages along with diminishing supplies of water.[19] The city of Pittsburgh's economic rebirth after the early 1980s shows how, through a host of partnerships with local colleges and universities, it is possible for a region to transform its economy from one based on a single modern industry—in that case, steel—to one based on education, pharmaceuticals, and technology.[20]

Even though it may take a number of years for a similar transformation to take place in the Gulf, there is no question that women in the region are well positioned to take advantage of it. This again points to one of my core themes in this book: we cannot understand the Gulf without taking into account the role of women. As I noted in Chapter 5, Gulf women have made impressive gains in literacy since the 1970s. Females often constitute as much as 60 percent of the student body at all levels of education, and women are serving in senior positions in government and business throughout the Gulf. They are the single group of Gulf nationals who have the skills to replace some expatriates in the region's workforce. Women are also a natural ally for the Gulf's leaders, who, since September 11, 2001, have sought to modify their region's austere image in order to win greater foreign investment and to combat extremist groups. Although issues linked to women's driving, voting, and working remain unresolved in several Gulf states, women are well on their way to recapturing or surpassing the socioeconomic roles they held in the region before the rise of the oil industry.

By contrast, men are falling further behind their female peers—another respect in which the Gulf states are remarkably similar to Western societies, where men have fallen behind women in educational achievement and have borne the brunt of the current economic downturn. For example, nearly 80 percent of the jobs lost in the United States between 2007 and 2009 were held by men.[21] Young men in the Gulf, on average, are far less literate than women and drop out of school earlier. Few find positions outside of family businesses or the military.

Although this is not a new social problem (British officials observed it as early as the 1950s), it has taken on greater social significance in recent years. With bleak career prospects and ample time on their hands, young men (and even some older ones) have gravitated toward antisocial behavior, including truancy, petty crime, drug abuse, religious extremism, and "drifting," a form of car racing in which drivers perform complex and dangerous maneuvers at extremely high speeds. Drifters throughout the Gulf post their performances on YouTube, where they are celebrities who are said to have their pick of young male sexual partners. Drifting has become so popular that Chevrolet and the energy drink Red Bull have begun to sponsor "drifting" races in Middle Eastern cities.[22]

Yet the dangers of drifting to Gulf society have been clear for many years. In 2005, three young boys died in Jeddah in the car crash of a Saudi naval officer, Faisal al-Otabi—better known as Abu Kab (or the One Who Wears a [Baseball] Cap)—who wrecked his car while attempting to perform a stunt-driving maneuver. Abu Kab's trial, which was front-page news in Saudi Arabia, caused considerable public outcry, especially after it was revealed that he had more than sixty speeding tickets. There have been similar deadly accidents in Jeddah and other cities in the Gulf. One of the most dangerous of terrorists was a drifter: Youssef al-Ayyeri headed Al-Qaida in Saudi Arabia until he died in a shootout with Saudi security forces in 2003.[23]

Drifting, especially when linked to other dangerous antisocial problems of young men, suggests that future "gender questions" in the Gulf will no longer focus exclusively on women, the veil, and other related issues—as they have for generations. Instead, they will revolve around how to integrate young men (including those in their twenties and thirties) into society and make them productive individuals before they engage in behavior that is dangerous to themselves and others.

It is significant that the problems of men in Gulf societies are analogous to those faced by men in the United States and elsewhere during the current economic downturn. A white paper produced by the Georgia Department of Labor in July 2009 called for the state radically to alter how it delivers social services to men, a significant percentage of whom are in grave danger of becoming "structurally unemployed." The report noted that men in Georgia and in other parts of the United States—much like men in the Arab Gulf states—lack basic modern skills and lag far behind women in educational achievement. The report also noted the striking statistic that the percentage of students who are female in Georgia's universities, colleges, and technical institutes is approximately 60 percent, a number that is in line with the percentages in the Gulf.[24]

Just as the question of gender may increasingly be viewed very differently in the Gulf (as well as in Georgia), one may well come to see expatriate workers and national security challenges understood in new ways. This goes back to one of my core arguments: that non-Muslims and non-Arabs are critical to understanding the politics of the Gulf. Although the global economic downturn since the fall of 2008 has led thousands of expatriates to leave the Gulf, or at least to contemplate leaving, foreigners still dominate many sectors of the private economy. A public opinion survey conducted in February 2009 found that half of the expatriates in the UAE plan to remain, and nearly two-thirds of them plan on starting their own businesses if they lose their current employment. One reason for the expatriates to stay is that economic conditions are even worse elsewhere, especially in their home countries. In fact, the poll showed that a number of expatriate workers today, much like missionaries and other non-Arabs and non-Muslims of previous eras, are sufficiently satisfied with life in the Gulf that they intend to remain there regardless of economic conditions or their social and political status.[25]

For Gulf Arabs, many of whom for decades have hoped to expel these workers, this development may prove to be enormously beneficial. These expatriates are precisely the type of hard-working and industrious people who are essential to the success of contemporary economies, especially those based on knowledge industries. If expatriates remain in the Gulf and do not move to Asia, Europe, or North America, they could transform the region's economy and produce a true postpetroleum economic system. The chief dilemma for Gulf Arabs ironically posed by expatriate workers will not be how to replace them but how to keep them from leaving.

One can see similar reversals in national security. For example, the chief foreign policy question for Gulf Arabs for half a century has been how to balance their dependence on Western security guarantees and financial ties with their populations' anger at Western policies toward Israel and the Palestinians. To achieve these almost irreconcilable goals, Gulf leaders have deployed flexible policy approaches. On the one hand, they refuse to recognize Israel, and they briefly boycotted oil shipments to Israel's allies in the 1970s. On the other hand, they maintain ironclad links to Israel's closest ally, the United States. Thanks to this approach, Gulf leaders have retained their credibility on the Arab-Israeli dispute, have profited from their Western investments, and have successfully repelled various external threats. In 1991, the Gulf states' multitrack approach paid off handsomely when the United States expelled Iraq from Kuwait and initiated negotiations that set the stage for the emergence of the Oslo Peace Process.

The decline of US power in the Middle East has raised new concerns, however, for the leaders in the Gulf. Despite the fact that Washington maintains tens of thousands of troops in the Middle East, the United States has proven unable to defend the Gulf Arabs' core interests in the Middle East or to protect their overseas wealth. In particular, Gulf governments are astonished that Washington has allowed Iran to gain unparalleled influence in Iraq, Lebanon, Yemen, and the Palestinian territories since 2003 and has permitted the US dollar to fall to such a low level that it sparked inflation in Gulf economies.[26]

Gulf leaders have good reasons for their fears. US power in the region will necessarily decline as the nation finally withdraws its troops from Iraq and begins to implement the deep cuts in defense spending that are needed to offset new increased domestic spending.[27] Although the United States will retain a naval presence in the Gulf and remain an important source of investment for some time, it will not again maintain the web of military facilities that it had between 1991 and 2003. It is also unlikely to have the resources necessary to launch an operation similar to the 1991 Gulf War.

Consequently, in future years, Gulf governments will no longer have to make the same compromises they once did in order to secure US friendship, but they will simultaneously no longer be able to depend on overwhelming US military power in a crisis. Which nation or nations might replace the United States in the Gulf is unclear, since no other major state—aside from Iran—currently has the capabilities to project power into the region.

As difficult as these various dilemmas are, they should be weighed against the enormous advantages that Gulf Arabs currently possess. To begin with, they produce a product, oil, that is critical to the international economy. Even if industrialized nations reduce their use of oil and adopt alternative fuels, this does not mean that they (or any other states) will abandon petroleum altogether. As Saudi prince Turki al-Faisal observed in *Foreign Policy* in August 2009, there is no fuel source in existence that can completely replace oil, and the United States and other nations will use it and other nonrenewable energy sources for decades to come. Rather than pursuing the impossible dream of energy independence, Faisal suggested, US, European, and other world leaders should acknowledge their "energy interdependence" with Saudi Arabia and other major oil-exporting nations.[28]

Faisal's comments remind us that it may take a very long time to reshape global energy markets—no matter how much money world governments devote to developing alternatives to oil. The internal combustion engine remains an efficient source of generating power. There are still millions of cars on the planet that run on gasoline, and they are likely to be utilized for many years to come. Fifty years ago, Americans reduced their use of coal in favor of oil, but coal still accounts for 23 percent of all US energy needs.[29] These major transitions take time. Even when global oil use inevitably declines, the Gulf states will still be able to fall back on their investments in alternative fuels, education, and other non-oil industries, which have the potential to yield significant economic growth in the future.

Although the Gulf states are facing immense problems, by international standards they are doing very well. They may be angst ridden, but they are also immensely rich. As the US songwriter Cole Porter put it, they are "down in the depths," but they are also "on the ninetieth floor."[30]

Notes

1. Kim Crane, "Halliburton Will Move HQ to Dubai," Associated Press, March 11, 2007; Steven Mufson and Dana Hedgpeth, "Halliburton's Chief Move to Dubai Evokes Warnings on the Hill," *Washington Post,* March 13, 2007.

2. Mufson and Hedgpeth, "Halliburton's Chief Move to Dubai Evokes Warnings on the Hill."

3. Hilary Hylton, "Goodbye, Houston. Hello, Dubai," *Time,* March 14, 2007 (available at http://www.time.com/).

4. For more on these arguments, see Keith Olbermann, "Dubai, and Good Luck" (includes interview with Philip Giraldi), *Countdown with Keith Olbermann,* MSNBC, March 12, 2007 (available at http://www.youtube.com/).

5. Hylton, "Goodbye, Houston. Hello, Dubai."

6. Halliburton was not the only oil services company or Houston-based company that was moving to Dubai in 2007. Two of Halliburton's competitors—Houston-based Baker Hughes and France's Schlumberger—were building major corporate facilities in Dubai at the time. Many Houston law firms and other service industries also had opened offices in the Gulf city. Ibid.

7. Clifford Krause, "Halliburton Moving C.E.O. from Houston to Dubai," *New York Times,* March 12, 2007.

8. "David Lesar Biography" (available at http://www.halliburton.com).

9. Richard Florida, "How the Crash Will Reshape America," *Atlantic Monthly,* March 2009 (available at http://www.theatlantic.com/); Tom Ashbrook "America's Post-Crash Geography" (includes interview with Richard Florida), *On Point with Tom Ashbrook,* February 23, 2009 (available at http://www.onpointradio.org).

10. Paul Harrison, *Doctor in Arabia* (New York: John Day, 1940), 300.

11. Thomas Friedman, "The Great Disruption," *New York Times,* March 8, 2009.

12. Andrew Revkin, "On Global Warming McCain and Obama Agree: Urgent Action Is Needed," *New York Times,* October 18, 2008.

13. Clifford Krauss, "As Oil and Gas Prices Drop, Drilling Frenzy Ends," *New York Times,* March 14, 2009; Jad Mouawad, "OPEC Achieves Cuts in Output, Halting Price Slide," *New York Times,* January 25, 2009.

14. Mohammed Elsidafy, "Unified GCC Sovereign Wealth Fund Is the 'Need of the Hour,'" *Emirates Business 24/7,* March 9, 2009 (available at http://www.business24-7.ae/).

15. David Jolly and Kate Galbraith, "Dubai's Move on Debt Rattles Markets Worldwide," *New York Times,* November 27, 2009, B1.

16. Camilla Hall, "Bankers Seek U.K.'s Help on $20 Billion Saudi Debt," Bloomberg.com, November 25, 2009 (available at http://www.bloomberg.com/)

17. "Arab Freedom of Expression Increasing: Saudi Author," Agence France-Presse—English, February 28, 2009.

18. For more on these schools, see Tamar Lewin, "U.S. Universities Rush to Set Up Outposts Abroad," *New York Times,* February 10, 2008.

19. Elizabeth Rosenthal, "Gulf Oil States Seeking a Lead in Clean Energy," *New York Times,* January 12, 2009.

20. David Streitfeld, "For Pittsburgh, There Is Life After Steel," *New York Times,* January 7, 2009.

21. Sarah Baxter, "Women Are Victors in 'Mancession'; Economics and Gender Roles Are Being Rewritten in America as Men Bear the Brunt of Job Losses," *Sunday Times* (London), June 7, 2009.

22. Tom Whitwell, "This Week: The Arab Drift," *Times,* August 16, 2008; Robert F. Worth, "Saudi Races Roar All Night Fueled by Boredom," *New York Times,* March 7, 2009.

23. Fatima Sidya, "Verdict in Abu Kab Case Today," *Arab News,* February 2, 2009 (available at http://www.arabnews.com/); Worth, "Saudi Races Roar All Night Fueled by Boredom."

24. Michael Thurmond, "Georgia Men Hit Hardest by the Recession, December 2007 to May 2009," Georgia Department of Labor: *White Paper on Georgia's Workforce, July 2009,* 7 (available at http://www.dol.state.ga.us/).

25. Shveta Pathak, "Expatriates Believe That the UAE Is the Best Bet," *Emirates Business 24/7,* March 2, 2009 (available at http://www.business24-7.ae/).

26. Iranian-Saudi tensions over Yemen became especially serious in November 2009 when Saudi Arabia deployed troops to northern Yemen to support Sana's campaign against Shia rebels known as the Hawthis. Riyadh repeatedly accused Iran of supporting the Hawthis, a charge Tehran vehemently denied. Some Saudis compared the Hawthis to the Shia organization Hezbollah in Lebanon and portrayed them as a threat to the future of Sunnisim in the Arabian peninsula. For

more on Iran-Saudi tensions over Yemen, see Donna Abu-Nasr, "Yemen Conflict Inflaming Saudi-Iranian Rivalry," Associated Press, November 24, 2009; Jeffrey Fleishman, "Yemen Teeters on the Brink of Failure," *Los Angeles Times*, December 6, 2009.

27. Christopher Drew, "Drilling Down on the Budget: Defense," *New York Times*, February 26, 2009; Christopher Drew and Thom Shanker, "Pentagon Expects Cuts in Military Spending," *New York Times*, November 2, 2008; Thom Shanker, "After Stimulus Package, Pentagon Officials Are Preparing to Pare Back," *New York Times*, February 17, 2009.

28. Turki al-Faisal, "Don't Be Crude: Why Barack Obama's Energy-Independence Talk Is Just Demagoguery," *Foreign Policy*, August 24, 2009 (available at http://www.foreignpolicy.com/).

29. Energy Information Administration, *Renewable Energy Consumption and Electricity Preliminary 2007 Statistics* (Washington, DC: US Government Printing Office, 2008) (available at http://www.eia.doe.gov/).

30. Cole Porter, "Down in the Depths," *Red Hot Blues*, in *The Complete Lyrics of Cole Porter*, ed. Robert Kimball (New York: Vintage Books, 1984), 206–207.

Acronyms

AOC	ARAMCO Overseas Company
APOC	Anglo-Persian Oil Company
ARABSAT	Arab Satellite Communications Organization
ARAMCO	Arab-American Oil Company
ARC	Advice and Reform Committee
ART	Arab Radio and Television
AWDS	Arab Women's Development Society
BAPCO	Bahrain Petroleum Company
CDLR	Committee for the Defense of Legitimate Rights
CIA	Central Intelligence Agency
CNN	Cable News Network
CSS	Cultural and Social Society
GCC	Gulf Cooperation Council
GDP	gross domestic product
IMF	International Monetary Fund
IPC	Iraq Petroleum Company
KOC	Kuwait Oil Company
LNG	liquified natural gas
MBC	Middle East Broadcasting Corporation
NATO	North Atlantic Treaty Organization
NGO	nongovernmental organization
OPEC	Organization of Petroleum Exporting Countries
SAMA	Saudi Arabian Monetary Agency
SCC	State Consultative Council (Oman)
TPC	Turkish Petroleum Company
TWA	Trans World Airlines
UAE	United Arab Emirates
UN	United Nations

Bibliography

Abdullah, Muhammad. *The United Arab Emirates*. New York: Barnes and Noble, 1978.

Abir, Mordechai. *Saudi Arabia in the Oil Era: Regime and Elites: Conflict and Collaboration*. Boulder, CO: Westview Press, 1988.

Aburish, Saïd K. *The Rise, Corruption, and Coming Fall of the House of Saud*. London: Bloomsbury, 1994.

Adnas, Malik ibn Malik. *Muwatta,* cited from the USC Center for Muslim-Jewish Engagement's Online Compendium of Muslim Texts. Available at http://www.usc.edu.

Ahroni, Reuben. *Jewish Immigration from the Yemen: Carpet Without Magic*. Richmond, Surrey, UK: Curzon, 2001.

Alawi, Jamil al-, and Mohammed Abdulrazzak. "Water in the Arabian Peninsula: Problems and Perspectives." In *Water in the Arab World,* edited by Peter Rogers and Peter Lynch, 171–202. Cambridge, MA: Harvard University Press, 1993.

Aldamer, Shafi. *Saudi Arabia and Britain: Changing Relations, 1939–1953*. Reading, England: Ithaca Press, 2003.

Alkanderi, Faisal. "Jews in Kuwait." *Islam and Christian-Muslim Relations* 17, no. 4 (October 2006): 445–456.

Allen, Calvin H. "The Indian Merchant Community of Masqat." *Bulletin School of Oriental and African Studies* 44, no. 1 (1981): 39–53.

———. *Oman: Modernization of the Sultanate*. Boulder, CO: Westview Press, 1987.

Alterman, Jon. *New Media, New Politics? From Satellite Television to the Internet in the Arab World*. Washington, DC: Washington Institute for Near East Policy, 1998.

Altorki, Soraya, and Donald P. Cole. *Arabian Oasis City: The Transformation of 'Unayzah*. Austin: University of Texas Press, 1989.

Anthony, T. A. "Documentation of the Modern Mistory of Bahrain from American Sources (1900–1938)." In *Bahrain Through the Ages*, edited by Shaikh Abdullah bin Khalid al-Khalifa and Michael Rice, 62–77. London: Kegan Paul International, 1993.

Arafa, Mohamed. "Qatar." In *Mass Media in the Middle East*, edited by Yahya R. Kamalipour and Hamid Mowlana, 229–241. Westwood, CT: Greenwood Press, 1994.

Arebi, Saddeka. *Women and Words in Saudi Arabia*. New York: Columbia University Press, 1984.

Armerding, Paul L. *Doctors for the Kingdom: The Work of the American Mission Hospitals in the Kingdom of Saudi Arabia*. Grand Rapids, MI: William B. Eerdmans Publishing, 2003.

Arnold, Fred, and Nasra M. Shah. "Asian Labor Migration to the Middle East." *International Migration Review* 18, no. 2 (Summer 1984): 294–318.

Bahgat, Gawdat. "Education in the Gulf Monarchies: Retrospect and Prospect." *International Review of Education/Internationale Zeitschrift für Erziehungswissenschaft/Revue Internationale de l'Éducation* 45, no. 2 (March 1999): 127–136.

Bahry, Louay. "The New Saudi Woman: Modernizing in an Islamic Framework." *Middle East Journal* 36, no. 4 (Autumn 1982): 502–515.

Bahry, Louay, and Phebe Marr. "Qatari Women: A New Generation of Leaders." *Middle East Policy* 12, no. 2 (2005): 104–119.

Bales, Kevin. *Disposable People: New Slavery in the Global Economy*. Berkeley: University of California Press, 2004.

Balfour-Paul, Glen. *End of Empire in the Middle East*. Cambridge: Cambridge University Press, 1999.

Baram, Amatzia. *Culture, History and Ideology in the Formation of Iraq*. New York: St. Martin's Press, 1991.

Beblawi, Hazem, and Giacomo Luciani, eds. *The Rentier State*. New York: Routledge, 1987.

Bergen, Peter. *Holy War Inc*. New York: A Touchstone Book/Simon and Schuster, 2002.

Bickerton, Ian J., and Carla L. Klausner. *A History of the Arab-Israeli Dispute*, 5th ed. New York: Pearson Prentice Hall, 2007.

Birks, J. S., I. J. Seccombe, and A. Sinclair. "Migrant Workers in the Arab Gulf: The Impact of Declining Oil Revenues." *International Migration Review* 20, no. 4 (Winter 1986): 799–814.

Birks, J. S., and C. A. Sinclair, "Preparations for Income After Oil: Bahrain's Example." *British Journal of Middle East Studies*, no. 1 (1979): 39–57.

Booth, Marilyn. "Translator v. Author: Girls of Riyadh Goes to New York." *Translation Studies* 1, no. 2 (July 2008): 197–211.

Bose, Sugata. *A Hundred Horizons: The Indian Ocean in the Age of Global Empire*. Cambridge, MA: Harvard University Press, 2006.

Boyd, Douglas A. "Saudi Arabian Television." *Journal of Broadcasting* 15, no. 1 (Winter 1970–1971): 73–78.

Boyne, Walter J. "The Pilgrim Airlift." *Air Force Magazine Online* 90, no. 3 (March 2007): 122–145.

Bukhari, Muhammad ibn Ismail. *Sahih Bukhari*, cited from the USC Center for Muslim-Jewish Engagement's Online Compendium of Muslim Texts. Available at http://www.usc.edu.

Bullard, Reader. *Two Kings in Arabia: Letters from Jeddah: 1923–5 and 1936–9*. Edited by E. C. Hodgkin. Reading, UK: Ithaca Press, 1993.

Bulmuş, Birsen. "The Plague in the Ottoman Empire, 1300–1838." Ph.D. diss., Georgetown University, 2008.

Burba, Evadna. *Seasoned with Sand: An American Housewife in Saudi Arabia, 1948–1966*. New York: Adne Press, 1981.

Calvert, John R, and Abdullah S. al-Shetaiwi. "Exploring the Mismatch Between Skills and Jobs for Women in Saudi Arabia in Technical and Vocational Areas: The Views of Saudi Arabian Private Sector Business Managers." *International Journal of Training and Development* 6, no. 2 (2002): 112–124.

Casey, Michael. *The History of Kuwait*. Westport, CT: Greenwood Press, 2007.

Champion, Daryl. "Saudi Arabia: Elements of Instability Within Stability." In *Crisis in the Contemporary Persian Gulf*, edited by Barry Rubin, 127–163. London: Frank Cass, 2002.

Chatty, Dawn. "Rituals of Royalty and the Elaboration of Ceremony in Oman: View from the Edge." *International Journal of Middle East Studies* 41, no. 1 (February 2009): 39–60.

Chaudhry, Kiren. *The Price of Wealth: Economies and Institutions in the Middle East*. Ithaca, NY: Cornell University Press, 1997.

Choudhury, Masudul. "Oil and Water Do Mix: The Case of Saudi Arabia." *The Journal of Developing Areas* 37, no. 2 (Spring 2004): 169–179.

Clark, Arthur P., Muhammad A Tahlawi, William Facey, and Thomas A Pledge. *A Land Transformed—The Arabian Peninsula, Saudi Arabia, and Aramco*. Dhahran: Saudi Arabian Oil Company; Houston, TX: ARAMCO Services, 2006.

Clarke, Angela. *Through the Changing Scenes of Life, 1893–1993: The American Mission Hospital Bahrain*. Bahrain: American Mission Hospital Society, 1993.

Coll, Steve. *The Bin Ladens: An Arabian Family in the American Century*. New York: Penguin Press, 2008.

———. *Ghost Wars*. New York: Penguin Books, 2004.

Commins, David. *The Wahhabi Mission and Saudi Arabia*. New York: I. B. Tauris, 2006.

Cordesman, Anthony. *Bahrain, Oman, Qatar, and the UAE: Challenges of Security*. Boulder, CO: Westview Press, 1997.

———. *Kuwait: Recovery and Security After the Gulf War*. Boulder, CO: Westview Press, 1997.

———. *Saudi Arabia Enters the Twenty-First Century*. New York: Praeger, 2003.

———. *US Forces in the Middle East*. Boulder, CO: Westview Press, 1997.

Cordesman, Anthony, and Ahmed S. Hashim. *Iraq: Sanctions and Beyond*. Boulder, CO: Westview Press, 1997.

Cordesman, Anthony, and Khalid al-Rodhan. *Gulf Military Forces in an Era of Asymmetric Wars*. Washington, DC: Center for Strategic and International Studies and Praeger Security International, 2007.

Crystal, Jill. *Kuwait: The Transformation of an Oil State*. Boulder, CO: Westview Press, 1992.

———. *Oil and Politics in the Gulf: Rulers and Merchants in Qatar*. Cambridge: Cambridge University Press, 1995.

Davidson, Christopher. *Dubai: The Vulnerability of Success*. New York: Columbia University Press, 2008.

———. *The United Arab Emirates: A Study in Survival*. Boulder, CO: Lynne Rienner Publishers, 2005.

Davies, R.E.G. *Saudi Arabian Airlines, an Airline and Its Aircraft: The Illustrated History of the Largest Airline in the Middle East*. McLean, VA: Paladwr Press, 1995.

Dawoud, Mohamed A. "The Role of Desalination in Augmentation of Water Supply in GCC Countries." *Desalination* 186 (December 30, 2005): 187–198.

Deen, Hana al-. "Oman." In *Mass Media in the Middle East,* edited by Yahya R. Kamalipour and Hamid Mowlana, 186–228. Westwood, CT, Greenwood Press, 1994.

DeLong-Bas, Natana. *Wahhabi Islam: From Revival and Reform to Global Islam.* Oxford: Oxford University Press, 2004.

Dew, Philip, and Jonathan Wallace. *Doing Business with Bahrain.* New York: Wiley, 2002.

Diederich, Mathias. "Indonesians in Saudi Arabia." In *Transnational Connections and the Arab Gulf,* edited by Madawi al-Rasheed, 128–146. New York: Routledge, 2005.

Dorr, Robert. *Desert Shield: The Build-Up: The Complete Story.* Osceola, WI: Motorbooks International, 1991.

Doumato, Eleanor. "Between Breadwinner and Domestic Icon?" In *Women and Power in the Middle East,* edited by Suad Joseph and Susan Slyomovics, 166–176. Philadelphia: University of Pennsylvania Press, 2001.

———. "Gender, Monarchy, and National Identity in Saudi Arabia." *British Journal of Middle Eastern Studies* 19, no. 1 (1992): 31–47.

———. "Saudi Arabia: The Society and Its Environment." In *Saudi Arabia: A Country Study,* edited by Helen Metz, 49–106. Washington, DC: Library of Congress Federal Research Division, 1993.

———. "The Saudis and the Gulf War: Gender, Power, and Revival of the Religious Right." In *Change and Development in the Gulf,* edited by Abbas Abdelkarim, 184–210. New York: Palgrave Macmillan, 1999.

———. "Women and Work in Saudi Arabia: How Flexible Are Islamic Margins?" *The Middle East Journal* 53, no. 4 (Autumn 1999): 568–583.

———. *Women, Islam, and Healing in Saudi Arabia and the Gulf.* New York: Columbia University Press, 2000.

Du Quenoy, Paul. *Stage Fright: Politics and the Performing Arts in Late Imperial Russia.* University Park: Pennsylvania State University Press, 2009.

Energy Information Administration. *Annual Energy Review 2007.* Washington, DC: US Government Printing Office.

———. *Renewable Energy Consumption and Electricity Preliminary 2007 Statistics.* Washington, DC: US Government Printing Office, 2008.

Esposito, John. *Islam: The Straight Path.* 3rd ed. Oxford: Oxford University Press, 1998.

———. *Unholy War: Terror in the Name of Islam.* Oxford: Oxford University Press, 2002.

Europa Publications. *Middle East and North Africa, 2003.* New York: Routledge, 2003.

Fakhro, Munira A. "The Uprising in Bahrain: An Assessment." In *The Persian Gulf at the Millennium: Essays in Politics, Economy, Security, and Religion,* edited by Gary G. Sick and Lawrence G. Potter, 167–188. New York: St. Martin's Press, 1997.

———. *Women at Work in the Gulf: A Case Study of Bahrain.* London: Kegan Paul International, 1990.

Fandy, Mamoun. *Saudi Arabia and the Politics of Dissent.* London: Macmillan, 1997.

———. *(UN)civil War of Words.* Westport, CT: Greenwood Publishing Group, 2007.

Fasano, Ugo, and Qing Wang. "Testing the Relationship Between Government Spending and Revenue: Evidence from the GCC Countries." IMF working paper, 2001, 3–12.

Fischbach, Michael. *Jewish Property Claims Against Arab Countries.* New York: Columbia University Press, 2008.

Florida, Richard. "How the Crash Will Reshape America." *Atlantic Monthly,* March 2009.

Foley, Sean. "The Gulf Arabs and the New Iraq: The Most to Gain and the Most to Lose?" *Middle Eastern Review of International Affairs* 7, no. 2 (2003): 24–43.

———. "The Gulf Arabs and the New Iraq: The Most to Gain, the Most to Lose." In *After the Dictator: The Rebirth of Iraq,* edited by Barry Rubin. New York: M. E. Sharpe, 2010.

———."History, Oil, and Ethnicity: The Story of Abu Musa and the Tunbs Islands," *Politica* 2, no. 2 (Spring 1996): 68–81.

———. "Kuwait, Bahrain, Qatar, Oman, and the UAE." In *Guide to Islamist Movements,* edited by Barry Rubin. New York: M. E. Sharpe, 2010.

———. "The Naqshbandiyya-Khalidiyya, Islamic Sainthood, and Religion in Modern Times." *The Journal of World History* 19, no. 4 (December 2008): 521–545.

———. "The UAE: Political Issues and Security Dilemmas." *Middle Eastern Review of International Affairs* 3, no. 1 (March 1999): 25–45. Available at http://meria.idc.ac.il.

———. "What Wealth Cannot Buy." In *Crisis in the Contemporary Persian Gulf,* edited by Barry Rubin, 33–74. London: Frank Cass, 2002.

Fuccaro, Nelida. "Mapping the Transnational Community: Persians and the Space of the City in Bahrain, c. 1869–1937." In *Transnational Connections and the Arab Gulf,* edited by Madawi al-Rasheed, 39–58. New York: Routledge, 2005.

Fuller, Graham, and Rend Francke. *The Arab Shi'a: The Forgotten Muslims.* New York: Macmillan, 2001.

Gause, Gregory. *Oil Monarchies: Domestic and Security Challenges in the Arab Gulf States.* New York: Council on Foreign Relations, 1994.

Ghabra, Shafeeq N. "Balancing State and Society: The Islamic Movement in Kuwait." In *Revolutionaries and Reformers: Contemporary Islamist Movements in the Middle East,* edited by Barry Rubin, 105–126. Binghamton: State University of New York Press, 2003.

Grimmett, Richard. *Conventional Arms Transfers to Developing Nations, 1993–2000.* Washington, DC: Congressional Research Service, 2001.

Hall, Richard. *Empires of the Monsoon.* New York: HarperCollins, 1996.

Hamdan, Amani. "Women and Education in Saudi Arabia: Challenges and Achievements." *International Education Journal* 6, no. 1 (2005): 42–64.

Harrison, Paul. *Doctor in Arabia*. New York: John Day, 1940.

Hart, Parker. "Application of Hanbalite and Decree Law to Foreigners in Saudi Arabia." *George Washington Law Review* 22, no. 65 (1953): 165–175.

Heard-Bey, Frauke. *From Trucial States to United Arab Emirates: A Society in Transition*. London: Longman, 1981.

Herb, Michael. *All in the Family: Absolutism, Revolution, and Democracy in the Middle Eastern Monarchies*. Albany: State University of New York Press, 1999.

———. "A Nation of Bureaucrats: Political Participation and Economic Diversification in Kuwait and the United Arab Emirates." *International Journal of Middle East Studies* 41, no. 3 (August 2009): 375–395.

Hillyard, Susan. *Before the Oil: A Personal Memoir of Abu Dhabi, 1954–1958*. Bakewell, Derbyshire, UK: Ashridge Press, 2002.

Hiro, Dilip. *The Second Gulf War: Desert Shield to Desert Storm*. New York: Universe, 2003.

Hogarth, David. *Hejaz Before World War I: A Handbook*. Cairo: Arab Bureau, 1917. Reprint Oxford: Falcon-Oleander, 1978.

Hooglund, Eric, and Anthony Toth. "United Arab Emirates." In *Persian Gulf States: Country Studies*, edited by Helen Metz, 197–246. Washington, DC: Federal Research Division, Library of Congress, 1994.

Humphreys, R. Stephen. *Between Memory and Desire: The Middle East in a Troubled Age*, 2nd ed. Berkeley: University of California Press, 2005.

Huntington, Samuel P. *Political Order in Changing Societies*. New Haven: Yale University Press, 1968.

Hylton, Hilary. "Goodbye, Houston. Hello, Dubai." *Time*, March 14, 2007.

Ingham, Bruce. "Men's Dress in the Arabian Peninsula: Historical and Present Perspectives." In *Languages of Dress in the Middle East*, edited by Nancy Lindisfarne-Tapper and Bruce Ingham, 40–54. Richmond, UK: Curzon Press, 1997.

International Monetary Fund. *Balance of Payments Statistics Yearbook: Part 1: Country Tables*. Washington, DC: IMF, 1993.

———. *Direction of Trade Statistics Quarterly: December 2004*. Washington, DC: IMF, 2004.

———. *Direction of Trade Statistics Quarterly: June 2006*. Washington, DC: IMF, 2006.

———. *Direction of Trade Statistics Quarterly: September 2008*. Washington, DC: IMF, 2008.

———. *International Financial Statistics Online*. Available at https://login.library.lausys.georgetown.edu.

Johnson, Nora. *You Can Go Home Again*. New York: Doubleday Books, 1982.

Kamrava, Mehron. *The Making of the Modern Middle East: A Political History Since World War I*. Berkeley: University of California Press, 2005.

Karabell, Zachary. "Backfire: U.S. Policy Towards Iraq, 1988–2 August, 1990." *Middle East Journal* 49, no. 1 (Winter 1995): 28–47.

Kechichian, Joseph. *Oman and the World: The Emergence of an Independent Foreign Policy*. Santa Monica, CA: Rand, 1995.

———. *Succession in Saudi Arabia*. New York: Palgrave Macmillan, 2001.

Khaldun, Ibn. *The Muqadimah*. Translated by Franz Rosenthal. Princeton, NJ: Princeton University Press, 1967.

Khalidi, Omar. "The Lotus and the Crescent: Hindus in the Islamic Lands." *Journal of the Institute of Muslim Minority Affairs* 14, no. 1 (January 1993): 85–93.

Khedouri, Nancy. *From Our Beginning to Present Day*. Manama, Bahrain: Al-Manar Press, 2007.

Kimball, Robert. ed. *The Complete Lyrics of Cole Porter*. New York: Vintage Books, 1984.

King, Geoffrey. "The Coming of Islam and the Islamic Period in the UAE." In *United Arab Emirates: A New Perspective*, edited by Ibrahim Abed and Peter Hellyer, 70–97. Naples, FL: Trident Press, 2001.

Klare, Michael T. *Rising Powers, Shrinking Planet: The New Geopolitics of Energy*. New York: Metropolitan Books, 2008.

Kondapi, C. *Indians Overseas, 1838–1949*. New Delhi: Indian Council of World Affairs, 1951.

Kuroda, Yasumasa. "A Structural Analysis of Instability and Conflict in the Gulf." In *The Gulf War and the New World Order: International Relations of the Middle East,* edited by Tareq Y. Ismael and Jacqueline S. Ismael, 52–76. Gainesville: University of Florida Press, 1994.

Labi, Nadya. "The Kingdom in the Closet." *Atlantic Monthly,* May 2007. Available at http://www.theatlantic.com.

Lacey, Robert. *The Kingdom: Arabia and the House of Saud*. New York: Avon, 1983.

Langfeldt, John. "Recently Discovered Early Christian Monuments in Northeastern Arabia." *Arabian Archaeology and Epigraphy* 5, no. 1 (2007): 32–60.

Lapidus, Ira. *A History of Islamic Societies*. Cambridge: Cambridge University Press, 2002. First published 1984 by Cambridge University Press.

Leatherdale, Clive. *Britain and Saudi Arabia: The Imperial Oasis*. London: Frank Cass, 1983.

Legrenzi, Matteo. *The Gulf Cooperation Council: Diplomacy, Security, and Economy in a Changing Region*. London: I. B. Tauris, 2008.

Lienhardt, Peter. *Disorientations: A Society in Flux: Kuwait in the 1950s*. Edited by Ahmed al-Shahi. Reading, UK: Ithaca Press, 1993.

———. *Sheikhdoms of Eastern Arabia*. Edited by Ahmed al-Shahi. New York: Palgrave, 2001.

Lippman, Thomas. *Inside the Mirage: America's Fragile Partnership with Saudi Arabia*. Boulder, CO: Westview Press, 2004.

Little, Douglas. *American Orientalism: The United States and the Middle East Since 1945*. London: I. B. Tauris, 2003.

Litwack, Robert. *Regime Change: U.S. Strategy Through the Prism of 9/11*. Baltimore, MD: Johns Hopkins University Press, 2007.

Longva, Anh. *Walls Built on Sand: Migration, Exclusion, and Society in Kuwait*. Boulder, CO: Westview Press, 1997.

Low, Michael. "Empire and the Hajj: Pilgrims, Plagues, and Pan-Islam Under British Surveillance, 1865–1908." *International Journal of Middle East Studies* 40, no. 2 (2008): 269–290.

Lynch, Marc. "Blogging the New Arab Public." *Arab Media and Society* 1 (February 2007): 1–30. Available at http://www.arabmediasociety.com.

———. *Voices of the New Arab Public: Iraq, al-Jazeera, and Middle East Politics Today*. New York: Columbia University Press, 2006.

Madani, Muhammad Mughairibi Futaih al-. *Al-Nahdhat al-Haditha fi Jazzirat al-Arab fil Malaka al-Arabiya al-Sadiya.* Cairo: Dar Ahya al-Kutub al-Arabiyya, 1952.

Mahon, Joseph A. Papers. Georgetown University Library Special Collections.

Maktum, Muhammad bin Rashid al-. *My Vision: Challenges in the Race to Excellence.* Beirut: Arab Institute for Research and Publication, 2006.

Marr, Phebe. *The Modern History of Iraq,* 2nd ed. Boulder, CO: Westview Press, 2004.

Mason, Alfred DeWitt, and Frederick J. Barny. *History of the Arabian Mission.* New York: Board of Foreign Missions, Reformed Church of America, 1926.

McIntosh, Clarence J. Papers. Georgetown University Library Special Collections.

McNeil, J. R. *Something New Under the Sun: An Environmental History of the Twentieth Century.* New York: W. W. Norton, 2001.

McNulty, Shannon. "A Lifetime of Servitude? Low-wage Labor in the Arabian Gulf." Master's thesis, Georgetown University, 2004.

Meade, Francis. *Honey and Onions: A Life in Saudi Arabia.* Philadelphia: Xlibris Corporation, 2004.

Mehden, Fred R. von der. *Two Worlds of Islam: Interactions Between Southeast Asia and the Middle East.* Gainesville: University of Florida Press, 1993.

Ménoret, Pascal. *The Saudi Enigma: A History.* Translated by Patrick Camiller. London: Zed Books, 2005.

Meron, Ya'akov. "Expulsion of Jews from Arab Countries: The Palestinians' Attitudes Towards It and Their Claims." In *The Forgotten Millions,* edited by Malka Hillel Shulewitz, 83–125. London: Cassell Press, 1999.

Miller, Michael. "Pilgrims' Progress: The Business of the Hajj." *Past and Present* 191, no. 1 (May 2006): 189–228.

Mohamedi, Fareed. "The Economy." In *Saudi Arabia: A Country Study,* edited by Helen Metz, 113–187. Washington, DC: Federal Research Division, Library of Congress, 1993.

———. "Oman." In *Persian Gulf States: Country Studies*, edited by Helen Metz, 251–318. Washington, DC: Library of Congress Federal Research Division, 1994.

Mughni, Haya al-. *Women in Kuwait: The Politics of Gender.* London: Saqi Books, 2001.

Mulligan, William. Papers. Georgetown University Library Special Collections.

Munif, Abdelrahman. *Cities of Salt.* Translated by Peter Theroux. New York: Vintage Books, 1989.

Nadelhoffer, Hans. *Cartier.* New York: Chronicle Books, 2007.

Nakash, Yitzhak. *Reaching for Power: The Shi'a in the Modern Arab World.* Princeton, NJ: Princeton University Press, 2006.

Nashmi, Eisa. "Political Discussions in the Arab World: A Look at Online Forums from Kuwait, Saudi Arabia, Jordan, and Egypt." Master's thesis, University of Florida, 2007.

Nordenson, Jon. "The Internet as a Public Sphere: A Case from Kuwait." Paper presented at the annual meeting of the Middle East Studies Association (MESA), Boston, MA, November 2009.

Norton, Mary Beth, David M. Katzman, Paul Escott, Howard Cudacoff, Thomas

Paterson, and William Tuttle. *A People and a Nation: A History of the United States*. Vol. 2, *Since 1865*. 3rd ed. Boston: Houghton Mifflin, 1990.
Nuri, Maqsud al-Hassan. "Regional Military Involvement: A Case Study of Iran Under the Shah." *Pakistan Horizon* 37, no. 4 (1984): 32–45.
Ochsenwald, William. "Islam and Loyalty in the Saudi Hijaz, 1926–1939." *Die Welt des Islams* 47, no. 1 (2007): 1–32.
Okruhlik, Gwenn. "The Irony of *Islah* (Reform)." *Washington Quarterly* 28, no. 4 (2005): 153–170.
———. "Making Conversation Permissible: Islamism and Reform in Saudi Arabia." In *Islamic Activism: A Social Movement Theory Approach,* edited by Quintan Wiktorowicz, 250–269. Indianapolis: Indiana University Press, 2004.
Onley, James. *The Arabian Frontier of the British Raj: Merchants, British, and Rulers in the Nineteenth-Century Gulf.* Oxford: Oxford University Press, 2007.
———. "Britain's Native Agents in Arabia in the Nineteenth Century." *Comparative Studies of South Asia, Africa, and the Middle East* 24, no. 1 (2004): 129–137.
O'Shea, Raymond. *The Sand Kings: The Experiences of an RAF Officer in the Little-Known Regions of Trucial Oman, Arabia*. London: Methuen, 1947.
Parfitt, Tudor. *The Road to Redemption*. Leiden: E. J. Brill, 1996.
Patrick, Neil. "Nationalism in the Gulf States." Research paper, Kuwait Programme on Development, Governance and Globalisation in the Gulf States, 2009.
Peaslee, Amos. *The Constitutions of Nations*. Vol. 3: *Nicaragua to Yugoslavia*. The Hague: M. Nijhoff, 1956. First edition published by the Rumford Press 1950.
Peters, F. E. *The Hajj: The Muslim Pilgrimage to Mecca and the Holy Places*. Princeton, NJ: Princeton University Press, 1994.
Philby, H.St.J.B. *Arabian Highlands*. Ithaca, New York: Cornell University Press for the Middle East Institute, 1952.
Philip, George. *The Political Economy of International Oil*. Edinburgh: Edinburgh University Press, 1994.
Political Diaries of the Persian Gulf. Vol. 8: *1928–1929*. Farnham Common, England: Archive Editions, 1990.
———. Vol. 9: *1930–1931*. Farnham Common, England: Archive Editions, 1990.
———. Vol. 11: *1934–1935*. Farnham Common, England: Archive Editions, 1989.
———. Vol. 13: *1938–1939*. Farnham Common, England: Archive Editions, 1990.
———. Vol. 20: *1955–1958*. Farnham Common, England: Archive Editions, 1990.
———. Vol. 21: *1947–1958*. Farnham Common, England: Archive Editions, 1990.
Porter, Cole. *The Complete Lyrics of Cole Porter.* Edited by Robert Kimball. New York: Vintage Books, 1984.
Qasimi, Nurah al-. *Al-Wujud al-Hindi fi al-Khalij al-Arabi, 1820–1947*. Al-Shariqa: Da'irat al-Thaqafa wa-al-I'lam, 1996.
Ramady, M. A. *The Saudi Arabian Economy: Policies, Achievements, and Challenges*. New York: Springer Press, 2005.
Rampal, Kuldip R. "Saudi Arabia." In *Mass Media in the Middle East*, edited by Yahya R. Kamalipour and Hamid Mowlana, 244–260. Westwood, CT, Greenwood Press, 1994.

Rasheed, Madawi al-. *A History of Saudi Arabia*. Cambridge: Cambridge University Press, 2002.

Reformed Church in America. *Acts and Proceedings of the Regular Session of the General Synod: 1939*. New York: Board of Publication and Bible-school Work, 1939.

Rihani, Ameen. *Around the Coasts of Arabia*. Boston: Houghton Mifflin, 1930.

Ross, Michael. "Oil, Islam, and Women." *American Political Science Review* 102, no. 1 (February 2008): 107–123.

Rudnyckyj, Daromir. "Technologies of Servitude: Governmentality and Indonesian Transnational Labor Migration." *Anthropological Quarterly* 77, no. 3 (2004): 407–434.

Rugh, William. *Arab Mass Media*. Westwood, CT: Greenwood Publishing Group, 2004.

Rush, Alan de Lacy, ed. *Records of the Hajj: A Documentary History of the Pilgrimage to Mecca*. Vol. 8: *The Saudi Period (Since 1952)*. Cambridge: Cambridge University Press Archive Editions, 1993.

Russell, Richard. *Weapons Proliferation in the Middle East*. New York: Routledge, 2005.

Saba, Michael. *King Abdulaziz . . . His Plane and His Pilot*. Sioux Falls, SD: Gulf America Press, 2009.

Sabban, Rima. "United Arab Emirates: Migrant Women in the United Arab Emirates: The Case of Female Domestic Workers." Gender Promotion Program Working Paper no. 10, International Labor Office, Geneva, 2006.

Said, Abeer Abu. *Qatari Women: Past and Present*. London: Longman Group, 1984.

Sakr, Naomi. *Satellite Realms: Transnational Television, Globalization, and the Middle East*. London: I. B. Tauris, 2001.

Sanea, Rajaa al-. *Girls of Riyadh*. Translated by Rajaa al-Sanea and Marilyn Booth. New York: Penguin Press, 2007.

Sanmiguel, Victor. *Christians in Kuwait*. Beirut: Beirut Press, 1970.

Sayegh, Fatima al-. "American Missionaries in the UAE Region in the Twentieth Century." *Middle Eastern Studies* 32, no. 1 (1996): 120–139.

———. "Women and Economic Changes in the Gulf: The Case of the United Arab Emirates." *Domes* 10, no. 2 (2001): 3–10.

Scheuer, Michael. *Imperial Hubris*. Dulles, VA: Potomac Books, 2004.

Scott, James. *The Moral Economy of the Peasant*. New Haven, CT: Yale University Press, 1976.

Seccombe, Ian J. "A Disgrace to American Enterprise: Italian Labour and the Arabian American Oil Company in Saudi Arabia, 1944–1954." *Immigrants and Minorities* 5, no. 3 (November 1986): 240–246.

Seccombe, Ian J., and R. I. Lawless. "Foreign Worker Dependence in the Gulf, and the International Oil Companies: 1910–50." *International Migration Review* 20, no. 3 (Autumn 1986): 548–574.

Seikaly, Mary. "Women and Religion in Bahrain: An Emerging Identity." In *Islam, Gender, and Social Change*, edited by Yvonne Haddad and John Esposito, 169–189. New York: Oxford University Press, 1997.

———. "Women and Social Change in Bahrain." *International Journal for Middle East Studies* 26, no. 3 (August 1994): 415–426.

Shayeb, Jafar al-. "Saudi Arabia: Municipal Councils and Political Reform." *Arab*

Reform Bulletin, November 2005. Available at http://www.carnegieendowment.org.

Sick, Gary. "The Coming Crisis." In *The Persian Gulf at the Millennium: Essays in Politics, Economy, Security, and Religion,* edited by Gary Sick and Lawrence Potter, 11–30. New York: St. Martin's Press, 1997.

Smith, Peter. *How CNN Fought the War: A View from the Inside.* Secaucus, NJ: Carol Publishing Group, 1991.

Sreberny-Mohammadi, Annabelle, and Ali Mohammadi. *Small Media, Big Revolution: Communication, Culture and the Iranian Revolution.* Minneapolis: University of Minnesota Press, 1994.

Steinberg, Guido. *Religion und Staat in Saudi Arabien: Die wahhabitischen Gelehrten, 1902–1953.* Würzburg: Ergon, 2002.

Stowasser, Barbara. "Old Shaykhs, Young Women, and the Internet: The Rewriting of Women's Political Rights in Islam." *The Muslim World* 91, no. 1–2 (2001): 99–119.

Suba'i, Ahmad al-. *My Days in Mecca.* Translated and edited by Deborah Akers and Abubaker Bagader. Boulder, CO: First Forum Press, 2009.

Sultan, Fawzi al-. *Averting Financial Crisis—Kuwait.* Washington, DC: World Bank, 1989.

Tajir, Mahdi al-. *Bahrain, 1920–1945: Britain, the Shaykh, and the Administration.* New York: Routledge and Kegan Paul, 1987.

Tartter, Jean. "Regional and National Security Considerations." In *Persian Gulf States: Country Studies,* edited by Helen Metz, 321–377. Washington, DC: Federal Research Division, Library of Congress, 1994.

Taryam, Abdullah. *The Establishment of the United Arab Emirates, 1950–85.* London: Croom Helm, 1987.

Teitelbaum, Joseph. "Pilgrimage Politics: The Hajj and the Saudi-Hashemite Rivalry, 1916–1925." In *The Hashemites in the Modern Arab World: Essays in Honor of the Late Professor Uriel Dann,* edited by Asher Susser and Aryeh Shmuelevitz, 75–84. London: Frank Cass, 1995.

Tétreault, Mary Ann. "A State of Two Minds: State Cultures, Women, and Politics in Kuwait." *International Journal of Middle East Studies* 33, no. 3 (May 2001): 203–220.

———. *Stories of Democracy: Politics and Society in Contemporary Kuwait.* New York: Columbia University Press, 2000.

Thomas, Amos. *Imaginations and Borderless Television: Media, Culture, and Politics Across Asia.* New York: Sage, 2005.

Thurmond, Michael. "Georgia Men Hit Hardest by the Recession, December 2007 to May 2009." *Georgia Department of Labor: White Paper on Georgia's Workforce.* 2009. Available at http://www.dol.state.ga.us.

Tobi, Joseph. *The Jews of Yemen: Studies in Their History and Culture.* Leiden: Brill, 1999.

Ulrich, Brian. "Historicizing Arab Blogs: Reflections on the Transmission of Ideas and Information in Middle Eastern History." *Arab Media and Society 8* (Spring 2009). Available at http://www.arabmediasociety.com.

United Nations Conference on Trade and Development. "World Investment Report 2007: Country Fact Sheet Bahrain." Available at http://www.unctad.org.

———. "World Investment Report 2007: Country Fact Sheet Kuwait." Available at http://www.unctad.org.

———. "World Investment Report 2007: Country Fact Sheet Oman." Available at http://www.unctad.org.

———. "World Investment Report 2007: Country Fact Sheet Qatar." Available at http://www.unctad.org.

———. "World Investment Report 2007: Country Fact Sheet Saudi Arabia." Available at http://www.unctad.org.

———. "World Investment Report 2007: Country Fact Sheet UAE." Available at http://www.unctad.org.

United Nations Department of Economic and Social Affairs. Population Division. *United Nations' World Population Prospects*. New York: United Nations Publications, 2008.

United Nations Office of Drugs and Crimes. *Surveys of Criminal Trends and Operations of Criminal Justice Systems*. Available at http://www.unodc.org.

United States Arms Control and Disarmament Agency. *World Military Expenditures and Arms Transfers 1997 Report*. Washington, DC: US Government Printing Office, 1997.

———. *World Military Expenditures and Arms Transfers, 1971–1980*. Washington, DC: US Government Printing Office, 1982.

United States Congress. House Committee on Foreign Affairs. *Mutual Security Act of 1958: Hearing Before the Committee on Foreign Affairs: House of Representatives, 85th Congress, Second Session*. Washington, DC: US Government Printing Office, 1958.

United States Department of Defense. "Active Duty Military Personnel Strengths by Regional Area and by Country." (309A). March 31, 2003. Available at http://siadapp.dior.whs.mil.

———. "Active Duty Military Personnel Strengths by Regional Area and by Country." (309A). June 30, 2003. Available at http://siadapp.dior.whs.mil.

———. "Active Duty Military Personnel Strengths by Regional Area and by Country." (309A). December 31, 2003. Available at http://siadapp.dior.whs.mil.

———. "Active Duty Military Personnel Strengths by Regional Area and by Country." (309A). June 30, 2004. Available at http://siadapp.dior.whs.mil.

United States Department of State. "Background Note: Saudi Arabia." 2009. Available at http://www.state.gov.

———. *Country Reports on Terrorism 2007*. Washington, DC: US Government Printing Office, 2008.

———. *Foreign Relations of the United States: 1955–1957*. Vol.13: *Foreign Relations: Near-East, Jordan*. Washington, DC: US Government Printing Office, 1989.

———. *Records of the Department of State Relating to Internal Affairs of Saudi Arabia, 1930–1944*. Washington, DC: National Archives, National Records and Archives Service, General Services Administration, 1974.

United States Department of State. Under Secretary for Democracy and Global Affairs, Bureau of Democracy, Human Rights, and Labor. *2006 Country Reports on Human Rights Practices*. "Saudi Arabia." Available at http://www.state.gov.

———."International Religious Freedom Report 2005: Saudi Arabia." Available at http://www.state.gov.

United States Department of State. Under Secretary for Democracy and Global Affairs, Office to Monitor and Combat Trafficking in Persons. "Trafficking in Persons: 2008 Report." Available at http://www.state.gov.

"U.S. Is the Pilgrim's Friend in Need." *Life Magazine,* September 8, 1952.

Vassiliev, Alexei. *The History of Saudi Arabia*. London: Saqi Books, 1998.

Viviano, Frank. "Kingdom on Edge: Saudi Arabia." *National Geographic* 204, no. 4 (October 2003): 3–41.

Vitalis, Robert. *America's Kingdom: Mythmaking on the Saudi Oil Frontier.* Stanford, CA: Stanford University Press, 2007.

Wehrey, Frederic, et al. *Saudi-Iranian Relations Since the Fall of Saddam: Rivalry, Cooperation, and Implications for U.S. Policy*. Santa Monica, CA: Rand Corporation, 2009.

Weiner, Myron. "International Migration and Development: Indians in the Persian Gulf." *Population and Development Review* 8, no. 1 (March 1982): 1–36.

Wilcke, Christoph. *The Ismalis of Najran*. New York: Human Rights Watch, 2008.

Wilford, Hugh. *The Mighty Wurlitzer: How the CIA Played America*. Cambridge, MA: Harvard University Press, 2008.

Winder, R. Bayly. *Saudi Arabia in the Nineteenth Century.* New York: St. Martin's Press, 1965.

Winkler, David. *Amirs, Admirals, and Desert Sailors: Bahrain, the U.S. Navy, and the Gulf.* Annapolis, MD: United States Naval Institute Press, 2007.

Woodward, Bob. *Veil, The Secret Wars of the CIA, 1981–1987*. New York: Simon and Schuster, 2005.

———. *The Commanders*. New York: Simon and Schuster, 1991.

World Bank. *Making the Most of Scarcity: Accountability for Better Water Management in the Middle East and North Africa*. Washington, DC: World Bank, 2007.

———. *The Status and Progress of Women in the Middle East and North Africa*. Washington, DC: World Bank Press, 2007.

———. *Women in the Middle East and North Africa: Women in the Public Sphere*. Washington, DC: World Bank Press, 2004.

Yamani, Mai. "Changing the Habits of a Lifetime: The Adaptation of Hejazi Dress to the New Social Order." In *Languages of Dress in the Middle East,* edited by Nancy Lindisfarne-Tapper and Bruce Ingham, 55–66. Richmond, UK: Curzon Press, 1997.

———. "Health, Education, Gender, and Security in the Gulf in the Twenty-First Century." In *Gulf Security in the Twenty-First Century*, edited by Christian Koch and David Long, 265–280. Abu Dhabi, United Arab Emirates: Emirates Center for Strategic Studies and Research, 1997.

———. "Some Observations on Women in Saudi Arabia." In *Feminism and Islam: Legal and Literary Perspectives,* edited by Mai Yamani, 263–282. New York: New York University Press, 1996.

Yergin, Daniel. *The Prize: The Epic Quest for Oil, Money, and Power.* New York: Free Press, 1991.

Zahlan, Rosemarie. "Anglo-American Rivalry in Bahrain, 1918–1947." In *Bahrain Through the Ages*, edited by Shaikh Abdullah bin Khalid al-Khalifa and Michael Rice, 567–587. London: Kegan Paul International, 1993.

Index

About the Book

If petroleum buys political legitimacy in the Arab Gulf states, how can we explain the rise of dissent and calls for political reform despite sustained oil revenues? The answer, according to Sean Foley, lies in political, social, and economic dynamics that have been brewing beneath the surface for more than a decade—and that are slowly shifting the balance of political power.

Though Foley does not disagree that oil revenues have been important in preserving the power of Gulf autocrats, he goes beyond popular stereotypes to identify other crucial forces that are conspiring to disrupt the status quo. Chief among these are the telecommunications revolution, which has brought news of democracy (as well as regime misdeeds) to people's homes, the lack of jobs for major segments of the male population, and the increasing economic power of women and minority groups. It is these complex issues, Foley shows us, that are at the forefront as the Arab Gulf states grapple with the challenges of both modernity and money.

Sean Foley is assistant professor of history at Middle Tennessee State University.